Held Captive by Indians

Held Captive by Indians

Selected Narratives 1642-1836

†

EDITED BY
RICHARD VANDERBEETS

THE UNIVERSITY OF TENNESSEE PRESS
KNOXVILLE

Library of Congress Catalog Card Number 73-3448
International Standard Book Number 0-87049-145-8

First Edition.

Library of Congress Cataloging in Publication Data

VanDerBeets, Richard, comp.
Held captive by Indians.

Bibliography: p. 367
1. Indians of North America—Captivities.
I. Title.
E85.V36 970.1 [B] 73-3448
ISBN 0-87049-145-8

For Marlene, Dirk, Scott, Ruth, and Mark

Contents

† † †

Illustrations

†††

Maps

I may say, that as none knows what it is to fight
and pursue such an enemy as this, but that they have
fought and pursued them: so none can imagine what it
is to be captivated, and enslaved to such . . .
but those that have tryed it.

†

—Preface to the Second Edition,
*A Narrative of the Captivity and Restauration of
Mrs. Mary Rowlandson*
(1682)

Introduction

†††

Civilized peoples have long recognized the value of tempering their joys with a play or story chronicling the misfortunes and tragedies of others. Because the earliest Americans countenanced neither playacting nor the unhealthy influences of the novel, they wrote and read true tales of tragedy and horror in the form of disasters, plagues, and shipwrecks—and of Indian massacres and captivities. As the frontier pushed westward under continuing conflict the tales of Indian captivity accompanied it, gradually becoming our first literature of catharsis in an era when native American fiction scarcely existed. The immense popularity of the Indian captivity narrative in its own time is unquestionable; first editions are rare today because they were quite literally read to pieces, and most narratives went through a remarkable number of editions. There are some thirty known editions of the Mary Rowlandson narrative; Jonathan Dickenson's account went to twenty-one, including translations into Dutch and German; there are over thirty editions of the Mary Jemison captivity; and the popularity of Peter Williamson's narrative carried it through forty-one editions.

American Indians took white or non-Indian captives for four principal reasons: to use as slaves; to ransom (to the English and, later, Americans); to sell (to the French or to other tribes); and to replace, by adoption, those members of the tribe lost or slain in battle. Except for the fur trader, who did not as a rule publish his observations, the captive shared Indian life more intimately and for a longer time than all other colonials or settlers. In addition to providing fascinating popular reading in America for over two centuries, the narratives of Indian captivity have from the beginning proved valuable documents for the ethnologist, historian, and cultural historian. The four surviving sixteenth-century captivity accounts—*Relation of Alvar Nunez Cabeza de Vaca* (1542), *The Captivity of Juan Ortiz* (1557), Hans Staden's *Warhaftige Historia* (1557), and Job Hortop's *The Travailes of an Englishman* (1591)—are not only remarkable firsthand tales of ordeal and adventure but also provide the earliest descriptions of the Indians of Texas, Florida, and Brazil. Captain John Smith's account of his three-week captivity (1607–1608) in Virginia contains excellent detail on Pamunkey Indian manners and customs, although this is never so well remembered as the description of his famous encounter with Powhatan and Pocahontas, first fully reported in his *General History of Virginia* (1624). While Smith's account is not technically a separately published captivity narrative, it does stand as the generic precursor of the later and discrete narratives of Indian captivity in America. A succession of later narratives such as Jonathan Dickenson's (1699) and those of John Gyles (1736), Robert Eastburn (1758), Marie LeRoy and Barbara Leininger (1759), Thomas Morris (1791), James Smith (1799), Mary Jemison (1824), Charles Johnston (1827), Rachel Plummer (1839), and Nelson Lee (1859) all contain, in addition to their personal adventures, significant and detailed observations of aboriginal life and customs—Seminole, Maliseet, Mohawk, Ottawa, Miami, Seneca, Shawnee, Comanche, and Apache, among others. Many captive-narrators were excellent observers, and their accounts of Indian warfare, hunting, customs and manners, religion, and council procedures are in some cases our only glimpses of these past realities. In this way their narratives constitute valuable specimens of ethnological reportage. For the historian, many of the narratives of Indian captivity are repositories of eyewitness information relating to the major Indian-white conflicts throughout the course of American history. The narrative of Mary Rowlandson (1682) provides additional insight into King Philip's War and even Philip himself, whom Mrs. Rowlandson met and spoke with during her captivity. Such eighteenth-century narratives as John Williams (1707), John Gyles (1736), Peter Williamson (1757), and Robert Eastburn (1758) give added dimension to the French and Indian War generally and to many campaigns and battles specifically.

Also, such nineteenth-century accounts as those of Rachel Plummer (1839), Nelson Lee (1859), and Fanny Kelly (1871) underscore the conflicts arising from the later westward movement.

In the context of American cultural history, however, the significances of the narratives of Indian captivity are shaped and differentiated largely by the society for which the narratives were intended. These cultural significances are in many ways discrete impulses and range from expressions of religious sentiment, to vehicles for anti-Indian propaganda, to blatantly visceral penny dreadfuls or pulp thrillers. The earliest Indian captivity narratives published in America, those of the seventeenth and early eighteenth centuries, are straightforward and generally unadorned religious documents, for the most part Puritan; a number of surviving Jesuit relations illustrate the Catholic experience. The captivity here takes on a typically symbolic and even typological value, reinforced by frequent scriptural citations. There are over fifty-five such references in the narrative of Father Isaac Jogues. The religious and largely didactic function is generally made explicit either in a prefatory note or very early in the narrative proper, though title pages more often than not provide succinct indicators: Mrs. Rowlandson's *The Soveraignty and Goodness of God, Together With the Faithfulness of His Promises Displayed* (1682); Jonathan Dickenson's *God's Protecting Providence Man's Surest Help in the Times of the Greatest Difficulty and Most Imminent Danger* (1699); John Williams' *The Redeemed Captive Returning to Zion* (1707). Interestingly, the first American Negro "slave narratives" are in fact Indian captivities of distinctly religious orientation: *A Narrative of the Uncommon Sufferings and Surprising Deliverance of Briton Hammon, A Negro Man* (1760), and *A Narrative of the Lord's Wonderful Dealings with John Marrant, a Black, Taken Down from His Own Relation* (1785). The religious expressions deriving from the captivity experience treat the salutary effects of the captivity, especially in the context of redemptive suffering; the captivity as test, trial, or punishment by God; and, finally and most demonstrably, the captivity as evidence of Divine Providence and of God's inscrutable wisdom.

Calvinists believing themselves to be God's chosen people newly arrived in the Promised Land to establish a New Zion, the

Puritan settlers extended their typology to encompass a view of the Indian inhabitants of the continent as Canaanites who the Lord had promised Moses would be driven from the land to make way for the Neo-Israelites. "Thus the Lord was pleased to smite our Enemies in the hinder Parts," concluded the 1638 report of the extermination of the Pequots at Fort Mystic wherein six hundred Indians were killed at the cost of two English lives, "and to give us their Land for an Inheritance." Believing also that the last great struggle between good and evil was to take place in their wilderness, a struggle between God's chosen and the agents of the Devil, they considered the natives of the wilderness to be under the direction of Satan and consequently enemies of God and His instruments in that struggle. Seventeenth-century records clearly reveal the extent to which the Puritans held the conception of Indian as Devil. Cotton Mather firmly believed in the magical powers of the Indian Powaw (powwow), an example to him of heathen black arts. The common view was that through the Devil's help, the Indians' charms were of force to produce effects of wonderment, and it was a widespread belief that the Devil held the Indians in thrall and even appeared in bodily shape to them. In *God's Controversy with New England* (1662), Michael Wigglesworth described the Indian forest, the scene of the prophesied last struggle between good and evil, as a "Devil's den" wherein "none inhabited / But hellish fiends, and brutish men / That devils worshipped."

If the savages were directly the instruments of Satan and indirectly so of God, then the torments of Indian captivity could be, and were, viewed as one of God's ways of testing, punishing, or instructing His creatures. "God strengthened them [Indians] to be a scourge to his People," writes Mary Rowlandson; "the Lord feeds and nourishes them up to be a scourge to the whole Land." The scriptural citation she uses for support is Hebrews 12:6: "For whom the Lord loveth he chasteneth, and scourgeth every Son whom he receiveth." In the course of her narrative, Mrs. Rowlandson turns to the Scriptures for comfort over sixty-five times, occasioned by reflections on a variety of incidents ranging from the death of her child (Genesis 42:36: "Me have ye bereaved of my

Children . . . ") to her staying dry while fording a river (Isaiah 43:2: "When thou passeth through the waters I will be with thee . . . "). Most of her citations are strikingly appropriate to her captivity experience: Jeremiah 31:16: "Refrain thy voice from weeping, and thine eyes from tears, for thy work shall be rewarded, and they shall come again from the land of the Enemy"; or Psalms 106:46: "He made them also to be pittied, of all those that carried them Captives." Father Isaac Jogues sees punishment for weakness even in the small details of his captivity. When his bonds give him pain and he asks to have them loosened, "God justly ordained that the more I pleaded, the more tightly they drew my chains." For the Jesuits, particularly, physical suffering was a redemptive and intensely religious aspect of captivity, an experience to delight in: "How long they spent their fury on me," relates Jogues, "he knows for whose love and sake I suffered all, and for whom it is delightful and glorious to suffer." When the Mohawks force a Christian Huron prisoner to cut off Jogues's left thumb, the priest observes that "surely it is pleasing to suffer at the hands of those for whom you would die, and for whom you chose to suffer . . . ." He then takes the severed thumb in his other hand and offers it to God.

For Protestant captives, however, the salutary effects of captivity generally lay in areas other than suffering, principally the morally instructive nature of the experience. There were spiritual lessons to be drawn. "How evident is it that the Lord hath made this Gentlewoman a gainer by all this affliction," runs the preface to the second edition of the Rowlandson narrative, "that she can say 'tis good for her yea better that she hath been, then that she should not have been thus afflicted . . . the worst of evils working together for the best good." Mrs. Rowlandson validates this theme in matters both large and small. On the first Sabbath of her captivity she recalls "how careless I had been of God's holy time, how many Sabbaths I had lost and misspent . . . . Yet the Lord still shewed mercy, and upheld me; and as he wounded me with one hand, so he healed me with the other." When, after her release, she is troubled with small matters ("a shadow, a blast, a bubble, and things of no continuance . . . "), she thinks upon her recent captivity: "It was but the other day that if I had had the world, I would have given it for my freedom.... I have learned to look beyond present and smaller troubles."

Perhaps the chief spiritual significance for both the captive-narrator and his reader lay in interpreting the captivity as an illustration of God's providence. "God was with me, in a wonderfull manner, carrying me along and bearing up my spirit... that I might see more of his Power," writes Mrs. Rowlandson. "Thus God wonderfully favored me," John Gyles reflects, "and carried me through the first year of my captivity.... Though I underwent extreme difficulties, yet I saw much of God's goodness." Father Jogues views his captivity as an opportunity, willed by God, to baptize and instruct the heathen in their very camp. Robert Eastburn blesses God for the "gracious interposure of Providence, in preserving me both from sin and danger" during his captivity. At one point, being interrogated about the strength of Fort Williams, Eastburn gives false information in the hope that the Indians will not attack the fort; when they do not, he sees the workings of a divine plan in his capture: "Hereby it evidently appeared that I was suffered to fall into the hands of the enemy to promote the good of my countrymen."

If the captive drew such lessons from his experience, he also felt obliged to pass them on to others who might profit from the morally instructive nature of Indian captivity. "One principall ground of my setting forth these lines," writes Mrs. Rowlandson, is "to declare the Works of the Lord, and his wonderfull power in carrying us along, preserving us in the Wilderness, while under the Enemies hand, and returning us to safety again...." In the introduction to his narrative, John Gyles states that one reason for compiling his "private memoirs" is "that we might have a memento ever ready at hand, to excite in ourselves gratitude and thankfulness to God." More importantly, he continues, "may the most powerful and benificent Being accept of this public testimony... and bless my experience to excite others to confide in his all-sufficiency." Elizabeth Hanson suggests the instructive, edifying design of her narrative by asserting that she related her "remarkable trials and wonderful deliverances" for one reason only: the hope that "thereby the merciful kindness and goodness of God may be magnified, and the reader hereof provoked with more care and fear to serve him in righteousness and humility." As test or punishment by God, as opportunity for redemptive suffering, and as evidence of divine providence, the Indian captivity experience was viewed by Puritan and Catholic captives as salutary and morally instructive. Late Protestant captives of firm religious convictions made comparable apprehensions, though principally that of the captivity as illustration of God's providence. Explicit or implicit in their narratives are the spiritual lessons they drew from captivity, lessons intended as well for the moral edification of the reader. In this mode and by these apprehensions, the Indian captivity narrative served as an intense and satisfying expression of profoundly felt religious experience.

From animosities dating back to Indian encounters during the Forest Wars of the later seventeenth century and aggravated by the initial conflicts of what was to become the French and Indian War, the captivity narratives of the early and middle eighteenth century became vehicles less for religious expression than for hatred of the Indian and, later, his French master in the struggle with England for control of the continent. Again, title pages are more than suggestive: *French and Indian Cruelty Exemplified in the Life and Various Vicissitudes of Fortune of Peter Williamson* (1757); *A Narrative of the Sufferings and Surprizing Deliverances of William and Elizabeth Fleming . . . Wherein it Fully Appears, That the Barbarities of the Indians is Owing to the French, and Chiefly their Priests* (1756). The propaganda value of the captivity narrative became more and more evident and was increasingly a factor in narratives treating experiences during the eighteenth century. The French and Indian War produced narratives markedly anti-Indian, anti-French, and anti-Catholic. The Revolution (often called "The British and Indian War"), during which many tribes shifted allegiance to the English against the settlers, called forth equally inflammatory accounts of Indian outrages, depredations, and captivities.

When John Gyles is offered a biscuit by a Jesuit, he is afraid to eat it and buries it, believing that the priest "had put something into it to make me love him. Being very young, and having heard much of the Papists torturing the Protestants," he relates, "I hated the sight of a Jesuit." Gyles's mother, also a captive, thinking that her son would be sold to the Jesuit, cries out: "I had rather follow you to your grave or never see you more in this world, than you should be sold to a Jesuit; for a Jesuit will ruin you, body and soul!" Gyles is instead sold to a French merchant and laments later that he has been turned over to "a people of that persuasion which my mother so much detested." Differences between the 1754 and 1760 editions of the narrative of Elizabeth Hanson illustrate the intrusion of specific anti-French sentiment into updated accounts of Indian captivity. In the 1754 version, Mrs. Hanson describes the scalping of her children, adding only the fact that the Indians were accustomed to "receiving sometimes a reward for every scalp." In the 1760 edition the phrase is replaced by propaganda: "And it has been currently reported, that the French, in their wars with the English, have given the Indians a pecuniary reward for every scalp they brought to them." Robert Eastburn's narrative, one of the most overtly anti-French and anti-Catholic, reports that "the pains the papists take to propagate such a bloody religion is truly surprising. . . . The zeal they employ to propagate superstition and idolatry should make Protestants ashamed of their lukewarmness." Eastburn tells of young boys taken at Oswego who were "delivered up a sacrifice to the Indian enemy, to be instructed in popish principles, and be employed in murdering their countrymen, yea, perhaps their own fathers, mothers, and bretheren! O horrible! O lamentable!" He suggests that the "insatiable thirst of the French for empire" is aided by the pardons they receive from the Pope and their priests for whatever crimes committed in the course of conquest. Eastburn especially damns the conduct of the French governor of Quebec, who even in time of peace had given the Indians encouragement to murder and capture the inhabitants of the frontiers: "a scandal to any civilized nation, and what many pagans would abhor." Observing that "our enemies seem to make a better use of a bad religion than we do of a good one" because they are united as one man while America is divided against itself, Eastburn warns that the French "leave no stone unturned to compass our ruin. They pray, work, and travel to bring it about, and are unwearied in the pursuit, while many among us sleep in a storm which . . . has laid a good part of our country desolate and threatens the whole with destruction."

Peter Williamson is equally assertive but more graphic. During his captivity he encountered other captives who gave him "some shocking accounts of the murders and devastations committed in their parts; a few instances of which will enable the reader to guess at the treatment the provincials have suffered in years past." There follows a catalog of horrors to demonstrate French-inspired Indian cruelties: entire families slaughtered and scalped; victims cut in pieces and given to the swine; a trader scalped, roasted while still alive, and his whole body eaten (including his head, of which is made an "Indian pudding"). These "instances of savage cruelty" lead Williamson to his main polemic: such horrors must "cause in every breast the utmost detestation," not only against the Indians but against those who, through "inattention, or pusillanimous or erroneous principles, suffered these savages at first, unrepelled, or even unmolested, to commit such outrages and incredible depradations and murders."

One of the "repeated injuries" cited in the Declaration of Independence is the British endeavor "to bring on the inhabitants of our frontiers the merciless Indian Savages, whose known rule of warfare is an undistinguished destruction of all ages, sexes, and conditions." It is not surprising, then, that Revolutionary War narratives of Indian captivity during the late eighteenth century serve in many ways as vehicles for anti-British propaganda of the kind directed against the French in the earlier French and Indian captivities. The "Account of the Destruction of the Settlements at Wyoming," one of the tidbits in the Manheim anthology of captivities, is largely designed as an attack on the British and Tories for their employment of Indian allies in the Revolution. "The following are a few of the more singular circumstances of the barbarity practiced in the attack upon Wyoming [the Wyoming Valley in western Pennsylvania]," the account begins, and then develops a tale of treachery, cruelty, and horror calculated to elicit the reader's wrath against the British and Royalists. The Reverend William Rogers, in his preface to John Corbly's narrative, also in the Manheim collection, refers to Great Britain during the Revolution as "a power, at that time, so lost to every human affection, that, rather than not subdue and make us slaves, they basely chose to encourage, patronize and reward, as their most faithful and beloved allies, the savages of the wilderness." The military, religious, and nationalistic considerations of both the French and Indian and the Revolutionary wars, then, find forceful expression in propagandistic narratives of Indian captivity and as such constitute another of their significant cultural impulses.

The infusion of melodrama and sensibility into the narratives, appropriately ornamented and stylistically embellished, capitalized on what became an increasingly profitable commercial market for properly "literary" narratives of Indian captivity in the later eighteenth and early nineteenth centuries. To be sure, the earlier propagandistic impulse deliberately played up Indian horrors and outrages, but more to solicit strong anti-Indian sentiments than to evoke pity and terror for the captive himself. It was but a short and almost inevitable step from narrative excesses for the purpose of propaganda to excesses in the interest of sensation and titillation, from promoting hatred to eliciting horror, from inspiring patriotism to encouraging sales, from chauvinism to commercialism. The chief concern was not for accuracy or fidelity to the hard facts of frontier life but rather for the salability of pulp thrillers, such penny dreadfuls as *Affecting History of the Dreadful Distresses of Frederic Manheim's Family* (1793), *An Affective Narrative of the Captivity and Sufferings of Mrs. Mary Smith* (1818), or *An Affecting Account of the Tragical Death of Major Swan, and the Captivity of Mrs. Swan and Infant Child* (1815). This particular application of the captivity narrative can be seen in three overlapping developments: accounts became more stylized, with every effort toward literary correctness; they became sensationalized, with an emphasis upon "effect" and the sensibility of horror; and, finally, they became so factually exaggerated and ultimately fictionalized that in some cases they were outright novels of sensibility based only slightly and speciously on actual captivities.

An illustration of the subtle shift toward more literary effect in the narratives is found in the versions of the captivity of Elizabeth Hanson. The 1754 edition, less simple and direct than the first (1728) edition but still a relatively straightforward account, was altered through "improved" diction and other rhetorical embellishments for the 1760 edition, the account of Mrs. Hanson's experience that was "Taken in Substance from her own Mouth" by one Samuel Bownas:

> [1754] In a few days after this, they got near their journey's end, where they had more plenty of corn, and other food. But flesh often fell very short, having no other way to depend on it but hunting; and when that failed, they had very short commons. It was not long ere my daughter and servant were likewise parted, and my daughter's master being sick, was not able to hunt for flesh; neither had they any corn in that place, but were forced to eat bark of trees for a whole week.
>
> [1760] Accordingly, in a few days after this, they drew near their journey's end, where they found greater plenty of corn and other food; but flesh often fell very short, as they had no other way of procuring it but hunting.
>
> It was not long before my daughter and servant were parted also; and my daughter's master falling sick, he was thereon disabled from hunting. All their corn was likewise spent; and so great were their distresses, that they were compelled to feed on the bark of trees for a whole week, being almost famished to death.

The worst offenders at this kind of stylistic embellishment were journalists or opportunists who "edited" for publication the accounts of captives. The development of sensationalism in the narratives can be discerned in two separate appeals: one to the reader's sensibilities through stylistic excesses and melodrama, the other to his capacity for horror through excesses of descriptive detail. Many narratives contain passages well within the tradition of the sentimental novel: in the Manheim anthology, Jackson Johonnot begins the narrative of his captivity as if it were indeed an affecting fiction, expressing his confident expectation that "the tender hearted will drop the tear of sympathy, when they realize the idea of the sufferings of such of our unfortunate country folks as fall into the hands of the western Indians, whose tender mercies are cruelties." Johonnot's attempt to confirm this expectation is in part stylistic: "Alas! how fluctuating are the scenes of life! how singularly precarious the fortunes of a soldier!" And, "Good God!

what were my feelings when, starting from my slumbers, I heard the most tremendous firing all around, with yellings, horrid whoopings and expiring groans in dreadful discord . . . ."

Given the circumstances and conditions of Indian captivity, it was an easy matter to elicit horror from the reader by playing up "barbarities terrible and shocking to human nature" as Peter Williamson did. This narrative, like others of its kind, displays many elements of the Gothic novel—depicting the reactions of a character to trying or appalling situations, holding the reader in suspense with the character, and the heaping of a succession of horrors upon the reader in order to shock and alarm him. The Williamson narrative very quickly plunges into a veritable orgy of horrors, excessively and even lovingly described. Two prisoners with Williamson have their bellies ripped open, entrails removed and burnt before their eyes; a third captive is buried upright to his neck, scalped, and a fire laid along-side his head until his brains boil and "till his eyes gushed out of their sockets." Jackson Johonnot describes the scalping of a companion, who is then stripped naked and stabbed with knives "in every sensitive part of the body" and left "weltering in blood, though not quite dead, a wretched victim to Indian rage and hellish barbarity." Such incidents had, for the most part, a basis in actual occurrence; it is the excessive and sensational treatment of them that affronts the modern reader. There are numerous examples, on the other hand, of incidents in many narratives that are either so greatly exaggerated as to strain credibility, such as Isaac Stewart's encounter with Welsh-speaking Indians or the circumstances surrounding Rachel Plummer's cave visitation, or are, in some cases, outright fictions lacking the all-important sense of authentically human experience that characterizes the earlier, genuine captivities. Because of these known fraudulent and fictionalized accounts, many writers of authentic narratives felt obliged to attest the veracity of their own accounts. As early as 1758, the Reverend Gilbert Tennent's preface to Robert Eastburn's narrative points out that Eastburn is a deacon of the church and that his testimony "may with safety be depended upon." The 1792 version of Jemima Howe's captivity ("A Genuine and Correct Account . . . ") given to the Reverend Bunker Gay was issued to remedy the excesses of a previously published version thought by Mrs. Howe to be "romantic and extravagant," containing errors of fact as well as excesses of style. By the early decades of the nineteenth century the credibility of captivity narratives was definitely in question, so much so in fact that one narrative was actually accompanied by an affidavit. Published in the 1820's, the later editions of the captivity of Matthew Bunn contained this testimony: "I, Matthew Bunn, the author of the above Narrative am duly sworn, and testify that the above Narrative is a true statement of the Life and Adventures of the above named Matthew Bunn...." Many nineteenth-century captives were reluctant to publish their stories at all. The most recently published original narrative of Indian captivity, the account of Frank Buckelew—who was taken in 1866 at the age of thirteen by Lipan Indians in Texas—was not related until 1932. The preface states that he "long hesitated to present his story as an Indian captive lest it be condemned as fiction, like so many Indian stories, and cast aside as worthless."

An egregious example of the entirely fictionalized captivity narrative is *An Account of a Beautiful Young Lady, Who Was Taken by the Indians and Lived in the Woods Nine Years* (1787), by Abraham Panther [pseud.]. Pure fiction in a pamphlet of less than a dozen pages, it was a best seller of sorts, running through twenty-five editions printed by small village presses and hawked by Yankee peddlers. Its popularity is not surprising in a time when reading fiction was improper but reading "true" stories was legitimate. The *Narrative of the Singular Adventures and Captivity of Mrs. Thomas Berry* (1800) is also regarded as another piece of "Indian fiction." Very likely the first novelist to work an Indian captivity into his narrative and pass it off to the public as a true adventure was W. R. Chetwood, whose *The Voyages, Dangerous Adventures and Imminent Escapes of Captain Richard Falconer* (1720) went through nine editions. The most elaborate eighteenth-century captivity in novelized form is Ann Eliza Bleecker's *The History of Maria Kittle. In a Letter to Miss Ten Eyck* (1797). This novel, a fictionalized story of the captivity of Maria Kittlehuyne and the massacre of her family during King George's War, is an outright novel of sensibility. Mrs. Bleecker's unabashed goal is to "open the sluice gate" of the reader's eyes by achieving "the luxury of sorrow" in her story. "O hell! are not thy flames impatient to cleave the center and engulph these wretches in thy ever burning waves?" soliloquizes her heroine at the high point in this tale of Indian devastations and cruelties; "Are there no thunders in Heaven—no avenging Angels—no God to take notice of such Heaven-defying cruelties?" The captivity narrative has here become whole-cloth sentimental fiction, a forerunner of many of the tales in Erastus Beadle's celebrated series of formularized dime novels, the first of which using the captivity experience appeared in 1860: Edward S. Ellis' *Seth Jones; or, The Captives of the Frontier*, followed by such others as Joseph E. Badger's *The Forest Princess; or, The Kickapoo Captives*, and *Nathan Todd; or, The Fate of the Sioux' Captive*. It is at this point and with this mode that, for all practical purposes and with few exceptions, the development of the narratives of Indian captivity culminates—in the travesty of the penny dreadful.

From beginning to end, one feature that the greater part of Indian captivity narratives have in common, as publications, is their current rarity. Printed in limited editions by small village presses, many first editions—like the first Mary Rowlandson—are not extant, and countless others survive in but a handful of copies. The popularity of Cotton Mather's *Good Fetch'd Out of Evil: A Collection of Memorables Relating to Our Captives* (1706) is indicated by its sale of one thousand copies the first week of its printing, yet only four known copies now exist, all imperfect. Despite this scarcity, the Edward E. Ayer Collection in the Newberry Library, Chicago, contains some 480 editions of the narratives of over two hundred different captives.

Narratives were generally written for immediate publication as soon as the captive had returned from the wilderness. The captive, usually at the urging of friends and relatives or just as often at the suggestion of enterprising journalists or printers, either composed his account in his own words ("Written by Himself" is a testament that frequently appears on title pages) or, if not literate, related the story to someone else who took it "in Substance from His Own Relation," as many other title pages report. Often the narratives were printed at the expense of their authors or agents; at other times, at the risk of their printers. Generally, in the earlier colonial period, only such staple items as psalters and psalm books were printed on order from booksellers. During the period from 1680 to 1716 colonial printing of captivity narratives was restricted largely to the Boston area presses, and bookselling in later colonial America was centered chiefly in Boston, New York, Philadelphia, and Charleston. In smaller towns and villages, the community printer's production was confined to almanacs, schoolbooks, chapbooks, and reprints of popular works of fiction, travel, and adventure. Among these were, in many instances, narratives of Indian captivity.

While the primary means of book distribution in the colonies was over-the-counter sale by the printer or retail bookseller, there were also other modes: subscription, traveling booksellers, and auctions. Very few captivity narratives were sold by subscription, but a great many were hawked by traveling book peddlers, most notably in the later period. Matthew Carey's celebrated agent Mason Weems ("Parson Weems," the prince of American book agents) covered the eastern seaboard from Pennsylvania to Georgia from 1794 to 1825. From before the Revolution to about 1860 the traveling agent was a popular means of bookselling in America, and many Indian captivity narratives found a wide readership through this mode of distribution. The book auction, called in colonial days the "vendue," began in America in 1713 at Boston. The principal difference between auctions then and now is that the colonial auction was used as a means for the disposal of new books as well as of old, and fresh captivities often found their way to the auction tables during the period.

The first Indian captivity narrative published in New England, Mary Rowlandson's *The Soveraignty and Goodness of God, Together With the Faithfulness of His Promises Displayed; Being a Narrative of the Captivity and Restauration of Mrs. Mary Rowlandson*, was printed in Boston by Samuel Green, Jr., in 1682 for John Ratcliffe and John Griffin, who commissioned the printing at their expense. The second edition was issued at Cambridge in the same year by Samuel Green the elder on authority of the General Court. This edition is accompanied by a sermon of the Reverend Joseph Rowlandson on the occasion of his wife's captivity. An adjunct of Harvard College, the Cambridge press was not strictly a private enterprise, and the product of the press was carefully watched and monitored by the General Court. The printing of the Rowlandson narrative, then, was more in the nature of a public service than a business venture, as were the two other principal publications of the press for 1682—Urian Oakes's *Fast Sermon* and Cotton Mather's *Ornaments for the Daughters of Zion.* Other early captivity narratives were issued under similar circumstances and proceeded from like motives: Increase Mather's *An Essay for the Recording of Illustrious Providences* (1684), printed by Green the younger in Boston, contains the first printing of the Quentin Stockwell captivity; Cotton Mather's *Humiliations Follow'd With Deliverances* (1697), printed by Bartholomew Green and John Allen in Boston, contains the narratives of Hannah Dustin (Dustan, Duston) and Hannah Swarton. Mather later reprinted the Dustin narrative in his *Decennium Luctuosum* (1699) and both the Swarton and the Dustin narratives in the *Magnalia* (1702). The first bookseller-publisher to specialize, as it were, in captivity narratives appears to have been Samuel Phillips, a Boston bookdealer who sold his wares "at the Brick-Shop at the West-End of the Town-House" and who founded a line of Boston booksellers that continued to do business until after the Revolution. The first edition of John Williams' *The Redeemed Captive Returning to Zion* (1707) was printed by Bartholomew Green at Boston for Samuel Phillips. Phillips, in other words, took the risk of (or "published") the title; the printer had no financial interest in the venture other than a stipulated payment for the printing. The second (1720) edition of the Williams narrative was also printed for Samuel Phillips, but by another Boston printer, Thomas Fleet. Phillips also issued the 1720 edition of the Rowlandson narrative.

After 1720 the publication of captivity narratives followed the manner of colonial printing generally: titles were issued at the risk of a single printer-bookseller who united the twin functions of the early book trade—production and distribution. The first edition of the Elizabeth Hanson narrative, *God's Mercy Surmounting Man's Cruelty* (1728), bears the title page notation "To be sold by Samuel Keimer [printer] in Philadelphia." Its publication was advertised in the *Pennsylvania Gazette*, December 24, 1728. The first edition of *Memoirs of Odd Adventures, Strange Deliverances, Etc., In the Captivity of John Gyles, Esq.* (1736) was printed and sold by S. Kneeland and T. Green in Boston. With the Gyles narrative began a spate of narratives growing out of the French and Indian War, popular enough to enable the publisher of *A Narrative of the Captivity of Nehemiah How* (Boston, 1748) to issue that narrative initially by subscription. The title page of the How narrative gives no publisher or printer, but a two-page list of subscribers is appended to the edition. *A Narrative of the Sufferings and Surprizing Deliverances of William and Elizabeth Fleming...* (Philadelphia, 1756) was "Printed for the Benefit of the Unhappy Sufferers, and Sold by Them Only." Issued at the height of the French and Indian conflict, the Fleming narrative was widely reprinted: in the same year of its original publication, reprint editions were issued in Lancaster, Massachusetts, by William Dunlap; in New York by J. Parker and W. Weyman; and in Germantown, Pennsylvania, a German translation by Christoph Saur appeared. Three other popular French and Indian captivity narratives were Peter Williamson's *French and Indian Cruelty ...* (1757), "Printed for the Author" in York; Robert Eastburn's *A Faithful Narrative of the Many Dangers and Sufferings, as well as Wonderful and Surprizing Deliverances of Robert Eastburn, During His Late Captivity Among the Indians* (1758), printed in Philadelphia by William Dunlap and immediately "Re-printed and sold by Green & Russell" in Boston the same year; and Thomas Brown's *A Plain Narrative of the Uncommon Sufferings and Remarkable Deliverance of Thomas Brown* (1760), "Printed and Sold by Fowle and Draper" in three editions of the same imprint and date.

Narratives of the period following the French and Indian War were sometimes printed first in newspapers or magazines. Frances Scott's *A True and Wonderful Narrative...*, for example, originally appeared in the *Freeman's Journal*, December 14, 1785, and was subsequently picked up and reprinted in other magazines before it was brought out in book form in Boston in 1786. Other narratives of this period were often solicited from captives for various reasons. Indian-hater Hugh Henry Brackenridge, who arranged for the publication of the John Knight and John Slover captivities, *Narratives of a Late Expedition Against the Indians*, in the Philadelphia *Freeman's Journal*, April 30–May 21, 1783, reported that Knight's account "was written by himself at my request; that of Slover was taken by myself from his own mouth as he related it." *A Journal of the Adventures of Matthew Bunn* (Providence, 1796) was published "by the particular request of a number of persons who have seen the manuscript" and was printed "for the author, and sold by him." Enterprising and shrewd Matthew Carey arranged, as bookseller, for the Philadelphia publication (1794) of the Manheim anthology, *Affecting History of the Dreadful Distresses . . .*, a highly successful commercial collection on Indian horrors and captivities compiled and first published in Exeter in 1793. This Philadelphia edition, "Printed (for Matthew Carey) by D. Humphreys," was followed by a later edition (1800) "Printed by Henry Switzer for Matthew Carey." Both editions became staples for Carey's traveling hawkers.

The publication and success of the Manheim anthology signaled the appearance of the collections of captivity narratives that began in the very early 1800's and continued throughout the century as individual captivities, less frequently issued, gradually gave way to staple anthologies of older accounts. Archibald Loudon's *A Selection of Some of the Most Interesting Narratives of Outrages Committed by the Indians, in Their Wars, With the White People* (1808–11) collects the narratives of John Knight and John Slover, Frances Scott, the Manheim anthology (Corbly, Morgan, Stewart, Herbeson, Williamson, Johonnot) and of James Smith, John M'Cullough, Robert Eastburn, Richard Bard, and Benjamin Gilbert. In 1821, Samuel L. Metcalf's *A Collection of Some of the Most Interesting Narratives of Indian Warfare* gathered the Knight and Slover, Morgan, Johonnot, Smith, and Daniel Boone captivities. Benjamin B. Thatcher's *Tales of the Indians* (1831), while largely a history of North American Indians, prints the captivities of Mrs. Rowlandson and Alexander Henry. The publication of *Chronicles of Border Warfare*, edited by Alexander Scott Withers, containing among others the Boone, Knight and Slover, and Williamson captivities, occurred in the same year. The best and most deservedly well-known collection appeared in 1839: Samuel Gardner Drake's *Indian Captivities, or Life in the Wigwam*, twenty-nine narratives complete and without alterations or editorial tinkering. Among these are the Rowlandson, Gyles, Hanson, How, Williamson, Smith, and Eastburn narratives, and the Manheim anthology. James Wimer's *Events in Indian History* (1841), taken largely from Drake and Thatcher, contains the Williams, Rowlandson, How, Stockwell, Gyles, Smith, Hanson, and M'Coy narratives. *Thrilling Adventures Among the Indians* (1854), edited by John Frost, includes the Scott, Stewart, and Frances Slocum narratives but is otherwise a collection of brief and undocumented anecdotes concerning fights, massacres, escapes, and "singular scenes" of Indian life. Joseph Pritts's *Incidents of Border Life* (1859) contains the Smith, Knight and Slover, Scott, Eastburn, Boone, and Slocum narratives, and the Manheim anthology.

In the twentieth century, Horace Kephart's *Captives among the Indians* (1915) collects but four narratives (Smith, Bressani, Rowlandson, and Herbeson), and Emma L. Coleman's *New England Captives Carried to Canada between 1677 and 1760 during the French and Indian Wars* (1925)—a continuation of C. Alice Baker's project, *True Stories of New England Captives Carried to Canada* (1897)—is not a collection of captivity narratives as such but rather a compilation by name, date, place of capture, and disposition of several hundred captives during that period. Carl Coke Rister's *Border Captives* (1940), a regional study describing the traffic in prisoners by Southern Plains Indians from 1835 to 1875, considers only the broad movement, interspersed at points by episode and incident and using brief captive sketches as types and examples. *Captured by Indians* (1954), by Howard H. Peckham, presents fourteen narratives in paraphrase ("retold for today's reading"), with occasional quotations from the originals for flavor; summarized are the Rowlandson, Williams, Jemison, Boone, Olive and Mary Ann Oatman, and Kelly narratives, among others. Finally, in a commercial enterprise "intended for the popular reader, not the historian or scholar" and titled *Scalps and Tomahawks* (1961), Frederick Drimmer offers fifteen narratives (actually seven condensed books and eight shorter pieces), freely revised to improve their "readability." In sum, there has been no significant and scholarly collection of Indian captivity narratives in the twentieth century. It is hoped that this volume, the first modern scholarly collection of uncut and unaltered narratives, will serve to redirect attention to this important body of distinctly native American materials.

The eighteen narratives collected here were chosen not only to present a chronological sampling of seventeenth-, eighteenth-, and nineteenth-century captivities (1642–1836, by dates of capture) but also to illustrate the principal significances and uses of the narratives collectively: cultural, historical, ethnological. In the context of American culture, for example, the narratives selected illuminate the concerns of the captivity experience itself in the light of the society for which the narratives were intended: those of predominantly religious orientation (Puritan in the Mary Rowlandson narrative, Catholic in Father Jogues's); those manifesting the propagandistic, anti-French and Indian tendency (John Gyles and Robert Eastburn narratives); and those increasingly stylized (Elizabeth Hanson and Mary Kinnan narratives) or sensationalized (the Manheim anthology). These are not, of course, mutually exclusive categories of concern, but they do differ significantly in respective focus. Added to these are the John Marrant narrative, one of the first American books by a Negro and one of the three most popular of all stories of Indian captivity; the Charles Johnston narrative, a historically and ethnologically interesting account; and the narrative of Rachel Plummer, a nineteenth-century example from the Southwest.

In a historical perspective, the selections provide both overview of and insight into major Indian-white conflicts in America as they are reflected in the narratives of Indian captivity: King Philip's War, 1675–76 (Rowlandson narrative); King William's War, 1689–97 (Gyles); French and Indian War, 1755–62 (Williamson, Eastburn); the Revolution, 1775–83 (Manheim anthology); the Western Wars, 1790–94 (Johnston, Kinnan); and nineteenth-century Plains warfare of the later westward movement (Plummer). Finally, the selections are of sufficient variety as to provide a wide range of ethnological data and commentary on American Indian tribes of New England, the Southeast, Plains, and Southwest that are represented as captors or in contact with captives: Mohawk, Huron, Maliseet, Penobscot, Cherokee, Shawnee, Comanche, and, peripherally, Wichita, Choctaw, Seneca, and Pawnee. The editorial materials are designed to develop the cultural, historical, and ethnological concerns of each of the narratives wherever appropriate and relevant. In addition to, and perhaps transcending, these significances and uses of the captivity narratives is the inherent appeal of the narratives themselves—tales of adventure, terror, ordeal, and fortitude that touch upon fundamental truths. More than cultural indices or curiosities, the narratives of Indian captivity draw and shape their materials from the very wellsprings of human experience.

Acknowledgments

For assistance and access to materials, grateful acknowledgment is made to the Special Collections Division, the Newberry Library (Edward E. Ayer Collection); the Reference Department of the Huntington Library; the University of Texas and University of Washington libraries; the State Library and Archives, Sacramento, California; the Documents and Loan Department of the San Jose State College Library; and for their early work with the narratives of Indian captivity, to Professors R. W. G. Vail, Roy Harvey Pearce, and Richard M. Dorson. Special acknowledgment and thanks are made to Professor William N. Fenton, Department of Anthropology, State University of New York at Albany, from whose suggestions and comments a great part of the ethnological data in this volume is derived; to Professor Richard Beale Davis, Department of English, University of Tennessee, who read the manuscript and offered both encouragement and advice.

Richard VanDerBeets

San Jose, California
April 26, 1972

Held Captive by Indians

I

Captivity of Father Isaac Jogues, of the Society of Jesus, Among the Mohawks

†††

Isaac Jogues was born at Orleans, France, in 1607 and became a member of the Society of Jesus in 1624. He sought a foreign mission and was assigned to Canada soon after his ordination in 1636. He lived in Huron country in upper Canada until 1642, when he was sent to Quebec for supplies to replenish his mission. On the return trip he was taken prisoner following an ambush by a band of marauding Mohawks. The narrative of the captivity of Father Jogues is in the form of a letter from Jogues to the provincial of the Jesuits in France, dated August 5, 1643. The Jesuit missionaries who came to the French territory in America during the seventeenth century were required to submit written annual reports to their superior at Quebec or Montreal. Annually, between 1632 and 1673, the superior compiled and edited a journal, or "Relation," of the most important materials and forwarded it to the provincial. Known collectively as the Jesuit Relations, *they were published in a series of volumes issued from the press of Sebastian Cramoisy in Paris. The* Jesuit Relations *are especially valuable to historians and ethnologists because the authors of the journals that formed the basis of the* Relations *were well-educated men and trained observers. They were explorers as well as priests, journalists as well as missionaries. Consequently, the folklore, the religion, the mythology, the manners and morals, and even the speech of the Indians have been well preserved in their accounts. The Jesuits in*

New France were very sparsely scattered from Cape Breton to the eastern shore of Lake Huron, a distance of over one thousand miles. Trading posts were located as near as possible to the lakes and navigable rivers: the principal highway was the St. Lawrence River; the Maurice, Ottawa, and Severn rivers opened up the north, while the Sorel River, Lake Champlain, and the Hudson River furnished a highway to the south. Over all this area there were only twenty-four Jesuits at the time Jogues landed at Quebec in 1636. The Hurons, in whose country Jogues labored, were bitter enemies of the Iroquois and had been driven westward to a relatively small area between Lakes Erie and Huron. They were friendly with the French, however, and were consequently considered a fruitful field for Jesuit missions. The Iroquois occupied roughly what is now New York State and the land between Lakes Ontario, Huron, and Erie. Jogues's captors, the Mohawks, were the fiercest of the Five Iroquois Nations (Mohawk, Oneida, Cayuga, Seneca, and Onondaga) and were universally feared warriors. The Hurons were in danger of total extermination from their wars with the Iroquois, who had also terrorized the French and all the Algonquin Nations up and down the St. Lawrence River. It was during the height of these internecine tribal conflicts that Jogues began his mission. The complete version of Jogues's captivity, from his original letter (a sworn copy of which is preserved at the College Sainte-Marie, Montreal), was printed in Philippe Alegambe, S.J., Mortres Illustres *(1655) and is the basis for John Gilmary Shea's version in* Perils of the Ocean and Wilderness *(Boston, 1857), the text reprinted here.*

† †

Narrative

Reverend Father in Christ—the Peace of Christ.—Wishing, as I do, to write to your reverence, I hesitate first in which language to address you, for, after such long disuse, almost equally forgetful of both, I find equal difficulty in each.[1] Two reasons, however, in-

[1] That is, French and Latin. Jogues's letter is in "the less common idiom," a pure and classic Latin. The Reverend Father to whom it is addressed is Father Jean Filleau, the provincial of the French Province of the Society of Jesus.

duce me to employ the less common idiom. I shall be better able to use the words of Holy Scripture, which have been, at all times, my greatest consolation: "Amid the tribulations which have found us exceedingly."—Psalms xlv. 2. I also wished this letter to be less open to all. The exceeding charity of your reverence, which, in other days, overlooked my manifold transgressions, will excuse, in a man for eight years a companion and associate of savages, nay, a savage now himself in form and dress, whatever may be wanting in decorum or correctness. I fear more that, wanting in language, I may be still more so in knowledge, "nor know the time of my visitation," nor remember what character I here bear imposed on me by God as a preacher of his gospel, a Jesuit and a priest. This induced me to write to your reverence that, if this letter should ever reach your hands, I may, though lying here in this hard land, amid Iroquois and Maaquas, be helped by your masses, and the prayers of your whole province. This, I am in hopes, will be more earnestly given, when, from the perusal of this letter, you shall see, both how much I am indebted to the Almighty, and in what need I am of the prayers of the pious, in which, I am aware, I have a powerful shield.

We sailed from the Huron territory on the 13th of June, 1642, in four small boats, here called canoes; we were twenty-three souls in all, five of us being French. This line of travel is, in itself, most difficult for many reasons, and especially because, in no less than forty places, both canoes and baggage had to be carried by land on the shoulders. It was now too full of danger from fear of the enemy, who, every year, by lying in wait on the roads to the French settlements, carry off many as prisoners; and, indeed, Father John Brebeuf [2] was all but taken the year before. Besides this, not long before they carried off two Frenchmen, but afterwards brought them back to their countrymen unharmed, demanding peace on most unjust terms, and then conducted themselves in a very hostile manner, so that they were driven off by the cannons of the fort. On this, they declared that, if they took another Frenchman prisoner, they would torture him cruelly, like their other captives, and burn him alive by a slow fire. The Superior,

[2] Father Jean de Brébeuf, who led the first attempt to Christianize the Hurons in 1624.

conscious of the dangers I was exposed to on this journey, which was, however, absolutely necessary for God's glory, so assigned the task to me, that I might decline it if I chose; "I did not, however, resist; I did not go back;" (Isaias 1. 5;) but willingly and cheerfully accepted this mission imposed upon me by obedience and charity.[3] Had I declined it, it would have fallen to another, far more worthy than myself.

Having, therefore, loosed from St. Mary's of the Hurons, amid ever-varying fears of the enemy, dangers of every kind, losses by land and water, we at last, on the thirtieth day after our departure, reached in safety the Conception of the Blessed Virgin. This is a French settlement or colony, called Three Rivers,[4] from a most charming stream near it, which discharges itself into the great river St. Lawrence, by three mouths. We returned hearty thanks to God, and remained here and at Quebec about two weeks.

The business which had brought us, having been concluded, we celebrated the feast of our holy Father Ignatius,[5] and, on the second of August, were once more on our way for Huronia.[6] The

3 It was necessary that one of the priests at Sainte Marie (St. Mary's of the Hurons) accompany the group to Quebec: reports and letters had to be delivered, letters and instructions had to be brought back, and supplies had to be gathered for the winter. The Superior, Father Jérôme Lalemant, chose the experienced Jogues for the journey.

4 Three Rivers had become a permanent settlement in 1634. It lay at the juncture of the St. Maurice River emptying into the St. Lawrence, about eighty miles from Quebec, and was a prehistoric trading and assembly place of the Indians, who called it *Metaberoutin*, the "Spot Exposed to All the Winds." The French had named it Three Rivers because the St. Maurice, divided by projecting islands, had the appearance of three distinct rivers at its mouth.

5 St. Ignatius of Loyola (1491–1556), the founder of the Society of Jesus. The order was formed in 1534 to combat the Reformation and to propagate the Roman Catholic faith among the heathen. Through its discipline, organization, and methods of secrecy the order acquired great political power. Jesuits were particularly active in three fields: education, missionary endeavor in non-Catholic lands, and the development of a deeper spiritual life.

6 That is, the land of the Hurons, some thousand miles westward from Quebec. The Hurons numbered about 35,000, occupying twenty villages. The two principal villages that Jogues and his fellow missionaries served were Ihonatiria and Ossossané. Ihonatiria was a major hamlet of the Nation of the Bear (the Attignawantans), who formed the original stock of the Wendat peoples whom the French referred to as Hurons. The name "Huron" was given them by the French owing to their fashion of wearing their hair in ridges, an inch or two wide, from the forehead to the nape of the neck, with furrows of the same width cut to the scalp. The resemblance of these ridges to the tufts on the head of the wild boar (*la hure*) suggested the name.

second day after our departure had just dawned, when, by the early light, some of our party discovered fresh foot-prints on the shore. While some were maintaining that they were the trail of the enemy, others, that of a friendly party, Eustace Ahatsistari,[7] to whom, for his gallant feats of arms, all yielded the first rank, exclaimed: "Brothers! be they the bravest of the foe, for such I judge them by their trail, they are no more than three canoes, and we number enough not to dread such a handful of the enemy." We were, in fact, forty, for some other had joined us.

We consequently urged on our way, but had scarcely advanced a mile, when we fell into an ambush of the enemy, who lay in two divisions on the opposite banks of the river, to the number of seventy in twelve canoes.[8]

As soon as we reached the spot where they lay in ambush, they poured in a volley of musketry from the reeds and tall grass, where they lurked. Our canoes were riddled, but, though well supplied with fire-arms, they killed none, one Huron only being shot through the hand. At the first report of the fire-arms, the Hurons, almost to a man, abandoned the canoes, which, to avoid the more rapid current of the centre of the river, were advancing close by the bank, and in head-long flight, plunged into the thickest of the woods. We, four Frenchmen,[9] left with a few, either already Christians, or at least Catechumens,[10] offering up a prayer to Christ, faced the enemy. We were, however, out-numbered, being scarcely twelve or fourteen against thirty; yet we fought on, till our comrades, seeing fresh canoes shoot out from the opposite bank of the river, lost heart and fled. Then a Frenchman named Rene Goupil, who was fighting with the bravest, was taken with some

7 Honored as one of the great war chiefs of the Huron Nations, and a recent convert of the Jesuits, Ahatsistari had already become a hero of legend. He was baptized in the chapel of Sainte Marie in March of 1642 and given the name of Eustace.

8 The place of the Iroquois attack and the capture of Jogues has been calculated as the north bank of the North Channel of the St. Lawrence, opposite Ile à l'Aigle, near the dividing line between Berthier and Maskinonge counties, Quebec.

9 René Goupil, Guillaume Coûture, Jogues, and a French workman. Goupil and Coûture were two of a new class of lay helpers, called *donnés,* bound by contract and by private, not religious, vow for life to serve and assist the Fathers in the Huron mission.

10 Neophytes.

of the Hurons. When I saw this, I neither could, nor cared to fly. Where, indeed, could I escape, barefooted as I was? Conceal myself amid the reeds and tall grass, I could indeed, and thus escape; but could I leave a countryman, and the unchristened Hurons already taken or soon to be? As the enemy, in hot pursuit of the fugitives, had passed on, leaving me standing on the battle-field, I called out to one of those who remained to guard the prisoners, and bade him make me a fellow captive to his French captive, that, as I had been his companion on the way, so would I be in his dangers and death. Scarce giving credit to what he heard, and fearful for himself, he advanced and led me to the other prisoners.

Dearest brother, I then exclaimed, wonderfully hath God dealt with us! "but he is the Lord, let him do what is good in his sight;" —1 Kings iii. 18. "As it hath pleased him, so hath it come to pass, blessed be his name;" then, hearing his confession, I gave him absolution. I now turned to the Huron prisoners, and, instructing them one by one, baptized them; as new prisoners were constantly taken in their flight, my labor was constantly renewed. At length Eustace Ahatsistari, that famous Christian chief, was brought in; when he saw me, he exclaimed, "Solemnly did I swear, brother, that I would live or die by thee." What I answered, I know not, so had grief overcome me. Last of all, William Couture was dragged in; he too, had set out from Huronia with me. When he saw all in confusion, he had, with the rest, taken to the woods, and, being a young man endowed with great gifts in body as well as in mind, had, by his great agility, left the enemy far behind. When he looked around and could see nothing of me, "Shall I," he said to himself," abandon my dear Father, a prisoner in the hands of savages, and fly without him? Not I." Then returning by the path which he had taken in flight, he gave himself up to the enemy. Would that he had fled, nor swelled our mournful band! for, in such a case, it is no comfort to have companions, especially those whom you love as yourself. Yet such are the souls, who, though but laymen, (with no views of earthly reward,) serve God and the Society among the Hurons.

It is painful to think, even, of all his terrible sufferings. Their hate was enkindled against all the French, but especially against him, as they knew that one of their bravest had fallen by his hand in the fight. He was accordingly first stripped naked, all his nails torn out, his very fingers gnawed, and a broad-sword driven through his right hand. Mindful of the wounds of our Lord Jesus Christ, he bore, as he afterwards told me, this pain, though most acute, with great joy.

When I beheld him, thus bound and naked, I could not contain myself, but, leaving my keepers, I rushed through the midst of the savages who had brought him, embraced him most tenderly, exhorted him to offer all this to God for himself, and those at whose hands he suffered. They at first looked on in wonder at my proceedings; then, as if recollecting themselves, and gathering all their rage, they fell upon me, and, with their fists, thongs, and a club, beat me till I fell senseless.[11] Two of them then dragged me back to where I had been before, and scarcely had I begun to breathe, when some others, attacking me, tore out, by biting, almost all my nails, and crunched my two fore-fingers with their teeth, giving me intense pain. The same was done to René Goupil, the Huron captives being left untouched.

When all had come in from the pursuit, in which two Hurons were killed, they carried us across the river, and there shared the plunder of the twelve canoes, (for eight had joined us.) This was very great, for, independent of what each Frenchman had with him, we had twenty packages containing church plate and vestments, books and other articles of the kind; a rich cargo indeed, considering the poverty of our Huron mission. While they were dividing the plunder, I completed the instruction of such as were unchristened, and baptized them. Among the rest was one sere, octogenarian chief, who, when ordered to enter the canoe to be borne off with the rest, exclaimed, "How shall I, a hoary old man, go to a strange and foreign land? Never! here will I die." As he absolutely refused to go, they slew him on the very spot where he had just been baptized.

Raising then a joyful shout which made the forest ring, "as conquerors who rejoice after taking a prey," (Isaias ix. 3,) they bore us off, twenty-two captives, towards their own land; three

[11] In effecting his brief escape, Coûture had slain one of the Mohawk chiefs. When Jogues embraced him the Indians, thinking he was congratulating Coûture, were enraged.

had been killed. By the favor of God our sufferings on that march, which lasted thirteen days, were indeed great—hunger, and heat, and menaces, the savage fury of the Indians, the intense pain of our untended and now putrefying wounds, swarming even with worms; but no trial came harder upon me than when, five or six days after, they would come up to us, weary with the march, and in cold blood, with minds in no wise aroused by passion, pluck out our hair and beard, and drive their nails, which are always very sharp, deep into parts most tender and sensitive to the slightest impression. But this was outward; my internal sufferings affected me still more when I beheld that funeral procession of doomed Christians pass before my eyes, among them five old converts, the main pillars of the infant Huron church.

Indeed, I ingenuously admit, that I was again and again unable to withhold my tears, mourning over their lot and that of my other companions, and full of anxious solicitude for the future. For I beheld the way to the Christian faith closed by these Iroquois, on the Hurons, and countless other nations, unless they were checked by some seasonable dispensation of Divine Providence.

On the eighth day we fell in with a troop of two hundred Indians going out to fight. And as it is the custom for the savages, when out on war parties, to initiate themselves as it were by cruelty, under the belief that their success will be greater as they shall have been more cruel, they thus received us. First rendering thanks to the sun, which they imagine presides over war,[12] they congratulated their countrymen by a joyful volley of musketry. Each then cut off some stout clubs in the neighboring wood in order to receive us. When, therefore, we landed from the canoes,

[12] The religion of the Iroquois was a sort of nature-dread, a belief that everything material had life and intelligence, had power to harm, and would exercise that power upon the slightest offense or neglect. Trees, rivers, mountains, winds, beasts, birds, and fishes were all embodied spirits capable of understanding the language of man and doing him good or harm. A storm, for example, was an angry wind spirit; an unsuccessful hunt, an offended deer spirit; an upset canoe, an angry river spirit; an unsuccessful crop, a displeased harvest spirit; and so on for all the occurrences of life. Iroquois also believed that some one material thing or animal possessed a particular spirit which was a personal deity, to be worshipped by a particular individual. The spirit was called an "oki" or "manitou." The Indian made an image of it which he always carried with him and to which he made supplications and offerings. Human life was frequently sacrificed to a "manitou" to placate or propitiate an offended spirit.

they fell upon us from both sides with their clubs, with such fury, that I, who was the last, and therefore most exposed to their blows, sank, overcome by their number and severity, before I had accomplished half the rocky way that led to the hill on which a stage had been erected for us.[13] I thought I should soon die there; and so, partly because I could not, partly because I cared not, I did not arise. How long they spent their fury on me, he knows for whose love and sake I suffered all, and for whom it is delightful and glorious to suffer.—Moved at length by a cruel mercy, and wishing to carry me into their country alive, they refrained from beating me. And, thus half dead, and drenched in blood, they bore me to the stage. I had scarce begun to breathe, when they ordered me to come down, to load me with scoffs and insults, and countless blows on my head and shoulders, and indeed on my whole body. I should be tedious were I to attempt to tell all that the French prisoners suffered. They burnt one of my fingers, and crunched another with their teeth; others already thus mangled, they so wrenched by the tattered nerve, that, even now, though healed, they are frightfully deformed. Nor indeed was the lot of my fellow-suffers much better.

But one thing showed that God watched over us, and was trying us rather than casting us off. One of these savages, breathing nought but blood and cruelty, came up to me, scarce able to stand on my feet, and, seizing my nose with one hand, prepared to cut it off with a large knife which he held in the other. What could

13 Jogues is describing the well-known gantlet, or "gauntlet," ritual of greeting captives as they enter a new village, a custom recurring in captivity accounts from the seventeenth to the nineteenth century and practiced by tribes of wide geographical divergence. John Heckewelder, in his work, "An Account of the History, Manners, and Customs, of the Indian Nations" (*Transactions of the Historical and Literary Committee of the American Philosophical Society* [Philadelphia, 1819], I, 212), describes the usual procedure: "On entering the village, [the new captive] is shewn a painted post at the distance from twenty to forty yards, and told to run to it.... On each side of him stand men, women, and children with axes, sticks, and other offensive weapons, ready to strike him as he runs, in the same manner as is done in the European armies when soldiers, as it is called, run the gauntlet." The Mohawks stripped Jogues and his companions completely naked and whipped them into file. Coûture was in the forefront; Goupil in the middle; and Jogues, as the greatest in dignity, was held to the last so that his punishment might be the greatest. The "stage" upon which the captives were flung was a platform, half the height of a man, roughly strung together from branches and wattles.

I do? Believing that I was soon to be burnt at the stake, unmoved, I awaited the stroke, groaning to my God in heart; when stayed, as if by a supernatural power, he drew back his hand in the very act of cutting. About a quarter of an hour after, he returned, and as if condemning his cowardice and faint-heartedness, again prepared to do it; when again held back by some unseen hand, he departed. Had he carried out his design, my fate was sealed, for it is not their custom to grant life to captives thus mutilated.[14] At length, late at night, and last of all, I was taken to my captors, without receiving a morsel of food, which I had scarcely touched for several days. The rest of the night I spent in great pain.

My sufferings, great in themselves, were heightened by the sight of what a like cruelty had wreaked on the Christian Hurons, fiercer than all in the case of Eustace; for they had cut off both his thumbs, and, through the stump of his left, with savage cruelty, they drove a sharp stake to his very elbow. This frightful pain he bore most nobly and piously.[15]

The following day we fell in with some other war-canoes, who cut off some of our companions' fingers, amid our great dread.

At last, on the tenth day, about noon, we left our canoes, and performed on foot, the rest of the journey, which lasted four days. Besides the usual hardships of the march, now came that of carrying the baggage. [Although my share of this was done quite remissly, both because I was unable, and because I disdained to do it, for my spirit was haughty, even in fetters and death; so that only a small package was given me to bear.] We were now racked by hunger, from the ever-increasing want of food. Thus, three days in succession, (and when, on the fourth, we were met by a party from the village,) we tasted nothing but some berries, once gathered on the way. [For my part, I had, in the beginning of the

[14] Jogues was aware that had the Mohawks mutilated him by striking off his nose he would have been put to death on the spot. It was the custom among them to kill outright those notably marred.

[15] Ahatsistari's composure under these torments was characteristic of the Indians on either side. From earliest youth they were trained to endure pain, and it was considered a weakness to wince under torture. Ordinarily a captive sang or laughed aloud while enduring pain; a victim who showed signs of suffering was despised and left for the women and children to inflict further torture. Ahatsistari would not disgrace his people or give satisfaction to his enemies by showing his sufferings.

march, neglected to avail myself of the food which our canoes had supplied abundantly, that I might not offer to their fire and torture, a strong and vigorous frame, for I ingenuously confess my weakness; and when my body worn down by fasting called for food, it found nothing but water; for, on the second day, when we halted, weary with our march, they set a large kettle on the fire as if to prepare food; but it was merely to enable us to drink as much as each chose of the water thus slightly warmed.]

At last, on the eve of the Assumption of the Blessed Virgin, we reached the first village of the Iroquois.[16] I thank our Lord Jesus Christ, that, on the day when the whole Christian world exults in the glory of his Mother's Assumption into heaven, he called us to some small share and fellowship of his sufferings and cross. Indeed, we had during the journey always foreseen that it would be a sad and bitter day for us. It would have been easy for René and myself to escape that day and the flames, for, being unbound and often at a distance from our guards, we might, in the darkness of night, have struck off from the road, and even though we should never reach our countrymen, we would at least meet a less cruel death in the woods. He constantly refused to do this, and I was resolved to suffer all that could befall me, rather than forsake, in death, Frenchmen and Christian Hurons, depriving them of the consolation which a priest can afford.

On the Eve of the Assumption then about 3 o'clock we reached a river which flows by their village. Both banks were filled with Iroquois and Hurons formerly captured, now coming forth to meet us, the latter to salute us by a warning that we were to be burnt alive; the former received us with clubs, fists and stones.

And as baldness or thin hair, a shaved, or lightly covered head is an object of their aversion, this tempest burst in its fury on my bare head. Two of my nails had hitherto escaped; these they tore out with their teeth, and with their keen nails stripped off the flesh beneath to the very bones. When satisfied with the cruelties and mockeries which we thus received by the river side, they led us to their village on the top of the hill.

16 This was Ossernenon, one of the three principal Mohawk palisaded villages, or "castles." The others were Andagaron and Tionontoguen. All were located on the south bank of the Mohawk River.

At its entrance we met the youth of all that district awaiting us with clubs, in a line on each side of the road.

Conscious that, if we withdrew ourselves from the ranks of those chastised, we no less withdrew ourselves from that of the children, we cheerfully offered ourselves to our God, thus like a father chastising us, that in us he might be well pleased. Our order was as follows: in the front of the line they placed a Frenchman, alas, entirely naked, not having even his drawers. René Goupil was in the centre, and I last of all closed the line, (we were more fortunate as they had left us our shirts and drawers.) The Iroquois scattered themselves through our lines between us and the Hurons, both to check our speed, and to afford more time and ease to our torturers, to strike us thus separately as we passed. Long and cruelly indeed did the "wicked work upon my back," (Ps. cxxviii. 3,) not with clubs merely, but even with iron rods, which they have in abundance from their proximity to the Europeans; [17] one of the first, armed with a ball of iron of the size of a fist, slung to a throng, dealt me so violent a blow that I should have fallen senseless, had not fear of a second given me strength and courage. Running then our long race amid this fearful hail of blows, we with difficulty reached the stage erected in the centre of the village.

If each here presented a face to excite compassion, that of René was certainly the most pitiable. Being by no means quick or active, he had received so many blows all over his body, but especially on his face, that nothing could be distinguished there but the white of his eyes; more beautiful truly as he more resembled him, whom we have beheld "as a leper, and smitten by God for us," "in whom there was no comeliness or beauty."—Isaias liii. 2.

We had but just time to gain breath on this stage, when one with a huge club gave us Frenchmen three terrible blows on the bare back; the savages now took out their knives and began to mount the stage and cut off the fingers of many of the prisoners; and, as a captive undergoes their cruelty in proportion to his dignity, they began with me, seeing, by my conduct, as well as by

[17] The Dutch, who then had two trading forts: New Amsterdam (New York) and Rensselaerwyck, or Fort Orange (Albany), about thirty miles from the first village of the Mohawks.

their words, that I was in authority among the French and Hurons. Accordingly, an old man and a woman approached the spot where I stood; he commanded his companion to cut off my thumb; she at first drew back, but at last, when ordered to do so three or four times by the old wretch, as if by compulsion she cut off my left thumb where it joins the hand. [She was an Algonquin, that is, one of that nation which dwells near the French, in New France; she had been captured a few months before, and was a Christian. Her name was Jane. Surely it is pleasing to suffer at the hands of those for whom you would die, and for whom you chose to suffer the greatest torment rather than leave them exposed to the cruelty of visible and invisible enemies.]

Then, taking in my other hand the amputated thumb, I offered it to thee, my true and living God, calling to mind the sacrifice which I had for seven years constantly offered thee in thy Church. At last, warned by one of my comrades to desist, since they might otherwise force it into my mouth and compel me to eat it as it was, I flung it from me on the scaffold and left it I know not where.

René had his right thumb cut off at the first joint. I must thank the Almighty that it was his will that my right should be untouched, thus enabling me to write this letter to beg my dear fathers and brothers to offer up their masses, prayers, supplications and entreaties in the holy church of God, to which we know that we are now entitled by a new claim, for she often prays for the afflicted and the captive.

On the following day, the Assumption of the Blessed Virgin, after spending the morning on the stage, we were taken about mid-day to another village, some two miles distant from the first. As I was on the point of marching, the Indian who had brought me, loth to lose my shirt, sent me off naked, except an old and wretched pair of drawers. When I beheld myself thus stripped, "Surely, brother," said I, "thou wilt not send me off thus naked, thou hast taken enough of our property to enrich thee." This touched him, and he gave me enough of the hempen bagging in which our packages had been put up, to cover my shoulders and part of my body. But my shoulders, mangled by their blows and stripes, could not bear this rough and coarse cloth. On the way, while scarcely and at last not at all covered by it, the heat of the sun was so intense, that my skin was dried as though in an oven, and peeled off from my back and arms.

As we entered the second village,[18] blows were not spared, though this is contrary to their usual custom, which is to be content with once bastinadoing the prisoners. The Almighty surely wished us to be somewhat likened in this point to his apostle, who glories that he was thrice beaten with rods; and although they received us with fewer blows than the last, their blows were the more cruel, since, being less embarrassed by the crowd, they were better aimed; some striking constantly on the shins to our exquisite pain.

The rest of the day we spent on the stage, and the night in a hut tied down half naked to the bare ground, at the mercy of all ages and sexes. For we had been handed over to the sport of the children and youth who threw hot coals on our naked bodies, which, bound as we were, it was no easy matter to throw off. In this manner they make their apprenticeship in cruelty, and from less, grow accustomed to greater. We spent there two days and nights with scarcely any food or sleep, in great anguish of mind as far as I was concerned. For, from time to time, they mounted the stage, cutting off the fingers of my Huron companions, binding hard cords around their fists with such violence, that they fainted, and, while each of them suffered but his own pain, I suffered that of all; I was afflicted with as intense grief as you can imagine a father's heart to feel at the sight of his children's misery; for, with the exception of a few old Christians, I had begotten them all recently in Christ by baptism.

Yet amid all this the Lord gave me such strength that, suffering myself, I was able to console the suffering Hurons and French. So that, both on the road and on the stage, when the tormenting crowd of "saluters," (for so they call those who wreak their cruelty on the captives as they arrive,) had dropped away, I exhorted them, at one time generally, at another individually, to preserve their patience, nor lose confidence which would have a great reward; to remember "that, by many tribulations it behooves us to

18 Andagaron.

enter the kingdom of heaven;" that the time was come indeed, foretold to us by God, when he said: "Ye shall lament and weep, but the world shall rejoice, but your sorrow shall be turned into joy;" that we were like to a "a woman in travail, who, when she brings forth, hath sorrow, because her hour is come; but, when she has brought forth, no longer remembers her anguish for joy that a man is born into the world;" (John xvi. 21;) so should they feel assured that, in a few days, these momentary pains would give place to never-ending joys. And surely I had reason to rejoice when I beheld them so well disposed, especially the older Christians, Joseph, Eustace, and the other two; for, on the very day that we reached the first village, Theodore had freed himself from his bonds; but, as during the battle he had had his shoulder blade broken by the but-end of a musket, he died on his way to the French.

Never till now had the Indian scaffold beheld French or other Christians captives. So that, contrary to usual custom, we were led around through all their villages to gratify the general curiosity. The third,[19] indeed, we entered scathless, but on the scaffold a scene met my eyes more heart-rendering than any torment; it was a group of four Hurons, taken elsewhere by some other party, and dragged here to swell our wretched company. Among other cruelties every one of these had lost some fingers, and the eldest of the band his two thumbs. Joining these, I at once began to instruct them, separately, on the articles of faith; then, on the very stage itself, I baptized two, with rain-drops gathered from the leaves of a stalk of Indian corn, given us to chew; the other two, I christened as we were led by a stream on our way to another village. At this place, cold setting in after the rain, we suffered extremely from it, as we were entirely uncovered. Often shivering with cold on the stage, I would without orders come down and enter some hut, but I had scarcely begun to warm myself when I was commanded to return to the scaffold.

William Couture had thus far lost none of his fingers; this, exciting the displeasure of an Indian in this village, he sawed off the fore finger of his right hand in the middle; the pain was most

[19] Tionontoguen, the most populous and most important of the Mohawk villages. The captives had been brought there to climax the triumphal celebrations.

excruciating as for this amputation he employed not a knife, but in its stead a kind of shell, there very abundant. As it could not cut the sinews which were hard and slippery he wrenched the finger so violently, that, when the sinews gave way, the poor fellows arm swelled fearfully up to the very elbow. An Indian, touched by mercy, took him to his hut and kept him there two days which we spent in that village; leaving me in ignorance and great anxiety as to his fate.

At nightfall, we were taken to a hut where the youth awaited us. They ordered us to sing as other captives are wont to do; we at last complied, for alas, what else could we do? but we sang the "Canticles of the Lord in a strange land." Torture followed the chanting, and its fury burst especially on René and myself, for the good savage still kept William in his hut. Accordingly, on me, and especially on René, they threw hot ashes and live coals, burning him terribly in the breast.

They next hung me up between two poles in the hut, tied by the arms above the elbow with coarse rope woven of the bark of trees. Then I thought I was to be burnt, for this is one of their usual preliminaries. And that I might know that, if I had thus far borne anything with fortitude or even with patience, these came not from myself, but from Him who gives strength to the weary; now, as though left to myself in this torture, I groaned aloud, for "I will glory in my infirmities that the power of Christ may dwell in me," (2 Cor. xii. 9,) and from my intense pain, I begged my torturers to ease me some little from those hard, rough ropes. But God justly ordained that the more I pleaded, the more tightly they drew my chains. At last when I had been hanging thus about a quarter of an hour, they unloosed me as I was on the point of fainting. I render thee thanks, O Lord Jesus, that I have been allowed to learn, by some slight experience, how much thou didst deign to suffer on the cross for me, when the whole weight of thy most sacred body hung not by ropes, but by thy hands and feet pierced by hardest nails! Other chains followed these, for we were tied to the ground to pass the rest of the night. What did they not then do to my poor Huron companions thus tied hand and foot? What did they not attempt on me? But once more I thank thee, Lord, that thou didst save me, thy priest, ever unsullied from the impure hands of the savages. When we had thus spent two days in that village, we were led back to the second which we had entered, that our fate might be finally determined.

We had now been for seven days led from village to village, from scaffold to scaffold, become a spectacle to God and to his angels, as we may hope from his divine goodness; a scoff and jeer to the vilest savages, when we were at last told that that day should end our lives amid the flames. Though, in sooth, this last act was not without its horrors, yet the good pleasure of God and the hope of a better life subject to no sin rendered it more one of joy. Then, addressing my French and Huron companions as it were for the last time, I bid them be of good heart, amid their mental and bodily sufferings to think "diligently upon him that had endured such opposition of sinners against himself not to be weary, fainting in their minds," (Heb. xii. 3,) but to hope that the morrow would unite us to our God to reign forever.

Fearing lest we might be torn from one another, I especially advised Eustace to look towards me when we could not be together, and by placing his hands on his breast and raising his eyes to heaven to show his contrition for his sins, so that I could absolve him, as I had already frequently done after hearing his confession on the way, and after our arrival. As advised, he several times made the signal.

The sachems, however, on further deliberation, resolved, that no precipitate step was to be taken with regard to the French, and, when they had summoned us before the council, they declared that our lives were spared. To almost all the Hurons likewise they granted their lives: three were excepted, Paul, Eustace and Stephen, who were put to death in the three villages which make up the tribe; Stephen in the village where we were, known as Andagoron, Paul in Ossernenon, and Eustace in Teonontogen. The last was burned in almost every part of his body and then beheaded; he bore all most piously, and while it is usual for dying captives to cry out:

> "Exoriatur nostris ex ossibus ultor,"
> "May an avenger arise from our ashes,"

he, on the contrary, in the Christian spirit which he had so deeply imbibed in baptism, implored his countrymen standing around, not to let any feeling for his fate prevent the concluding of a peace with the Iroquois. Paul Ononhoratoon, who, after going through the usual fiery ordeal was tomahawked in the village of Ossernenon, was a young man of about twenty-five, full of life and courage; for such they generally put to death, to sap as it were the life-blood of the hostile tribe. With a noble contempt of death arising, as he openly professed on the way, from his hope of a better life, this generous man had repeatedly, when the Iroquois came up to me to tear out my nails, or inflict some other injury, offered himself to them, begging them to leave me and turn their rage on him. May the Lord return him a hundred fold with usury for that heroic charity, which led him to give his life for his friends, and for those who had begotten him in Christ in bondage!

Towards evening of that day they carried off William Couture, whom they regarded as a young man of unparalleled courage, to Teonontogen, the farthest village of their territory, and gave him to an Indian family. It is the custom of these savages, when they spare a prisoner's life, to adopt him into some family to supply the place of a deceased member, to whose rights he in a manner succeeds; he is subject thenceforward to no man's orders except those of the head of that family, who, to acquire this right, offers some presents.[20] But seeing that René and I were less vigorous, they led us to the first village, the residence of the party that had captured us, and left us there till some new resolution should be taken.

After so many a long day spent fasting, after so many sleepless nights, after so many wounds and stripes, and especially after such heart-rendering anguish of mind, when at last time was, so to speak, given us to feel our sufferings, we sank into a state of helplessness, scarce able to walk, or even stand erect: neither night nor day brought a moment of repose; this resulted from many causes, but chiefly from our still untended wounds; this state was rendered more trying by the myriads of lice, fleas and bedbugs, of which the maimed and mutilated state of our fingers did not permit us to

[20] Adoption of captives was a widespread, almost universal practice among American Indians and was usually accompanied by elaborate ceremony and ritual. In addition to supplying the place of a deceased member, as Jogues notes, adoption was also used as payment (by substitution) for killing a member of the tribe.

clear our persons. Besides this, we suffered from hunger; more truly here than elsewhere is the saying,

> "Cibus non utilis ægro."
> "Food is hurtful to the sick."

So that, with nothing to add to their American corn, (which in Europe we call Turkish,) carelessly bruised between two stones, but unripe squashes, we were brought to the brink of the grave; and René, especially, whose stomach refused this food, and who, from his many wounds, had almost lost his sight.

The Indians then, seeing us fail day by day, hunted up in the village some small fishes and some bits of meat dried by the fire and sun, and, pounding these, mixed them with our sagamity.[21]

After three weeks, we were just recovering from our illness when they sought to put us to death.

The two hundred Indians who had maltreated us so on the way, advanced into New France, to the point where the River Iroquois, so called from them, empties into the great river St. Lawrence; here, seeing a party of the French engaged in laying the foundations of Fort Richelieu,[22] they thought they could easily kill some and carry off the rest as prisoners. Accordingly, to the number of two hundred, in a single column and almost all armed with muskets, they rushed almost unexpected upon the whites engaged in the various works. At the first onset of the foe, the French, though but a handful compared to the number of the savages, flew to arms, and so bravely and successfully repulsed their fierce assailants, that, after killing two, and wounding many more, they put the rest to flight. The war party returned furious, and, as though they had been greatly wronged who had gone forth to do wrong, demanded the death of those of us who were yet alive. They asserted it to be a shame that three Frenchmen should live quietly among them when they had so lately slain three Iroquois. By these complaints, René's safety, especially, and my own, were in great

[21] Sagamite, a kind of thin porridge, or mush.

[22] Located on the promontory overlooking the juncture of the Richelieu and St. Lawrence rivers. Governor Charles Huault de Montmagny and Father Barthélemy Vimont, the superior of New France, had accompanied workmen there to supervise construction of the fort.

jeopardy. He alone, who, as he gave, protecteth life, warded off the blow.

On the eve of the Nativity of the Blessed Virgin, one of the principal Hollanders,[23] who have a settlement not more than twenty leagues from these Indians, came with two others, to endeavor to effect our liberation. He remained there several days, offered much, promised more, obtained nothing. But, as they are a wily and cunning race of savages, in order not to appear to refuse all that a friend asked, but to concede something to his desires, they lyingly asserted that they would, in a few days, restore us to our countrymen. This was, perhaps, the wish of some of them, but, in the latter part of September; (for constant rain had put the matter off till that time,) a final council was held on our fate, although provisions had been prepared and men appointed to take us back. Here the opinion of the few well inclined was rejected. Confusion carried the day, and some clamorous chiefs declared that they would never suffer a Frenchman to be taken back alive. The council broke up in alarm, and each, as if in flight, returned home, even those who came from other villages. Left thus to the cruelty of bloodthirsty men, attempts were constantly made on our lives. Some, tomahawk in hand, prowled around the cabins to find and despatch us. However, towards the close of the council, God had inspired me with some thought that induced me to draw my companions together without the village in a field belonging to the house where I was; here, ignorant of what had transpired, we lay hid as it were in safety, until the storm, beneath which we should all have fallen, had we remained in the village, was somewhat calmed.[24]

William was, after this, taken back by his master, to his own village; René and I, perceiving that there was now no hope of our

[23] This was Arendt VanCorlaer, who was acting on orders from the director-general of New Netherlands, Willem Kieft. The two men with VanCorlaer were Jacob Jansen and Jan Labatie.

[24] The Mohawks were in this case torn by indecision and dissension. Three dominant tribes within the Mohawk council were in conflict: the Wolf and Turtle clans favored peace with the French if they would separate from their alliance with the Hurons and Algonquins; the warriors of the Bear clan, however, were convinced that the French would never consent to a separate peace, and were therefore pushing for war. Jogues and Goupil were caught in the middle of this contention. The Wolf and Turtle urged that the captives be released as a gesture toward future peace; the Bear demanded they be executed as a gesture of defiance against the French.

return, withdrew to a neighboring hill, which commands the village, in order to pray. Here, remote from every witness, and from all officious intrusion, we resigned ourselves entirely to God and to his holy will; on our road back to the village, we were reciting our beads, and had already completed four decades of the rosary, when we met two young men who commanded us to return to the village. "Dear brother," said I, "we know not what may be, in this period of general excitement, the design of these men. Let us commend ourselves earnestly to God, and to the most Blessed Virgin, our good Mother." We had reached the village in prayer, when, at its very entrance, one of the two whom we had met, plucking forth his tomahawk which was concealed in his dress, dealt René so deadly a blow on the head, that he fell lifeless, invoking the most holy name of Jesus as he fell. We had happily, mindful of the indulgence thereby gained, often reminded each other to close our life by uttering, with our dying voice, that most holy name.

At the sight of the reeking hatchet, I knelt down on the spot, and uncovering my head, awaited a like blow. But, when I had been there a moment or two, they bade me rise, as they had no right to kill me, for I was the slave of another family. Rising then in haste, I ran to my still breathing companion, and conferred absolution, which I was in the habit of giving him after his confession every other day; then two other blows, dealt before my very face, added him to the number of the blessed. He was thirty-five years of age, eminent for his simplicity of manners, his innocence of life, his patience in adversity, entirely submissive to God, whom he, in all things, regarded as present before his eyes, and resigned to his most holy will in love. Most worthy is he, Reverend Father, to be counted among thy children, not only because he had spent several months in one of the novitiates of the Society, in a most edifying manner, and had afterwards, by the command of the Superiors, to whom he gave the entire disposal of his life, proceeded to Huronia, to aid the Christian population by his medical knowledge, but especially does he merit it from the fact, that, a few days before his death, impelled by a desire of uniting himself more closely to God, he pronounced the usual vows of the Society to subject himself to it as far as in him lay. And certain it is that, in life as in death, where his last word was the most holy name of Jesus, he had proved himself no unworthy son of the Society. Nay, I not only love him as a brother, but revere him as a martyr —martyr to obedience, and still more, a martyr to the faith and to the cross. As he was very pious, and accustomed to be with the Christians, or such as were most intimate with our Christians, he daily spent a long time in prayer, to the wonder and even suspicion of the savages, so novel did it seem to them. These suspicions were confirmed in their minds when one day, taking off the cap of a child in the hut where he lived, he made him make a sign of the cross on his breast and forehead; for a superstitious old Indian, the grandfather of the boy, seeing this, ordered him to be killed. This I afterwards learned from the boy's mother, who told me that he had been killed by the old man for that reason.

But to resume my narrative: after I had been seated a little while in our hut, where my life had been pretty quiet, I was taken to another, the hut of him who had cut off my thumb, a most bitter enemy of the Algonquins, and consequently of the French. Here, not I alone, but the other Iroquois, every moment expected to see me tomahawked. Accordingly, some who had given me articles of clothing, that I might, in part at least, cover my person, now asked them back, for fear of losing them by my death.

The next day, I was filled with the greatest anxiety to know what had become of my dear companion, that I resolved to look for his body at all hazards, and commit it, if possible, to the earth. After stripping it entirely, they had contemptuously tied a rope around the neck, and dragging it through the village, had flung it into a ravine at a considerable distance. As I was going out of the village, I met the old man in whose hut I had formerly been; he advised me to stay at home. "Whither art thou hurrying?" he exclaimed, "thou art scarce alive; they seek thee everywhere to slay thee, and yet thou goest to find an already putrefying corpse; dost thou not see those fierce young braves, who are about to kill thee?" Some, in fact, went out of the village armed, just before me; but I fearlessly pursued my way; for, in my bitter anguish, it was a pain to live, a gain to die in such a work of charity. When the old man saw me so resolute, he asked another Indian to go with me. By his assistance, I found the body, which the dogs had begun to gnaw about the hips, and, sinking it in the deepest part of the torrent, covered it with a heap of stones, intending to return the next day with a spade, and bury it secretly and alone, for I was afraid they would disinter it.

As I re-entered our hut, two young men were waiting to take me to their village to put me to death. Aware of their design, I told them that I was in the hands of those with whom I lived, that if they gave the slightest consent, I would accompany them, and would in fact have done so. Seeing that they gained nothing in this way, the next day one of them who, at the time of our capture, had been wounded with his brother, seeing me in the field whither I had gone to execute some order of my owners, seized a hatchet and was rushing on me to kill me, when he was stopped by an old man of our family, and prevented from accomplishing his design. Thus did the Almighty teach me "to cast all my solicitude on him," knowing that he hath care of me, and that I should not fear the face of a man when the Almighty was the protector of my life, without whose permission not a hair could fall from my head.

As I could not that day accomplish my design, early the next morning I proceeded to the spot with a spade or hoe to inter the body, but alas, they had carried off my brother. I returned to the spot; I descended the mount at the foot of which the torrent ran; I descended again; I searched the wood on the opposite side,—all, all in vain. The torrent ran swollen by the night rains, but, unrestrained by either its depth or the cold, for it was the first of October, I tried the bottom with my stick and feet, as I thought that the stream might have borne it to another spot; I asked all whom I met, whether they knew anything of him; but as they are a most lying race, and always give an affirmative answer without regard to truth, they falsely told me that he had been dragged to a quite distant river. What groans did I not utter then! What tears did I not shed, mingling them with the waters of that mountain stream, chanting to thee, my God, the psalms thy holy Church employs in the service of the dead!

When, however, the snows had melted away, I heard from the young men that they had seen the scattered bones of the Frenchman. Hurrying to the spot, I gathered up the half-gnawed bones, the remnants left by the dogs, the foxes and the crows, and especially the skull fractured in many places; these reverently kissing, I committed to the earth, that I might, one day, if such were God's will, bear with me as a great treasure to a consecrated Christian land.

From many other dangers, which I knew and knew not, did the Lord rescue me, in spite of all the ill will and hate of the Iroquois, unwilling and furious as the Iroquois were. But the following I should not omit. There was in our cabin an idiot who asked me to let him cut off two hands' breadth from a wretched bit of cloth not seven palms long, yet all that I had to cover me. Brother! said I, you see me shivering every night under this short thin covering; yet do as thou wilt. My modest excuse offended him, and when soon after I went to the huts of the baptized Hurons, whom I daily instructed and bore again till Christ should be formed in them, (Gal. iv. 19,) he came in search of me, and fiercely bade me return. When I had entered our cabin, René's murderer was sent for, that the same hand might end both our lives; they looked for him in vain, he could not be found. I was accordingly sent the next day into a field of my master's with two women, under the pretext of bringing back some article or other, but in fact to expose me to death; for, two days before, the only son of one of their noble women had died in our cabin, and I was to be sacrificed to his *manes*.[25]

These women had with them the squashes, corn and other articles of the kind which were to be the fee of my executioner. "But I, like a deaf man, heard not" the vain things they devised, "and like a dumb man opened not my mouth, and I became like a man that heareth not, nor hath a reply in his mouth," (Ps. xxxvii. 14,) "because in thee, O Lord, have I hoped;" but, mindful of his meekness "who was led like a lamb to the slaughter," (Acts viii. 32,) I went to my death, begging the Lord with David "to turn away evil from my enemies and scatter them in his truth."—Ps: liii. 7. About midway we met the looked-for murderer; seeing him coming at a distance, I commended myself for the last time to God, begging him to receive my life spent with care and anguish;

[25] The spirit, or shade, of a dead person.

but my sins still rendered me unworthy. He passed quietly by us, and meeting his mother, she addressed some words, of what import I know not, to those who conducted me; on this, trembling and fleeing as it were, they left me in the road, for they saw that I was aware of their design.

Amid this frequent fear and death, while every day I die, or rather drag on a life more bitter than any death, two months glided away. During this time I made no effort to learn their language, for why should I, who every moment expected to die? The village was a prison for me. I avoided being seen. I loved the wild wood, where I begged the Lord not to disdain to speak to his servant, to give me strength in such fearful trials, in which, indeed, if I have become a prodigy to many, God was my stout Helper, and often by his unfailing goodness roused my drooping spirits. I had recourse to the Holy Scriptures, my only refuge in the tribulations, which had found me exceedingly: these did I venerate; with these I wished to die. Of all the books which we were carrying to Huronia for the use of the Frenchmen living there, none had fallen into my hands but the Epistle of St. Paul to the Hebrews, with the paraphrase of the Rt. Rev. Anthony Godeau, Bishop of Gratz. This little book, with a picture of St. Bruno, the illustrious founder of the Carthusian Order, to which some indulgences were attached, and a rude wooden cross which I had made, I always carried about me, so that, whenever death, which I had ever present before my eyes, should strike me down, I could most cheerfully die with the Holy Scriptures which had ever been my greatest consolation, with the graces and indulgences of my most holy Mother the Church, whom I had always greatly, but now most tenderly, loved, and with the cross of my Lord and Savior.

And now the middle of October was come when the Indians leave their villages to go and hunt deer, which they take by traps, or kill with their guns, in the use of which they are very skilful. This season, to the Indians one of relaxation and enjoyment, brought its new burden of sorrows for me; for I was given to a party, who were first amazed at me, then ridiculed, and at last began to hate me.

Mindful of the character imposed upon me by God, I began with modesty to discourse with them of the adoration of one only

God, of the observance of his commandments, of heaven, hell, and the other mysteries of our Faith, as fully as I was able. At first, indeed, they listened, but when they saw me constantly recur to these things, and especially when the chase did not meet with the desired success, then they declared that I was an Otkon,[26] who caused them to take so little game. But what turned their ill-will into perfect rage and fury, so to speak, was this: It is a custom with all these nations to have recourse, in their hunting, fishing, war, sickness, and the like, to a certain demon whom they call Aireskoi. Whoever desires his fishing, hunting, or other expeditions to be successful, takes meat, and other of the better articles of food, and begs the oldest of the house or village to *bless* them for him, if I may use the term; and there are some to whose blessings they attach more value than to others. The old man, standing opposite the one that holds the meat, in a loud and distinct voice, speaks thus: "O, demon Aireskoi, behold, we offer this meat to thee, and from it we prepare thee a banquet, that thou mayest eat thereof, and show us where the deer are lurking, mayest lead them into our traps;"—(if not during the chase)—"that by thee we may again behold the spring, taste the new harvest, and again engage in the chase in the fall;"—(if in illness)—"that by these we may recover health." [27]

The very first time I heard a formula couched in such words, I was filled with a deep detestation of this savage superstition, and firmly resolved to abstain forever from meats thus offered. They interpreted this abstinence on my part, and this contempt of their demon, as the cause of their taking so little game; "the wicked have hated me without cause."—John xv. 25. As, under the influence of this hate, they would neither listen to my instructions, nor help me to acquire their language, in which I refuted their fables, I resolved to devote my time entirely to spiritual exercises. Accordingly, I went forth every morning from the midst of this Babylon, that is, our hut where constant worship was paid to the devil and to dreams, and "saved myself in the mountain," (Genesis xix. 17,) a neighboring hill. Here I had formed a large

[26] Sorcerer.

[27] Aireskoi, the demon of the chase and holder of the heavens, was the great god of the Mohawks. The sacrifice was repeated each day of the hunt.

cross on a majestic tree by stripping off the bark, and, at its foot, I spent the whole day with my God, whom, almost alone in those vast regions, I worshipped and loved; sometimes in meditation or in prayer, at other times reading an "Imitation of Christ,"[28] which I had just before recovered. This for some time was unperceived; but, on one occasion, finding me, as was my wont, in prayer before my cross, they attacked me most violently, saying that they hated the cross; that it was a sign that they and their friends the neighbors, (Europeans,) knew not, alluding to the Dutch Protestants.

Upon this, I changed my conduct, and whereas I had before carefully avoided praying or kneeling in their hut, that I might not give them the slightest reason to complain, (for we should, especially among savages, but little accustomed to such things, act in all prudence,) I now conceived that I should no longer refrain from those pious exercises which make up a spiritual life, a life I far preferred to my temporal one. This I believed would be serviceable to them when the moment of their conversion should come, "which the Father hath put in his own power."—Acts i. 7.

While thus an object of their enmity, I certainly suffered much from hunger and cold, the contempt of the lowest of the men, the bitter hatred of their women.

The latter, who are the greatest gainers by the hunting season, regarded me as the cause of their want and poverty. I suffered most from hunger; for, as almost all the venison on which they chiefly lived had been offered to the devil in these oblations, I spent many days fasting; and, almost every night, when I came in fasting, I would see our Egyptians sitting over their flesh-pots, which my severe, though self-imposed law, prevented my touching. And, although reasons occurred to me, at times dissuading me from this course, yet, by God's grace, I never suffered myself to break my resolution, but in hunger said to my God: "We shall be filled with the good things of thy house."—Psalms lxiv. 5. "I shall be satisfied when thy glory shall appear."—Ib. xvi. 15. "When thou wilt truly fill the desire of thy hungry servants in thy holy city, Jerusalem, which thou wilt fill forever with the fat of corn." —Ib. cxlvii. 14.

28 *De Imitatione Christi* (1426), a religious treatise commonly ascribed to Thomas à Kempis.

I suffered also greatly from cold, amid the deep snows under my scanty, worn-out cloak, especially at night, when ordered to sleep uncovered on the bare ground on some rough bark; for, though they had plenty of deerskins, perfectly useless to them, not one was given to me; nay, when sometimes on a very bitter night, I would, overcome by the cold, secretly take one, they rose at once and pulled it from me; so great was their enmity against me. My skin was now in such a state that I could with David say: "It had withered with the filth of dust."—Job vii. 5. It burst with cold, and gave me great pain all over my body. But when inward afflictions came crowding on these outward cares, then indeed my grief became intolerable. I remembered that I had been recently covered with the life's blood of my dearest companion; and those who came from William's village told me he had already been put to death with exquisite tortures,[29] and that I myself, on my return, was to meet the same fate. With this came up the rememberance of my past life, stained with so many sins, and so unfaithful to God, and I grieved that I was thus to be torn away unaided by any of the sacraments in the very midst of my course, rejected as it were by God, with no good works sent on to plead my cause. In this state, loathing life, yet shrinking from death, I uttered many a mournful cry, and said unto my God: "When shall sorrows and miseries have an end? How long wilt thou forget our want and our tribulation? When, after this tempest, wilt thou give us calm, and, after weeping, joy and exultation? And, had not those days been shortened, my flesh had not been saved."—Mark xiii. 20.

I had recourse to my wonted refuge of the Scriptures, my usual retreat, and passages which my memory had retained taught me how I should think of God in goodness, even though not upheld by sensible devotion; that I should know that the just man lives by faith. I searched them; I followed their stream, and sought, as it were, to quench my daily thirst. "I meditated on the law of God night and day."—Psalms i. 2; and, "had not the law of God been my meditation, I had then, perhaps, perished in my abjection."—Psalms cviii. 92. "And my soul had passed through a water unsupportable."—Psalms cxxiii. 5. "But, blessed be God, who did

[29] Jogues later learned this was untrue; Coûture was at that time alive and in good health.

not give us a prey to the teeth of our enemies."—Psalms cxxii. 6. "Whose hour had come and the power of darkness."—Luke xxii. 53. In which we "were overmuch oppressed."—2 Cor. i. 8. So that I was weary of life, and could say with Job, though in a different meaning, "Although he should kill me, I will trust in him."—Job. xiii. 15.

Thus passed two months away in this retreat, where, like St. Bernard, the disciple of the trees of the forest, I thought of naught but God, until become an object too hateful to all to be any longer borne with, I was sent back to the village before the usual time. During the way, which took us eight days, "I was become like a beast of burden before God," (Psalms lxxii. 23,) under the heavy load of venison which I carried; and, being ignorant what fate might await me at the village, endeavored to be ever united with him, for a party that had gone before had spread many reports about me. My sufferings in this journey, from the intense cold, were extreme; for I was nearly naked, and we generally passed the night in the open air.

My unhealed fingers were another source of misery; for the wounds were hardly closed by the middle of January. In the village, however, a thin skin was added to my worn out cloak; in this wretched guise I traversed the streets of our village, begging that the Lord would one day join me with his saints who formerly served him in "sheepskins and goatskins, distressed, afflicted, of whom the world was not worthy."—Hebrews xi. 37. And I daily saw the Indians well dressed in the cloth and garments which our baggage had plentifully supplied, while I was shivering night and day with cold; but this was little; more was I moved to see these heathen men unworthily profane things dedicated to the service of God. One of them had made himself leggings of two of the veils used at mass: "Non hos servatum munus in usus." [30]

I can in truth say, before God, of all that period up to mid-January, "Even unto this hour, we both hunger and thirst, and are naked and are buffeted, and have no fixed abode. And we labor, working with our hands; we are reviled, and we bless; we are persecuted, and we suffer it; we are ill-spoken of and we entreat; we

30 "An object not destined to such a use."

are made as the refuse of this world, the off-scouring of all even until now."—1 Cor. iv. 11.

When, in the middle of January, my owners returned from the chase, they, in a manner, dressed me in skins, until a Lorrainese who lived among our Dutch neighbors, hearing that I suffered greatly from cold, sent me from his house, a dress, such as they usually sell to the Indians. This brought some slight alleviation to my pains, but I found still greater in the care of an old woman, whose only son had died not long before. She was of very noble rank in the nation, for barbarism, too, has its nobles; she took care of me, and the Lord gave me grace in her eyes, yet all this was but a slight solace in such woe.

When I saw that my life was at last in some sort spared, I applied myself to the study of the language,[31] and, as our cabin was the council hall, not only of the village, but of almost all that country, I began to instruct the oldest on the articles of our faith. They, too, put me many questions, as to the sun, and moon, the face, which seemed to appear on his disk, of the circumference of the earth, of the size of the ocean, its tides, whether, as they had heard, the heavens and the earth anywhere met each other; adapting my philosophy to their reach, I satisfied them on all these; then, indeed, they began to wonder, and say, "Indeed, we should have lost a great treasure, had we put this man to death, as we have been so often on the point of doing." Then I endeavored to raise their minds from creatures, to a knowledge of the Creator; I confuted their old wives' tales of the creation of the world, which their fable makes out to have been created by a tortoise; [32] the sun was I showed them, not only without an intellect, but even a lifeless mass, much less a God; "that if, delighted by its appearance, they believed it to be a God, they should know that the Lord was much more more beautiful than it;" that Aireskoi, whom they falsely asserted to be the Author and Preserver of life, and the Giver of all

[31] The Iroquois dialect was a kindred language to the Huron, which Jogues could speak fluently, but with notable variations in vocabulary, in inflections, and in pronunciation. The complexity of both the Huron and the Iroquois tongues amazed the French: all words were inflected, verbs were conjugated in tenses and numbers in as many ways as in Greek, and compound words, made up of substantives joined with adjectives and pronouns, abounded.

[32] The Iroquois Creation Myth is at once a Flood Myth, in which the world arose from the waters on the back of the tortoise.

the good things which they enjoyed, was not a God but a demon. Were they as easy in belief as they are easy to be convinced, the matter would soon be settled. But the prince of the world [33] expelled from almost every quarter of the globe, by the power of the cross, seems to have retreated into these regions, as his last stronghold; so that the kingdom which this strong man armed has possessed here for so many thousand years, can be overthrown only in lapse of time, and by unconquerable constancy on the part of the soldiers of Christ. From time to time, however, Christ, their true Lord and Lord of all, chooses some for himself, not only among the infants, many of whom are now in heaven, but even among adults, some of whom I baptized in sickness or in bondage.

Many other native adults I instructed, but some refused to listen to me, others rejected me, others assented with their lips, merely from a kind of politeness which makes them consider it rude to contradict you; and without attention to which, many would be deceived. I sometimes even made excursions to the neighboring villages, to console and instruct the Christian Hurons, "who had not bent their knee before Baal," and to absolve them after hearing their confessions; to announce God everywhere as far as I was able, to succor the dying, but especially to save infants in danger of death. This was my only solace in my bitterest mental pangs; and once, with this view, I visited a neighboring village, and there baptized five children; I learnt, soon after, in another excursion, that all had been called to heaven.

In these and like exercises, therefore, and attempts to study their language, (for what study can there be without writing?) two months glided by. About the middle of March, when the snow had melted away, they took me with them to their fishing ground. We accordingly started; the party consisted of the old man and woman, a little boy and myself; four days' travel brought us to a lake where we caught nothing but a few little fishes.

The intestines of these generally served as a seasoning for our sagamity, the fish being laid by to carry back to the village.

Such food as this, with the intestines of deer full of blood, and half putrefied excrement, and mushrooms boiled, and rotten

33 **Satan.**

oysters, and frogs, which they eat whole, head and feet, not even skinned or cleaned; such food, had hunger, custom, and want of better, made, I will not say tolerable, but even pleasing. How often, in those journeys, and in that quiet wilderness, "did we sit by the rivers of Babylon, and weep, while we remembered thee, Sion," not only exulting in heaven, but even praising thy God on earth! "How often, though in a strange land, did we sing the canticle of the Lord;" and mountain and wildwood resound with the praises of their Maker, which from their creation they had never heard! How often, on the stately trees of the forest, did I carve the most sacred name of Jesus, that, seeing it, the demons might fly, who tremble when they hear it! How often on them too, did I not strip off the bark, to form the most holy Cross of the Lord, that the foe might fly before it, and that by it, thou, O Lord, my king, "mightst reign in the midst of thy enemies," the enemies of thy cross, the misbelievers and the pagans who dwell in that land, and the demons who rule so powerfully there! I rejoice, too, that I had been led by the Lord into the wilderness, at the very time when the church recalls the story of his Passion, so that I might more uninterruptedly remember the course of its bitterness and gall, and my soul might pine away at the rememberance.—Jer. iii. 20.

Accordingly, after performing the services which I owed as slave to my masters, the slave of savages, (my occupation being to cut and bring in wood for the hut,) I spent almost all my time before a large cross which I had formed on a huge tree at a considerable distance from the hut. But I was not long allowed to enjoy this holy repose; indeed, too many days had I passed, unharmed by my wonted terrors. On Monday, in Holy Week, an Indian came to us from our village; the reason of his coming was this. Ten Iroquois, among whom was the son of the man who had cut off my thumb, and in whose hut I now dwelt, had gone out on a war-party about mid-summer.[34] (Summer, fall, and even the whole winter, passed without their being heard of,) they were consequently given up, especially as neighboring nations said that they had fallen victims to the cruelty of the enemy. But when, early in the spring, a captive was brought in during our absence,

34 Against the Abenakis, an Algonquin Nation.

who, being also questioned as to them, gave the same answer, and said that they had been killed; then, indeed, deeming beyond a doubt, what they already believed to be true, they sacrificed that very captive to the *manes* of the young brave, the son of my master.

But the soul of this captive seemed too vile to atone for the life of the noble youth. I was accordingly sent for, from the lake where we were, that, together with him, I might compensate for the death of the chief. Such, at least, was the conclusion to which one or two old women and a decrepit old man had come. We consequently set out the next day, as if in flight, and, as a pretext, they said that parties of the enemy were around us. We reached the village towards evening, on Maundy Thursday. The morrow, which had closed the Savior's life, was now to close mine also! when it pleased him, who, by dying on that day, had given life to my spirit, to give it also to my body. Accordingly, on that day when I was to have been put to death, a rumor was first spread without any good authority, that those supposed to be dead were still alive; then it came that they had joined another war party, and were now bringing in twenty-two captives.

Thus did God scatter the malignant designs of the savages, instructing and showing me that he took care of me, that I should cast myself wholly on him, conscious that he would not recoil and let me fall.

Although I naturally rejoiced to be rescued from these and other dangers, yet I sighed to see myself again given over to new sorrows and heart-breaking torments, compelled me to drag on a life more painful than the most cruel death. For the success, as well as the reverses of these men, fell heavily on me alone; if any one was slain in battle, I was at once demanded as a victim to be offered to his shade. But if, as was generally the case, they brought in prisoners after having killed more, my heart was always rent with grief, for they were either Frenchmen or allies of the French.

Naturally, therefore, did I prefer retirement and solitude, where, far from the villages, I was no longer dismayed at the wonted cruelty of these savages, and where I could better and more freely hold converse with God. Yet knowing, that, though Lia was blear-eyed, she was more fruitful than Rachel, and bore more children; mindful, too, of the Institute of our Society, which prefers our neighbor's salvation to our private spiritual delights, I reluctantly remained at home; for the village enabled me to make greater progress in the language, and to secure the salvation of infants and adults by baptism; for I was greatly grieved whenever, during my absence, an adult died without instruction or a child without baptism.

To return to our war party: they came in bringing twenty-two prisoners, but belonging to a nation with whom they had as yet never been at war; still, in violation of all right and justice, they were beaten with clubs and stripes, and mutilated by the usual cutting off of fingers. Five of them were to be put to death, for all the rest, being boys and girls, or women, were kept as slaves. Their instruction was now an object of my solicitude, for I was ignorant of their language; yet by God's grace I was able, by a few words that I picked up, but chiefly by the kindness of one who knew both languages, to instruct and baptize them. This happened at Easter. At Whitsuntide, they brought in new prisoners, three women with their little children, the men having been killed near the French settlements. They were led into the village entirely naked, not even with any kind of petticoat on; and, after being severely beaten on the way, had their thumbs cut off. One of them, a thing not hitherto done, was burnt all over her body, and afterwards thrown into a huge pyre. And worthy of note is a strange rite I then beheld, when this woman was burnt at each wound which they inflicted, by holding lighted torches to her body, an old man in a loud voice exclaimed, "Demon Aireskoi, we offer thee this victim, whom we burn for thee, that thou mayst be filled with her flesh, and render us ever anew victorious over our enemies." Her body was cut up, sent to the various villages and devoured; for about mid-winter, grieving as it were, that they had refrained from eating the flesh of some prisoners, they had in a solemn sacrifice of two bears, which they offered to their demon, uttered the words, "Justly dost thou punish us, oh, Demon Aireskoi; lo! this long time we have taken no captives; during the summer and fall, we have taken none of the Algonquins. (These they consider properly their enemies.) We have sinned against thee, in that we ate not the last captives thrown into our hands;

but, if we shall ever again capture any, we promise thee to devour them as we now consume these two bears"; and they kept their word.[35] This poor woman I baptized in the midst of the flames, unable to do so before, and then only while raising a drink to her parched lips.

On the eve of St. John the Baptist, of whom it is written "that many shall rejoice at his birth," a new weight was added to my usual sorrows; eleven Hurons and a Frenchman were brought in; three Frenchmen and ten Hurons, among them some of the most celebrated Christians, had been killed, treacherously circumvented by a show of friendship. Of these, they bore the scalps or hair, which they tear off with the skin, from their fallen enemies.[36] I certainly felt, in my own person, this punishment deserved by my sins, and pronounced of old by God to his people, when he said "that their new moons, their festivals, and solemnities should be turned into grief and sorrow," as Easter and Whitsuntide, and the nativity of St. John the Baptist, each brought sorrows on me, to be afterwards increased to agony by the slaughter of a hundred Hurons, most of whom, racked by fearful torments, were burnt to death in the neighboring cantons. "Wo is me, wherefore was I born to see the ruin of my people."—1 Mach. ii. 7.

Verily, in these, and like heart-rendering cares, "my life is wasted with grief, and my years with sighs;" (Ps. xxx. 2,) "for the

35 Cannibalism, a practice rather more widespread among American Indians than is commonly understood, encompassed a geographical span of tribes ranging from New England forest Indians to tribes of the Great Lakes to the Indians of the Southwest. The practice of eating the flesh of an enemy derived from the belief that the eater could acquire the courage and strength of his victim, a belief that is part of a primitive system of sympathetic or homeopathic magic. It was a common custom of these Indians, when returning from battle, to make a feast from among the slain enemy. For tribes that practiced it, cannibalism was a ritual of war like their purification rites. For an analysis of ritual and archetypal features in the narratives collectively, see my "The Indian Captivity Narrative as Ritual," *American Literature*, XLIII (Jan., 1972), 548–62.

36 The taking of scalps, a practice popularly thought to have originated with the American Indian, was in part a manifestation of far older beliefs ascribing magical powers to the hair. The hair is also a principal feature of the primitive conception of the external or separable soul. American Indians, like many other primitive peoples, attributed special powers to the hair and believed the scalp to be somehow connected with a person's fate. Scalps were generally desired in a diameter of approximately two inches (although more than that was often taken in haste), a fact that tends to substantiate the symbolic as opposed to merely evidential significance of the practice.

Lord hath corrected me for mine iniquity, and hath made my soul waste away as a spider."—xxxviii. 12. "He hath filled me with my bitterness, he hath inebriated me with wormwood, (Lament. iii. 15,) because the comforter, the relief of my soul, is far from me," (i. 16.) "but, in all these things, we overcome," and by the favor of God will overcome, "because of him that hath loved us," (Rom. viii. 37,) until "he come that is to come and will not delay (Heb. x. 37,) until my day like that of a hireling come, (Job vii. 1,) or my change be made."—xiv. 14. Although I could, in all probability, escape either through the Europeans or the savage nations around us, did I wish to fly, yet on this cross, to which our Lord has nailed me beside himself, am I resolved by his grace to live and die. For who in my absence would console the French captives? who absolve the penitent? who remind the christened Huron of his duties? who instruct the prisoners to be brought in from time to time? who baptize the dying, encourage them in their torments? who cleanse the infants with the saving waters? who provide for the safety of the dying adults, the instruction of those in health? And indeed I cannot but think it a peculiar interposition of divine goodness, that while on one side a nation fallen from the true Catholic religion barred the entrance of the faith to these regions, and on the other a fierce war between savage nations, and on their account with the French did the same, I should have fallen into the hands of these Indians, who, by the will of God, reluctantly, and, I may say, against their will, have, thus far, spared my life, that through me, though unworthy, those might be instructed, believe and be baptized, who are predestined to eternal life. Since the time when I was taken, I have baptized seventy, children, young and old, of five different nations and languages, that of every tribe, and people, and tongue, they might stand in the sight of the Lamb. —Apoc. vii. 9.

Therefore do I daily bow my knees to the Lord and to the Father of my Lord, that, if it be for his glory, he may confound all the designs of the Europeans and savages, for ransoming me or sending me back to the whites. For many of the Indians speak of my being restored, and the Dutch, among whom I write this, have frequently offered, and now again offer, to rescue me and my companions. I have twice visited them and been most kindly welcomed;

they leave no stone unturned to effect our deliverance; and have made many presents to the Indians with whom I am, to induce them to treat me humanely.[37]

But I am now weary of so long and so prolix a letter; I therefore earnestly beg your reverence, ever to recognize me, though unworthy, as one of yours; for, though a savage in dress and manner, and almost without God in so tossed a life, yet, as I have ever lived a son of the most holy Church of Rome, and of the Society, so do I wish to die. Obtain for me from God, Reverend Father, by your holy sacrifices, that although I have hitherto but ill employed the means he gave me to attain the highest sanctity, I may at least employ well this last occasion which he offers me. Your bounty owes this surely to your son who has recourse to you, for I lead a truly wretched life, where every virtue is in danger. Faith in the dense darkness of paganism; hope in so long and hard trials; charity amid so much corruption, deprived of all the Sacraments. Purity is not indeed here endangered by delights, yet it is amid this promiscuous and intimate intercourse of both sexes; in the perfect liberty of each to hear and do what he please, and most of all in their constant nakedness. For here, willing or not, you must often see what elsewhere is shut out, not only from wandering, but even from curious eyes. Hence I daily groan to my God, begging him not to leave me without help amid the dead; begging him, I say, that amid so much impurity and such superstitious worship of the devil to which he has exposed me, naked as

37 The families with whom Jogues's captors were traveling had taken him with them to spend a few days trading at the Dutch settlement at Fort Orange (Rensselaerwyck), where the Iroquois and Dutch had established cordial but guarded relations. The Dutch at Rensselaerwyck were genuinely concerned about Jogues's plight. While they had no love for the French and detested Catholicism, they deemed it an outrage that any white man should be enslaved by the savages. It was during the few days Jogues spent at Rensselaerwyck that he wrote this report of himself to his Superior. Shortly after he had written the letter, the circumstances of a French attack on the Iroquois up-country decided the Mohawks to take him back to their village and there kill him. Convinced that he was now absolutely condemned to execution and that it would be more for God's glory and the salvation of souls for him to escape death, he accepted the refuge offered him by the Dutch and eventually made his way from Canada to France. In the spring of 1644 he returned to his missionary work in Canada, and in 1646 was again taken into captivity by the Mohawks, who this time killed him and exhibited his severed head on a pole over their palisaded village. See Francis Talbot, S. J., *Saint Among Savages* (New York, 1935), and John J. Birch, *The Saint of the Wilderness* (New York, 1936).

it were, and unarmed, "my heart may be undefiled in his justifications," (Ps. cxviii. 80,) so that, when that good Shepherd shall come, "who will gather together the dispersed of Israel," (Ps. cxlvi. 2,) he may gather us from among the nations to bless his holy name. Amen! Amen!—Ps. cv. 47.

Your Reverence's
Most humble servant and son in Christ,
Isaac Jogues.

Permit me, through your Reverence, to salute all my dear Fathers and Brothers, whom I tenderly love and cherish in Christ, and to commend myself to their Holy Sacrifices and Prayers.

Your most humble servant and son in Christ,
Isaac Jogues.

Renssalaerswyck in New Netherland,
August 5, 1643.

II

The Soveraignty and Goodness of God, Together with the Faithfulness of His Promises Displayed; Being a Narrative of the Captivity and Restauration of Mrs. Mary Rowlandson.

†††

The first and most deservedly well-known New England Indian captivity narrative and, except for sixteenth-century Spanish accounts, the first captivity published in North America, Mary Rowlandson's narrative has appeared in over thirty editions since its first publication in 1682. Mrs. Mary White Rowlandson (c.1635–c.1678) was the wife of the Reverend Joseph Rowlandson, pastor of the church at Lancaster, Massachusetts. Disputes between English settlers and the southern New England tribes—Narragansett, Nipmuck, and Wampanoag—over territory and hunting and fishing rights erupted into the most serious Indian conflict of the seventeenth century, King Philip's War. Led by the Wampanoag sachem Metacomet, called Philip by the English, Indian war parties swept down on New England communities in June of 1675. The war continued through the winter until the Colonial army under Josiah Winslow and Benjamin Church won a decisive battle at Kingston, Rhode Island. After several subsequent minor and anticlimactic skirmishes, the uprising was put down and Philip was executed in August of 1676. Mrs. Rowlandson was captured at the attack on Lancaster February 20, 1676, and spent eleven weeks and five days with her captors. She was ransomed and freed at Redemption Rock in Princeton, Massachusetts, on May 2, 1676. Because Puritan religious attitudes engendered a view of the American ab-

origines as directly the instruments of Satan and indirectly so of God, the experience of Indian captivity was apprehended as one of God's ways of testing, punishing, or instructing His creatures. Mrs. Rowlandson's simple, direct account reflects these attitudes with particular emphasis on the salutary and morally instructive nature of the captivity as well as its use as an illustration of God's protecting providence. In this mode and by these apprehensions, her captivity narrative serves as an intense and satisfying expression of profoundly felt religious experience. The first edition of the Rowlandson Narrative, *of which no complete copy is known to exist, was printed by Samuel Green, Jr., at Boston in 1682. The second edition ("The second Addition Corrected and amended") was printed in the same year at Cambridge by Samuel Green, Sr. A facsimile of this edition, reprinted in* Narratives of the Indian Wars, *ed. C. H. Lincoln (New York, 1913), is the basis for the text which follows.*

† †

A Narrative of the Captivity and Restauration of Mrs. Mary Rowlandson

On the tenth of February 1675,[1] Came the Indians with great numbers upon Lancaster: Their first coming was about Sun-rising; hearing the noise of some Guns, we looked out; several Houses were burning, and the Smoke ascending to Heaven. There were five persons taken in one house, the Father, and the Mother and a sucking Child, they knockt on the head; the other two they took and carried away alive. There were two others, who being out of their Garison upon some occasion were set upon; one was knockt on the head, the other escaped: Another their was who running along was shot and wounded, and fell down; he begged of them his life, promising them Money (as they told me) but they

[1] Thursday, Feb. 10, 1675/6; Feb. 20, New Calendar. The fifty or so families of Lancaster had fortified six of their houses with stockades for protection at night; the Rowlandson house sheltered thirty-seven people. The Reverend Mr. Rowlandson was absent at the time of the attack, having gone with his brother-in-law to Boston in an attempt to secure troops for Lancaster. Mary Rowlandson remained with her three children: Joseph, little Mary, and the baby, Sarah. With them were Mary's two sisters and their families, and some neighbors.

would not hearken to him but knockt him in head, and stript him naked, and split open his Bowels. Another seeing many of the Indians about his Barn, ventured and went out, but was quickly shot down. There were three others belonging to the same Garison who were killed; the Indians getting up upon the roof of the Barn, had advantage to shoot down upon them over their Fortification. Thus these murtherous wretches went on, burning, and destroying before them.

At length they came and beset our own house, and quickly it was the dolefullest day that ever mine eyes saw. The House stood upon the edg of a hill; some of the Indians got behind the hill, others into the Barn, and others behind any thing that could shelter them; from all which places they shot against the House, so that the Bullets seemed to fly like hail; and quickly they wounded one man among us, then another, and then a third, About two hours (according to my observation, in that amazing time) they had been about the house before they prevailed to fire it (which they did with Flax and Hemp, which they brought out of the Barn, and there being no defence about the House, only two Flankers [2] at two opposite corners and one of them not finished) they fired it once and one ventured out and quenched it, but they quickly fired it again, and that took. Now is the dreadfull hour come, that I have often heard of (in time of War, as it was the case of others) but now mine eyes see it. Some in our house were fighting for their lives, others wallowing in their blood, the House on fire over our heads, and the bloody Heathen ready to knock us on the head, if we stirred out. Now might we hear Mothers and Children crying out for themselves, and one another, Lord, What shall we do? Then I took my Children (and one of my sisters, hers) to go forth and leave the house: but as soon as we came to the dore and appeared, the Indians shot so thick that the bullets rattled against the House, as if one had taken an handfull of stones and threw them, so that we were fain to give back. We had six stout Dogs belonging to our Garrison, but none of them would stir, though another time, if any Indian had come to the door, they were ready to fly upon him and tear him down. The Lord hereby would make us the more acknowledge his hand, and to see that our

[2] Projections from which blank walls, or curtains, could be positioned.

help is always in him. But out we must go, the fire increasing, and coming along behind us, roaring, and the Indians gaping before us with their Guns, Spears and Hatchets to devour us. No sooner were we out of the House, but my Brother in Law [3] (being before wounded, in defending the house, in or near the throat) fell down dead, wherat the Indians scornfully shouted, and hallowed, and were presently upon him, stripping off his cloaths, the bulletts flying thick, one went through my side, and the same (as would seem) through the bowels and hand of dear Child in my arms. One of my elder Sisters Children, named William, had then his Leg broken, which the Indians perceiving, they knockt him on head. Thus were we butchered by those merciless Heathen, standing amazed, with the blood running down to our heels. My eldest Sister being yet in the House, and seeing those wofull sights, the Infidels haling Mothers one way, and Children another, and some wallowing in their blood: and her elder Son telling her that her Son William was dead, and my self was wounded, she said, And, Lord, let me dy with them; which was no sooner said, but she was struck with a Bullet, and fell down dead over the threshold. I hope she is reaping the fruit of her good labours, being faithfull to the service of God in her place. In her younger years she lay under much trouble upon spiritual accounts, till it pleased God to make that precious Scripture take hold of her heart, 2 Cor. 12. 9. *And he said unto me, my Grace is sufficient for thee.* More then twenty years after I have heard her tell how sweet and comfortable that place was to her. But to return: The Indians laid hold of us, pulling me one way, and the Children another, and said, Come go along with us; I told them they would kill me: they answered, If I were willing to go along with them, they would not hurt me.

Oh the dolefull sight that now was to behold at this House! *Come, behold the works of the Lord, what dissolations he has made in the Earth.* Of thirty seven persons who were in this one House, none escaped either present death, or a bitter captivity, save only one,[4] who might say as he, Job 1. 15, *And I only am escaped alone*

3 John Divoll, the husband of Mrs. Rowlandson's younger sister, Hannah.

4 One Ephraim Roper. Unknown to Mrs. Rowlandson, three children had also escaped. Various contemporary accounts estimate the size of the garrison at between 37 and 55.

to tell the News. There were twelve killed, some shot, some stab'd with their Spears, some knock'd down with their Hatchets. When we are in prosperity, Oh the little that we think of such dreadfull sights, and to see our dear Friends, and Relations ly bleeding out their heart-blood upon the ground. There was one who was chopt into the head with a Hatchet, and stript naked, and yet was crawling up and down. It is a solemn sight to see so many Christians lying in their blood, some here, and some there, like a company of Sheep torn by Wolves, All of them stript naked by a company of hell-hounds, roaring, singing, ranting and insulting, as if they would have torn our very hearts out; yet the Lord by his Almighty power preserved a number of us from death, for there were twenty-four of us taken alive and carried Captive.

I had often before this said, that if the Indians should come, I should chuse rather to be killed by them then taken alive but when it came to the tryal my mind changed; their glittering weapons so daunted my spirit, that I chose rather to go along with those (as I may say) ravenous Beasts, then that moment to end my dayes; and that I may the better declare what happened to me during that grievous Captivity, I shall particularly speak of the severall Removes we had up and down the Wilderness.

THE FIRST REMOVE.

Now away we must go with those Barbarous Creatures, with our bodies wounded and bleeding, and our hearts no less than our bodies. About a mile we went that night, up upon a hill within sight of the Town, where they intended to lodge. There was hard by a vacant house (deserted by the English before, for fear of the Indians). I asked them whither I might not lodge in the house that night to which they answered, what will you love English men still? this was the dolefullest night that ever my eyes saw. Oh the roaring, and singing and danceing, and yelling of those black creatures in the night, which made the place a lively resemblance of hell. And as miserable was the wast that was there made, of Horses, Cattle, Sheep, Swine, Calves, Lambs, Roasting Pigs, and Fowl (which they had plundered in the Town) some roasting, some lying and burning, and some boyling to feed our merciless Enemies; who were joyful enough though we were disconsolate. To add to the dolefulness of the former day, and the dismalness of the present night: my thoughts ran upon my losses and sad bereaved condition. All was gone, my Husband gone (at least separated from me, he being in the Bay,[5] and to add to my grief, the Indians told me they would kill him as he came homeward) my Children gone, my Relations and Friends gone, our House and home and all our comforts within door, and without, all was gone, (except my life) and I knew not but the next moment that might go too. There remained nothing to me but one poor wounded Babe, and it seemed at present worse than death that it was in such a pitiful condition, bespeaking Compassion, and I had no refreshing for it, nor suitable things to revive it. Little do many think what is the savageness and bruitishness of this barbarous Enemy, I [6] even those that seem to profess more than others among them, when the English have fallen into their hands.

Those seven that were killed at Lancaster the summer before upon a Sabbath day, and the one that was afterward killed upon a week day, were slain and mangled in a barbarous manner, by one-ey'd John, and Marlborough's Praying Indians,[7] which Capt. Mosely brought to Boston, as the Indians told me.

THE SECOND REMOVE.[8]

But now, the next morning, I must turn my back upon the Town, and travel with them into the vast and desolate Wilderness, I knew not whither. It is not my tongue, or pen can express the sorrows of my heart, and bitterness of my spirit, that I had at this departure: but God was with me, in a wonderfull manner, carrying me along, and bearing up my spirit, that it did not quite fail. One of the Indians carried my poor wounded Babe upon a horse, it went moaning all along, I shall dy, I shall dy. I went on foot after it, with sorrow that cannot be exprest. At length I took it off the horse, and carried it in my armes till my strength failed, and I fell down with it: Then they set me upon a horse with my

[5] At Massachusetts Bay, i. e., at or near Boston.

[6] Ay.

[7] One-eyed John was also known as Monoco and Apequinsah. "Marlborough's Praying Indians" refers to a settlement of Christianized Indians at Marlborough, Mass.

[8] The second remove was to Princeton, Mass.

wounded Child in my lap, and there being no furniture upon the horse back, as we were going down a steep hill, we both fell over the horses head, at which they like inhumane creatures laught, and rejoyced to see it, though I thought we should there have ended our dayes, as overcome with so many difficulties. But the Lord renewed my strength still, and carried me along, that I might see more of his Power; yea, so much that I could never have thought of, had I not experienced it.

After this it quickly began to snow, and when night came on, they stopt: and now down I must sit in the snow, by a little fire, and a few boughs behind me, with my sick Child in my lap; and calling much for water, being now (through the wound) fallen into a violent Fever. My own wound also growing so stiff, that I could scarce sit down or rise up; yet so it must be, that I must sit all this cold winter night upon the cold snowy ground, with my sick Child in my armes, looking that every hour would be the last of its life; and having no Christian friend near me, either to comfort or help me. Oh, I may see the wonderfull power of God, that my Spirit did not utterly sink under my affliction: still the Lord upheld me with his gracious and mercifull Spirit, and we were both alive to see the light of the next morning.

THE THIRD REMOVE.[9]

The morning being come, they prepared to go on their way. One of the Indians got up upon a horse, and they set me up behind him, with my poor sick Babe in my lap. A very wearisome and tedious day I had of it; what with my own wound, and my Childs being so exceeding sick, and in a lamentable condition with her wound. It may be easily judged what a poor feeble condition we were in, there being not the least crumb of refreshing that came within either of our mouths, from Wednesday night to Saturday night, except only a little cold water. This day in the afternoon, about an hour by Sun, we came to the place where they intended, *viz.* an Indian Town, called Wenimesset, Norward of Quabaug. When we were come, Oh the number of Pagans (now merciless enemies) that there came about me, that I may say as David,

9 The third remove (Feb. 12–27) ended at an Indian village, Menameset (Wanimesset), on the Ware River in what is now New Braintree, Mass.

Psal. 27. 13, *I had fainted, unless I had believed*, etc. The next day was the Sabbath: I then remembered how careless I had been of Gods holy time, how many Sabbaths I had lost and mispent, and how evily I had walked in Gods sight; which lay so close unto my spirit, that it was easie for me to see how righteous it was with God to cut off the thread of my life, and cast me out of his presence for ever. Yet the Lord still shewed mercy to me, and upheld me; and as he wounded me with one hand, so he healed me with the other. This day there came to me one Robbert Pepper (a man belonging to Roxbury) who was taken in Captain Beers his Fight, and had been now a considerable time with the Indians; and up with them almost as far as Albany, to see king Philip,[10] as he told me, and was now very lately come into these parts. Hearing, I say, that I was in this Indian Town, he obtained leave to come and see me. He told me, he himself was wounded in the leg at Captain Beers his Fight; and was not able some time to go, but as they carried him, and as he took Oaken leaves and laid to his wound, and through the blessing of God he was able to travel again.[11] Then I took Oaken leaves and laid to my side, and with the blessing of God it cured me also; yet before the cure was wrought, I may say, as it is in Psal. 38. 5, 6. *My wounds stink and are corrupt, I am troubled, I am bowed down greatly, I go mourning all the day long.* I sat much alone with a poor wounded Child in my lap, which moaned night and day, having nothing to revive the body, or cheer the spirits of her, but in stead of that, sometimes one Indian would come and tell me one hour, that your Master will knock your Child in the head, and then a second, and then a third, your Master will quickly knock your Child in the head.

This was the comfort I had from them, miserable comforters are ye all, as he said. Thus nine dayes I sat upon my knees, with my Babe in my lap, till my flesh was raw again; my Child being even ready to depart this sorrowfull world, they bade me carry it out to another Wigwam (I suppose because they would not be troubled with such spectacles) Whither I went with a very heavy

[10] The Wampanoag leader Metacomet (see headnote); Philip's winter quarters had been east of Albany, N. Y.

[11] The use of oak leaves for staunching wounds is an Indian remedy which persists in modern herbalism.

heart, and down I sat with the picture of death in my lap. About two houres in the night, my sweet Babe like a Lambe departed this life, on Feb. 18, 1675. It being about six yeares, and five months old. It was nine dayes from the first wounding, in this miserable condition, without any refreshing of one nature or other, except a little cold water. I cannot, but take notice, how at another time I could not bear to be in the room where any dead person was, but now the case is changed; I must and could ly down by my dead Babe, side by side all the night after. I have thought since of the wonderfull goodness of God to me, in preserving me in the use of my reason and senses, in that distressed time, that I did not use wicked and violent means to end my own miserable life. In the morning, when they understood that my child was dead they sent for me home to my Masters Wigwam: (by my Master in this writing, must be understood Quanopin, who was a Saggamore, and married King Phillips wives Sister; not that he first took me, but I was sold to him by another Narrhaganset Indian, who took me when first I came out of the Garison). I went to take up my dead child in my arms to carry it with me, but they bid me let it alone: there was no resisting, but goe I must and leave it. When I had been at my masters wigwam, I took the first opportunity I could get, to go look after my dead child: when I came I askt them what they had done with it? then they told me it was upon the hill: then they went and shewed me where it was, where I saw the ground was newly digged, and there they told me they had buried it: There I left that Child in the Wilderness, and must commit it, and my self also in this Wilderness-condition, to him who is above all. God having taken away this dear Child, I went to see my daughter Mary, who was at this same Indian Town, at a Wigwam not very far off, though we had little liberty or opportunity to see one another. She was about ten years old, and taken from the door at first by a Praying Ind and afterward sold for a gun. When I came in sight, she would fall a weeping; at which they were provoked, and would not let me come near her, but bade me be gone; which was a heart-cutting word to me. I had one Child dead, another in the Wilderness, I knew not where, the third they would not let me come near to: *Me* (as he said) *have ye bereaved of my Children, Joseph is not, and Simeon is not, and ye will take*

Benjamin also, all these things are against me. I could not sit still in this condition, but kept walking from one place to another. And as I was going along, my heart was even overwhelm'd with the thoughts of my condition, and that I should have Children, and a Nation which I knew not ruled over them. Whereupon I earnestly entreated the Lord, that he would consider my low estate, and shew me a token for good, and if it were his blessed will, some sign and hope of some relief. And indeed quickly the Lord answered, in some measure, my poor prayers: for as I was going up and down mourning and lamenting my condition, my Son came to me, and asked me how I did; I had not seen him before, since the destruction of the Town, and I knew not where he was, till I was informed by himself, that he was amongst a smaller percel of Indians, whose place was about six miles off; with tears in his eyes, he asked me whether his Sister Sarah was dead; and told me he had seen his Sister Mary; and prayed me, that I would not be troubled in reference to himself. The occasion of his coming to see me at this time, was this: There was, as I said, about six miles from us, a smal Plantation of Indians, where it seems he had been during his Captivity: and at this time, there were some Forces of the Ind. gathered out of our company, and some also from them (among whom was my Sons master) to go to assault and burn Medfield: In this time of the absence of his master, his dame brought him to see me. I took this to be some gracious answer to my earnest and unfeigned desire. The next day, *viz.* to this, the Indians returned from Medfield, all the company, for those that belonged to the other smal company, came thorough the Town that now we were at. But before they came to us, Oh! the outragious roaring and hooping that there was: They began their din about a mile before they came to us. By their noise and hooping they signified how many they had destroyed (which was at that time twenty three.) [12] Those that were with us at home, were gathered together as soon as they heard the hooping, and every time that the other went over their number, these at home gave a shout, that the very Earth rung again: And thus they continued till those that had been upon the expedition were come up to the

[12] The custom of whooping by a returning war party signaled the number of enemy killed and captured in the battle.

Sagamores Wigwam; and then, Oh, the hideous insulting and triumphing that there was over some Englishmens scalps that they had taken (as their manner is) and brought with them, I cannot but take notice of the wonderfull mercy of God to me in those afflictions, in sending me a Bible. One of the Indians that came from Medfield fight, had brought some plunder, came to me, and asked me, if I would have a Bible, he had got one in his Basket. I was glad of it, and asked him, whether he thought the Indians would let me read? he answered, yes: So I took the Bible, and in that melancholy time, it came into my mind to read first the 28. Chap. of Deut.,[13] which I did, and when I had read it, my dark heart wrought on this manner, That there was no mercy for me, that the blessings were gone, and the curses come in their room, and that I had lost my opportunity. But the Lord helped me still to go on reading till I came to Chap. 30 the seven first verses, where I found, There was mercy promised again, if we would return to him by repentance; and though we were scatered from one end of the Earth to the other, yet the Lord would gather us together, and turn all those curses upon our Enemies. I do not desire to live to forget this Scripture, and what comfort it was to me.[14]

Now the Ind. began to talk of removing from this place, some one way, and some another. There were now besides my self nine English Captives in this place (all of them Children, except one Woman). I got an opportunity to go and take my leave of them; they being to go one way, and I another, I asked them whether they were earnest with God for deliverance, they told me, they did as they were able, and it was some comfort to me, that the Lord stirred up Children to look to him. The Woman *viz.* Goodwife Joslin told me, she should never see me again, and that she could

[13] A recital of blessings for obedience to God and curses for disobedience.

[14] As Mrs. Rowlandson subsequently relates, this Bible became "my Guid by day, and my Pillow by night." Other captives, however, were less fortunate: elsewhere during the period a certain Wright of Providence, R.I., was ripped open by his Indian captors and his Bible thrust into his belly ("A New and Further Narrative of the state of New-England" [1676], in Samuel Gardner Drake, *The Old Indian Chronicle* [Boston, 1867], pp. 223–24). Jonathan Dickenson and his party, captured in 1696, were stripped of their clothes and given, for use as breechcloths, pages torn out of a large Bible belonging to the party (*God's Protecting Providence Man's Surest Help and Defence in the Times of the Greatest Difficulty and Most Imminent Danger* [Philadelphia, 1699]).

find in her heart to run away; I wisht her not to run away by any means, for we were near thirty miles from any English Town, and she very big with Child, and had but one week to reckon; and another Child in her Arms, two years old, and bad Rivers there were to go over, and we were feeble, with our poor and course entertainment. I had my Bible with me, I pulled it out, and asked her whether she would read; we opened the Bible and lighted on Psal. 27, in which Psalm we especially took notice of that, *ver. ult., Wait on the Lord, Be of good courage, and he shall strengthen thine Heart, wait I say on the Lord.*

THE FOURTH REMOVE.[15]

And now I must part with that little Company I had. Here I parted from my Daughter Mary, (whom I never saw again till I saw her in Dorchester, returned from Captivity), and from four little Cousins and Neighbours, some of which I never saw afterward: the Lord only knows the end of them. Amongst them also was that poor Woman before mentioned, who came to a sad end, as some of the company told me in my travel: She having much grief upon her Spirit, about her miserable condition, being so near her time, she would be often asking the Indians to let her go home; they not being willing to that, and yet vexed with her importunity, gathered a great company together about her, and stript her naked, and set her in the midst of them; and when they had sung and danced about her (in their hellish manner) as long as they pleased, they knockt her on head, and the child in her arms with her: when they had done that, they made a fire and put them both into it, and told the other Children that were with them, that if they attempted to go home, they would serve them in like manner: The Children said, she did not shed one tear, but prayed all the while. But to return to my own Journey; we travelled about half a day or little more, and came to a desolate place in the Wilderness, where there were no Wigwams or Inhabitants before; we came about the middle of the afternoon to this place, cold and wet, and snowy, and hungry, and weary, and no refreshing, for man, but the cold ground to sit on, and our poor Indian cheer.

15 From Feb. 28 to Mar. 3. The camp was at the Indian village of Nichewaug.

Heart-aking thoughts here I had about my poor Children, who were scattered up and down among the wild beasts of the forrest: My head was light and dissey (either through hunger or hard lodging, or trouble or altogether) my knees feeble, my body raw by sitting double night and day, that I cannot express to man the affliction that lay upon my Spirit, but the Lord helped me at that time to express it to himself. I opened my Bible to read, and the Lord brought that precious Scripture to me, Jer. 31. 16. *Thus saith the Lord, refrain thy voice from weeping, and thine eyes from tears, for thy work shall be rewarded, and they shall come again from the land of the Enemy.* This was a sweet Cordial to me, when I was ready to faint, many and many a time have I sat down, and weept sweetly over this Scripture. At this place we continued about four dayes.

THE FIFTH REMOVE.[16]

The occasion (as I thought) of their moving at this time, was, the English Army, it being near and following them: For they went, as if they had gone for their lives, for some considerable way, and then they made a stop, and chose some of their stoutest men, and sent them back to hold the English Army in play whilst the rest escaped: And then, like Jehu, they marched on furiously, with their old, and with their young: some carried their old decrepit mothers, some carried one, and some another. Four of them carried a great Indian upon a Bier;[17] but going through a thick Wood with him, they were hindered, and could make no hast; whereupon they took him upon their backs, and carried him, one at a time, till they came to Bacquaug River. Upon a Friday, a little after noon we came to this River. When all the company was come up, and were gathered together, I thought to count the number of them, but they were so many, and being somewhat in motion, it was beyond my skil. In this travel, because of my wound, I was somewhat favoured in my load; I carried only my knitting

16 The fifth remove (Mar. 3–5) included crossing the Baquag River in Orange. The "Army" following consisted of Massachusetts and Connecticut forces under Captain Thomas Savage.

17 Cartier at Montreal in 1535 was the first early observer to mention the carrying of a distinguished person on a litter. The custom was widespread in the eastern woodlands, particularly in the southeast.

work and two quarts of parched meal: [18] Being very faint I asked my mistriss to give me one spoonfull of the meal, but she would not give me a taste. They quickly fell to cutting dry trees, to make Rafts to carry them over the river: and soon my turn came to go over: By the advantage of some brush which they had laid upon the Raft to sit upon, I did not wet my foot (which many of themselves at the other end were mid-leg deep) which cannot but be acknowledged as a favour of God to my weakned body, it being a very cold time. I was not before acquainted with such kind of doings or dangers. *When thou passeth through the waters I will be with thee, and through the Rivers they shall not overflow thee,* Isai. 43. 2. A certain number of us got over the River that night, but it was the night after the Sabbath before all the company was got over. On the Saturday they boyled an old Horses leg which they had got, and so we drank of the broth, as soon as they thought it was ready, and when it was almost all gone, they filled it up again.

The first week of my being among them, I hardly ate any thing; the second week, I found my stomach grow very faint for want of something; and yet it was very hard to get down their filthy trash: but the third week, though I could think how formerly my stomach would turn against this or that, and I could starve and dy before I could eat such things, yet they were sweet and savoury to my taste. I was at this time knitting a pair of white cotton stockins for my mistriss; and had not yet wrought upon a Sabbath day; when the Sabbath came they bade me go to work; I told them it was the Sabbath day, and desired them to let me rest, and told them I would do as much more to morrow; to which they answered me, they would break my face. And here I cannot but take notice of the strange providence of God in preserving the heathen: They were many hundreds, old and young, some sick, and some lame, many had Papooses at their backs, the greatest number at this time with us, were Squaws, and they travelled with all they had, bag and baggage, and yet they got over this River aforesaid; and on Munday they set their Wigwams on fire, and away they went: On that very day came the English Army after them to this River, and saw the smoak of their Wigwams, and yet

[18] Parched meal was a favorite traveling food.

this River put a stop to them. God did not give them courage or activity to go over after us; we were not ready for so great a mercy as victory and deliverance; if we had been, God would have found out a way for the English to have passed this River, as well as for the Indians with their Squaws and Children, and all their Luggage. *Oh that my People had hearkened to me, and Israel had walked in my ways, I should soon have subdued their Enemies, and turned my hand against their Adversaries*, Psal. 81: 13.14.

THE SIXTH REMOVE.[19]

On Munday (as I said) they set their Wigwams on fire, and went away. It was a cold morning, and before us there was a great Brook with ice on it; some waded through it, up to the knees and higher, but others went till they came to a Beaver-dam, and I amongst them, where through the good providence of God, I did not wet my foot. I went along that day mourning and lamenting, leaving farther my own Country, and travelling into the vast and howling Wilderness, and I understood something of Lot's Wife's Temptation, when she looked back: we came that day to a great Swamp, by the side of which we took up our lodging that night. When I came to the brow of the hil, that looked toward the Swamp, I thought we had been come to a great Indian Town (though there were none but our own Company) The Indians were as thick as the trees: it seemed as if there had been a thousand Hatchets going at once: if one looked before one, there was nothing but Indians, and behind one, nothing but Indians, and so on either hand, I my self in the midst, and no Christian soul near me, and yet how hath the Lord preserved me in safety? Oh the experience that I have had of the goodness of God, to me and mine!

THE SEVENTH REMOVE.[20]

After a restless and hungry night there, we had a wearisome time of it the next day. The Swamp by which we lay, was, as it were, a deep Dungeon, and an exceeding high and steep hill before

19 This remove was on Monday, Mar. 6, and ended near a swamp in Northfield, Mass.

20 The seventh remove carried Mrs. Rowlandson to Squakeag, near Beer's Plain in Northfield.

it. Before I got to the top of the hill, I thought my heart and legs, and all would have broken, and failed me. What through faintness, and soreness of body, it was a grievous day of travel to me. As we went along, I saw a place where English Cattle had been: that was comfort to me, such as it was: quickly after that we came to an English Path, which so took with me, that I thought I could have freely lyen down and dyed. That day, a little after noon, we came to Squaukheag, where the Indians quickly spread themselves over the deserted English Fields, gleaning what they could find; some pickt up ears of Wheat that were crickled down, some found ears of Indian Corn, some found Ground-nuts.[21] and others sheaves of Wheat that were frozen together in the shock, and went to threshing of them out. My self got two ears of Indian Corn, and whilst I did but turn my back, one of them was stolen from me, which much troubled me. There came an Indian to them at that time, with a basket of Horse-liver. I asked him to give me a piece: What, sayes he, can you eat Horse-liver? I told him, I would try, if he would give a piece, which he did, and I laid it on the coals to rost; but before it was half ready they got half of it away from me, so that I was fain to take the rest and eat it as it was, with the blood about my mouth, and yet a savoury bit it was to me: *For to the hungry Soul every bitter thing is sweet.* A solemn sight methought it was, to see Fields of wheat and Indian Corn forsaken and spoiled: and the remainders of them to be food for our merciless Enemies. That night we had a mess of wheat for our Supper.

THE EIGHT REMOVE.[22]

On the morrow morning we must go over the River, *i. e.* Connecticot, to meet with King Philip; two Cannoos ful, they had carried over, the next Turn I my self was to go; but as my foot was upon the Cannoo to step in, there was a sudden out-cry among them, and I must step back; and instead of going over the River, I must go four or five miles up the River farther North-

[21] The custom of eating groundnuts (*Apios tuberosa*) is mentioned numerous times. They were eaten either boiled or roasted and parched for provisions. The path of fleeing Indians could be traced by holes dug for the tubers.

[22] To Coasset in South Vernon, Vt. Here Mrs. Rowlandson met King Philip for the first time as he was returning from New York State to take up the campaign of 1676.

ward. Some of the Indians ran one way, and some another. The cause of this rout was, as I thought, their espying some English Scouts, who were thereabout. In this travel up the River, about noon the Company made a stop, and sate down; some to eat, and others to rest them. As I sate amongst them, musing of things past, my Son Joseph unexpectedly came to me: we asked of each others welfare, bemoaning our dolefull condition, and the change that had come upon uss. We had Husband and Father, and Children, and Sisters, and Friends, and Relations, and House, and Home, and many Comforts of this Life: but now we may say, as Job, *Naked came I out of my Mothers Womb, and naked shall I return: The Lord gave, and the Lord hath taken away, Blessed be the Name of the Lord.* I asked him whither he would read; he told me, he earnestly desired it, I gave him my Bible, and he lighted upon that comfortable Scripture, Psal. 118. 17, 18. *I shall not dy but live, and declare the works of the Lord: the Lord hath chastened me sore, yet he hath not given me over to death.* Look here, Mother (sayes he) did you read this? And here I may take occasion to mention one principall ground of my setting forth these Lines: even as the Psalmist sayes, To declare the Works of the Lord, and his wonderfull Power in carrying us along, preserving us in the Wilderness, while under the Enemies hand, and returning of us in safety again, And His goodness in bringing to my hand so many comfortable and suitable Scriptures in my distress. But to Return, We travelled on till night; and in the morning, we must go over the River to Philip's Crew. When I was in the Cannoo, I could not but be amazed at the numerous crew of Pagans that were on the Bank on the other side. When I came ashore, they gathered all about me, I sitting alone in the midst: I observed they asked one another questions, and laughed, and rejoyced over their Gains and Victories. Then my heart began to fail: and I fell a weeping which was the first time to my remembrance, that I wept before them. Although I had met with so much Affliction, and my heart was many times ready to break, yet could I not shed one tear in their sight: but rather had been all this while in a maze, and like one astonished: but now I may say as, Psal. 137. 1. *By the Rivers of Babylon, there we sate down: yea, we wept when we remembered Zion.* There one of them asked me, why I wept, I could hardly tell what to say: yet I answered, they would kill me: No, said he, none will hurt you. Then came one of them and gave me two spoon-fulls of Meal to comfort me, and another gave me half a pint of Pease; which was more worth than many Bushels at another time. Then I went to see King Philip, he bade me come in and sit down, and asked me whether I woold smoke it (a usual Complement nowadayes amongst Saints and Sinners) but this no way suited me. For though I had formerly used Tobacco, yet I had left it ever since I was first taken. It seems to be a Bait, the Devil layes to make men loose their precious time: I remember with shame, how formerly, when I had taken two or three pipes, I was presently ready for another, such a bewitching thing it is: But I thank God, he has now given me power over it; surely there are many who may be better imployed than to ly sucking a stinking Tobacco-pipe.[23]

Now the Indians gather their Forces to go against North-Hampton: over-night one went about yelling and hooting to give notice of the design. Whereupon they fell to boyling of Ground-nuts, and parching of Corn (as many as had it) for their Provision: and in the morning away they went. During my abode in this place, Philip spake to me to make a shirt for his boy, which I did, for which he gave me a shilling: I offered the mony to my master, but he bade me keep it: and with it I bought a piece of Horse flesh. Afterwards he asked me to make a Cap for his boy, for which he invited me to Dinner. I went, and he gave me a Pancake, about as big as two fingers; it was made of parched wheat, beaten, and fryed in Bears grease, but I thought I never tasted pleasanter meat in my life. There was a Squaw who spake to me to make a shirt for her *Sannup*,[24] for which she gave me a piece of Bear.[25] Another asked me to knit a pair of Stockins, for which she gave me a quart of Pease: I boyled my Pease and Bear together, and invited my master and mistriss to dinner, but the proud Gossip, because

23 The use of tobacco was widespread among early American women as well as men. Colonial New England ladies were said to "smoke in bed, smoke as they knead their bread, smoke whilst they're cooking." Quoted in Robert K. Heimann, *Tobacco and Americans* (New York, 1960).

24 Husband.

25 Payment in kind for services rendered. New England Indians were eager to have tailored and knit clothes, and captives were often kept busy making garments.

I served them both in one Dish, would eat nothing, except one bit that he gave her upon the point of his knife. Hearing that my son was come to this place, I went to see him, and found him lying flat upon the ground: I asked him how he could sleep so? he answered me, That he was not asleep, but at Prayer; and lay so, that they might not observe what he was doing. I pray God he may remember these things now he is returned in safety. At this Place (the Sun now getting higher) what with the beams and heat of the Sun, and the smoak of the Wigwams, I thought I should have been blind. I could scarce discern one Wigwam from another. There was here one Mary Thurston of Medfield, who seeing how it was with me, lent me a Hat to wear: but as soon as I was gone, the Squaw (who owned that Mary Thurston) came running after me, and got it away again. Here was the Squaw that gave me one spoonfull of Meal. I put it in my Pocket to keep it safe: yet notwithstanding some body stole it, but put five Indian Corns in the room of it: which Corns were the greatest Provisions I had in my travel for one day.

The Indians returning from North-Hampton, brought with them some Horses, and Sheep, and other things which they had taken: I desired them, that they would carry me to Albany, upon one of those Horses, and sell me for Powder: for so they had sometimes discoursed. I was utterly hopless of getting home on foot, the way that I came. I could hardly bear to think of the many weary steps I had taken, to come to this place.

THE NINTH REMOVE.[26]

But instead of going either to Albany or homeward, we must go five miles up the River, and then go over it. Here we abode a while. Here lived a sorry Indian, who spoke to me to make him a shirt. When I had done it, he would pay me nothing. But he living by the River side, where I often went to fetch water, I would often be putting of him in mind, and calling for my pay: at last he told me if I would make another shirt, for a Papoos not yet born, he would give me a knife, which he did when I had done it. I carried the knife in, and my master asked me to give it him, and I was not a little glad that I had any thing that they would accept of, and be

[26] To the Ashuelot Valley in New Hampshire.

pleased with. When we were at this place, my Masters maid came home, she had been gone three weeks into the Narrhaganset Country, to fetch Corn, where they had stored up some in the ground: she brought home about a peck and half of Corn. This was about the time that their great Captain, Naananto, was killed in the Narrhaganset Countrey.[27] My Son being now about a mile from me, I asked liberty to go and see him, they bade me go, and away I went: but quickly lost my self, travelling over Hills and thorough Swamps, and could not find the way to him. And I cannot but admire at the wonderfull power and goodness of God to me, in that, though I was gone from home, and met with all sorts of Indians, and those I had no knowledge of, and there being no Christian soul near me; yet not one of them offered the least imaginable miscarriage to me. I turned homeward again, and met with my master, he shewed me the way to my Son: When I came to him I found him not well: and withall he had a boyl on his side, which much troubled him: We bemoaned one another awhile, as the Lord helped us, and then I returned again. When I was returned, I found my self as unsatisfied as I was before. I went up and down mourning and lamenting: and my spirit was ready to sink, with the thoughts of my poor Children: my Son was ill, and I could not but think of his mournfull looks, and no Christian Friend was near him, to do any office of love for him, either for Soul or Body. And my poor Girl, I knew not where she was, nor whither she was sick, or well, or alive, or dead. I repaired under these thoughts to my Bible (my great comfort in that time) and that Scripture came to my hand, *Cast thy burden upon the Lord, and He shall sustain thee*, Psal. 55. 22.

But I was fain to go and look after something to satisfie my hunger, and going among the Wigwams, I went into one, and there found a Squaw who shewed her self very kind to me, and gave me a piece of Bear. I put it into my pocket, and came home, but could not find an opportunity to broil it, for fear they would get it from me, and there it lay all that day and night in my stinking pocket. In the morning I went to the same Squaw, who had a Kettle of Ground nuts boyling; I asked her to let me boyle

[27] Naananto, better known as Canonchet, was one of the important leaders in the war. He was killed Apr. 3, 1676.

my piece of Bear in her Kettle, which she did, and gave me some Ground-nuts to eat with it: and I cannot but think how pleasant it was to me. I have sometime seen Bear baked very handsomly among the English, and some like it, but the thoughts that it was Bear, made me tremble: but now that was savoury to me that one would think was enough to turn the stomach of a bruit Creature.

One bitter cold day, I could find no room to sit down before the fire: I went out, and could not tell what to do, but I went in to another Wigwam, where they were also sitting round the fire, but the Squaw laid a skin for me, and bid me sit down, and gave me some Ground-nuts, and bade me come again: and told me they would buy me, if they were able, and yet these were strangers to me that I never saw before.

THE TENTH REMOVE.[28]

That day a small part of the Company removed about three quarters of a mile, intending further the next day. When they came to the place where they intended to lodge, and had pitched their wigwams, being hungry I went again back to the place we were before at, to get something to eat: being encouraged by the Squaws kindness, who bade me come again; when I was there, there came an Indian to look after me, who when he had found me, kickt me all along: I went home and found Venison roasting that night, but they would not give me one bit of it. Sometimes I met with favour, and sometimes with nothing but frowns.

THE ELEVENTH REMOVE.[29]

The next day in the morning they took their Travel, intending a dayes journey up the River, I took my load at my back, and quickly we came to wade over the River: and passed over tiresome and wearisome hills. One hill was so steep that I was fain to creep up upon my knees, and to hold by the twiggs and bushes to keep my self from falling backward. My head also was so light, that I usually reeled as I went; but I hope all these wearisome steps

28 Apparently only a change to another location in the same Ashuelot Valley.

29 This remove, in Apr. 1676, carried Mrs. Rowlandson as far north as she was taken. The camp was in or near Chesterfield, N. H., where she remained until the twelfth remove on Sunday, Apr. 9.

that I have taken, are but a forewarning to me of the heavenly rest. *I know, O Lord, that thy Judgements are right, and that thou in faithfulness hast afflicted me*, Psal. 119. 71.[30]

THE TWELFTH REMOVE.

It was upon a Sabbath-day-morning, that they prepared for their Travel. This morning I asked my master whither he would sell me to my Husband; he answered me *Nux*,[31] which did much rejoyce my spirit. My mistriss, before we went, was gone to the burial of a Papoos, and returning, she found me sitting and reading in my Bible; she snatched it hastily out of my hand, and threw it out of doors; I ran out and catcht it up, and put it into my pocket, and never let her see it afterward. Then they packed up their things to be gone, and gave me my load: I complained it was too heavy, whereupon she gave me a slap in the face, and bade me go; I lifted up my heart to God, hoping the Redemption was not far off: and the rather because their insolency grew worse and worse.

But the thoughts of my going homeward (for so we bent our course) much cheared my Spirit, and made my burden seem light, and almost nothing at all. But (to my amazement and great perplexity) the scale was soon turned: for when we had gone a little way, on a sudden my mistriss gives out, she would go no further, but turn back again, and said, I must go back again with her, and she called her *Sannup*, and would have had him gone back also, but he would not, but said, He would go on, and come to us again in three dayes. My Spirit was upon this, I confess, very impatient, and almost outragious. I thought I could as well have dyed as went back: I cannot declare the trouble that I was in about it; but yet back again I must go. As soon as I had an opportunity, I took my Bible to read, and that quieting Scripture came to my hand, Psal. 46. 10. *Be still, and know that I am God.* Which stilled my spirit for the present: But a sore time of tryal, I concluded, I had to go through, My master being gone, who seemed to me the best friend that I had of an Indian, both in cold and hunger, and quickly so it proved. Down I sat, with my heart as full as it could hold, and yet

30 This quotation is from Ps. 119:75.
31 Yes.

so hungry that I could not sit neither: but going out to see what I could find, and walking among the Trees, I found six Acorns, and two Ches-nuts, which were some refreshment to me. Towards Night I gathered me some sticks for my own comfort, that I might not ly a-cold: but when we came to ly down they bade me go out, and ly some-where-else, for they had company (they said) come in more than their own: I told them, I could not tell where to go, they bade me go look; I told them, if I went to another Wigwam they would be angry, and send me home again. Then one of the Company drew his sword, and told me he would run me thorough if I did not go presently. Then was I fain to stoop to this rude fellow, and to go out in the night, I knew not whither. Mine eyes have seen that fellow afterwards walking up and down Boston, under the appearance of a Friend-Indian, and severall others of the like Cut. I went to one Wigwam, and they told me they had no room. Then I went to another, and they said the same; at last an old Indian bade me come to him, and his Squaw gave me some Ground-nuts; she gave me also something to lay under my head, and a good fire we had: and through the good providence of God, I had a comfortable lodging that night. In the morning, another Indian bade me come at night, and he would give me six Ground-nuts, which I did. We were at this place and time about two miles from Connecticut River. We went in the morning to gather Ground-nuts, to the River, and went back again that night. I went with a good load at my back (for they when they went, though but a little way, would carry all their trumpery with them) I told them the skin was off my back, but I had no other comforting answer from them than this, That it would be no matter if my head were off too.

THE THIRTEENTH REMOVE.[32]

Instead of going toward the Bay, which was that I desired, I must go with them five or six miles down the River into a mighty Thicket of Brush: where we abode almost a fortnight. Here one asked me to make a shirt for her Papoos, for which she gave me a mess of Broth, which was thickened with meal made of the Bark of a Tree, and to make it the better, she had put into it about a

[32] The encampment seems to have been temporarily shifted to Hinsdale, N. H.

handfull of Pease, and a few roasted Ground-nuts. I had not seen my son a pritty while, and here was an Indian of whom I made inquiry after him, and asked him when he saw him: he answered me, that such a time his master roasted him, and that himself did eat a piece of him, as big as his two fingers, and that he was very good meat: But the Lord upheld my Spirit, under this discouragement; and I considered their horrible addictedness to lying, and that there is not one of them that makes the least conscience of speaking of truth. In this place, on a cold night, as I lay by the fire, I removed a stick that kept the heat from me, a Squaw moved it down again, at which I lookt up, and she threw a handfull of ashes in mine eyes; I thought I should have been quite blinded, and have never seen more: but lying down, the water run out of my eyes, and carried the dirt with it, that by the morning, I recovered my sight again. Yet upon this, and the like occasions, I hope it is not too much to say with Job, *Have pitty upon me, have pitty upon me, O ye my Friends, for the Hand of the Lord has touched me.* And here I cannot but remember how many times sitting in their Wigwams, and musing on things past, I should suddenly leap up and run out, as if I had been at home, forgetting where I was, and what my condition was: But when I was without, and saw nothing but Wilderness, and Woods, and a company of barbarous heathens, my mind quickly returned to me, which made me think of that, spoken concerning Sampson, who said, *I will go out and shake my self as at other times, but he wist not that the Lord was departed from him.* About this time I began to think that all my hopes of Restoration would come to nothing. I thought of the English Army, and hoped for their coming, and being taken by them, but that failed. I hoped to be carried to Albany, as the Indians had discoursed before, but that failed also. I thought of being sold to my Husband, as my master spake, but in stead of that, my master himself was gone, and left behind, so that my Spirit was now quite ready to sink. I asked them to let me go out and pick up some sticks, that I might get alone, And poure out my heart unto the Lord. Then also I took my Bible to read, but I found no comfort here neither, which many times I was wont to find: So easie a thing it is with God to dry up the Streames of Scripture-comfort from us. Yet I can say, that in all my sorrows

The forced marches of Father Isaac Jogues, Mrs. Mary Rowlandson, and John Gyles.

and afflictions, God did not leave me to have my impatience work towards himself, as if his wayes were unrighteous. But I knew that he laid upon me less then I deserved. Afterward, before this dolefull time ended with me, I was turning the leaves of my Bible, and the Lord brought to me some Scriptures, which did a little revive me, as that Isai. 55. 8, *For my thoughts are not your thoughts, neither are your wayes my ways, saith the Lord.* And also that, Psal. 37. 5, *Commit thy way unto the Lord, trust also in him, and he shal bring it to pass.* About this time they came yelping from Hadly, where they had killed three English men, and brought one Captive with them, *viz.* Thomas Read. They all gathered about the poor Man, asking him many Questions. I desired also to go and see him; and when I came, he was crying bitterly, supposing they would quickly kill him. Whereupon I asked one of them, whether they intended to kill him; he answered me, they would not: He being a little cheared with that, I asked him about the wel-fare of my Husband, he told me he saw him such a time in the Bay, and he was well, but very melancholly. By which I certainly understood (though I suspected it before) that whatsoever the Indians told me respecting him was vanity and lies. Some of them told me, he was dead, and they had killed him: some said he was Married again, and that the Governour wished him to Marry; and told him he should have his choice, and that all perswaded I was dead. So like were these barbarous creatures to him who was a lyer from the beginning.

As I was sitting once in the Wigwam here, Phillips Maid came in with the Child in her arms, and asked me to give her a piece of my Apron, to make a flap for it, I told her I would not: then my Mistriss bad me give it, but still I said no: the maid told me if I would not give her a piece, she would tear a piece off it: I told her I would tear her Coat then, with that my Mistriss rises up, and takes up a stick big enough to have killed me, and struck at me with it, but I stept out, and she struck the stick into the Mat of the Wigwam. But while she was pulling of it out, I ran to the Maid and gave her all my Apron, and so that storm went over.

Hearing that my Son was come to this place, I went to see him, and told him his Father was well, but melancholly: he told me he was as much grieved for his Father as for himself; I wondered at his speech, for I thought I had enough upon my spirit in reference to my self, to make me mindless of my Husband and every one else: they being safe among their Friends. He told me also, that a while before, his Master (together with other Indians) where[33] going to the French for Powder; but by the way the Mohawks met with them, and killed four of their Company which made the rest turn back again,[34] for it might have been worse with him, had he been sold to the French, than it proved to be in his remaining with the Indians.

I went to see an English Youth in this place, one John Gillberd of Springfield. I found him lying without dores, upon the ground; I asked him how he did? he told me he was very sick of a flux,

[33] Were.

[34] That Mohawks attacked Philip's Indians sheds light on intertribal relations during King Philips's War.

with eating so much blood: They had turned him out of the Wigwam, and with him an Indian Papoos, almost dead, (whose Parents had been killed) in a bitter cold day, without fire or clothes: the young man himself had nothing on, but his shirt and wastcoat. This sight was enough to melt a heart of flint. There they lay quivering in the Cold, the youth round like a dog; the Papoos stretcht out, with his eyes and nose and mouth full of dirt, and yet alive, and groaning. I advised John to go and get to some fire: he told me he could not stand, but I perswaded him still, lest he should ly there and die: and with much adoe I got him to a fire, and went my self home. As soon as I was got home, his Masters Daughter came after me, to know what I had done with the English man, I told her I had got him to a fire in such a place. Now had I need to pray Pauls Prayer, 2 Thess. 3. 2. *That we may be delivered from unreasonable and wicked men.* For her satisfaction I went along with her, and brought her to him; but before I got home again, it was noised about, that I was running away and getting the English youth, along with me; that as soon as I came in, they began to rant and domineer: asking me Where I had been, and what I had been doing? and saying they would knock him on the head: I told them, I had been seeing the English Youth, and that I would not run away, they told me I lyed, and taking up a Hatchet, they came to me, and said they would knock me down if I stirred out again; and so confined me to the Wigwam. Now may I say with David, 2 Sam. 24. 14. *I am in a great strait.* If I keep in, I must dy with hunger, and if I go out, I must be knockt in head. This distressed condition held that day, and half the next; And then the Lord remembred me, whose mercyes are great. Then came an Indian to me with a pair of stockings that were too big for him, and he would have me ravel them out, and knit them fit for him. I shewed my self willing, and bid him ask my mistriss if I might go along with him a little way; she said yes, I might, but I was not a little refresht with that news, that I had my liberty again. Then I went along with him, and he gave me some roasted Ground-nuts, which did again revive my feeble stomach.

Being got out of her sight, I had time and liberty again to look into my Bible: Which was my Guid by day, and my Pillow by night. Now that comfortable Scripture presented it self to me,

Isa. 54. 7. *For a smal moment have I forsaken thee, but with great mercies will I gather thee.* Thus the Lord carried me along from one time to another, and made good to me this precious promise, and many others. Then my Son came to see me, and I asked his master to let him stay a while with me, that I might comb his head, and look over him, for he was almost overcome with lice. He told me, when I had done, that he was very hungry, but I had nothing to relieve him; but bid him go into the Wigwams as he went along, and see if he could get any thing among them. Which he did, and it seems tarried a little too long; for his Master was angry with him, and beat him, and then sold him. Then he came running to tell me he had a new Master, and that he had given him some Groundnuts already. Then I went along with him to his new Master who told me he loved him: and he should not want. So his Master carried him away, and I never saw him afterward, till I saw him at Pascataqua in Portsmouth.

That night they bade me go out of the Wigwam again: my Mistrisses Papoos was sick, and it died that night, and there was one benefit in it, that there was more room. I went to a Wigwam, and they bade me come in, and gave me a skin to ly upon, and a mess of Venson and Ground-nuts, which was a choice Dish among them. On the morrow they buried the Papoos, and afterward, both morning and evening, there came a company to mourn and howle with her: though I confess, I could not much condole with them. Many sorrowfull dayes I had in this place: often getting alone; *like a Crane, or a Swallow, so did I chatter: I did mourn as a Dove, mine eyes ail with looking upward. Oh, Lord, I am oppressed; undertake for me,* Isa. 38. 14. I could tell the Lord as Hezeckiah, ver. 3. *Remember now O Lord, I beseech thee, how I have walked before thee in truth.* Now had I time to examine all my wayes: my Conscience did not accuse me of un-righteousness toward one or other: yet I saw how in my walk with God, I had been a careless creature. As David said, *Against thee, thee only have I sinned:* and I might say with the poor Publican, *God be merciful unto me a sinner.* On the Sabbath-dayes, I could look upon the Sun and think how People were going to the house of God, to have their Souls refresht; and then home, and their bodies also: but I was destitute of both; and might say as the poor Prodigal, *he would fain have filled his belly with the husks that the Swine did eat, and no man gave unto him*, Luke 15. 16. For I must say with him, *Father I have sinned against Heaven, and in thy sight*, ver. 21. I remembred how on the night before and after the Sabbath, when my Family was about me, and Relations and Neighbours with us, we could pray and sing, and then have a comfortable Bed to ly down on: but in stead of all this, I had only a little Swill for the body, and then like a Swine, must ly down on the ground. I cannot express to man the sorrow that lay upon my Spirit, the Lord knows it. Yet that comfortable Scripture would often come to my mind, *For a small moment have I forsaken thee, but with great mercies will I gather thee.*

THE FOURTEENTH REMOVE.[35]

Now must we pack up and be gone from this Thicket, bending our course toward the Bay-towns, I haveing nothing to eat by the way this day, but a few crumbs of Cake, that an Indian gave my girle the same day we were taken. She gave it me, and I put it in my pocket: there it lay, till it was so mouldy (for want of good baking) that one could not tell what it was made of; it fell all to crumbs, and grew so dry and hard, that it was like little flints; and this refreshed me many times, when I was ready to faint. It was in my thoughts when I put it into my mouth, that if ever I returned, I would tell the World what a blessing the Lord gave to such mean food. As we went along, they killed a Deer, with a young one in her, they gave me a piece of the Fawn, and it was so young and tender, that one might eat the bones as well as the flesh, and yet I thought it very good. When night came on we sate down; it rained, but they quickly got up a Bark Wigwam, where I lay dry that night. I looked out in the morning, and many of them had line in the rain all night, I saw by their Reaking. Thus the Lord dealt mercifully with me many times. and I fared better than many of them. In the morning they took the blood of the

35 The fourteenth to the nineteenth removes covered the period from Apr. 20 to Apr. 28. Here the route retraced the path taken earlier: from Hinsdale, N. H., the trail led to the camp on Miller's River in Orange, thence to Nichewaug in Petersham, to Menameset on Barre Plains, and to Mount Wachusett in Princeton, where the negotiations for ransom began.

Deer, and put it into the Paunch, and so boyled it;[36] I could eat nothing of that, though they ate it sweetly. And yet they were so nice in other things, that when I had fetcht water, and had put the Dish I dipt the water with, into the Kettle of water which I brought, they would say, they would knock me down; for they said, it was a sluttish trick.[37]

THE FIFTEENTH REMOVE.

We went on our Travel. I having got one handfull of Groundnuts, for my support that day, they gave me my load, and I went on cheerfully (with the thoughts of going homeward) haveing my burden more on my back than my spirit: we came to Baquaug River again that day, near which we abode a few dayes. Sometimes one of them would give me a Pipe, another a little Tobacco, another a little Salt: which I would change for a little Victuals. I cannot but think what a Wolvish appetite persons have in a starving condition: for many times when they gave me that which was hot, I was so greedy, that I should burn my mouth, that it would trouble me hours after, and yet I should quickly do the same again. And after I was thoroughly hungry, I was never again satisfied. For though sometimes it fell out, that I got enough, and did eat till I could eat no more, yet I was as unsatisfied as I was when I began. And now could I see that Scripture verified (there being many Scriptures which we do not take notice of, or understand till we are afflicted) Mic. 6. 14. *Thou shalt eat and not be satisfied.* Now might I see more than ever before, the miseries that sin hath brought upon us: Many times I should be ready to run out against the Heathen, but the Scripture would quiet me again, Amos 3. 6, *Shal there be evil in the City, and the Lord hath not done it?* The Lord help me to make a right improvement of His Word, and that I might learn that great lesson, Mic. 6. 8, 9. *He hath shewed thee (Oh Man) what is good, and what doth the Lord require of thee, but to do justly, and love mercy, and walk humbly with thy God? Hear ye the rod, and who hath appointed it.*

36 Skin-boiling (in this instance in the paunch of a deer) was a common food custom as was the eating of the fetus of various animals, mentioned earlier (cf. also Eastburn narrative, p. 163).

37 A taboo on putting one's dipper or cup into a kettle of water used by the community.

THE SIXTEENTH REMOVE.

We began this Remove with wading over Baquag River: the water was up to the knees, and the stream very swift, and so cold that I thought it would have cut me in sunder. I was so weak and feeble, that I reeled as I went along, and thought there I must end my dayes at last, after my bearing and getting thorough so many difficulties; the Indians stood laughing to see me staggering along: but in my distress the Lord gave me experience of the truth, and goodness of that promise, Isai. 43. 2. *When thou passest thorough the Waters, I will be with thee, and through the Rivers, they shall not overflow thee.* Then I sat down to put on my stockins and shoos, with the teares running down myne eyes, and many sorrowfull thoughts in my heart, but I gat up to go along with them. Quickly there came up to us an Indian, who informed them, that I must go to Wachusit to my master, for there was a Letter come from the Council to the Saggamores, about redeeming the Captives, and that there would be another in fourteen dayes, and that I must be there ready. My heart was so heavy before that I could scarce speak or go in the path; and yet now so light, that I could run. My strength seemed to come again, and recruit my feeble knees, and aking heart: yet it pleased them to go but one mile that night, and there we stayed two dayes. In that time came a company of Indians to us, near thirty, all on horseback. My heart skipt within me, thinking they had been English-men at the first sight of them, for they were dressed in English Apparel, with Hats, white Neckcloths, and Sashes about their wasts, and Ribbonds upon their shoulders: [38] but when they came near, their was a vast difference between the lovely faces of Christians, and the foul looks of those Heathens, which much damped my spirit again.

THE SEVENTEENTH REMOVE.

A comfortable Remove it was to me, because of my hopes. They gave me a pack, and along we went chearfully; but quickly my will proved more than my strength; having little or no refreshing my strength failed me, and my spirit were almost quite gone. Now may I say with David, Psal. 119. 22, 23, 24. *I am poor and*

[38] New England tribes often affected Puritan dress (see n. 25, above).

needy, and my heart is wounded within me. I am gone like the shadow when it declineth: I am tossed up and down like the locust; my knees are weak through fasting, and my flesh faileth of fatness. At night we came to an Indian Town, and the Indians sate down by a Wigwam discoursing, but I was almost spent, and could scarce speak. I laid down my load, and went into the Wigwam, and there sat an Indian boyling of Horses feet (they being wont to eat the flesh first, and when the feet were old and dried, and they had nothing else, they would cut off the feet and use them). I asked him to give me a little of his Broth, or Water they were boiling in; he took a dish, and gave me one spoonfull of Samp,[39] and bid me take as much of the Broth as I would. Then I put some of the hot water to the Samp, and drank it up, and my spirit came again. He gave me also a piece of the Ruff or Ridding of the small Guts, and I broiled it on the coals; and now may I say with Jonathan, *See, I pray you, how mine eyes have been enlightened, because I tasted a little of this honey*, 1 Sam. 14. 29. Now is my Spirit revived again; though means be never so inconsiderable, yet if the Lord bestow his blessing upon them, they shall refresh both Soul and Body.

THE EIGHTEENTH REMOVE.

We took up our packs and along we went, but a wearisome day I had of it. As we went along I saw an English-man stript naked, and lying dead upon the ground, but knew not who it was. Then we came to another Indian Town, where we stayed all night. In this Town there were four English Children, Captives; and one of them my own Sisters. I went to see how she did, and she was well, considering her Captive-condition. I would have tarried that night with her, but they that owned her would not suffer it. Then I went into another Wigwam, where they were boyling Corn and Beans,[40] which was a lovely sight to see, but I could not get a taste thereof. Then I went to another Wigwam, where there were two of the English Children; the Squaw was boyling Horses feet, then she cut me off a little piece, and gave one of the English

39 A porridge made from coarse hominy. The word is from the Narragansett *nasaump*, "corn mush."

40 The familiar succotash; the word itself is of Algonquin origin.

Children a piece also. Being very hungry I had quickly eat up mine, but the Child could not bite it, it was so tough and sinewy, but lay sucking, gnawing, chewing and slabbering of it in the mouth and hand, then I took it of the Child, and eat it my self, and savoury it was to my taste. Then I may say a Job, Chap. 6. 7. *The things that my soul refused to touch, are as my sorrowfull meat.* Thus the Lord made that pleasant refreshing, which another time would have been an abomination. Then I went home to my mistresses Wigwam; and they told me I disgraced my master with begging, and if I did so any more, they would knock me in head: I told them, they had as good knock me in head as starve me to death.

THE NINETEENTH REMOVE.

They said, when we went out, that we must travel to Wachuset this day. But a bitter weary day I had of it, travelling now three dayes together, without resting any day between. At last, after many weary steps, I saw Wachuset hills, but many miles off. Then we came to a great Swamp, through which we travelled, up to the knees in mud and water, which was heavy going to one tyred before. Being almost spent, I thought I should have sunk down at last, and never gat out; but I may say, as in Psal. 94. 18, *When my foot slipped, thy mercy, O Lord, held me up.* Going along, having indeed my life, but little spirit, Philip, who was in the Company, came up and took me by the hand, and said, Two weeks more and you shal be Mistress again. I asked him, if he spake true? he answered, Yes, and quickly you shal come to your master again; who had been gone from us three weeks. After many weary steps we came to Wachuset, where he was: and glad I was to see him. He asked me, When I washt me? I told him not this month, then he fetcht me some water himself, and bid me wash, and gave me the Glass to see how I lookt; and bid his Squaw give me something to eat: so she gave me a mess of Beans and meat, and a little Groundnut Cake. I was wonderfully revived with this favour shewed me, Psal. 106. 46, *He made them also to be pittied, of all those that carried them Captives.*

My master had three Squaws, living sometimes with one, and sometimes with another one, this old Squaw, at whose Wigwam

I was, and with whom my Master had been those three weeks.[41] Another was Wattimore,[42] with whom I had lived and served all this while: A severe and proud Dame she was, bestowing every day in dressing her self neat as much time as any of the Gentry of the land: powdering her hair, and painting her face, going with Neck-laces, with Jewels in her ears, and Bracelets upon her hands: When she had dressed her self, her work was to make Girdles of Wampom and Beads. The third Squaw was a younger one, by whom he had two Papooses. By that time I was refresht by the old Squaw, with whom my master was, Wettimores Maid came to call me home, at which I fell a weeping. Then the old Squaw told me, to encourage me, that if I wanted victuals, I should come to her, and that I should ly there in her Wigwam. Then I went with the maid, and quickly came again and lodged there. The Squaw laid a Mat under me, and a good Rugg over me; the first time I had any such kindness shewed me. I understood that Wettimore thought, that if she should let me go and serve with the old Squaw, she would be in danger to loose, not only my service, but the redemption-pay also. And I was not a little glad to hear this; being by it raised in my hopes, that in Gods due time there would be an end of this sorrowfull hour. Then came an Indian, and asked me to knit him three pair of Stockins, for which I had a Hat, and a silk Handkerchief. Then another asked me to make her a shift, for which she gave me an Apron.

Then came Tom and Peter,[43] with the second Letter from the Council, about the Captives. Though they were Indians, I gat them by the hand, and burst out into tears; my heart was so full that I could not speak to them; but recovering my self, I asked them how my husband did, and all my friends and acquaintance? they said, They are all very well but melancholy. They brought me two Biskets, and a pound of Tobacco. The Tobacco I quickly gave away; when it was all gone, one asked me to give him a pipe of Tobacco, I told him it was all gone; then began he to rant and threaten. I told him when my Husband came I would give

[41] Polygyny was not uncommon among New England tribes.

[42] Weetamoo.

[43] Tom Dublet (*Nepanet*) and Peter Conway (*Tatatiquinea*) were Christian Indians who were conducting the negotiations for ransom.

him some: Hang him Rogue (sayes he) I will knock out his brains, if he comes here. And then again, in the same breath they would say, That if there should come an hundred without Guns, they would do them no hurt. So unstable and like mad men they were. So that fearing the worst, I durst not send to my Husband, though there were some thoughts of his coming to Redeem and fetch me, not knowing what might follow. For there was little more trust to them then to the master they served. When the Letter was come, the Saggamores met to consult about the Captives, and called me to them to enquire how much my husband would give to redeem me, when I came I sate down among them, as I was wont to do, as their manner is: Then they bade me stand up, and said, they were the General Court. They bid me speak what I thought he would give. Now knowing that all we had was destroyed by the Indians, I was in a great strait: I thought if I should speak of but a little, it would be slighted, and hinder the matter; if of a great sum, I knew not where it would be procured: yet at a venture, I said Twenty pounds, yet desired them to take less; but they would not hear of that, but sent that message to Boston, that for Twenty pounds I should be redeemed. It was a Praying-Indian that wrote their Letter for them. There was another Praying Indian, who told me, that he had a brother, that would not eat Horse; his conscience was so tender and scrupulous (though as large as hell, for the destruction of poor Christians). Then he said, he read that Scripture to him, 2 Kings, 6. 25. *There was a famine in Samaria, and behold they beseiged it, untill an Asses head was sold for fourscore pieces of silver, and the fourth part of a Kab of Doves dung, for five pieces of silver.* He expounded this place to his brother, and shewed him that it was lawfull to eat that in a Famine which is not at another time. And now, sayes he, he will eat Horse with any Indian of them all. There was another Praying-Indian, who when he had done all the mischief that he could, betrayed his own Father into the English hands, thereby to purchase his own life. Another Praying-Indian was at Sudbury-fight, though, as he deserved, he was afterward hanged for it.[44] There was another Praying Indian, so wicked and cruel,

44 "Sudbury-fight" took place on Apr. 18; some thirty Englishmen were killed in ambush.

as to wear a string about his neck, strung with Christians fingers.[45] Another Praying-Indian, when they went to Sudbury-fight, went with them, and his Squaw also with him, with her Papoos at her back: Before they went to that fight, they got a company together to *Powaw;* the manner was as followeth.[46] There was one that kneeled upon a Deer-skin, with the company round him in a ring who kneeled, and striking upon the ground with their hands, and with sticks, and muttering or humming with their mouths; besides him who kneeled in the ring, there also stood one with a Gun in his hand: Then he on the Deer-skin made a speech, and all manifested assent to it: and so they did many times together. Then they bade him with the Gun go out of the ring, which he did, but when he was out, they called him in again; but he seemed to make a stand, then they called the more earnestly, till he returned again: Then they all sang. Then they gave him two Guns, in either hand one: And so he on the Deer-skin began again; and at the end of every sentence in his speaking, they all assented, humming or muttering with their mouthes, and striking upon the ground with their hands. Then they bade him with the two Guns go out of the ring again; which he did, a little way. Then they called him in again, but he made a stand; so they called him with greater earnestness; but he stood reeling and wavering as if he knew not whither he should stand or fall, or which way to go. Then they called him with exceeding great vehemency, all of them, one and another: after a little while he turned in, staggering as he went, with his Armes stretched out, in either hand a Gun. As soon as he came in, they all sang and rejoyced exceedingly a while. And then he upon the Deer-skin, made another speech unto which they all assented in a rejoicing manner: and so they ended their business, and forthwith went to Sudbury-fight. To my thinking they went without any scruple, but that they should prosper, and gain the victory. And they went out not so rejoycing, but they came home with as great a Victory. For they said they had killed two Captains, and almost an hundred men. One English-man they brought along with them:

45 Wearing a necklace of human fingers is a practice that survived well into the nineteenth century among Plains Indians.

46 An excellent and valuable description of the powwow preparatory to battle. Note that the ceremony involved ritual conjuring for omens of victory.

and he said, it was too true, for they had made sad work at Sudbury, as indeed it proved. Yet they came home without that rejoycing and triumphing over their victory, which they were wont to shew at other times, but rather like Dogs (as they say) which have lost their ears. Yet I could not perceive that it was for their own loss of men: They said, they had not lost above five or six: and I missed none, except in one Wigwam. When they went, they acted as if the Devil had told them that they should gain the victory: and now they acted, as if the Devil had told them they should have a fall. Whither it were so or no, I cannot tell, but so it proved, for quickly they began to fall, and so held on that Summer, till they came to utter ruine. They came home on a Sabbath day, and the *Powaw* that kneeled upon the Deer-skin came home (I may say, without abuse) as black as the Devil. When my master came home, he came to me and bid me make a shirt for his Papoos, of a holland-laced Pillowbeer. About that time there came an Indian to me and bid me come to his Wigwam, at night, and he would give me some Pork and Ground-nuts. Which I did, and as I was eating, another Indian said to me, he seems to be your good Friend, but he killed two Englishmen at Sudbury, and there ly their Cloaths behind you: I looked behind me, and there I saw bloody Cloaths, with Bullet-holes in them; yet the Lord suffered not this wretch to do me any hurt; Yea, instead of that, he many times refresht me: five or six times did he and his Squaw refresh my feeble carcass. If I went to their Wigwam at any time, they would alwayes give me something, and yet they were strangers that I never saw before. Another Squaw gave me a piece of fresh Pork, and a little Salt with it, and lent me her Pan to Fry it in; and I cannot but remember what a sweet, pleasant and delightfull relish that bit had to me, to this day. So little do we prize common mercies when we have them to the full.

THE TWENTIETH REMOVE.[47]

It was their usual manner to remove, when they had done any mischief, lest they should be found out: and so they did at this time. We went about three or four miles, and there they built a great

47 The twentieth remove (Apr. 28–May 2) was to an encampment near the southern end of Wachusett Lake, Princeton, Mass.

Wigwam, big enough to hold an hundred Indians, which they did in preparation to a great day of Dancing.[48] They would say now amongest themselves, that the Governour would be so angry for his loss at Sudbury, that he would send no more about the Captives, which made me grieve and tremble. My Sister being not far from the place where we now were, and hearing that I was here, desired her master to let her come and see me, and he was willing to it, and would go with her: but she being ready before him, told him she would go before, and was come within a Mile or two of the place; Then he overtook her, and began to rant as if he had been mad; and made her go back again in the Rain; so that I never saw her till I saw her in Charlestown. But the Lord requited many of their ill doings, for this Indian her Master, was hanged afterward at Boston. The Indians now began to come from all quarters, against their merry dancing day. Among some of them came one Goodwife Kettle. I told her my heart was so heavy that it was ready to break: so is mine too said she, but yet said, I hope we shall hear some good news shortly. I could hear how earnestly my Sister desired to see me, and I as earnestly desired to see her: and yet neither of us could get an opportunity. My Daughter was also now about a mile off, and I had not seen her in nine or ten weeks, as I had not seen my Sister since our first taking. I earnestly desired them to let me go and see them: yea, I intreated, begged, and perswaded them, but to let me see my Daughter; and yet so hard hearted were they, that they would not suffer it. They made use of their tyrannical power whilst they had it: but through the Lords wonderfull mercy, their time was now but short.

On a Sabbath day, the Sun being about an hour high in the afternoon, came Mr. John Hoar (the Council permitting him, and his own foreward spirit inclining him) together with the two forementioned Indians, Tom and Peter, with their third Letter from the Council. When they came near, I was abroad: though I saw them not, they presently called me in, and bade me sit down and not stir. Then they catched up their Guns, and away they ran, as if an Enemy had been at hand; and the Guns went off apace.

48 The building of a festival wigwam and the dance that follows may be taken as a ceremonial farewell to the captives prior to ransom and release.

I manifested some great trouble, and they asked me what was the matter? I told them, I thought they had killed the English-man (for they had in the mean time informed me that an English-man was come) they said, No; They shot over his Horse and under, and before his Horse; and they pusht him this way and that way, at their pleasure: shewing what they could do: Then they let them come to their Wigwams. I begged of them to let me see the English-man, but they would not. But there was I fain to sit their pleasure. When they had talked their fill with him, they suffered me to go to him. We asked each other of our welfare, and how my Husband did, and all my Friends? He told me they were all well, and would be glad to see me. Amongst other things which my Husband sent me, there came a pound of Tobacco: which I sold for nine shillings in Money: for many of the Indians for want of Tobacco, smoaked Hemlock, and Ground-Ivy. It was a great mistake in any, who thought I sent for Tobacco: for through the favour of God, that desire was overcome. I now asked them, whither I should go home with Mr. Hoar? They answered No, one and another of them: and it being night, we lay down with that answer; in the morning, Mr. Hoar invited the Saggamores to Dinner; but when we went to get it ready, we found that they had stollen the greatest part of the Provision Mr. Hoar had brought, out of his Bags, in the night. And we may see the wonderfull power of God, in that one passage, in that when there was such a great number of the Indians together, and so greedy of a little good food; and no English there, but Mr. Hoar and my self: that there they did not knock us in the head, and take what we had: there being not only some Provision, but also Trading cloth, a part of the twenty pounds agreed upon: But instead of doing us any mischief, they seemed to be ashamed of the fact, and said, it were some Matchit Indian [49] that did it. Oh, that we could believe that there is no thing too hard for God! God shewed his Power over the Heathen in this, as he did over the hungry Lyons when Daniel was cast into the Den. Mr. Hoar called them betime to Dinner, but they ate very little, they being so busie in dressing themselves, and getting ready for their Dance: which was carried

49 That is, a bad Indian.

on by eight of them, four Men and four Squaws: My master and mistress being two. He was dressed in his Holland shirt, with great Laces sewed at the tail of it, he had his silver Buttons, his white Stockins, his Garters were hung round with Shillings, and he had Girdles of Wampom upon his head and shoulders. She had a Kersey Coat, and covered with Girdles of Wampom from the Loins upward: her armes from her elbows to her hands were covered with Bracelets; there were handfulls of Necklaces about her neck, and severall sorts of Jewels in her ears. She had fine red Stokins and white Shoos, her hair powdered and face painted Red, that was alwayes before Black. And all the Dancers were after the same manner. There were two other singing and knocking on a Kettle for their musick. They keept hopping up and down one after another, with a Kettle of water in the midst, standing warm upon some Embers, to drink of when they were dry. They held on till it was almost night, throwing out Wampom to the standers by. At night I asked them again, if I should go home? They all as one said No, except my Husband would come for me. When we were lain down, my Master went out of the Wigwam, and by and by sent in an Indian called James the Printer, who told Mr. Hoar, that my Master would let me go home to morrow, if he would let him have one pint of Liquors. Then Mr. Hoar called his own Indians, Tom and Peter, and bid them go and see whither he would promise it before them three: and if he would, he should have it; which he did, and he had it. Then Philip smeling the business cal'd me to him, and asked me what I would give him, to tell me some good news, and speak a good word for me. I told him, I could not tell what to give him, I would any thing I had, and asked him what he would have? He said, two Coats and twenty shillings in Mony, and half a bushel of seed Corn, and some Tobacco. I thanked him for his love: but I knew the good news as well as the crafty Fox. My Master after he had had his drink, quickly came ranting into the Wigwam again, and called for Mr. Hoar, drinking to him, and saying, He was a good man: and then again he would say, Hang him Rogue: Being almost drunk, he would drink to him, and yet presently say he should be hanged. Then he called for me. I trembled to hear him, yet I was fain to go to him, and he drank to me, shewing no incivility. He was the first Indian I saw drunk all the while that I was amongst them.[50] At last his Squaw ran out, and he after her, round the Wigwam, with his mony jingling at his knees: But she escaped him: But having an old Squaw he ran to her: and so through the Lords mercy, we were no more troubled that night. Yet I had not a comfortable nights rest: for I think I can say, I did not sleep for three nights together. The night before the Letter came from the Council, I could not rest, I was so full of feares and troubles, God many times leaving us most in the dark, when deliverance is nearest: yea, at this time I could not rest night nor day. The next night I was overjoyed, Mr. Hoar being come, and that with such good tidings. The third night I was even swallowed up with the thoughts of things, *viz.* that ever I should go home again; and that I must go, leaving my Children behind me in the Wilderness; so that sleep was now almost departed from mine eyes.

On Tuesday morning they called their General Court (as they call it) to consult and determine, whether I should go home or no: And they all as one man did seemingly consent to it, that I should go home; except Philip, who would not come among them.[51]

But before I go any further, I would take leave to mention a few remarkable passages of providence, which I took special notice of in my afflicted time.

1. Of the fair opportunity lost in the long March, a little after the Fort-fight, when our English Army was so numerous, and in pursuit of the Enemy, and so near as to take several and destroy them: and the Enemy in such distress for food, that our men might track them by their rooting in the earth for Ground-nuts, whilest they were flying for their lives. I say, that then our Army should want Provision, and be forced to leave their pursuit and return homeward: and the very next week the Enemy came upon our Town, like Bears bereft of their whelps, or so many ravenous Wolves, rending us and our Lambs to death. But what shall I say? God seemed to leave his People to themselves, and order all things for his own holy ends. *Shal there be evil in the City and the Lord*

[50] A striking testimony, perhaps attributable less to the discipline among this particular band of Indians than to the remoteness of their successive removes.

[51] This is consistent with the requirement of unanimity in all council decisions. Philip, who disagreed, absented himself in order that consent be unanimous. Majority rule was not a procedural practice among New England tribes until after the Revolution.

hath not done it? They are not grieved for the affliction of Joseph, therefore shal they go Captive, with the first that go Captive. It is the Lords doing, and it should be marvelous in our eyes.

2. I cannot but remember how the Indians derided the slowness, and dulness of the English Army, in its setting out. For after the desolations at Lancaster and Medfield, as I went along with them, they asked me when I thought the English Army would come after them? I told them I could not tell: It may be they will come in May, said they. Thus did they scoffe at us, as if the English would be a quarter of a year getting ready.

3. Which also I have hinted before, when the English Army with new supplies were sent forth to pursue after the enemy, and they understanding it, fled before them till they came to Baquaug River, where they forthwith went over safely; that that River should be impassable to the English. I can but admire to see the wonderfull providence of God in preserving the heathen for farther affliction to our poor Countrey. They could go in great numbers over, but the English must stop: God had an over-ruling hand in all those things.

4. It was thought, if their Corn were cut down, they would starve and dy with hunger: and all their Corn that could be found, was destroyed, and they driven from that little they had in store, into the Woods in the midst of Winter; and yet how to admiration did the Lord preserve them for his holy ends, and the destruction of many still amongst the English! strangely did the Lord provide for them; that I did not see (all the time I was among them) one Man, Woman, or Child, die with hunger.

Though many times they would eat that, that a Hog or a Dog would hardly touch; yet by that God strengthned them to be a scourge to his People.

The chief and commonest food was Ground-nuts: They eat also Nuts and Acorns, Harty-choaks,[52] Lilly roots, Ground-beans, and several other weeds and roots, that I know not.

They would pick up old bones, and cut them to pieces at the joynts, and if they were full of wormes and magots, they would scald them over the fire to make the vermine come out, and then

[52] The Jerusalem artichoke (*Helianthus tuberosus*) was wild in North America and cultivated by New England Indians for its edible tuber.

boile them, and drink up the Liquor, and then beat the great ends of them in a Morter, and so eat them. They would eat Horses guts, and ears, and all sorts of wild Birds which they could catch: also Bear, Vennison, Beaver, Tortois, Frogs, Squirrels, Dogs, Skunks, Rattle-snakes; yea, the very Bark of Trees; besides all sorts of creatures, and provision which they plundered from the English. I can but stand in admiration to see the wonderful power of God, in providing for such a vast number of our Enemies in the Wilderness, where there was nothing to be seen, but from hand to mouth. Many times in a morning, the generality of them would eat up all they had, and yet have some forther supply against they wanted. It is said, Psal. 81. 13, 14. *Oh, that my People had hearkned to me, and Israel had walked in my wayes, I should soon have subdued their Enemies, and turned my hand against their Adversaries.* But now our perverse and evil carriages in the sight of the Lord, have so offended him, that instead of turning his hand against them, the Lord feeds and nourishes them up to be a scourge to the whole Land.

5. Another thing that I would observe is, the strange providence of God, in turning things about when the Indians was at the highest, and the English at the lowest. I was with the Enemy eleven weeks and five dayes, and not one Week passed without the fury of the Enemy, and some desolation by fire and sword upon one place or other. They mourned (with their black faces) for their own lossess, yet triumphed and rejoyced in their inhumane, and many times devilish cruelty to the English. They would boast much of their Victories; saying, that in two hours time they had destroyed such a Captain, and his Company at such a place; and such a Captain and his Company in such a place; and such a Captain and his Company in such a place: and boast how many Towns they had destroyed, and then scoffe, and say, They had done them a good turn, to send them to Heaven so soon.[53] Again, they would say, This Summer that they would knock all the Rogues in the head, or drive them into the Sea, or make them flie the Countrey:

53 The custom of boasting about one's achievements in war was common. A later manifestation is found among the Plains Indians' practice of counting coup, a game of status in which war exploits were graded according to the dangers involved. The exploit itself was known as the coup, and "counting coups" referred to the recital of war deeds.

thinking surely, Agag-like, *The bitterness of Death is past.* Now the Heathen begins to think all is their own, and the poor Christians hopes to fail (as to man) and now their eyes are more to God, and their hearts sigh heaven-ward: and to say in good earnest, *Help Lord, or we perish:* When the Lord had brought his people to this, that they saw no help in any thing but himself: then he takes the quarrel into his own hand: and though they had made a pit, in their own imaginations, as deep as hell for the Christians that Summer, yet the Lord hurll'd them selves into it. And the Lord had not so many wayes before to preserve them, but now he hath as many to destroy them.

But to return again to my going home, where we may see a remarkable change of Providence: At first they were all against it, except my Husband would come for me; but afterwards they assented to it, and seemed much to rejoyce in it; some askt me to send them some Bread, others some Tobacco, others shaking me by the hand, offering me a Hood and Scarfe to ride in; not one moving hand or tongue against it. Thus hath the Lord answered my poor desire, and the many earnest requests of others put up unto God for me. In my travels an Indian came to me, and told me, if I were willing, he and his Squaw would run away, and go home along with me: I told him No: I was not willing to run away, but desired to wait Gods time, that I might go home quietly, and without fear. And now God hath granted me my desire. O the wonderfull power of God that I have seen, and the experience that I have had: I have been in the midst of those roaring Lyons, and Salvage Bears, that feared neither God, nor Man, nor the Devil, by night and day, alone and in company: sleeping all sorts together, and yet not one of them ever offered me the least abuse of unchastity to me, in word or action.[54] Though some are ready to say, I speak it for my

[54] Eastern Indians did not abuse or violate female captives. This restraint, however, derived from ritual rather than ethical considerations: braves customarily made elaborate preparations before taking up the hatchet in war, and this included the practice of continence as well as purification rites. The sexual abuse of a female captive would have been thought to weaken the Indians' "medicine." Cf. Elizabeth Hanson's statement: "The Indians are very civil towards their captive women, not offering any incivility by any indecent carriage." In the nineteenth century, however, there are reports of violation of white female captives by Indians west of the Mississippi as well as evidence that Southwestern tribes also abused women prisoners.

own credit; But I speak it in the presence of God, and to his Glory. Gods Power is as great now, and as sufficient to save, as when he preserved Daniel in the Lions Den: or the three Children in the fiery Furnace. I may well say as his Psal. 107. 12, *Oh give thanks unto the Lord for he is good, for his mercy endureth for ever.* Let the Redeemed of the Lord say so, whom he hath redeemed from the hand of the Enemy, especially that I should come away in the midst of so many hundreds of Enemies quietly and peacably, and not a Dog moving his tongue. So I took my leave of them, and in coming along my heart melted into tears, more then all the while I was with them, and I was almost swallowed up with the thoughts that ever I should go home again. About the Sun going down, Mr. Hoar, and my self, and the two Indians came to Lancaster, and a solemn sight it was to me. There had I lived many comfortable years amongst my Relations and Neighbours, and now not one Christian to be seen, nor one house left standing. We went on to a Farm house that was yet standing, where we lay all night: and a comfortable lodging we had, though nothing but straw to ly on. The Lord preserved us in safety that night, and raised us up again in the morning, and carried us along, that before noon, we came to Concord. Now was I full of joy, and yet not without sorrow: joy to see such a lovely sight, so many Christians together, and some of them my Neighbours: There I met with my Brother, and my Brother in Law, who asked me, if I knew where his Wife was? Poor heart! he had helped to bury her, and knew it not; she being shot down by the house was partly burnt: so that those who were at Boston at the desolation of the Town, and came back afterward, and buried the dead, did not know her. Yet I was not without sorrow, to think how many were looking and longing, and my own Children amongst the rest, to enjoy that deliverance that I had now received, and I did not know whither ever I should see them again. Being recruited with food and raiment we went to Boston that day, where I met with my dear Husband, but the thoughts of our dear Children, one being dead, and the other we could not tell where, abated our comfort each to other. I was not before so much hem'd in with the merciless and cruel Heathen, but now as much with pittiful, tender-hearted and compassionate Christians. In that poor, and destressed, and beggerly condition I was received in, I was kindly entertained in severall Houses: so much love I received from several (some of whom I knew, and others I knew not) that I am not capable to declare it. But the Lord knows them all by name: The Lord reward them seven fold into their bosoms of his spirituals, for their temporals. The twenty pounds the price of my redemption was raised by some Boston Gentlemen, and Mrs. Usher, whose bounty and religious charity, I would not forget to make mention of. Then Mr. Thomas Shepard of Charlstown received us into his House, where we continued eleven weeks; and a Father and Mother they were to us. And many more tender-hearted Friends we met with in that place. We were now in the midst of love, yet not without much and frequent heaviness of heart for our poor Children, and other Relations, who were still in affliction. The week following, after my coming in, the Governour and Council sent forth to the Indians again; and that not without success; for they brought in my Sister, and Good-wife Kettle: Their not knowing where our Children were, was a sore tryal to us still, and yet we were not without secret hopes that we should see them again. That which was dead lay heavier upon my spirit, than those which were alive and amongst the Heathen; thinking how it suffered with its wounds, and I was no way able to relieve it; and how it was buried by the Heathen in the Wilderness from among all Christians. We were hurried up and down in our thoughts, sometime we should hear a report that they were gone this way, and sometimes that; and that they were come in, in this place or that: We kept enquiring and listning to hear concerning them, but no certain news as yet. About this time the Council had ordered a day a publick Thanks-giving: [55] though I thought I had still cause of mourning, and being unsettled in our minds, we thought we would ride toward the Eastward, to see if we could hear any thing concerning our Children. And as we were riding along (God is the wise disposer of all things) between Ipswich and Rowly we met with Mr. William Hubbard, who told us that our Son Joseph was come in to Major Waldrens, and another with him, which was my Sisters Son. I asked him how he knew it? He said, the Major himself told him so. So along we went till we came to Newbury; and their Minister being absent, they desired my Husband to Preach

55 This was the Thanksgiving of June 29, 1676.

the Thanks giving for them; but he was not willing to stay there that night, but would go over to Salisbury, to hear further, and come again in the morning; which he did, and Preached there that day. At night, when he had done, one came and told him that his Daughter was come in at Providence: Here was mercy on both hands: Now hath God fulfiled that precious Scripture which was such a comfort to me in my distressed condition. When my heart was ready to sink into the Earth (my Children being gone I could not tell whither) and my knees trembled under me, And I was walking through the valley of the shadow of Death: Then the Lord brought, and now has fulfilled that reviving word unto me: *Thus saith the Lord, Refrain thy voice from weeping, and thine eyes from tears, for thy Work shall be rewarded, saith the Lord, and they shall come again from the Land of the Enemy*. Now we were between them, the one on the East, and the other on the West: Our Son being nearest, we went to him first, to Portsmouth, where we met with him, and with the Major also: who told us he had done what he could, but could not redeem him under seven pounds; which the good People thereabouts were pleased to pay. The Lord reward the Major, and all the rest, though unknown to me, for their labour of Love. My Sisters Son was redeemed for four pounds, which the Council gave order for the payment of. Having now received one of our Children, we hastened toward the other; going back through Newbury, my Husband preached there on the Sabbath-day: for which they rewarded him many fold.

On Munday we came to Charlstown, where we heard that the Governour of Road-Island had sent over for our Daughter, to take care of her, being now within his Jurisdiction: which should not pass without our acknowledgments. But she being nearer Rehoboth than Road-Island, Mr. Newman went over, and took care of her, and brought her to his own House. And the goodness of God was admirable to us in our low estate, in that he raised up passionate [56] Friends on every side to us, when we had nothing to recompance any for their love. The Indians were now gone that way, that it was apprehended dangerous to go to her: But the Carts which carried Provision to the English Army, being guarded, brought her with them to Dorchester, where we received her safe: blessed be

[56] Compassionate.

the Lord for it, For great is his Power, and he can do whatsoever seemeth him good. Her coming in was after this manner: She was travelling one day with the Indians, with her basket at her back; the company of Indians were got before her, and gone out of sight, all except one Squaw; she followed the Squaw till night, and then both of them lay down, having nothing over them but the heavens, and under them but the earth. Thus she travelled three dayes together, not knowing whither she was going: having nothing to eat or drink but water, and green Hirtle-berries.[57] At last they came into Providence, where she was kindly entertained by several of that Town. The Indians often said, that I should never have her under twenty pounds: But now the Lord hath brought her in upon free-cost, and given her to me the second time. The Lord make us a blessing indeed, each to others. Now have I seen that Scripture also fulfilled, Deut. 30: 4, 7. *If any of thine be driven out to the outmost parts of heaven, from thence will the Lord thy God gather thee, and from thence will he fetch thee. And the Lord thy God will put all these curses upon thine enemies, and on them which hate thee, which persecuted thee.* Thus hath the Lord brought me and mine out of that horrible pit, and hath set us in the midst of tender-hearted and compassionate Christians. It is the desire of my soul, that we may walk worthy of the mercies received, and which we are receiving.

Our Family being now gathered together (those of us that were living) the South Church in Boston hired an House for us: Then we removed from Mr. Shepards, those cordial Friends, and went to Boston, where we continued about three quarters of a year: Still the Lord went along with us, and provided graciously for us. I thought it somewhat strange to set up House-keeping with bare walls; but as Solomon sayes, *Mony answers all things;* and that we had through the benevolence of Christian-friends, some in this Town, and some in that, and others: And some from England, that in a little time we might look, and see the House furnished with love. The Lord hath been exceeding good to us in our low estate, in that when we had neither house nor home, nor other necessaries; the Lord so moved the hearts of these and those towards us, that we wanted neither food, nor raiment for our selves or ours, Prov. 18. 24.

57 Huckleberries.

There is a Friend which sticketh closer than a Brother. And how many such Friends have we found, and now living amongst? And truly such a Friend have we found him to be unto us, in whose house we lived, *viz.* Mr. James Whitcomb, a Friend unto us near hand, and afar off.

I can remember the time, when I used to sleep quietly without workings in my thoughts, whole nights together, but now it is other wayes with me. When all are fast about me, and no eye open, but his who ever waketh, my thoughts are upon things past, upon the awfull dispensation of the Lord towards us; upon his wonderfull power and might, in carrying of us through so many difficulties, in returning us in safety, and suffering none to hurt us. I remember in the night season, how the other day I was in the midst of thousands of enemies, and nothing but death before me: It is then hard work to perswade my self, that ever I should be satisfied with bread again. But now we are fed with the finest of the Wheat, and, as I may say, With honey out of the rock: In stead of the Husk, we have the fatted Calf: The thoughts of these things in the particulars of them, and of the love and goodness of God towards us, make it true of me, what David said of himself, Psal. 6. 5.[58] *I watered my Couch with my tears.* Oh! the wonderfull power of God that mine eyes have seen, affording matter enough for my thoughts to run in, that when others are sleeping mine eyes are weeping.

I have seen the extrem vanity of this World: One hour I have been in health, and wealth, wanting nothing: But the next hour in sickness and wounds, and death, having nothing but sorrow and affliction.

Before I knew what affliction meant, I was ready sometimes to wish for it. When I lived in prosperity, having the comforts of the World about me, my relations by me, my Heart chearfull, and taking little care for any thing; and yet seeing many, whom I preferred before my self, under many tryals and afflictions, in sickness, weakness, poverty, losses, crosses, and cares of the World, I should be sometimes jealous least I should have my portion in this life, and that Scripture would come to my mind, Heb. 12. 6 *For whom the Lord loveth he chasteneth, and scourgeth every Son whom he re-*

[58] Ps. 6:6.

ceiveth. But now I see the Lord had his time to scourge and chasten me. The portion of some is to have their afflictions by drops, now one drop and then another; but the dregs of the Cup, the Wine of astonishment, like a sweeping rain that leaveth no food, did the Lord prepare to be my portion. Affliction I wanted, and affliction I had, full measure (I thought) pressed down and running over; yet I see, when God calls a Person to any thing, and through never so many difficulties, yet he is fully able to carry them through and make them see, and say they have been gainers thereby. And I hope I can say in some measure, As David did, *It is good for me that I have been afflicted.* The Lord hath shewed me the vanity of these outward things. That they are the Vanity of vanities, and vexation of spirit; that they are but a shadow, a blast, a bubble, and things of no continuance. That we must rely on God himself, and our whole dependance must be upon him. If trouble from smaller matters begin to arise in me, I have something at hand to check my self with, and say, why am I troubled? It was but the other day that if I had had the world, I would have given it for my freedom, or to have been a Servant to a Christian. I have learned to look beyond present and smaller troubles, and to be quieted under them, as Moses said, Exod. 14. 13. *Stand still and see the salvation of the Lord.*[59]

Finis.

[59] After spending the winter in Boston, the Reverend Mr. Rowlandson secured a church in Wethersfield, Conn., and moved his family there in 1677. He died the next year, and the town voted Mary a pension of £30 a year for as long as she remained a widow. Nothing more is known of her after that time.

III

Memoirs of Odd Adventures, Strange Deliverances, etc., in the Captivity of John Gyles, Esq., Commander of the Garrison on St. George River, in the District of Maine. Written by Himself.

†††

John Gyles was taken at the age of nine by Maliseet Indians, invading what is now Maine, on August 2, 1689. Released in June of 1698 at the age of eighteen, he had spent six years with the Indians and three years with a French master to whom he had been sold. Gyles's family had settled in Pemaquid, a spot midway between the Kennebec and Penobscot rivers, soon after the close of King Philip's War in 1676. The attack on Pemaquid in 1689 was one of a number directed at white settlements in Maine, New Hampshire, and Massachusetts during the early stages of King William's War, the first major conflict in the French-English struggle for control of the continent. King Louis XIV of France had determined to drive the English out of North America in concert with his declaration of war against England in support of the deposed James II and against the ascendance of King William. Military strategist Count Frontenac had been sent to Quebec as governor of New France, and his officers began leading Indian war parties on guerrilla raids into New England and New York. Missionaries from France worked diligently among the Micmac Indians of northern and eastern New Brunswick and Nova Scotia, the Passamaquoddies of the Passamaquoddy Bay coast, the Penobscots of Maine, and the Maliseets of the St. John River area to ensure loyalty to the French cause. North Yarmouth was attacked in the fall of 1688, Saco was assaulted in January of 1689, and Quochech (Dover) in New Hampshire was ravaged in July of that year. Fort Charles, the English garrison guarding the sea approach to Pemaquid, had been reduced to one-fifth its troop strength in order to supply reinforcements for border outposts, leaving vulnerable both the village and its environs. On the second of August, 1689, war parties of Micmacs, Passamaquoddies, Penobscots, and Maliseets reached Pemaquid. So began John Gyles's long adventure.

Along the St. John River Valley and up to the Rivière du Loup lived one thousand Maliseets (or Etchemins or Wulastukwiuks) of Algonquin stock, who roamed the river system on the Atlantic seaboard south of the St. Lawrence. To the west in Maine were the Maliseets' blood relatives, the Penobscots. Beyond the Penobscots, in New England, were numerous tribes both large and small: Narragansetts, Massachusetts, Wampanoags, Nipmucks, Nashuas, and Podunks, among others. Less is recorded historically and culturally about the early life and customs of the Maliseet Indians than those of any other Eastern tribe. The narrative of John Gyles's captivity among them provides a valuable storehouse of firsthand observation. Gyles's narrative, or Memoirs, *was first published at Boston in 1736. The text reprinted here is from Samuel Gardner Drake's* Indian Captivities *(Auburn, 1850).*

††

INTRODUCTION.—These private memoirs were collected from my minutes, at the earnest request of my second consort,[1] for the use of our family, that we might have a memento ever ready at hand, to excite in ourselves gratitude and thankfulness to God; and in our offspring a due sense of their dependence on the Sovereign of the universe, from the precariousness and vicissitudes of all sublunary enjoyments. In this state, and for this end, they have laid by me for

[1] By 1736, Gyles, aged fifty-six, had married, lost his first wife, and wed a second time.

some years. They at length falling into the hands of some, for whose judgment I had a value, I was pressed for a copy for the public. Others, desiring of me to extract particulars from them, which the multiplicity and urgency of my affairs would not admit, I have now determined to suffer their publication. I have not made scarce any addition to this manual, except in the chapter of creatures, which I was urged to make much larger. I might have greatly enlarged it, but I feared it would grow beyond its proportion. I have been likewise advised to give a particular account of my father, which I am not very fond of, having no dependence on the virtues or honors of my ancestors to recommend me to the favor of God or men; nevertheless, because some think it is a respect due to the memory of my parents, whose name I was obliged to mention in the following story, and a satisfaction which their posterity might justly expect from me, I shall give some account of him, though as brief as possible.

The flourishing state of New England, before the unhappy eastern wars, drew my father hither, whose first settlement was on Kennebeck river, at a place called Merrymeeting Bay, where he dwelt for some years; until on the death of my grand parents, he, with his family, returned to England, to settle his affairs. This done, he came over with the design to have returned to his farm; but on his arrival at Boston, the eastern Indians had begun their hostilities.[2] He therefore begun a settlement on Long Island. The air of that place not so well agreeing with his constitution, and the Indians having become peaceable, he again proposed to resettle his lands in Merrymeeting Bay; but finding that place deserted, and that plantations were going on at Pemmaquid, he purchased several tracts of land of the inhabitants there. Upon his highness the duke of York resuming a claim to those parts, my father took out patents under that claim; and when Pemmaquid was set off by the name of the county of Cornwall, in the province of New York, he was commissioned chief justice of the same by Gov. Duncan [Dongan].[3] He was a strict sabbatarian, and met with considerable difficulty in

2 That is, King Philip's War (1675–76); see headnote to Rowlandson narrative.
3 Col. Thomas Dongan had been appointed governor of New York in 1682.

the discharge of his office, from the immoralities of a people who had long lived lawless. He laid out no inconsiderable income, which he had annually from England, on the place, and at last lost his life there, as will hereafter be related.

I am not insensible of the truth of an assertion of Sir Roger L'Estrange,[4] that "Books and dishes have this common fate: no one of either ever pleased all tastes." And I am fully of his opinion in this: "It is as little to be wished for as expected; for a universal applause is, at least, two thirds of a scandal." To conclude with Sir Roger, "Though I made this composition principally for my family, yet, if any man has a mind to take part with me, he has free leave, and is welcome; "but let him carry this consideration along with him, "that he is a very unmannerly guest who forces himself upon another man's table, and then quarrels with his dinner."

CHAPTER I.—*Containing the occurrences of the first year.* On the second day of August, 1689, in the morning, my honored father, THOMAS GYLES, Esq., went with some laborers, my two elder brothers and myself, to one of his farms, which laid upon the river about three miles above fort Charles,[5] adjoining Pemmaquid falls, there to gather in his English harvest, and we labored securely till noon. After we had dined, our people went to their labor, some in one field to their English hay, the others to another field of English corn. My father, the youngest of my two brothers, and myself, tarried near the farm-house in which we had dined till about one of the clock; at which time we heard the report of several great guns at the fort. Upon which my father said he hoped it was a signal of good news, and that the great council had sent back the soldiers, to cover the inhabitants; (for on report of the revolution they had deserted.) But to our great surprise, about thirty or forty Indians, at that moment, discharged a volley of shot at us, from behind a

4 Sir Roger L'Estrange (1616–1704), English journalist and writer of pamphlets, was surveyor of printing presses and licenser of the press under Charles II and James II.

5 "Fort Charles stood on the spot where fort Frederick was, not long since, founded by Colonel Dunbar. The township adjoining thereto was called Jamestown, in honor of the duke of York. In this town, within a quarter of a mile of the fort, was my father's dwelling-house, from which he went out that unhappy morning." [Gyles's note].

rising ground, near our barn. The yelling of the Indians,[6] the whistling of their shot, and the voice of my father, whom I heard cry out, "What now! what now!" so terrified me, (though he seemed to be handling a gun,) that I endeavoured to make my escape. My brother ran one way and I another, and looking over my shoulder, I saw a stout fellow, painted, pursuing me with a gun, and a cutlass glittering in his hand, which I expected every moment in my brains. I soon fell down, and the Indian seized me by the left hand. He offered me no abuse, but tied my arms, then lifted me up, and pointed to the place where the people were at work about the hay, and led me that way. As we went, we crossed where my father was, who looked very pale and bloody, and walked very slowly. When we came to the place, I saw two men shot down on the flats, and one or two more knocked on their heads with hatchets, crying out, "O Lord," &c. There the Indians brought two captives, one a man, and my brother James, who, with me, had endeavored to escape by running from the house, when we were first attacked. This brother was about fourteen years of age. My oldest brother, whose name was Thomas, wonderfully escaped by land to the Barbican, a point of land on the west side of the river, opposite the fort, where several fishing vessels lay. He got on board one of them and sailed that night.

After doing what mischief they could, they sat down, and made us sit with them. After some time we arose, and the Indians pointed for us to go eastward. We marched about a quarter of a mile, and then made a halt. Here they brought my father to us. They made proposals to him, by old Moxus,[7] who told him that those were strange Indians who shot him, and that he was sorry for it. My father replied that he was a dying man, and wanted no favor of them, but to pray with his children. This being granted him, he recommended us to the protection and blessing of God Almighty; then gave us the best advice, and took his leave for this life, hoping in God that we should meet in a better. He parted with a cheerful voice, but looked very pale, by reason of his great loss of blood,

6 "The Indians have a custom of uttering a most horrid howl when they discharge guns, designing thereby to terrify those whom they fight against" [Gyles].

7 A friendly Indian of the Pemaquid region, "Old Moxus" was of the Kennebec tribe.

which now gushed out of his shoes. The Indians led him aside!—I heard the blows of the hatchet, but neither shriek not groan! I afterwards heard that he had five or seven shotholes through his waistcoat or jacket, and that he was covered with some boughs.

The Indians led us, their captives, on the east side of the river, towards the fort, and when we came within a mile and a half of the fort and town, and could see the fort, we saw firing and smoke on all sides. Here we made a short stop, and then moved within or near the distance of three quarters of a mile from the fort, into a thick swamp. There I saw my mother and my two little sisters, and many other captives who were taken from the town. My mother asked my about my father. I told her he was killed, but could say no more for grief. She burst into tears, and the Indians moved me a little farther off, and seized me with cords to a tree.

The Indians came to New Harbor, and sent spies several days to observe how and where the people were employed, &c., who found the men were generally at work at noon, and left about their houses only women and children. Therefore the Indians divided themselves into several parties,[8] some ambushing the way between the fort and the houses, as likewise between them and the distant fields; and then alarming the farthest off first, they killed and took the people, as they moved towards the town and fort, at their pleasure, and very few escaped to it. Mr. Pateshall was taken and killed, as he lay with his sloop near the Barbican.

On the first stir about the fort, my youngest brother was at play near it, and running in, was by God's goodness thus preserved. Captain Weems, with great courage and resolution, defended the weak old fort two days;[9] when, being much wounded, and the best of his men killed, he beat for a parley, which eventuated in these conditions:

1. That they, the Indians, should give him Mr. Pateshall's sloop. 2. That they should not molest him in carrying off the few people that had got into the fort, and three captives that they had taken.

[8] The whole company of Indians, led by French officers, numbered about one hundred.

[9] The fort commanded by Weems had only two guns aloft and an outwork nine feet high, with two bastions in the opposite angles containing two cannon each. Another cannon was mounted at the gateway.

3. That the English should carry off in their hands what they could from the fort.

On these conditions the fort was surrendered, and Captain Weems went off; and soon after, the Indians set on fire the fort and houses, which made a terrible blast, and was a melancholy sight to us poor captives, who were sad spectators! [10]

After the Indians had thus laid waste Pemmaquid, they moved us to New Harbor, about two miles east of Pemmaquid, a cove much frequented by fishermen. At this place, there were, before the war, about twelve houses. These the inhabitants deserted as soon as the rumor of war reached the place. When we turned our backs on the town, my heart was ready to break! I saw my mother. She spoke to me, but I could not answer her. That night we tarried at New Harbor, and the next day went in their canoes for Penobscot. About noon, the canoe in which my mother was, and that in which I was, came side by side; whether accidently or by my mother's desire I cannot say. She asked me how I did. I think I said "pretty well," but my heart was so full of grief I scarcely knew whether audible to her. Then she said, "O, my child! how joyful and pleasant it would be, if we were going to old England, to see your uncle Chalker, and other friends there! Poor babe, we are going into the wilderness, the Lord knows where!" Then bursting into tears, the canoes parted. That night following, the Indians with their captives lodged on an island.

A few days after, we arrived at Penobscot fort, where I again saw my mother, my brother and sisters, and many other captives. I think we tarried here eight days. In that time, the Jesuit of the place had a great mind to buy me. My Indian master made a visit to the Jesuit, and carried me with him. And here I will note, that the Indian who takes a captive is accounted his master, and has a

[10] Unknown to Gyles, the Indians reneged on their part of the agreement. Although Weems and six of his garrison reached the shallop safely, eight of the others were attacked and killed as they ran for the shore. The question of whether the French officers approved this or were simply unable to control their Indian allies touches on a problem that persisted throughout the series of French and Indian wars from 1689 to 1760. Another such incident during King William's War occurred at Fort Loyal in 1690; the most shocking episode of this nature was the massacre of English men, women, and children at the surrender of Fort William Henry in 1757.

perfect right to him, until he gives or sells him to another. I saw the Jesuit show my master pieces of gold, and understood afterwards that he was tending them for my ransom. He gave me a biscuit, which I put into my pocket, and not daring to eat it, buried it under a log, fearing he had put something into it to make me love him. Being very young, and having heard much of the Papists torturing the Protestants, caused me to act thus; and I hated the sight of a Jesuit.[11] When my mother heard the talk of my being sold to a Jesuit, she said to me, "Oh, my dear child, if it were God's will, I had rather follow you to your grave, or never see you more in this world, than you should be sold to a Jesuit; for a Jesuit will ruin you, body and soul!" It pleased God to grant her request, for she never saw me more! Yet she and my two little sisters were, after several years' captivity, redeemed, but she died before I returned. My brother who was taken with me, was, after several years' captivity, most barbarously tortured to death by the Indians.

My Indian master carried me up Penobscot river, to a village called *Madawamkee*,[12] which stands on a point of land between the main river and a branch which heads to the east of it. At home I had ever seen strangers treated with the utmost civility, and being a stranger, I expected some kind treatment here; but I soon found myself deceived, for I presently saw a number of squaws, who had got together in a circle, dancing and yelling. An old grim-looking one took me by the hand, and leading me into the ring, some seized me by my hair, and others by my hands and feet, like so many furies; but my master presently laying down a pledge, they released me.

A captive among the Indians is exposed to all manner of abuses, and to the extremest tortures, unless their master, or some of their master's relations, lay down a ransom; such as a bag of corn, a blanket, or the like, which redeems them from their cruelty for that dance. The next day we went up that eastern branch of Penobscot river many leagues; carried over land to a large pond, and from one

[11] The "Jesuit of the place" was Father M. Thury, who had accompanied the French-Indian assault on Pemaquid as chaplain. Gyles's father had been a devoutly iron-willed Puritan whose antipathy toward alien religions had instilled in his children a great fear of the blandishments of popery. It was not uncommonly believed that Jesuits had the power of winning over heretics by mysterious arts.

[12] Mattawamkeag.

pond to another, till, in a few days, we went down a river, called Medocktack,[13] which vents itself into St. John's river. But before we came to the mouth of this river, we passed over a long carrying place, to Medocktack fort, which stands on a bank of St. John's river. My master went before, and left me with an old Indian and two or three squaws. The old man often said, (which was all the English he could speak,) "By and by come to a great town and fort." I now comforted myself in thinking how finely I should be refreshed when I came to this great town.

After some miles' travel we came in sight of a large cornfield, and soon after of the fort, to my great surprise. Two or three squaws met us, took off my pack, and led me to a large hut or wigwam, where thirty or forty Indians were dancing and yelling round five or six poor captives, who had been taken some months before from Quochech, at the time Major Waldron was so barbarously butchered by them.[14] And before proceeding with my narrative I will give a short account of that action.

Major Waldron's garrison was taken on the night of the 27th of June, 1689. I have heard the Indians say at a feast that as there was a truce for some days, they contrived to send in two squaws to take notice of the numbers, lodgings and other circumstances of the people in his garrison, and if they could obtain leave to lodge there, to open the gates and whistle. (They said the gates had no locks, but were fastened with pins, and that they kept no watch.) The squaws had a favorable season to prosecute their projection, for it was dull weather when they came to beg leave to lodge in the garrison. They told the major that a great number of Indians were not far from thence, with a considerable quantity of beaver, who would be there to trade with him the next day. Some of the people were very much against their lodging in the garrison, but the major said, "Let the poor creatures lodge by the fire." The squaws went into every

[13] The Meductic, or Eel River, a stream that the Maliseets had originally named *Madawamketook,* "Rocky at the Mouth." They had reached this point after successive portages to the Cheputnedticook Lakes.

[14] Thirteen years earlier, at the end of King Philip's War, Maj. Richard Waldron had invited 400 hostile Indians to meet with him under truce at the Quochech garrison; when they appeared he attacked with two companies of troops and killed or seized over 200 of them. With the commencement of King William's War in 1689, the Indians took their revenge on the seventy-four-year-old soldier in the manner described here by Gyles.

apartment, and observing the numbers in each, when all the people were asleep, arose and opened the gates, gave the signal, and the other Indians came to them; and having received an account of the state of the garrison, they divided according to the number of people in each apartment, and soon took and killed them all. The major lodged within an inner room, and when the Indians broke in upon him, he cried out, "What now! what now!" and jumping out of bed with only his shirt on, seized his sword and drove them before him through two or three doors; but for some reason, turning about towards the apartment he had just left, an Indian came up behind him, knocked him on the head with his hatchet, which stunned him, and he fell. They now seized upon him, dragged him out, and setting him upon a long table in his hall, bid him "judge Indians again." Then they cut and stabbed him, and he cried out, "O, Lord! O, Lord!" They bid him order his book of accounts to be brought, and to cross out all the Indians' debts, (he having traded much with them.) After they had tortured him to death, they burned the garrison and drew off. The narration I had from their own mouths, at a general meeting, and have reason to think it true. But to return to my narrative.

I was whirled in among this circle of Indians, and we prisoners looked on each other with a sorrowful countenance. Presently one of them was seized by each hand and foot, by four Indians, who, swinging him up, let his back fall on the ground with full force. This they repeated, till they had danced, as they called it, round the whole wigwam, which was thirty or forty feet in length. But when they torture a boy they take him up between two. This is one of their customs of torturing captives. Another is to take up a person by the middle, with his head downwards, and jolt him round till one would think his bowels would shake out of his mouth. Sometimes they will take a captive by the hair of the head, and stooping him forward, strike him on the back and shoulder, till the blood gushes out of his mouth and nose. Sometimes an old shrivelled squaw will take up a shovel of hot embers and throw them into a captive's bosom. If he cry out, the Indians will laugh and shout, and say, "What a brave action our old grandmother has done." Sometimes they torture them with whips, &c.

The Indians looked on me with a fierce countenance, as much as to say, it will be your turn next. They champed cornstalks, which they threw into my hat, as I held it in my hand. I smiled on them, though my heart ached. I looked on one, and another, but could not perceive that any eye pitied me. Presently came a squaw and a little girl, and laid down a bag of corn in the ring. The little girl took me by the hand, making signs for me to go out of the circle with them. Not knowing their custom, I supposed they designed to kill me, and refused to go. Then a grave Indian came and gave me a short pipe, and said in English, "Smoke it;" then he took me by the hand and led me out. My heart ached, thinking myself near my end. But he carried me to a French hut, about a mile from the Indian fort. The Frenchman was not at home, but his wife, who was a squaw, had some discourse with my Indian friend, which I did not understand. We tarried about two hours, then returned to the Indian village, where they gave me some victuals. Not long after this I saw one of my fellow-captives, who gave me a melancholy account of their sufferings after I left them.

After some weeks had passed, we left this village and went up St. John's river about ten miles, to a branch called *Medockscenecasis,* where there was one wigwam. At our arrival an old squaw saluted me with a yell, taking me by the hair and one hand, but I was so rude as to break her hold and free myself. She gave me a filthy grin, and the Indians set up a laugh, and so it passed over. Here we lived upon fish, wild grapes, roots, &c., which was hard living to me.

When the winter came on we went up the river, till the ice came down, running thick in the river, when, according to the Indian custom, we laid up our canoes till spring. Then we travelled sometimes on the ice, and sometimes on the land, till we came to a river that was open, but not fordable, where we made a raft, and passed over, bag and baggage. I met with no abuse from them in this winter's hunting, though I was put to great hardships in carrying burdens and for want of food. But they underwent the same difficulty, and would often encourage me, saying, in broken English, "*By and by great deal moose.*" Yet they could not answer any question I asked them. And knowing little of their customs and way of life, I thought it tedious to be constantly moving from place to place, though it might be in some respects an advantage;

for it ran still in my mind that we were travelling to some settlement; and when my burden was over-heavy, and the Indians left me behind, and the still evening coming on, I fancied I could see through the bushes, and hear the people of some great town; which hope, though some support to me in the day, yet I found not the town at night.

Thus we were hunting three hundred miles from the sea, and knew no man within fifty or sixty miles of us. We were eight or ten in number, and had but two guns, on which we wholly depended for food. If any disaster had happened, we must all have perished. Sometimes we had no manner of sustenance for three or four days; but God wonderfully provides for all creatures. In one of these fasts, God's providence was remarkable. Our two Indian men, who had guns, in hunting started a moose, but there being a shallow crusted snow on the ground, and the moose discovering them, ran with great force into a swamp. The Indians went round the swamp, and finding no track, returned at night to the wigwam, and told what had happened. The next morning they followed him on the track, and soon found him lying on the snow. He had, in crossing the roots of a large tree, that had been blown down, broken through the ice made over the water in the hole occasioned by the roots of the tree taking up the ground, and hitched one of his hind legs among the roots, so fast that by striving to get it out he pulled his thigh bone out of its socket at the hip; and thus extraordinarily were we provided for in our great strait. Sometimes they would take a bear, which go into dens in the fall of the year, without any sort of food, and lie there four or five months without food, never going out till spring; in which time they neither lose nor gain in flesh. If they went into their dens fat they came out so, and if they went in lean they came out lean. I have seen some which have come out with four whelps, and both very fat, and then we feasted. An old squaw and a captive, if any present, must stand without the wigwam, shaking their hands and bodies as in a dance, and singing, "WEGAGE OH NELO WOH," which in English is, "Fat is my eating." This is to signify their thankfulness in feasting times. When one supply was spent we fasted till further success.

The way they preserve meat is by taking the flesh from the bones and drying it in smoke, by which it is kept sound months or years without salt. We moved still further up the country after moose when our store was out, so that by the spring we had got to the northward of the Lady mountains.[15] When the spring came and the rivers broke up, we moved back to the head of St. John's river, and there made canoes of moose hides, sewing three or four together and pitching the seams with balsam mixed with charcoal. Then we went down the river to a place called Madawescook.[16] There an old man lived and kept a sort of trading house, where we tarried several days; then went farther down the river till we came to the greatest falls in these parts, called Checanekepeag,[17] where we carried a little way over the land, and putting off our canoes we went down-stream still. And as we passed down by the mouths of any large branches, we saw Indians; but when any dance was proposed, I was bought off. At length we arrived at the place where we left our birch canoes in the fall, and putting our baggage into them, went down to the fort.

There we planted corn, and after planting went a fishing, and to look for and dig roots, till the corn was fit to weed. After weeding we took a second tour on the same errand, then returned to hill our corn. After hilling we went some distance from the fort and field, up the river, to take salmon and other fish, which we dried for food, where we continued till corn was filled with milk: some of it we dried then, the other as it ripened. To dry corn when in the milk, they gather it in large kettles and boil it on the ears, till it is pretty hard, then shell it from the cob with clam-shells, and dry it on bark in the sun. When it is thoroughly dry, a kernel is no bigger than a pea, and would keep years, and when it is boiled again it swells as large as when on the ear, and tastes incomparably sweeter than other corn. When we had gathered our corn and dried it in the way already described, we put some into Indian barns, that is, into holes in the ground lined and covered with bark, and then with dirt. The rest we carried up the river upon our next winter's hunting. Thus God wonderfully favored me, and carried me through the first year of my captivity.

15 Called by the French *Monts Notre Dame*. This indicates that Gyles was then on the borders of the St. Lawrence, to the north of the head of Chaleur Bay.

16 Madawaska.

17 Grand Falls, or *Checanekepeag,* "The Destroying Giant," some 200 miles from the sea.

CHAPTER II.—*Of the abusive and barbarous treatment which several captives met with from the Indians.* When any great number of Indians met, or when any captives had been lately taken, or when any captives desert and are retaken, they have a dance, and torture the unhappy people who have fallen into their hands. My unfortunate brother, who was taken with me, after about three years' captivity, deserted with another Englishman, who had been taken from Casco Bay, and was retaken by the Indians at New Harbor, and carried back to Penobscot fort. Here they were both tortured at a stake by fire, for some time; then their noses and ears were cut off, and they made to eat them. After this they were burnt to death at the stake; the Indians at the same time declaring that they would serve all deserters in the same manner. Thus they divert themselves in their dances.

On the second spring of my captivity, my Indian master and his squaw went to Canada, but sent me down the river with several Indians to the fort, to plant corn. The day before we came to the planting ground, we met two young Indian men, who seemed to be in great haste. After they had passed us, I understood they were going with an express [18] to Canada, and that there was an English vessel at the mouth of the river. I not being perfect in their language, not knowing that English vessels traded with them in time of war, supposed a peace was concluded on, and that the captives would be released; I was so transported with this fancy, that I slept but little if any that night. Early the next morning we came to the village, where my ecstacy ended; for I had no sooner landed, but three or four Indians dragged me to the great wigwam, where they were yelling and dancing round James Alexander, a Jersey man, who was taken from Falmouth, in Casco Bay. This was occasioned by two families of Cape Sable Indians,[19] who, having lost some friends by a number of English fishermen, came some hundreds of miles to revenge themselves on poor captives. They soon came to me, and tossed me about till I was almost breathless, and then threw

[18] Message.

[19] These were Micmacs, whom the Maliseets called *Mateweswesweskitchinuuk*, "the Porcupine People," from their use of dyed porcupine quills for ornamentation. The Micmacs, in turn, called the Maliseets *Kuuswekitchinuuk*—"the muskrat people," owing to their love of muskrat meat. The Maliseets called themselves *Wulastukwiuk*, "the People of the Goodly River."

me into the ring to my fellow-captive; and taking him out, repeated their barbarities on him. Then I was hauled out again by three Indians, who seized me by the hair of the head; and bending me down by my hair, one beat me on the back and shoulders so long that my breath was almost beat out of my body. Then others put a *tomhake* [tomahawk] [20] into my hands, and ordered me to get up and sing and dance Indian, which I performed with the greatest reluctance, and while in the act, seemed determined to purchase my death, by killing two or three of those monsters of cruelty, thinking it impossible to survive their bloody treatment; but it was impressed on my mind that it was not in their power to take away my life, so I desisted.

Then those Cape Sable Indians came to me again like bears bereaved of their whelps, saying, "Shall we, who have lost relations by the English, suffer an English voice to be heard among us?" &c. Then they beat me again with the axe. Now I repented that I had not sent two or three of them out of the world before me, for I thought I had much rather die that suffer any longer. They left me the second time, and the other Indians put the tomhake into my hands again, and compelled me to sing. Then I seemed more resolute than before to destroy some of them; but a strange and strong impulse that I should return to my own place and people supressed it, as often as such a motion rose in my breast. Not one of them showed the least compassion, but I saw the tears run down plentifully on the cheeks of a Frenchman who sat behind, though it did not alleviate the tortures that poor James and I were forced to endure for the most part of this tedious day; for they were continued till the evening, and were the most severe that ever I met with in the whole six years that I was a captive with the Indians.

After they had thus inhumanly abused us, two Indians took us up and threw us out of the wigwam, and we crawled away on our hands and feet, and were scarce able to walk for several days. Some time after they again concluded on a merry dance, when I was at some distance from the wigwam dressing leather, and an Indian was

20 "The *tomhake* is a warlike club, the shape of which may be seen in cuts of ETOWOHKOAM, one of the four Indian chiefs, which cuts are common amongst us" [Gyles]. The reference is to woodcut portraits of four Iroquois chiefs who visited England during the reign of Queen Anne.

so kind as to tell me that they had got James Alexander, and were in search for me. My Indian master and his squaw bid me run for my life into a swamp and hide, and not to discover myself unless they both came to me; for then I might be assured the dance was over. I was now master of their language, and a word or a wink was enough to excite me to take care of one. I ran to the swamp, and hid in the thickest place I could find. I heard hallooing and whooping all around me; sometimes some passed very near me, and I could hear some threaten and others flatter me, but I was not disposed to dance. If they had come upon me, I had resolved to show them a pair of heels, and they must have had good luck to have catched me. I heard no more of them till about evening, for I think I slept, when they came again, calling, "Chon! Chon!" but John would not trust them. After they were gone, my master and his squaw came where they told me to hide, but could not find me; and, when I heard them say, with some concern, they believed the other Indians had frightened me into the woods, and that I was lost, I came out, and they seemed well pleased. They told me James had had a bad day of it; that as soon as he was released he ran away into the woods, and they believed he was gone to the Mohawks. James soon returned, and gave a melancholy account of his sufferings, and the Indian's fright concerning the Mohawks passed over. They often had terrible apprehensions of the incursions of those Indians.[21] They are called also *Maquas*, a most ambitious, haughty and blood-thirsty people, from whom the other Indians take their measures and manners, and their modes and changes of dress, &c. One very hot season, a great number gathered together at the village, and being a very droughty [thirsty] people, they kept James and myself night and day fetching water from a cold spring, that ran out of a rocky hill about three quarters of a mile from the fort. In going thither, we crossed a large interval cornfield, and then a descent to a lower interval, before we ascended the hill to the spring. James being almost dead, as well as I, with this continual fatigue, contrived to frighten the Indians. He told me of his plan, but conjured me to secrecy, yet

[21] Both the Maliseets and the Penobscots possessed an almost pathological fear of the Mohawks, as much for their cannibalism as for their legendary ferocity. The Maliseets' palisaded forts, such as Meductic, were built as protection against the Mohawks, not the English.

said he knew I could keep counsel! The next dark night, James, going for water, set his kettle down on the descent to the lowest interval, and running back to the fort, puffing and blowing as though in the utmost surprise, told his master that he saw something near the spring that looked like Mohawks, (which were only stumps.) His master, being a most courageous warrior, went with him to make discovery. When they came to the brow of the hill, James pointed to the stumps, and withal touching his kettle with his toe, gave it motion down the hill; at very turn its bail clattered, which caused James and his master to see a Mohawk in every stump, and they lost no time in "turning tail to," and he was the best fellow who could run the fastest. This alarmed all the Indians in the village. They were about thirty or forty in number, and they packed off, bag and baggage, some up the river and others down, and did not return under fifteen days; and then the heat of the weather being finally over, our hard service was abated for this season. I never heard that the Indians understood the occasion of their fright; but James and I had many a private laugh about it.

But my most intimate and dear companion was one John Evans, a young man taken from Quochecho. We, as often as we could, met together, and made known our grievances to each other, which seemed to ease our minds; but, as soon as it was known by the Indians, we were strictly examined apart, and falsely accused of contriving to desert. We were too far from the sea to have any thought of that, and finding our stories agreed, did not punish us. An English captive girl about this time, who was taken by Medocawando, would often falsely accuse us of plotting to desert; but we made the truth so plainly appear, that she was checked and we were released. But the third winter of my captivity, John Evans went into the country, and the Indians imposed a heavy burden on him, while he was extremely weak from long fasting; and as he was going off the upland over a place of ice, which was very hollow, he broke through, fell down, and cut his knee very much. Notwithstanding, he travelled for some time, but the wind and cold were so forcible, that they soon overcame him, and he sat or fell down, and all the Indians passed by him. Some of them went back the next day after him, or his pack, and found him, with a dog in his arms, both frozen to death. Thus all of my fellow-captives were dispersed and dead, but through infinite and unmerited goodness I was supported under and carried through all difficulties.

CHAPTER III.—*Of further difficulties and deliverances.* One winter, as we were moving from place to place, our hunters killed some moose. One lying miles from our wigwams, a young Indian and myself were ordered to fetch part of it. We set out in the morning, when the weather was promising, but it proved a very cold, cloudy day. It was late in the evening before we arrived at the place where the moose lay, so that we had no time to provide materials for fire or shelter. At the same time we came on a storm of snow, very thick, which continued until the next morning. We made a small fire with what little rubbish we could find around us. The fire, with the warmth of our bodies, melted the snow upon us as fast as it fell; and so our clothes were filled with water. However, early in the morning we took our loads of moose flesh, and set out to return to our wigwams. We had not travelled far before my moose-skin coat (which was the only garment I had on my back, and the hair chiefly worn off) was frozen stiff round my knees, like a hoop, as were my snow-shoes and shoe-clouts to my feet. Thus I marched the whole day without fire or food. At first I was in great pain, then my flesh became numb, and at times I felt extremely sick, and thought I could not travel one foot farther; but I wonderfully revived again.

After long travelling I felt very drowsy, and had thought of sitting down, which had I done, without doubt I had fallen on my final sleep, as my dear companion, Evans, had done before. My Indian companion, being better clothed, had left me long before. Again my spirits revived as much as if I had received the richest cordial. Some hours after sunset I reached the wigwam, and crawling in with my snow-shoes on, the Indians cried out, "The captive is frozen to death!" They took off my pack, and the place where that lay against my back was the only one that was not frozen. They cut off my shoes, and stripped off the clouts from my feet, which were as void of feeling as any frozen flesh could be. I had not sat long by the fire before the blood began to circulate, and my feet to my ankles turned black, and swelled with bloody blisters, and were inexpressibly painful. The Indians said one to another,

"His feet will rot, and he will die." Yet I slept well at night. Soon after, the skin came off my feet from my ankles, whole, like a shoe, leaving my toes naked, without a nail, and the ends of my great toe bones bare, which, in a little time, turned black, so that I was obliged to cut the first joint off with my knife. The Indians gave me rags to bind up my feet, and advised me to apply fir balsam, but withal added that they believed it was not worth while to use means, for I should certainly die. But, by the use of my elbows, and a stick in each hand, I shoved myself along as I sat upon the ground over the snow from one tree to another, till I got some balsam. This I burned in a clam-shell till it was of a consistence like salve, which I applied to my feet and ankles, and, by the divine blessing, within a week I could go about upon my heels with my staff.[22] And, through God's goodness, we had provisions enough, so that we did not remove under ten or fifteen days. Then the Indians made two little hoops, something in the form of a snow-shoe, and sewing them to my feet, I was able to follow them in their tracks, on my heels, from place to place, though sometimes half leg deep snow and water, which gave me the most acute pain imaginable; but I must walk or die. Yet within a year my feet were entirely well; and the nails came on my great toes, so that a very critical eye could scarcely perceive any part missing, or that they had been frozen at all.

In a time of great scarcity of provisions, the Indians chased a large moose into the river, and killed him. They brought the flesh to the village, and raised it on a scaffold, in a large wigwam, in order to make a feast. I was very officious in supplying them with wood and water, which pleased them so well that they now and then gave me a piece of flesh half boiled or roasted, which I ate with eagerness, and I doubt not without due thankfulness to the divine Being who so extraordinarily fed me. At length the scaffold bearing the moose meat broke, and I being under it, a large piece

[22] Maliseet medicine made use of almost all native trees and plants. Hemlock bark steeped into a tea was used for colds and rheumatism and, applied externally, for bruises, swellings, and sprains. Steeped poplar bark was a remedy for headache, impure blood, and loss of appetite. Coughs and skin ailments were treated with sarsparilla-root tonic, and bunchberry tea was taken for fits and convulsions. Cornmeal, steeped fir roots, and puffball applied as a soft surgical dressing could stop bleeding; mountain ash was used as a purgative.

fell, and knocked me on the head. The Indians said I lay stunned a considerable time. The first I was sensible of was a murmuring noise in my ears, then my sight gradually returned, with an extreme pain in my hand, which was very much bruised; and it was long before I recovered, the weather being very hot.

I was once fishing with an Indian for sturgeon, and the Indian darting one, his feet slipped, and he turned the canoe bottom upward, with me under it. I held fast to the cross-bar, as I could not swim, with my face to the bottom of the canoe; but turning myself, I brought my breast to bear on the cross-bar, expecting every minute the Indian to tow me to the bank. But "he had other fish to fry." Thus I continued a quarter of an hour, [though] without want of breath, till the current drove me on a rocky point where I could reach bottom. There I stopped, and turned up my canoe. On looking about for the Indian, I saw him half a mile off up the river. On going to him, I asked him why he had not towed me to the bank, seeing he knew I could not swim. He said he knew I was under the canoe, for there were no bubbles any where to be seen, and that I should drive on the point. So while he was taking care of his fine sturgeon, which was eight or ten feet in length, I was left to sink or swim.

Once, as we were fishing for salmon at a fall of about fifteen feet of water, I came near being drownded in a deep hole at the foot of the fall. The Indians went into the water to wash themselves, and asked me to go with them. I told them I could not swim, but they insisted, and so I went in. They ordered me to dive across the deepest place, and if I fell short of the other side they said they would help me. But, instead of diving across the narrowest part, I was crawling on the bottom into the deepest place. They not seeing me rise, and knowing whereabouts I was by the bubbling of the water, a young girl dived down, and brought me up by the hair, otherwise I had perished in the water. Though the Indians, both male and female, go into the water together, they have each of them such covering on that not the least indecency can be observed, and neither chastity nor modesty is violated.

While at the Indian village, I had been cutting wood and binding it up with an Indian rope, in order to carry it to the wigwam; a stout, ill-natured young fellow, about twenty years of age, threw me backward, sat on my breast, pulled out his knife, and said he would kill me, for he had never yet killed one of the English. I told him he might go to war, and that would be more manly than to kill a poor captive who was doing their drugery for them. Notwithstanding all I could say, he began to cut and stab me on my breast. I seized him by the hair, and tumbling him off of me, followed him with my fists and knee with such application that he soon cried "enough." But when I saw the blood run from my boson, and felt the smart of the wounds he had given me, I at him again, and bid him get up, and not lie there like a dog; told him of his former abuses offered to me, and other poor captives, and that if ever he offered the like to me again, I would pay him double. I sent him before me, and taking up my burden of wood, came to the Indians, and told them the whole truth, and they commended me. And I do not remember that ever he offered me the least abuse afterwards, though he was big enough to have despatched two of me.

CHAPTER IV.—*Of remarkable events of Providence in the deaths of several barbarous Indians.* The priest of this river[23] was of the order of St. Francis, a gentleman of a humane, generous disposition. In his sermons he most severely reprehended the Indians for their barbarities to captives. He would often tell them that, excepting their errors in religion, the English were a better people than themselves, and that God would remarkably punish such cruel wretches, and had begun to execute his vengeance upon such already! He gave an account of the retaliations of Providence upon those murderous Cape Sable Indians above mentioned; one of whom got a splinter into his foot, which festered and rotted his flesh till it killed him. Another run a fish-bone into her hand or arm, and she rotted to death, notwithstanding all means that were used to prevent it. In some such manner they all died, so that not one of those two families lived to return home. Were it not for these remarks of the priest, I had not, perhaps, have noticed these providences.

There was an old squaw who ever endeavored to outdo all others in cruelty to captives. Wherever she came into a wigwam,

[23] Father Simon, the Récollet missionary of Meductic.

where any poor, naked, starved captives were sitting near the fire, if they were grown persons, she would stealthily take up a shovel of hot coals, and throw them into their bosoms. If they were young persons, she would seize them by the hand or leg, drag them through the fire, &c. The Indians with whom she lived, according to their custom, left their village in the fall of the year, and dispersed themselves for hunting. After the first or second removal, they all strangely forgot that old squaw and her grandson, about twelve years of age. They were found dead in the place where they were left some months afterwards, and no farther notice was taken of them by their friends. Of this the priest made special remark, forasmuch as it is a thing very uncommon for them to neglect either their old or young people.

In the latter part of summer, or beginning of autumn, the Indians were frequently frightened by the appearance of strange Indians, passing up and down this river in canoes, and about that time the next year died more than one hundred persons, old and young; all, or most of those who saw those strange Indians! The priest said it was a sort of plague. A person seeming in perfect health would bleed at the mouth and nose, turn blue in spots, and die in two or three hours. It was very tedious to me to remove from place to place this cold season. The Indians applied red ochre to my sores, [which had been occasioned by the affray before mentioned,] which by God's blessing cured me. This sickness being at the worst as winter came on, the Indians all scattered; and the blow was so great to them, that they did not settle or plant at their village while I was on the river, [St. Johns,] and I know not whether they have to this day. Before they thus deserted the village, when they came in from hunting, they would be drunk and fight for several days and nights together, till they had spent most of their skins in wine and brandy, which was brought to the village by a Frenchman called Monsieur *Sigenioncour*.

CHAPTER V.—*Of their familiarity with and frights from the devil, &c.* The Indians are very often surprised with the appearance of ghosts and demons. Sometimes they are encouraged by the devil, for they go to him for success in hunting, &c. I was once hunting with Indians who were not brought over to the Romish faith, and after several days they proposed to inquire, according to their custom, what success they should have. They accordingly prepared many hot stones, and laying them in a heap, made a small hut covered with skins and mats; then in a dark night two of the powwows[24] went into this hot house with a large vessel of water, which at times they poured on those hot rocks, which raised a thick steam, so that a third Indian was obliged to stand without, and lift up a mat, to give it vent when they were almost suffocated. There was an old squaw who was kind to captives, and never joined with them in their powwowing, to whom I manifested an earnest desire to see their management. She told me that if they knew of my being there they would kill me, and that when she was a girl she had known young persons to be taken away by a hairy man, and therefore she would not advise me to go, lest the hairy man should carry me away. I told her I was not afraid of the hairy man, not could he hurt me if she would not discover me to the powwows. At length she promised me she would not, but charged me to be careful of myself. I went within three or four feet of the hot house, for it was very dark, and heard strange noises and yellings, such as I never heard before. At times the Indian who tended without would lift up the mat, and a steam would issue which looked like fire. I lay there two or three hours, but saw none of their hairy men, or demons. And when I found they had finished their ceremony, I went to the wigwam, and told the squaw what had passed. She was glad I had escaped without hurt, and never discovered what I had done. After some time inquiry was made of the powwows what success we were likely to have in our hunting. They said they had very likely signs of success, but no real ones as at other times. A few days after we moved up the river, and had pretty good luck.

One afternoon as I was in a canoe with one of the powows the dog barked, and presently a moose passed by within a few rods of us, so that the waves he made by wading rolled our canoe. The Indian shot at him, but the moose took very little notice of it, and went into the woods to the southward. The fellow said, "I will try if I can't fetch you back for all your haste." The evening following, we built our two wigwams on a sandy point on the upper end

24 Conjurers.

of an island in the river, north-west of the place where the moose went into the woods; and here the Indian powwowed the greatest part of the night following. In the morning we had a fair track of a moose round our wigwams, though we did not see or taste of it. I am of opinion that the devil was permitted to humor those unhappy wretches sometimes, in some things.

That it may appear how much they were deluded, or under the influence of satan, read the two stories which were related and believed by the Indians. The first, of a boy who was carried away by a large bird called a *Gulloua*, who buildeth her nest on a high rock or mountain. A boy was hunting with his bow and arrow at the foot of a rocky mountain, when the gulloua came diving through the air, grasped the boy in her talons, and although he was eight or ten years of age, she soared aloft and laid him in her nest, food for her young. The boy lay still on his face, but observed two of the young birds in the nest with him, having much fish and flesh to feed upon. The old one seeing they would not eat the boy, took him up in her claws and returned him to the place from whence she took him. I have passed near the mountain in a canoe, and the Indians have said, "There is the nest of the great bird that carried away the boy." Indeed there seemed to be a great number of sticks put together like a nest on the top of the mountain. At another time they said, "There is the bird, but he is now as a boy to a giant to what he was in former days." The bird which we saw was a large and speckled one, like an eagle, though somewhat larger.

When from the mountain tops, with hideous cry
And clattering wings, the hungry harpies fly,
They snatched
And whether gods or birds obscene they were,
Our vows for pardon and for peace prefer.

DRYDEN'S VIRGIL

The other notion is, that a young Indian in his hunting was belated, and losing his way, was on a sudden introduced to a large wigwam full of dried eels, which proved to be a beaver's house, in which he lived till the spring of the year, when he was turned out of the house, and being set upon a beaver's dam, went home and related the affair to his friends at large.

CHAPTER VI.—*A description of several creatures commonly taken by the Indians on St. John's river.*

I. OF THE BEAVER.—The beaver has a very thick, strong neck; his fore teeth, which are two in the upper and two in the under jaw, are concave and sharp like a carpenter's gouge. Their side teeth are like a sheep's, for they chew the cud. Their legs are short, the claws something longer than in other creatures. The nails on the toes of their hind feet are flat like an ape's, but joined together by a membrane, as those of the water-foul, their tails broad and flat like the broad end of a paddle. Near their tails they have four bottles, two of which contain oil, the others gum; the necks of these meet in one common orifice. The latter of these bottles contain the proper castorum, and not the testicles, as some have fancied, for they are distinct and separate from them, in the males only; whereas the castorum and oil bottles are common to male and female. With this oil and gum they preen themselves, so that when they come out of the water it runs off of them, as it does from a fowl. They have four teats, which are on their breasts, so that they hug up their young and suckle them, as women do their infants. They have generally two, and sometimes four in a litter. I have seen seven or five in the matrix, but the Indians think it a strange thing to find so many in a litter; and they assert that when it so happens the dam kills all but four. They are the most laborious creatures that I have met with. I have known them to build dams across a river, thirty or forty perches [25] wide, with wood and mud, so as to flow many acres of land. In the deepest part of a pond so raised they build their houses, round, in the figure of an Indian wigwam, eight or ten feet high, and six or eight in diameter on the floor, which is made descending to the water, the parts near the centre about four, and near the circumference between ten and twenty inches above the water. These floors are covered with strippings of wood, like shavings. On these they sleep with their tails in the water; and if the freshets rise, they have the advantage of rising on their floor to the highest part. They feed on the leaves and bark of trees, and pond lily roots. In the fall of the year they lay in their provision for the approaching winter; cutting down trees great and small. With one end in their mouths they

[25] A unit of length, equivalent to the rod (16.5 feet).

drag their branches near to their house, and sink many cords of it. (They will cut [gnaw] down trees of a fathom in circumference.) They have doors to go down to the wood under the ice. And in case the freshets rise, break down and carry off their store of wood, they often starve. They have a note for conversing calling and warning each other when at work or feeding; and while they are at labor they keep out a guard, who upon the first approach of an enemy so strikes the water with his tail that he may be heard half a mile. This so alarms the rest that they are all silent, quit their labor, and are to be seen no more for that time. If the male or female die, the survivor seeks a mate, and conducts him or her to their house, and carry on affairs as above.

II. Of the Wolverene. (*Gulo Luscus* of L.) The wolverene is a very fierce and mischievous creature, about the bigness of a middling dog; having short legs, broad feet and very sharp claws, and in my opinion may be reckoned a species of cat.[26] They will climb trees and wait for moose and other animals which feed below, and when opportunity presents, jump upon and strike their claws in them so fast that they will hang on them till they have gnawed the main nerve in their neck asunder, which causes their death. I have known many moose killed thus. I was once travelling a little way behind several Indians, and hearing them laugh merrily, when I came up I asked them the cause of their laughter. They showed me the track of a moose, and how a wolverene had climbed a tree, and where he had jumped off upon a moose. It so happened that after the moose had taken several large leaps, it came under the branch of a tree, which striking the wolverene, broke his hold and tore him off; and by his tracks in the snow it appeared he went off another way, with short steps, as if he had been stunned by the blow that had broken his hold. The Indians imputed the accident to the cunning of the moose, and were wonderfully pleased that it had thus outwitted the mischievous wolverene.

These wolverenes go into wigwams which have been left for a time, scatter the things abroad, and most filthily pollute them with

[26] The wolverine, a carnivorous mammal and the largest member of the weasel family, was variously called by the Maliseets the "Black Devil" and the *carcajou* (from the Algonquin *karkajou*). White men, however, referred to the wolverine as "the Indian Devil."

ordure. I have heard the Indians say that this animal has sometimes pulled their guns from under their heads while they were asleep, and left them so defiled. An Indian told me that having left his wigwam with sundry things on the scaffold, among which was a birchen flask containing several pounds of powder, he found at his return, much to his surprise and grief, that a wolverene had visited it, mounted the scaffold, hove down bag and baggage. The powder flask happening to fall into the fire, exploded, blowing up the wolverene, and scattering the wigwam in all directions. At length he found the creature, blind from the blast, wandering backward and forward, and he had the satisfaction of kicking and beating him about! This in a great measure made up their loss, and then they could contentedly pick up their utensils and rig out their wigwam.

III. Of the Hedgehog, (*Histrix Dorsata,*) or Urchin, [*Urson?*] Our hedgehog or urchin is about the bigness of a hog of six months old. His back, sides and tail are full of sharp quills, so that if any creature approach him, he will contract himself into a globular form, and when touched by his enemy, his quills are so sharp and loose in the skin they fix in the mouth of the adversary. They will strike with great force with their tails, so that whatever falls under the lash of them are certainly filled with their prickles; but that they shoot their quills, as some assert they do, is a great mistake, as respects the American hedgehog, and I believe as to the African hedgehog or porcupine also. As to the former, I have taken them at all seasons of the year.

IV. Of the Tortoise. It is needless to describe the freshwater tortoise, whose form is so well known in all parts; but their manner of propagating their species is not so universally known. I have observed that sort of tortoise whose shell is about fourteen or sixteen inches wide. In their coition they may be heard half a mile, making a noise like a woman washing her linen with a batting staff. They lay their eggs in the sand, near some deep, still water, about a foot beneath the surface of the sand, with which they are very curious in covering them; so that there is not the least mixture of it amongst them, nor the least rising of sand on the beach where they are deposited. I have often searched for them with the Indians, by thrusting a stick into the sand at random, and brought up some part of an egg clinging to it; when, uncovering the place, we have found near one hundred and fifty in one nest. Both their eggs and flesh are good eating when boiled. I have observed a difference as to the length of time in which they are hatching, which is between twenty and thirty days; some sooner than others. Whether this difference ought to be imputed to the various quality or site of the sand in which they are laid, (as to the degree of cold or heat,) I leave to the conjecture of the virtuosi. As soon as they are hatched, the young tortoise breaks through the sand and betake themselves to the water, and, as far as I could discover, without any further care or help of the old ones.

CHAPTER VIII.—*Of their feasting.* 1. *Before they go to war.* When the Indians determine on war, or are entering upon a particular expedition, they kill a number of their dogs, burn off their hair and cut them to pieces, leaving only one dog's head whole. The rest of the flesh they boil, and make a fine feast of it. Then the dog's head that was left whole is scorched, till the nose and lips have shrunk from the teeth, leaving them bare and grinning. This done, they fasten it on a stick, and the Indian who is proposed to be chief in the expedition takes the head into his hand, and sings a warlike song, in which he mentions the town they design to attack, and the principal man in it; threatening that in a few days he will carry that man's head and scalp in his hand, in the same manner. When the chief has finished singing, he so places the dog's head as to grin at him who he supposes will go his second, who, if he accepts, takes the head in his hand and sings; but if he refuses to go, he turns the teeth to another; and thus from one to another till they have enlisted their company.

The Indians imagine that dog's flesh makes them bold and courageous. I have seen an Indian split a dog's head with a hatchet, take out the brains hot, and eat them raw with the blood running down his jaws! [27]

2. *When a relative dies.* In a still evening, a squaw will walk on the highest land near her abode, and with a loud and mournful voice will exclaim, "*Oh hawe, hawe, hawe,*" with a long, mournful

[27] Another manifestation of the primitive belief in sympathetic magic (see Jogues narrative, n. 35).

tone to each *hawe,* for a long time together. After the mourning season is over, the relations of the deceased make a feast to wipe off tears, and the bereaved may marry freely. If the deceased was a squaw, the relations consult together, and choose a squaw, (doubtless a widow,) and send her to the widower, and if he likes her he takes her to be his wife, if not, he sends her back, and the relations choose and send till they find one that he approves of.

If a young fellow determines to marry, his relations and the Jesuit advise him to a girl. He goes into the wigwam where she is, and looks on her. If he likes her appearance, he tosses a chip or stick into her lap, which she takes, and with a reserved, side look, views the person who sent it; yet handles the chip with admiration, as though she wondered from whence it came. If she likes him she throws the chip to him with a modest smile, and then nothing is wanting but a ceremony with the Jesuit to consummate the marriage. But if she dislikes her suitor, she, with a surly countenance, throws the chip aside, and he comes no more there.

If parents have a daughter marriageable they seek a husband for her who is a good hunter. If she has been educated to make *monoodah,* (Indian bags,) birch dishes, to lace snow-shoes, make Indian shoes, string wampum belts, sew birch canoes, and boil the kettle, she is esteemed a lady of fine accomplishments. If the man sought out for her husband have a gun and ammunition, a canoe, spear, and hatchet, a monoodah, a crooked knife, looking-glass and paint, a pipe, tobacco, and knot-bowl to toss a kind of dice in, he is accounted a gentleman of plentiful fortune. Whatever the new-married man procures the first year belongs to his wife's parents. If the young pair have a child within a year and nine months they are thought to be very forward and libidinous persons.

By their play with dice they lose much time, playing whole days and nights together; sometimes staking their whole effects; [28] though this is accounted a great vice by the old men.

[28] The dice game, called *al-te-sta-gen* by the Maliseets, was popular among the Eastern tribes generally. It was played with discs of bone, blackened on one side, thrown into the air to land on a blanket. Points were scored according to the number of discs that showed most black or white on each throw. A variation of this game, played with peach-pits tossed in a bowl, was called *Hub-Bub* (originally an Algonquin word) to describe the clamor made by the participants. In Indian mythology, this "Great Bowl" game symbolized the contest between the Creator and his evil twin for control of the world.

A digression.—There is an old story told among the Indians of a family who had a daughter that was accounted a finished beauty, having been adorned with the precious jewel, an Indian education! She was so formed by nature, and polished by art, that they could not find for her a suitable consort. At length, while this family were once residing upon the head of Penobscot river, under the White hills, called *Teddon,* this fine creature was missing, and her parents could learn no tidings of her. After much time and pains spent, and tears showered in quest of her, they saw her diverting herself with a beautiful youth, whose hair, like her own, flowed down below his waist, swimming, washing, &c., in the water; but they vanished upon their approach. This beautiful person, whom they imagined to be one of those kind spirits who inhabit the Teddon, they looked upon as their son-in-law; and, according to their custom, they called upon him for moose, bear, or whatever creature they desired, and if they did but go to the water-side and signify their desire, the animal would come swimimng to them! I have heard an Indian say that he lived by the river, at the foot of the Teddon, the top of which he could see through the hole of his wigwam left for the smoke to pass out. He was tempted to travel to it, and accordingly set out on a summer morning, and labored hard in ascending the hill all day, and the top seemed as distant from the place where he lodged at night as from his wigwam, where he began his journey. He now concluded the spirits were there, and never dared to make a second attempt.

I have been credibly informed that several others have failed in like attempts. Once three young men climbed towards its summit three days and a half, at the end of which time they became strangely disordered with delirium, &c., and when their imagination was clear, and they could recollect where they were, they found themselves returned one day's journey. How they came to be thus transported they could not conjecture, unless the genii of the place had conveyed them. These White hills, at the head of Penobscot river, are, by the Indians, said to be much higher than those called Agiockochook, above Saco.

But to return to an Indian feast, of which you may request a bill of fare before you go. If you dislike it, stay at home. The ingredients are fish, flesh, or Indian corn, and beans boiled together; sometimes hasty pudding made of pounded corn, whenever and as often as these are plenty. An Indian boils four or five large kettles full, and sends a messenger to each wigwam door, who exclaims, "*Kuh menscoorebah!*" that is, "I come to conduct you to a feast." The man within demands whether he must take a spoon or knife in his dish, which he always carries with him. They appoint two or three young men to mess it out, to each man his portion, according to the number of his family at home. This is done with the utmost exactness. When they have done eating, a young fellow stands without the door, and cries aloud, "*Mensecommook*," "come and fetch!" Immediately each squaw goes to her husband and takes what he has left, which she carries home and eats with her children. For neither married women, nor any youth under twenty, are allowed to be present; but old widow squaws and captive men may sit by the door. The Indian men continue in the wigwam; some relating their warlike exploits, others something comical, others narrating their hunting exploits. The seniors give maxims of prudence and grave counsel to the young men; and though every one's speech be agreeable to the run of his own fancy, yet they confine themselves to rule, and but one speaks at a time. After every man has told his story, one rises up, sings a feast song, and others succeed alternately as the company sees fit.[29]

Necessity is the mother of invention. If an Indian loses his fire, he can presently take two sticks, one harder than the other, (the drier the better,) and in the softest one make a hollow, or socket, in which one end of the hardest stick being inserted, then holding the softest piece firm between his knees, whirls it round like a drill, and fire will kindle in a few minutes.

If they have lost or left their kettle, it is but putting their victuals into a birch dish, leaving a vacancy in the middle, filling it with water, and putting in hot stones alternately; they will thus thoroughly boil the toughest neck of beef.

CHAPTER VIII.—*Of my three years captivity with the French.*—When about six years of my doleful captivity had passed, my sec-

[29] Warriors customarily narrated their adventures in sequence and sang in rotation, according to rigid tribal prescriptions. A French innovation, the saying grace by the oldest member of the assembled company, often preceded feasts during this period.

ond Indian master died, whose squaw and my first Indian master disputed whose slave I should be.[30] Some malicious persons advised them to end the quarrel by putting a period to my life; but honest father Simon, the priest of the river, told them that it would be a heinous crime, and advised them to sell me to the French. There came annually one or two men of war to supply the fort, which was on the river about 34 leagues from the sea. The Indians having advice of the arrival of a man of war at the mouth of the river,[31] they, about thirty or forty in number, went on board; for the gentlemen from France made a present to them every year, and set forth the riches and victories of their monarch, &c. At this time they presented the Indians with a bag or two of flour with some prunes, as ingredients for a feast. I, who was dressed up in an old greasy blanket, without cap, hat, or shirt, (for I had had no shirt for the six years, except the one I had on at the time I was made prisoner,) was invited into the great cabin, where many well-rigged gentlemen were sitting, who would fain have had a full view of me. I endeavoured to hide myself behind the hangings, for I was much ashamed; thinking how I had once worn clothes, and of my living with people who could rig as well as the best of them. My master asked me whether I chose to be sold to the people of the man of war, or to the inhabitants of the country. I replied, with tears, that I should be glad if he would sell me to the English from whom I was taken; but that if I must be sold to the French, I wished to be sold to the lowest inhabitants on the river, or those nearest to the sea, who were about twenty-five leagues from the mouth of the river; for I thought that, if I were sold to the gentlemen in the ship, I should never return to the English. This was the first time I had seen the sea during my captivity, and the first time I had tasted salt or bread.

My master persently went on shore, and a few days after all the Indians went up the river. When we came to a house which I had spoken to my master about, he went on shore with me, and tarried all night. The master of the house spoke kindly to me in

[30] Gyles had previously been sold by his first master to another Indian in the tribe. The point at issue was whether he was the property of the widow of this second master or if ownership reverted to his former master.

[31] At Menagoueche, or St. John.

Indian, for I could not then speak one word of French. Madam also looked pleasant on me, and gave me some bread. The next day I was sent six leagues further up the river to another French house. My master and the friar tarried with Monsieur Dechouffour,[32] the gentleman who had entertained us the night before. Not long after, father Simon came and said, "Now you are one of us, for you are sold to that gentleman by whom you were entertained the other night. I replied, "Sold!—to a Frenchman!" I could say no more, went into the woods alone, and wept till I could scarce see or stand! The word *sold*, and that to a people of that persuasion which my dear mother so much detested, and in her last words manifested so great fears of my falling into! These thoughts almost broke my heart.

When I had thus given vent to my grief I wiped my eyes, endeavoring to conceal its effects, but father Simon, perceiving my eyes were swollen, called me aside, and bidding me not to grieve, for the gentleman, he said, to whom I was sold, was of a good humor; that he had formerly bought two captives, both of whom had been sent to Boston. This, in some measure, revived me; but he added he did not suppose I would ever wish to go to the English, for the French religion was so much better. He said, also, he should pass that way in about ten days, and if I did not like to live with the French better than with the Indians he would buy me again. On the day following, father Simon and my Indian master went up the river, six and thirty leagues, to their chief village, and I went down the river six leagues with two Frenchmen to my new master. He kindly received me, and in a few days madam made me an osnaburg [33] shirt and French cap, and a coat out of one of my master's old coats. Then I threw away my greasy blanket and Indian flap, and looked as smart as—. And I never more saw the old friar, the Indian village, or my Indian master, till about fourteen years after, when I saw my old Indian master at Port Royal, whither I had been sent by the government with a flag of truce for

[32] That is, the Sieur de Chauffours, to whom Gyles was sold. His wife was Marguerite Guyon de Chauffours. The Frenchman's estate was at a place called *Jemseg*, "Great Marshes," where a small river of that name linked through a large lake with the St. John River. A small plantation, de Chauffours' estate had 65 acres under cultivation and some livestock.

[33] A heavy, coarse cotton fabric.

the exchange of prisoners; and again, about twenty-four years since, he came to St. John's to fort George, to see me, where I made him very welcome.[34]

My French master held a great trade with the Indians, which suited me very well, I being thorough in the languages of the tribes at Cape Sable and St. Johns.

I had not lived long with this gentleman before he committed to me the keys of his store, &c., and my whole employment was trading and hunting, in which I acted faithfully for my master, and never, knowingly, wronged him to the value of one farthing.

They spoke to me so much in Indian that it was some time before I was perfect in the French tongue. Monsieur generally had his goods from the men-of-war which came there annually from France.

In the year 1696, two men-of-war came to the mouth of the river. In their way they had captured the Newport, Captain Payson, and brought him with them. They made the Indians some presents, and invited them to join in an expedition to Pemmaquid. They accepted it, and soon after arrived there. Capt. Chubb, who commanded that post, delivered it up without much dispute to Monsieur D'Iberville, as I heard the gentleman say, with whom I lived, who was there present.[35]

Early in the spring I was sent with three Frenchmen to the mouth of the river, for provision, which came from Port Royal. We carried over land from the river to a large bay, where we were driven on an island by a north-east storm, where we were kept seven days, without any sustenance, for we expected a quick passage, and carried nothing with us. The wind continuing boisterous,

[34] After his release, Gyles, who could speak English, French, Maliseet, and Micmac, was in demand as an interpreter for peace negotiations and prisoner exchanges. In 1700 he was given a lieutenant's commission and began a military career that culminated in his appointment as commander of the garrison at St. George's River, near what is now Thomaston, Maine. Gyles died in 1755 in retirement at Roxbury, Massachusetts, at the age of seventy-four. See Stuart Trueman, *The Ordeal of John Gyles* (Toronto, 1966), and R. W. G. Vail, *The Voice of the Old Frontier* (Philadelphia, 1949).

[35] Two English warships cruising outside Menagoueche had been engaged by two French ships from Quebec under the command of d'Iberville and Bonaventure. One of the English ships escaped, but the *Newport* and her captain were captured. Captain Pascoe Chubb, the commander of the post at Pemaquid, was later court-martialed and relieved of his commission.

we could not return back, and the ice prevented our going forward. After seven days the ice broke up and we went forward, though we were so weak that we could scarce hear each other speak. The people at the mouth of the river were surprised to see us alive, and advised us to be cautious and abstemious in eating. By this time I knew as much of fasting as they, and dieted on broth, and recovered very well, as did one of the others; but the other two would not be advised, and I never saw any persons in greater distress, till at length they had action of the bowels, when they recovered.

A friar, who lived in the family, invited me to confession, but I excused myself as well as I could at that time. One evening he took me into his apartment in the dark and advised me to confess to him what sins I had committed. I told him I could not remember a thousandth part of them, they were so numerous. Then he bid me remember and relate as many as I could, and he would pardon them; signifying he had a bag to put them in. I told him I did not believe it was in the power of any but God to pardon sin. He asked me whether I had read the Bible. I told him I had, when I was a little boy, but it was so long ago I had forgotten most of it. Then he told me he did not pardon my sins, but when he knew them he prayed to God to pardon them; when, perhaps, I was at my sports and plays. He wished me well and hoped I should be better advised, and said he should call for me in a little time. Thus he dismissed me, nor did he ever call me to confession afterwards.

The gentleman with whom I lived had a fine field of wheat, in which great numbers of black-birds continually collected and made great havoc in it. The French said a Jesuit would come and banish them. He did at length come, and having all things prepared, he took a basin of holy water, a staff with a little brush, and having on his white robe, went into the field of wheat. I asked several prisoners who had lately been taken by privateers, and brought in there, viz. Mr. Woodbury, Cocks [Cox?] and Morgan, whether they would go and see the ceremony. Mr. Woodbury asked me whether I designed to go, and I told him yes. He then said I was as bad as a papist, and a d—d fool. I told him I believed as little of it as he did, but that I was inclined to see the ceremony, that I might tell it to my friends.

With about thirty following in procession, the Jesuit marched through the field of wheat, a young lad going before him bearing the holy water. Then the Jesuit, dipping his brush into the holy water, sprinkled the field on each side of him; a little bell jingling at the same time, and all singing the words *Ora pro nobis.*[36] At the end of the field they wheeled to the left about, and returned. Thus they passed and repassed the field of wheat, the black-birds all the while rising before them only to light behind. At their return I told a French lad that the friar had done no service, and recommended them to shoot the birds. The lad left me, as I thought, to see what the Jesuit would say to my observation, which turned out to be the case, for he told the lad that the sins of the people were so great that he could not prevail against those birds. The same friar as vainly attempted to banish the musketoes from Signecto, but the sins of the people there were also too great for him to prevail, but, on the other hand, it seemed that more came, which caused the people to suspect that some had come for the sins of the Jesuit also.

Some time after, Col. Hawthorne attempted the taking of the French fort up this river.[37] We heard of him some time before he came up, by the guard which Governor Villebon had stationed at the river's mouth. Monsieur, my master, had gone to France, and madam, his wife, advised with me. She desired me to nail a paper on the door of her house, which paper read as follows:

"I entreat the general of the English not to burn my house or barn, nor destroy my cattle. I don't suppose that such an army comes here to destroy a few inhabitants, but to take the fort above us. I have shown kindness to the English captives, as we were capacitated, and have bought two, of the Indians, and sent them to Boston. We have one now with us, and he shall go also when a convenient opportunity presents, and he desires it."

When I had done this, madam said to me, "Little English," [which was the familiar name she used to call me by,] "we have shown you kindness, and now it lies in your power to serve or disserve us, as you know where our goods are hid in the woods,

36 "Pray for us."

37 Hawthorne had combined forces with Maj. Benjamin Church, who had burned the French villages at Chignecto, for an attack on Nachouac.

and that monsieur is not at home. I could have sent you to the fort and put you under confinement, but my respect to you and your assurance of love to us have disposed me to confide in you; persuaded you will not hurt us or our affairs. And, now, if you will not run away to the English, who are coming up the river, but serve our interest, I will acquaint monsieur of it on his return from France, which will be very pleasing to him; and I now give my word, you shall have liberty to go to Boston on the first opportunity, if you desire it, or any other favor in my power shall not be denied you." I replied:

"Madam, it is contrary to the nature of the English to requite evil for good. I shall not endeavor to serve you and your interest. I shall not run to the English, but if I am taken by them I shall willingly go with them and yet endeavor not to disserve you eithr in your person or goods."

The place where we lived was called Hagimsack,[38] twenty-five leagues from the river's mouth, as I have before stated.

We now embarked and went in a large boat and canoe two or three miles up an eastern branch of the river that comes from a large pond,[39] and on the following evening sent down four hands to make discovery. And while they were sitting in the house the English surrounded it and took one of the four. The other three made their escape in the dark and through the English soldiers, and coming to us, gave a surprising account of affairs. Upon this news madam said to me, "Little English now you can go from us, but I hope you will remember your word." I said, "Madam, be not concerned. I will not leave you in this strait." She said, "I know not what to do with my two poor little babes!" I said, "Madam, the sooner we embark and go over the great pond the better." Accordingly we embarked and went over the pond. The next day we spoke with Indians, who were in a canoe, and they gave us an account that Signecto town was taken and burnt. Soon after we heard the great guns at Gov. Villebon's fort, which the English engaged several days. They killed one man, then drew off down the river; fearing to continue longer, for fear of being frozen in for the winter, which in truth they would have been.

[38] That is, Jemseg.
[39] Grand Lake.

Hearing no report of cannon for several days, I, with two others, went down to our house to make discovery. We found our young lad who was taken by the English when they went up the river. The general had shown himself so honorable, that on reading the note on our door, he ordered it not to be burnt, nor the barn. Our cattle and other things he preserved, except one or two and the poultry for their use. At their return they ordered the young lad to be put on shore. Finding things in this posture, we returned and gave madam an account of it.

She acknowledged the many favors which the English had showed her, with gratitude, and treated me with great civility. The next spring monsieur arrived from France in the man-of-war. He thanked me for my care of his affairs, and said he would endeavor to fulfil what madam had promised me.

Accordingly, in the year 1698, peace being proclaimed, a sloop came to the mouth of the river with ransom for one Michael Cooms. I put monsieur in mind of his word, telling him there was now an opportunity for me to go and see the English. He advised me to continue with him; said he would do for me as for his own, &c. I thanked him for his kindness, but rather chose to go to Boston, hoping to find some of my relations yet alive. Then he advised me to go up to the fort and take my leave of the governor, which I did, and he spoke very kindly to me. Some days after I took my leave of madam, and monsieur went down to the mouth of the river with me, to see me safely on board. He asked the master, Mr. Starkee, a Scotchman, whether I must pay for my passage, and if so, he would pay it himself rather than I should have it to pay at my arrival in Boston, but he gave me not a penny. The master told him there was nothing to pay, and that if the owner should make any demand he would pay it himself, rather than a poor prisoner should suffer; for he was glad to see any English person come out of captivity.

On the 13th of June, I took my leave of monsieur, and the sloop came to sail for Boston, where we arrived on the 19th of the same, at night. In the morning after my arrival, a youth came on board and asked many questions relating to my captivity, and at length gave me to understand that he was my little brother, who was at play with some other children at Pemmaquid when I was taken captive, and who escaped into the fort at that perilous time. He told me my elder brother, who made his escape from the farm, when it was taken, and our two little sisters, were alive, but that our mother had been dead some years. Then we went on shore and saw our elder brother.

On the 2d of August, 1689, I was taken, and on the 19th of June, 1698, I arrived at Boston; so that I was absent eight years, ten months, and seventeen days. In all which time, though I underwent extreme difficulties, yet I saw much of God's goodness. And may the most powerful and beneficent Being accept of this public testimony of it, and bless my experiences to excite others to confide in his all-sufficiency, through the infinite merits of JESUS CHRIST.

IV

An Account of the Captivity of Elizabeth Hanson, Now or Late of Kachecky, in New-England: Who, with Four of her Children and Servant-Maid, was taken captive by the Indians, and carried into Canada. Setting forth The various remarkable Occurrences, sore Trials, and wonderful Deliverances which befel them after their Departure, to the Time of their Redemption. Taken in Substance from her own Mouth, by Samuel Bownas.

†††

Elizabeth Hanson was taken captive with her four children and a maidservant at Kachecky, in Dover township, on August 27, 1724. She was redeemed by her husband, John Hanson, the following year after five months' captivity among the Indians and one month with the French. Three of Mrs. Hanson's children and the maid were ransomed with her, but the oldest daughter was not given up and later married a Frenchman. The narrative of Elizabeth Hanson provides little information of value about her Indian captors —not sufficient, indeed, even to identify them with any certainty. Apparently, she was taken by Indians from Maine or eastern Canada, for she was carried to Port Royal, where her husband found her. The significance of her narrative lies in its publishing history and successive editions, indicating the early and subtle shift toward literary "correctness" and stylization in the narratives of Indian captivity. There are two versions of the text of the Hanson narrative; the American editions follow one version and the English editions the other. The first American edition (Philadelphia, 1728) is titled God's Mercy Surmounting Man's Cruelty, Exemplified in the Captivity and Redemption of Elizabeth Hanson . . . ; *The second American edition was published in Philadelphia in 1754. The first English edition (London, 1760) is titled* An Account of the Captivity of Elizabeth Hanson . . . Taken in Substance from her own Mouth, by Samuel Bownas. *According to his own account, the Reverend Samuel Bownas visited Mrs. Hanson during his trip to America in 1727; he states in his autobiography,* An Account of the Life, Travels, and Christian Experiences of the Work of the Ministry of Samuel Bownas *(London, 1756), "I went to visit the widow Hanson, who had been taken into captivity by the Indians, an account of which I took from her own mouth. . . ." Yet Bownas nowhere claims authorship of the 1728 American version, and it appears without his name. Both American and English versions of the complete narrative are written in the first person, presumably by, or at least dictated by, Mrs. Hanson herself. The American editions are signed "E. H."; the English editions (1760, 1787, and 1791) assert that the narrative was taken down by Bownas from the captive's dictation. Yet the two versions are so close in content, structure, and matters other than style that they cannot have been taken down on separate occasions. Whoever brought out the first English edition, then, worked directly from a copy of the first or second American edition, very likely that of 1754. The American and English versions differ significantly, not in content but in treatment of the material. The 1728 and 1754 American editions are relatively natural and straightforward accounts told in the homely language of the period, while the 1760 London version has been lengthened, worked over, and "improved" in an attempt to give it a more polished style. The shift toward rhetorical emphasis and stylistic embellishment, begun here, would develop fully during the next hundred years in such narratives as* Remarkable Adventures of Jackson Johonnot *(1793), collected in the Manheim anthology; the overwrought* A True Narrative of the Sufferings of Mary Kinnan *(1795); the entirely fictionalized and sentimentalized* History of Maria Kittle *(1797); and ultimately in the pulp thrillers and formularized dime novels of the 1860's. Viewed in this light, the two versions of the Hanson narrative provide early evidence of the impulse toward stylization in the narratives of Indian captivity. The text of the "improved" English edition of 1760 is reprinted here, with representative examples from the American version of 1754 in the notes for comparison.*

††

The Remarkable Captivity of the Wife and Children of John Hanson.

ON the 27th of the Sixth Month, called August,[1] 1725, my husband and all our men-servants being abroad, eleven Indians, armed with tomahawks and guns, who had some time before been skulking about the fields, and watching an opportunity of our mens absence, came furiously into the house. No sooner were they entered, than they murdered one of my children upon the spot; intending no doubt, by this act of cruelty, to strike the greater degree of terror into the minds of us who survived. After they had thus done, their captain came towards me, with all the appearance of rage and fury it is possible to imagine: nevertheless, upon my earnest request for quarter, I prevailed with him to grant it.

I had with me a servant-maid and six children; but two of my little-ones were at that time playing in the orchard. My youngest child was but fourteen days old; and myself, of consequence, in a poor weak condition, and very unfit to endure the hardships I afterwards met with, as by the sequel will appear.

The next step they took was to rifle the house; which they did with much hurry and precipitation; being apprehensive in all probability of a surprise. And as it was late in the afternoon, they pack'd up what linen, woollen, and other things they liked, and forthwith turned us out of the house.[2]

1 England and the American colonies adopted the New Style calendar in March, 1752; consequently, August was considered the sixth month.

2 Compare the same paragraph in the 1754 version: "They went to rifling the

Being now at the door, my two children who had been playing in the orchard (the one six, the other four years of age) came in sight; and being terrified at the appearance of the naked Indians, they cried aloud. On which one of the Indians ran up to them; and taking one under each arm, brought them to us. My maid prevailed with the biggest to be still; but the other would not be pacified by any means, but continued shrieking and crying very much. Wherefore, to ease themselves of the noise, and prevent the danger of a discovery that might arise from it, they made no more to do, but knock'd out its brains before my face.

I bore this as well as the nature of so mournful a circumstance would permit; not daring to discover much of my uneasiness, lest it should provoke them to commit the like outrage upon the rest: [3] but could have been glad they had kept out of sight till we had been gone from the house.

The Indians having now killed two of my children, the next thing they did was to scalp them; a practice common with them whenever they kill any English people. This they do by cutting off the skin from the crown of the head; which they take with them as an evidence of the number they have slain. And it has been currently reported, that the French, in their wars with the English, have given the Indians a pecuniary reward for every scalp they brought to them.[4]

---

house in a great hurry, (fearing, as I suppose, a surprise from our people, it being late in the afternoon,) and pack'd up some linen, woolen and what other things pleased them best, and when they had done what they would, they turned out of the house immediately." The diction and syntax of the two passages show marked contrasts: e.g., in the 1760 version the substitution/addition of such words as *precipitation, apprehensive,* and *forthwith;* the insertion of transitional devices ("The next step..."; "And as..."); the change to the infinitive form of *rifling;* and the shifting of the modifier "late in the afternoon" from one clause to another. The result, ironically, is not only to spoil the immediacy and naturalness of the earlier version but actually to render it ambiguous in one instance and distorted in another: "it being late in the afternoon" (1754) is meant to explain the great hurry of the Indians, who knew that other settlers might be returning from the fields at that time of day; but "And as it was late in the afternoon" (1760), modifying the clause "they pack'd...," is, at best, ambiguous and makes little sense in that position. The distortion occurs in the difference in meaning between "they turned out of the house" (1754) and "they... turned us out of the house" (1760), which suggests that the Hansons also went outside, not just the Indians.

3 1754: "I bore this as well as I could, not daring to appear disturbed or to show much uneasiness, lest they should do the same to the others."

4 An example not only of increased stylization but also of alteration to conform with the heightened English sentiment against the French during the final

This being done, they prepared to leave the house in great haste, without committing any other violence than taking what they had packed up, together with myself and little babe fourteen days old, my little boy of six years, one daughter about sixteen, another about fourteen, and my maid-servant.

It was now, as I said before, but fourteen days since my lying-in; and being very tender and weakly, and turned out from a warm room, with every thing suitable to my circumstances, it increased the severity of the hardships I underwent exceedingly. Nevertheless I found the case was such, that I must either go or die; for I could make no resistance, neither would any persuasions avail.

Accordingly we began our journey, each having some of the plunder to carry, and I my infant: the other three were able to travel alone. But my new master, the Indian captain, was sometimes humane enough to carry my babe in his arms; which I looked upon as a singular favour, because he had besides a very heavy burden, and considerably more than he could take up without the help of his men.

We passed through several swamps and brooks; carefully avoiding all beaten paths, and every track that looked like a road, lest we should be surprised by our footsteps.

We travelled that night I suppose near ten miles in a direct line, and then we halted. The Indians kindled a fire, and we took up our quarters by it. They took it in turn to rest themselves, while a party of them kept watch, in order to prevent a surprise. For my part, I was very wet, as well as weary; and having no other lodging but the cold ground in the open woods, could get but little rest. Nevertheless, when day-light appeared, we set forward again, and travelled very hard all that day, passing through several swamps, rivers, and brooks, and still avoiding all beaten paths, for the reason already mentioned.

When night came on, I found myself again very wet, and heartily tired, having the same lodging, the cold ground and open woods.—Thus did we travel for twenty-six days successively, and

phase of the French and Indian War; the 1754 version reads "whenever they kill any enemies" for "whenever they kill any English people," and states simply that the Indians carry scalps with them "for a testimony and evidence that they have killed so many, receiving sometimes a reward for every scalp."

in general very hard; though sometimes we were helped a little by water, over lakes and ponds.—We climbed up abundance of high mountains; some of which were so steep, that I was fain to crawl up them on my hands and knees: But when I was under these difficulties, my Indian master would for the most part carry my infant: and this I esteemed as a favour from the Almighty, in that his heart was so tenderly inclined to assist me. Nay, he would sometimes take my very blanket; so that, having no incumbrance, I was enabled to give some assistance to my little boy, and now-and-then carry him in my arms.

When we came to any difficult place, my master would lend me his hand: or if it were steep, he frequently used to push me up before him. In all which he discovered more civility and humanity than I could have expected; and for which I was thankful to God, as the moving cause.

We had now some very great runs of water and brooks to pass; in wading through which we sometimes met with great difficulty, being frequently up to our middles, and some of the children to their shoulders and chins. But the Indians carried my babe (that is, my little boy) through them on their shoulders.

At the side of one of these rivers, the Indians would have had my eldest daughter sing them a song. Whereupon a passage in the cxxxviith Psalm was brought to her remembrance; to wit, *By the rivers of* Babylon *there we sat down. Yea, we wept, when we remembered* Zion. *We hanged our harps on the willows in the midst thereof. For they that carried us away captive, required of us a song; and they that wasted us, required of us mirth.*

When my poor child had given me this account, it affected me greatly, and my heart was filled with sorrow. Yet on her account I rejoiced that she had so good an inclination; which she still further manifested, by wishing for a Bible, that we might have the comfort of reading the Holy Text at leisure times, for our spiritual consolation under the afflictions we then suffered.

Next to the difficulty of crossing the rivers, were the prodigious swamps and thickets, which were very hard to pass through. But here also my master would sometimes lend me his hand; and as they passed through quickly one after the other, it became pretty tolerable for the hindmost. But the greatest difficulty of all, and which deserves first to be named, was our want of proper sustenance: for we were now reduced to very great extremity: having often nothing to eat but pieces of old beaver-skin match-coats,[5] which the Indians, in their journey to our settlement, had concealed (for they came to us naked, as I said before), but now, in their return, took along with them. They were used more for food than raiment, being cut out in long narrow straps, of which they gave us some little pieces. These, after their example, we laid upon the fire till the furr was sindged off, and then ate them as dainty morsels; experimentally knowing, that *to the hungry every bitter thing is sweet.*

Of this diet, mean as it was, we had but a scanty allowance. And what still further increased my affliction, was the complaints and moans of my poor children. Sometimes indeed the Indians caught a squirrel, or a beaver; at others, we met with nuts, berries, and roots; and sometimes we ate the bark of trees; but had no corn for a long while; till a party of the younger Indians went back and brought some from the English inhabitants, of which they gave us a very short allowance. But when they killed a beaver, we lived high while it lasted; as their custom was to allow me the guts and garbage for myself and children; but they would by no means suffer us to wash and cleanse them; which occasioned this kind of diet to be very loathsome; and indeed nothing but pining hunger would have made it in the least degree tolerable.

My distresses did not all center here. I had yet another affliction no less severe than the former; and this was it. By daily travel and hard living, my milk was almost dried up; and how to preserve my poor babe's life, was a matter of no little concern to me; having many times no other sustenance for it than cold water; which I took into my mouth, and dropped on my breast for it to suck in when I gave it the teat, with what little milk it could draw from thence. At other times, when I could procure any broth of beaver's guts, I fed it with that: by which means, and keeping it as warm as I could, its life was preserved till I came to Canada, where I met with better food.

5 "Match-coats" were mantles or similarly loose coverings of fur worn extensively by New England Indians. The term derives from the Powhatan *matshcore.*

When we were pretty far advanced in our journey, the Indians divided; and, to our great sorrow, divided us amongst them. My eldest daughter was taken away first, and carried to another part of the country, far distant from us, And we had not travelled far, before they parted again, and took from me my second daughter and my servant-maid; so that I had now only the babe at my breast, and my little boy of six years old. We three remained with the captain; but my daughter and servant underwent very great sufferings after they were taken from us; travelling very hard for three days together, without any sustenance but cold water; and on the third day the servant fell down in a swoon as dead; at which the Indians seemed surprised, and began to shew some signs of tenderness; not being willing to lose any of their captives by death, after they had brought them so near their own home; hoping, no doubt in case they lived, to obtain a considerable price for their ransom. Accordingly, in a few days after this, they drew near their journey's end, where they found greater plenty of corn and other food; but flesh often fell very short, as they had no other way of procuring it but hunting.

It was not long before my daughter and servant were parted also; and my daughter's master falling sick, he was thereon disabled from hunting. All their corn was likewise spent; and so great were their distresses, that they were compelled to feed on the bark of trees for a whole week, being almost famished to death.[6]

In this sore extremity it was providentially ordered, that some other Indians, hearing of their misery, came to visit them (for they are very kind and helpful one to another) and brought with them the guts and liver of a beaver; which, as they were but four in number (viz. the Indian and his wife and daughter, and my daughter) afforded them a good repast.

By this time my master and our company got to their journey's end; where we met with better entertainment, having corn, venison, wild fowl, and whatever else the Indians took in hunting. But

[6] 1754: "It was not long ere my daughter and servant were likewise parted, and my daughter's master being sick, was not able to hunt for flesh; neither had they any corn in that place, but were forced to eat bark of trees for a whole week."

my master's family being fifteen in number, it sometimes occasioned us to have very short commons, especially when game was scarce.

Our lodging was still on the cold ground, in a poor little wigwam, which is a kind of small shelter, made with rinds of trees and matts for its covering, after the manner of a tent. These are so easily set up and taken down, that they often remove them from place to place. Our shoes, stockings, and other clothes being worn out in this long journey through bushes and swamps, and the season coming on very sharp and cold, we were poorly defended from the injuries of the weather; which now grew so severe, that one of my own feet, one of my babe's, and both my little boy's, were frozen with the cold. But although this brought no small exercise upon me, yet through mercy we all did well.

Notwithstanding we were now come to the end of our journey, the Indians abode not long in one place; but often removed from one spot to another, carrying their wigwams, which were not a little troublesome, whithersoever they went.—These frequent removals were made for the sake of hunting; but were attended with great inconveniences, by reason of the dampness of the ground whereon the wigwams were pitched; which rendered our lodging much more unpleasant and unwholesome than if we had continued in one place.[7]

At length we arrived at the Indian fort, where many of the people came to visit my master and his family, and congratulate him on his safe return, and the success of his expedition. Publick rejoicings were made upon it (which in their way perhaps were a kind of thanksgiving); and these were attended with dancing, firing of guns, beating on hollow trees instead of drums, shouting, drinking, and feasting for several days together with much excess.

But while the Indians were in their mirth and jollity, my mind was earnestly exercised towards the Lord, that I, with my dear

7 1754: "Now, though we got to our journey's end, we were never long in one place, but very often removed from one place to another, carrying our wigwams with us, which we could do without much difficulty. This, being for the convenience of hunting, made our accommodations much more unpleasant, than if we had continued in one place, by reason the coldness and dampness of the ground, where our wigwams were pitched, made it very unwholesome, and unpleasant lodging."

The unhappy sojourns of Elizabeth Hanson, Robert Eastburn, and John Marrant.

children, who were now separated from me, might be preserved from repining against God under our present affliction. But that, on the other hand, we might have our dependence upon him, who rules in the hearts of men, and can do what he pleases in the kingdoms of the earth; knowing that his care is over those who put their trust in him.—But I found it very difficult to keep my mind under that patient resignation, so necessary to be found in such sore trials and afflictions as then fell to my lot: Being under various fears and doubts concerning my daughters, who were separated from me, which greatly increased my troubles: so that I can say my afflictions were not to be set forth by words to the full extent of them.

We had not long been arrived, before my master went abroad to hunt for provisions for the family, and was absent about a week. Before he set out, he ordered me to procure wood, and gather nuts: in doing which I was very diligent, during the time of his absence, cutting the wood, and putting it up in order. But no sooner was he returned, than I quickly perceived he was very much displeased; for he had met with no success in his hunting expedition; and so strongly did his disappointment work upon him, that he began to revenge it on us his captives. He allowed me, however, a little boiled corn for myself and child; but looking upon us with a very angry countenance, he threw a stick at me with so much violence, as plainly demonstrated that he grudged us the food we had received from him.

Hereupon his squaw and daughter broke forth in a violent fit of crying; which occasioned me to fear that some mischief was intended against us; and in consequence of this I instantly withdrew from his presence into another wigwam. He soon followed me; and in great fury tore my blanket from my back; then taking my little boy from me, he knocked him down as he went along before him. But the poor child, not being hurt, but only frightened with the fall, started up, and ran away without crying.

My Master then left us; but his wife's mother came and sat down by me, telling me I must sleep there that night. After this she went out for a while, and then returned with a small skin to cover my feet; giving me to understand withal, that my master was now determined to kill us.

I was very desirous to know the cause of this determination; urging to her that I had been very diligent, during his absence, to do as he had ordered me; and in the best manner I was able endeavoured to make her sensible how unreasonable he was; although we had no other means of making ourselves intelligible to each other but by signs. She still continued to make signs to me that I must die; advising me (by pointing upwards) to pray to God; and endeavouring, by other signs, and tears intermixed, to instruct me in that which was most needful, to prepare for death, which now appeared to be nigh at hand from my bloody master; who had conceived evil against me without any just cause; but his ill success in hunting, and the scarcity of provisions, had made him quite outrageous.

The poor old squaw, his mother-in-law, was very kind and tender to me; and all that night would not leave me; but came and laid herself down at my feet, signifying her intention to use her endeavours to appease his wrath.—For my own part, I got but little rest that night; though my babe slept sweetly by my side: but I dreaded the tragical design of my master, and looked every hour when he would enter the wigwam to execute his bloody purpose.—But here again kind providence interposed. For being weary with hunting, and having toiled in the woods without success, he went to rest, and forgot to put in practice the horrid purpose he had formed.

The morning being come, he went forth again to hunt. I dreaded his return emptyhanded; and prayed in my heart that he might take something to satisfy his hunger, and quell his ill humour. And before he had been long gone, he returned with booty; having shot some wild ducks. He now appeared in a better temper, and ordered the fowls to be dressed speedily. For these Indians, whenever they are in possession of plenty, spend it as freely as they take it: often consuming in the space of two days, through gluttony and drunkenness, as much as with prudent management might serve a week. And thus they live, for the most part, either in riot and excess; or undergo very great hardships for want of necessaries.

As this was a time of plenty, I felt the comfort of it, together with the rest of the family; having a part sent to me and my children; which was very acceptable.—I was now ready to think the bitterness of death was past for this time, and my spirit grew a little easier; yet this lasted not long before my master threatened my life again. But of this I took notice, that whenever this ill temper predominated, he was always pinched with hunger; and that when success attended his hunting, he was much better-humored; though indeed he was naturally hot and passionate, and often threw sticks and stones at me, or whatever else lay in his way, by reason whereof my life was continually in danger; but that God whose providence is over all his works, so preserved me, that I never received any great damage from this Indian; for which mercy I ever desire to be thankful to my Creator.

When flesh was scarce, we were only allowed the guts and garbage; but were not permitted to cleanse them any other way than just by emptying the dung out of them, and afterwards boiling them together with the broth of fowls; which would have been extremely nauseous, had not hunger compelled us to eat; but in time this kind of food, which often fell to our lot, became pretty tolerable to a keen appetite; though at another time I could by no means have dispensed with it.[8] And this led me to consider that none are able to say what hardships they can suffer till the trial comes upon them. For that which in time past I had thought not fit for food in my own family, I should now have esteemed a sweet morsel, and a dainty dish.

By this time I was reduced so low, through fatigue of spirits, hard labour, mean diet, and the frequent want of natural rest, that my milk was intirely dried up again, and my helpless babe very poor and weak, appearing to be little more than skin and bones; for I could perceive every joint of it, from one end of its back to the other; and how to procure any thing that might suit its weak appetite, I was at a very great loss. Whereupon one of the Indian squaws, perceiving my uneasiness, began some discourse with me, and withal advised me to take the kernels of walnuts, and after I had cleansed them, to beat them up with a little water; which ac-

[8] 1754: "Not being permitted to cleanse the guts any other wise than emptying the dung, without so much as washing them, as before is noted; in that filthy pickle we must boil them and eat them, which was very unpleasant. But hunger made up that difficulty, so that this food, which was very often our lot, became pretty tolerable to a sharp appetite, which otherwise could not have been dispensed with."

cordingly I did, and the water looked like milk. Then she bid me add to this water a little of the finest Indian corn meal, and just boil it up together. I did so; and found it very palatable, and soon perceived that it nourished my babe, for it quickly began to thrive and look well; which gave me great comfort.—I afterwards understood, that with this kind of diet the Indian children were often fed.

But the comfort I received on my dear child's recovery from the brink of death, was soon mixed with bitterness and trouble. For my master observing its thriving condition, used often to look upon it, and say, that when it was fat enough, he'd have it killed and eaten. Pursuant to this threat, he obliged me to fetch a stick, which he said he had prepared to roast my babe upon. And as soon as I had brought it, he made me sit down by him, and undress the infant. The child now being naked, he began to feel its arms, legs, and thighs; and having passed this examination upon it, he informed me, that as it was not yet fat enough, I must dress it again, till it was in better case. But notwithstanding he thus acted, I could not persuade myself he was in earnest, but that he did it with a view to afflict and aggravate me: neither could I think but that our lives would be preserved from his barbarous hands, by the overruling power of Him, in whose Providence I put my trust both night and day.

A little while after this, my master fell sick; and during his illness, as he lay in his wigwam, he ordered his own son to beat mine. But the old Squaw, the Indian boy's grandmother, would not suffer him to do it. Whereupon the father was so much provoked, that he seized hold on a stick, very sharp at one end, and threw it at my little boy with such violence, that it struck him so severe a blow on the breast, as made his countenance change as pale as death, through pain.—I intreated him not to cry; and though he was but six years old, and his breast very much bruised, he bore it with wonderful patience, not so much as once complaining. So that the patience of the child restrained his barbarity; which it is hardly to be doubted would have transported him further in his resentment, had he cried; for complaining always aggravated his passion greatly, and his anger grew hotter upon it.

A short time after on the same day, he got upon his feet; but was much out of order. But notwithstanding he was sick, his wife and daughter let me know that he still purposed to kill us; which made me now very fearful, unless Providence interposed, in what manner it would end.—I therefore laid down my child; and going out of his presence, went to cut wood for the fire, as I used to do, hoping this would in part abate his passion; but I still feared that before I returned to the wigwam, my two children would be killed.

In this situation I had no way left but to cast my care upon God, who had hitherto helped and protected me and mine.—But while my master remained in this feud, the old squaw (his mother-in-law) left him; but my mistress and her daughter still remained with him in the wigwam.

As soon as I returned with my wood, the daughter came to me. I asked her if her father had killed my children? She answered me by a sign that he had not; and seemed to be pleased that he had forborn it. For instead of venting his fury on me and mine, the Lord, in whom I had put my trust, interposed in the needful time, and mercifully delivered us from the cruel purpose he had threatened to put in execution.[9] Nor was he himself without some sense of the same, and that the hand of God was concerned therein, as he afterwards confessed to those who were about him. For a little time after he had got upon his feet he was struck with violent pains, and such a grievous sickness, that he uttered his complaints in a very doleful and hideous manner. Which when I understood (not having yet seen him) I went to another squaw, who was come to visit him, and could speak English, and asked her if my mistress (for so I used to call the Indian's wife) thought my master would die? She answered, it was very likely he would; for he grew worse and worse. I then told her he had struck my little boy a dreadful blow, without any provocation; and had threatened, in his fury, to kill us all. The squaw confessed that the abuse he had offered to my child, and the mischief he had done him, was the cause why God afflicted him with that sickness and pain; and told me that he had promised never to abuse us in such sort again.

9 1754: "When I came with my wood, the daughter came to me, whom I asked if her father had killed my child, and she made me a sign, no, with a countenance that seemed pleased it was so; for instead of his further venting his passion on me and my children, the Lord in whom I trusted did seasonable interpose, and I took it as a merciful deliverance from him."

After this he recovered; but I do not remember that from thenceforward he either struck me or my children so as to hurt us, or with that mischievous intent as he before used to do; nor was he so passionate afterwards as he had been accustomed to be.—All which I looked upon as the Lord's doing, and marvellous it was in my eyes.

A few weeks after this, my master made another remove; which was the largest he had ever made, being two days journey, and mostly over the ice. The first day the ice was bare; but some snow falling on the second, it made it very difficult to travel over. I received much hurt by frequent falls: having, besides, the care of my infant, which increased my trouble not a little. It was night when we arrived at our camp; and I was ordered to go and fetch water; but having sat a while on the cold ground, I could neither stand nor go, by reason that my limbs were so benumbed with cold. Yet I dared not refuse; and therefore attempted it by crawling on my hands and knees; but a young Indian squaw, belonging to another family, being come to see our people, she in compassion took the kettle; and knowing where to go, which I did not, fetched the water for me; which I took as a great favour, in that her heart was inclined to do me this service.

I now saw the design of this journey. My master, as I suppose, being weary of keeping us, was willing to make what ransom he could of us; and therefore went farther towards the French settlements, leaving his family at this place; where they had a great dance, several other Indians coming to our people. This held some time; and while they were employed in it, I got out of their way as far as I could into a corner of the wigwam. But every time they came by me in their dancing, they would bow my head towards the ground, and frequently kick me with great fury. Divers of them were barefooted, and the rest had only mocksans on. The dance lasted some time; and they made, in their manner, great rejoicing and noise.

It was not many days before my master returned from the French; but in such an ill humour, that he would not suffer me to abide in his presence. I had a little shelter made with boughs; having first digged through the snow, which was then pretty deep, quite to the ground. In this hole I and my poor children were put to lodge; and as the weather was then very sharp, and the frosts hard (it being then the month called January) our lodging was extremely bad. But our stay was not long in this wretched place, before my master took me and my children to the French, in order to get a chapman [10] for us. When we came among them, I was exposed to sale, and the price my master put upon me was 800 livres. But nobody appearing disposed to comply with his demands, and a Frenchman offering no more than 600 livres, it threw him into such a rage, that he said in his passion, if he could not have his price, he would burn me and the babe in the view of the city of Port-Royal. The Frenchman bade him make the fire; and added, "I will help you, if you think that will do you more good than 600 livres;" calling him fool, and roughly bidding him begone: but at the same time he was very civil to me; and for my encouragement bade me be of good cheer, for I should be redeemed, and not go back with the Indian again.—I was obliged, however, to retire with my master that night; but the next morning I was redeemed for 600 livres.

In driving the bargain with my master, the Frenchman asked him why he demanded so much for the little babe's ransom? urging, that when it came to have its belly-full it would die. The Indian said, No; it would not die; having already lived twenty-six days on nothing but water; and that he believed it was a devil. The Frenchman said, No; but the child is ordered for longer life; and it hath pleased God to preserve it to admiration. My master answered, No; that was not the case; but it was a devil; and he believed it would not die, unless they took a hatchet, and knocked out its brains.

This ended their discourse; and I was redeemed as aforesaid, with my little babe, for 600 livres. My little boy was likewise redeemed for an additional sum. And by this means we exchanged our lodging and diet much for the better, the French being kind and civil to me beyond what I could expect or desire.

The day after I was redeemed, a Romish priest took my babe from me; and according to their custom they baptized it; urging that if it died before, it would be damned; and accordingly they

10 Buyer.

gave it the name of Mary Ann Trossways; telling it, that if it died then, it would be saved, being baptized.[11] And my landlord also, speaking to the priest who performed the ceremony, said, it would be well if Trossways were to die then, being in a state of salvation. But the priest replied, that the child having been miraculously preserved through so many hardships, it might be designed for some great work, and, by its life being continued, might glorify God much more than if it were to die then. A very seasonable remark; and I wish it may prove true.

I had then been about five months among the Indians, and one month with the French, when my dear husband, to my unspeakable joy and comfort, came to me. He was much concerned for the redemption of his children; two of our daughters, and the servant-maid, being still in the hands of the Indians; and only myself and the two little-ones redeemed.

Accordingly, after much difficulty and trouble, he recovered our younger daughter and the maid; but we could by no means obtain our eldest from them. For the squaw to whom she was given had a son; and she intended a match between my daughter and him, hoping in time to prevail upon her to comply: for the Indians are seldom guilty of any indecent carriage towards their captive women, unless much overtaken in liquor.— [12] The affection they had for my daughter made them refuse all offers and terms of ransom. So that after my husband had waited, and used his utmost endeavours to obtain our child, we were at last obliged to depart homewards, and leave our daughter, to our great grief, amongst the Indians.

We accordingly set forward over the lake, with three of our children and servant, in company with sundry others; and, by the

[11] 1754: "But the next day after I was redeemed, the Romish Priest took my babe from me, and according to their custom, they baptized her, urging if she died before that, she would be damned, like some of our modern pretended reformed priests, and they gave her a name as pleased them best, which was Mary Ann Trossways, telling me my child, if she now died, would be saved, being baptized." Note the excision in the 1760 version of the phrase "like some of our modern pretended reformed priests."

[12] This is consistent with most reports of captives among the eastern tribes. See Rowlandson narrative, note 54, and Manheim anthology, note 21. The 1754 version of the Hanson narrative reads here: "The Indians are very civil towards their captive women, not offering any incivility by any indecent carriage, (unless they be much overcome in liquor,) which is commendable in them, so far."

kindness of Providence, got well home on the 1st of the Seventh Month, called September, in the year 1725. From which it appears, that I had been from home amongst the Indians and French, and on my journey, twelve months and twenty-six days.[13] In which series of time, the many deliverances and wonderful providences of God to us, have been, and I hope will remain to be, a continued obligation ever to live in fear, love, and obedience to God Almighty; hoping, by the assistance of his grace, with meekness and wisdom to approve myself in holiness of life, and godliness of conversation, to the praise of him who has called me; who is God, blessed for ever.

But my dear husband could not enjoy himself with satisfaction, because of the absence of our dear daughter Sarah, who, as I said before, was left behind. For which reason, not being willing to omit any thing which lay in his power for procuring her redemption, he concluded to make a second attempt. In order to this he began his journey about the 19th of the Second Month,[14] 1727, in company with a kinsman and his wife, who went to redeem some of their children, and were successful enough to obtain their desire. But my dear husband was taken sick by the way, and grew worse and worse. And as he was very sensible he should not get over it, he told my kinsman, that if it were the Lord's will he should die in the wilderness, he was freely given up to it. And at length, under a good composure of mind, and sensible to his last moments, he died, as near as they could guess, at the distance of about halfway between Albany and Canada, in my kinsman's arms; and is, I doubt not, at rest in the Lord. And although mine and my childrens loss is very great, yet his gain I hope is much greater. I therefore desire and pray that the Lord will enable me patiently to submit to his will in all things;—earnestly beseeching the God and Father of all our mercies to be a father to my fatherless children, and give them that blessing which makes truly rich, and adds no sorrow with it; that as they grow in years, they may grow in grace, and experience the joy of his salvation, which is come by Jesus Christ, our Lord and Savior. Amen.

[13] The 1754 version states "about twelve months and six days," which is more accurate.

[14] That is, April. See n. 1, above.

After the death of my dear husband, my kinsman proceeded on his journey; and when he arrived at Canada, he used all possible means to obtain my daughter's freedom, but all his endeavours proved ineffectual; she being still in the hands of the same old squaw, who designed at any rate to oblige my daughter to marry her son, and for that reason utterly rejected any proposal for her redemption. But herein she missed of her aim; for whilst she was endeavouring to bring my daughter to consent, a Frenchman, who had taken a great liking to her, interposed. He spared no pains by persuasion to gain her consent; setting before her the immediate privilege she would obtain by becoming his wife, to wit, her freedom from captivity among the Indians; for in such a case it seems they have no pretence to detain their captives any longer after marrying a Frenchman; but the woman then becomes the sole property of her husband. These remonstrances and persuasions, added to the improbability of her being redeemed from the Indians by any other means, at last prevailed; and accordingly she was married to the Frenchman, and settled amongst that people.[15]

Thus, as well as I was able by the help of memory (not having been in a condition to keep a journal) I have given a short but true account of some of the remarkable trials, and wonderful deliverances that have befallen me and mine. Which I never intended to publish, but that I hoped the merciful kindness and goodness of God might thereby be manifested; and the reader stirred up with more care and fear to righteousness and humility; and then will my purpose be answered.

N. B. The substance of the foregoing account was taken from her own mouth by Samuel Bownas. And in the Seventh Month,

[15] 1754: "Now, though my husband died, by reason of which his labor was ended, yet my kinsman prosecuted the thing, and left no stone unturned, that he thought, or could be advised, was proper to the obtaining my daughter's freedom; but could by no means prevail; for, as is before said, she being in another part of the country distant from where I was, and given to an old squaw, who intended to marry her in time to her son, using what persuasion she could to effect her end, sometimes by fair means, and sometimes by severe. In the meantime a Frenchman interposed, and they by persuasions enticing my child to marry, in order to obtain her freedom, by reason that those captives married by the French are, by that marriage, made free among them, the Indians having then no pretence longer to keep them as captives; she therefore was prevailed upon, for the reasons afore assigned, to marry, and she was accordingly married to the said Frenchman."

called September, 1741, Samuel Hopwood was with her, and received the relation much to the same purpose; at which time he saw the child (then grown a young woman) who was sucking at her breast when she was carried into captivity.

FINIS.

V

A Faithful Narrative, of the many Dangers and Sufferings, as well as wonderful Deliverances of Robert Eastburn, during his late Captivity among the Indians: Together with some Remarks upon the Country of Canada, and the Religion, and Policy of its Inhabitants; the whole intermixed with devout Reflections.

†††

Robert Eastburn's Faithful Narrative *(1758) is considered one of the valuable, because one of the undoubtedly original, documents relating to the French and Indian War. A member of a party en route to the frontier post of Oswego, New York, to engage in the Indian trade, Eastburn was captured in 1756 by a force of French soldiers and Indians between the Mohawk River and Wood Creek. Carried to Canada, where he was adopted into an Indian family, he remained for almost two years. The events leading to the battle in which Eastburn was captured are briefly these: with the defeat of Washington at Fort Necessity in 1755 and the French triumph over Braddock's forces at Fort Duquesne in the same year, the ravages of the French and Indian wars that for fifty years had desolated the frontiers of New England began to spread over the Alleghenies. It was in the midst of the aggressions of these war parties that Robert Eastburn, a blacksmith and a deacon in the First Presbyterian Church of Philadelphia, traveled into the wilderness bound for the most advanced post on the American frontier, Oswego. At the opening of the campaign of 1756, the French held Ticonderoga, as well as Fort Duquesne, and all borders of the Great Lakes except the one post of Oswego. The English planned an expedition to attack Niagara and another to try to reduce Ticonderoga and Crown Point. In concert with this maneuver, large quantities of English provisions had been sent forward toward Oswego, many of which were piled in the storehouses at the carrying place between the Mohawk and Wood Creek. The French commander Vaudreuil moved to destroy the forts and stores at the carrying place by sending a force of 360 men—soldiers, rangers, and Indians. This force arrived at the road leading from Fort Williams to Fort Bull on the morning of March 26, 1756. There they found a party of twelve teamsters, including an unnamed Negro, who were on their way with goods to Fort Bull. These they attacked, killing or capturing all the party except the Negro, who escaped to Fort Williams to give the alarm that Eastburn reports in the opening lines of his narrative. Fort Williams immediately sent out a scouting party; in this party marched Deacon Robert Eastburn. The first edition of Eastburn's* Faithful Narrative *was printed in Philadelphia by William Dunlap in 1758 and reprinted the same year in Boston by Green & Russell. The recommendatory Preface is by the Reverend Gilbert Tennent, of the Philadelphia Presbyterian Meeting. The narrative was subsequently reprinted in Ashbel Green's* Memoirs of Rev. Joseph Eastburn *(Philadelphia, 1828) and in the second edition of that work (Hartford, 1843). The Burrows edition (Cleveland, 1904), a reprint of Dunlap's original 1758 edition, is the basis for the text which follows.*

††

Preface

Candid Reader, The Author (and Subject) of the ensuing Narrative (who is a Deacon of our Church, and has been so for many Years) is of such an established good Character, that he needs no Recommendation of others, where he is known: a Proof of which, was the general Joy of the Inhabitants of this City, occasioned by his Return from a miserable Captivity! Together with the Readiness of divers Persons, to contribute to the Relief of himself, and necessitous Family, without any Request of his, or the least Motion of that Tendency!—But, seeing the following Sheets, are like to spread into many Places, where he is not known, permit me to say, That upon long Acquaintance, I have found him to be a Person of Candor, Integrity, and sincere Piety; whose Testimony, may with Safety, be depended upon; which give his Narrative the greater Weight, and may induce to read it with the greater Pleasure; The Design of it is evidently Pious, the Matters contained in it, and Manner of handling them, will, I hope, be esteemed by the Impartial, to be entertaining and improving: I heartily wish it may, by the divine Benediction, be of great and durable Service. I am thy sincere Servant, in the Gospel of Jesus Christ.

GILBERT TENNENT

PHILADELPHIA,
JAN. 19, 1758.

KIND READERS, On my Return from my Captivity, I had no Thoughts of publishing any Observations of mine to the World, in this Manner; as I had no Opportunity to keep a Journal, and my Memory being broken, and Capacity small, I was disinclined to undertake it; but a Number of my Friends were pressing in their Perswasions, that I should do it; with whose Motion I complied, from a sincere Regard to God, my King, and Country, so far as I know my own Heart: The following Pages contain, as far as I can remember, the most material Passages that happened within the Compass of my Observation, while a Prisoner in Canada; the Facts therein related are certainly true, but the Way of representing some Things especially, is not so regular, clear, and strong, as I could wish; but I trust it will be some Apology, that I am not so much acquainted with Performances of this Kind, as many others; who may be hereby excited to give better Representatives of Things, far beyond my Knowledge.

I remain Your unfeigned Well-Wisher,
and humble Servant,
ROBERT EASTBURN.

PHILADELPHIA,
JAN. 19, 1758.

A Faithful Narrative, &c.

About Thirty Tradesmen, and myself, arrived at Captain William's Fort,[1] (at the Carrying Place) in our Way to Oswego, the 26th of March, 1756; who informed me, that he was like to be cumbered in the Fort, and therefore advised us to take the Indian-House for our Lodging. About Ten o'Clock next Day, a Negro Man[2] came running down the Road, and reported, That our Slaymen were all taken by the Enemy; Captain Williams, on hearing this, sent a Serjeant, and about 12 Men, to see if it was true; I being at the Indian-House, and not thinking myself safe there, in Case of an Attack, and being also sincerely willing to serve my King and Country, in the best Manner I could in my present Circumstances, asked him if he would take Company? He replied, with all his Heart! Hereupon, I fell into the Rear, with my arms, and marched after them; when we had advanced about a Quarter of a Mile, we heard a Shot, followed with doleful Cries of a dying man, which excited me to advance, in order to discover the Enemy, who I soon perceived were prepared to receive us: In this difficult Situation, seeing a large Pine-Tree near, I repaired to it for Shelter; and while the Enemy were viewing our Party, I having a good Chance of killing two at a Shot, quickly discharged at them, but could not certainly know what Execution was done, till some Time after; our Company likewise discharged, and retreated: Seeing myself in Danger of being surrounded, I was obliged to Retreat a different Course, and to my great Surprize, fell into a deep Mire, which the Enemy, by following my Track in a light Snow, soon discovered, and obliged me to surrender, to prevent a cruel death. (They stood ready to drive their Darts into my Body, in case I refused to deliver up my Arms.) Presently after I was taken, I was surrounded by a great Number, who stripped me of my Cloathing, Hat, and Neckcloth (so that I had nothing left but a

[1] Where Rome, New York, now stands. Fort Williams was built to guard the south end of the carrying place (a land passage between two navigable bodies of water, in this case the Mohawk River and Wood Creek) on the route from Albany to Oswego. The fort was destroyed by the English after Oswego fell to the French.

[2] The only survivor of the party of twelve teamsters attacked enroute to Fort Bull with provisions and trader's goods (see headnote).

Flannel Vest, without Sleeves) put a Rope on my Neck, bound my Arms fast behind me, put a long Band round my Body,[3] and a large Pack on my Back, struck me on the Head (a severe Blow,) and drove me through the Woods before them: It is not easy to conceive, how distressing such a Condition is! In the mean Time, I endeavoured with all my little remaining Strength, to lift up my Eyes to God, from whom alone I could with Reason expect Relief!

Seventeen or Eighteen Prisoners, were soon added to our Number, one of which informed me, that the Indians were angry with me, and reported to some of their Chiefs, that I had fired on them, wounded one, and killed another; for which he doubted they would kill me. Hereupon I considered that the Hearts of all Men are in the Hand of God, and that one Hair of our Head cannot fall to the Ground without his Permission: I had not as yet learned what Numbers the Enemy's Parties consisted of; there being only about 100 Indians who had lain in Ambush on the Road, to kill or take into Captivity all that passed between the two Forts. Here an Interpreter came to me, to enquire what Strength Capt. Williams had to defend his Fort? After a short Pause, I gave such a discouraging Answer (yet consistent with Truth) as prevented their attacking it, and of Consequence the Effusion of much Blood; a gracious Providence, which I desire ever to retain a grateful Sense of; for hereby it evidently appeared, that I was suffered to fall into the Hands of the Enemy, to promote the Good of my Countrymen, to better Purpose than I could, by continuing with them; verily the Almighty is wise in Council, and wonderful in Working.

In the mean Time, the Enemy determined to destroy Bull's Fort, (at the Head of Wood-Creek) which they soon effected, all being put to the Sword, except five Persons, the Fort burnt, the Provision and Powder destroyed; (saving only a little for their own Use) then they retired to the Woods, and joined their main Body, which inclusive, consisted of 400 French, and 300 Indians, commanded by one of the principal Gentlemen of Quebec;[4] as

3 Eastburn is describing the Mohawk "prisoner tie," a variation of the decorated burden-strap. These straps were woven from fibres of elm bark, milkwood, and native hemp.

4 Joseph Chaussegros de Léry. Fort Bull, little more than a palisade around storehouses, was garrisoned by only thirty men. De Léry attacked it with a force of over two hundred.

soon as they got together (having a Priest with them) they fell on their knees, and returned Thanks for their Victory; an Example this, worthy of Imitation! an Example which may make prophane pretended Protestants blush, (if they are not lost to all Sense of Shame) who instead of acknowledging a God, or Providence, in their military Undertakings, are continually reproaching him with Oaths and Curses; is it any Wonder, that the Attempts of such, are blasted with Disappointment and Disgrace!

The Enemy had several wounded Men, both French and Indians among them, which they carried on their Backs; besides which, about Fifteen of their Number were killed, and of us about Forty: it being by this Time near dark, and some Indians drunk, they only marched about 4 Miles and encamped; the Indians untied my Arms, cut Hemlock Bowes, and strewed round the Fire, tied my Band to two Trees, with my Back on the green Bowes, (by the Fire) covered me with an old Blanket, and lay down across my Band, on each Side, to prevent my Escape, while they slept.

Sunday the 28th, rose early, the Commander ordered a hasty Retreat towards Canada, for fear of General Johnson; [5] in the mean Time, one of our men said, he understood the French and Indians designed to join a strong Party, and fall on Oswego, before our Forces there, could get any Provision or Succours; having, as they thought, put a Stop to our relieving them for a Time: When we encamped in the Evening, the Commanding-Officer ordered the Indians to bring me to his Tent, and asked me, by an Interpreter, If I thought General Johnson would follow them, I told him I judged not, but rather thought he would proceed to Oswego (which was indeed my Sentiment, grounded upon prior Information, and then expressed to prevent the Execution of their Design.) He farther enquired, what was my Trade? I told him that of a Smith; he then perswaded me, when I got to Canada, to send for my Wife, 'for said he, you can, get a rich Living there;' but when he saw that he could not prevail, he asked no more Questions, but commanded me to return to my Indian Master: Having this Opportunity of Conversation, I informed the General, that his Indian Warriors had stripped me of my Cloathing, and would be glad he

[5] Sir William Johnson, who, on hearing of the attack, sent reinforcements up the Mohawk but arrived too late to intercept the enemy.

would be good enough to order me some Relief; to which he replied, that I would get Cloaths when I came to Canada, which was cold Comfort to one almost frozen! On my Return, the Indians perceiving I was unwell, and could not eat their coarse Food, ordered some Chocolate (which they had brought from the Carrying-Place) to be boiled for me, and seeing me eat that, appeared pleased. A strong Guard was kept every Night; One of our Men being weakened by his Wounds, and rendered unable to keep Pace with them, was killed and scalped on the Road!—I was all this Time almost naked, traveling through deep Snow, and wading through Rivers cold as Ice!

After Seven Days March, we arrived at Lake Ontario, where I eat some Horse-Flesh, which tasted very agreeably, for to the hungry Man, as Solomon observes, every bitter Thing is sweet.[6] The French carried several of their wounded Men all the Way upon their Backs, (many of them wore no Breeches in their Travels in this cold Season, they are strong, hardy Men.) The Indians had Three of their Party wounded, which they likewise carried on their Backs, I wish there was more of this Hardness so necessary for War, in our Nation, which would open a more encouraging Scene than appears at present! The Prisoners were so divided, that but few could Converse together on our March, and (which was still more disagreeable and distressing) an Indian, who had a large Bunch of green Scalps, taken off our Men's Heads, marched before me, and another with a sharp Spear behind, to drive me after him; by which Means, the Scalps were very often close to my Face, and as we marched, they frequently every Day gave the *Dead Shout*, which was repeated as many Times, as there were Captives and Scalps taken! [7] In the Midst of this gloomy Scene, when I con-

[6] "On the Friday before we arrived at the Lake, the Indians killed a Porcupine, which is in bigness equal to a large Racoon, with short Legs, is covered with long Hair, intermixed with sharp Quills, which are their Defence: It is indeed dangerous coming very near them, because they cast their Quills (which are like barbed Irons or Darts) at any Thing that opposeth them, which when they pierce, are not easy to be drawn out; for, though their Points are sharp and smooth, they have a kind of Beard, which makes them stick fast: However, the Indians threw it on a large Fire, burnt off the Hair and Quills, roasted and eat of it, with whom I had a Part." [Eastburn's note.] It was commonly believed in Eastburn's time that porcupines could cast or throw their quills.

[7] When approaching a village, the Indians announced their victory by these whoops. See Rowlandson, n. 12.

sidered, how many poor Souls were hurried into a vast Eternity, with Doubts of their Unfitness for such a Change, it made me lament and expostulate in the Manner following; O Sin what hast thou done! what Desolation and Ruin hast thou brought into this miserable World? What am I, that I should be thus spared! My Afflictions are certainly far less than my Sins deserve! Through the exceeding Riches of divine Goodness and Grace, I was in this distressing Situation supported and comforted, by these Passages of sacred Scripture, viz. That our light Afflictions, which last but for a Moment, shall work for us a far more exceeding and eternal Weight of Glory. And that, though no Afflictions are for the present joyous, but grievous; yet nevertheless, they afterwards yield the peaceable Fruits of Righteousness, to them who are exercised thereby. And farther, that all Things shall work togther for Good, to them that love God; to them who are the Called, according to his Purpose. But to return,

I May, with Justice and Truth observe, That our Enemies leave no Stone unturned to compass our ruin; they pray, work, and travel to bring it about, and are unwearied in the Pursuit; while many among us sleep in a Storm, that has laid a good Part of our Country desolate, and threatens the Whole with Destruction: O may the Almighty awake us, cause us to see our Danger, before it be too late, and grant us Salvation! O that we may be of good Courage, and play the Man, for our People, and the Cities of our God! But alas, I am obliged to turn my Face towards cold Canada, among inveterate Enemies, and innumerable Dangers! O Lord, I pray three, be my safe Guard; thou hast already covered me in the Hollow of thy Hand; when Death cast Darts all around me, and many fell on every Side, I beheld thy Salvation!

April 4th, Several French Battoes [8] met us, and brought a large Supply of Provision; the Sight of which caused great Joy, for we were in great Want; then a Place was soon erected to celebrate Mass in, which being ended, we all went over the Mouth of a River, where it empties itself into the East-End of Lake Ontario, a great Part of our Company set off on Foot towards Oswegotchy; [9] while

[8] That is, *bateaux*—light, flat-bottomed boats used especially in Canada.

[9] A settlement of converted Iroquois Indians, established in 1794 where Ogdensburg, New York, now stands.

the rest were ordered into Battoes, and carried towards the Entrance of St Lawrence (where that River takes its Beginning) but by reason of bad Weather, Wind, Rain, and Snow, whereby the Waters of the Lake were troubled, we were obliged to lie-by, and hall our Battoes on Shore; here I lay on the cold Shore two Days. Tuesday set off, and entered the Head of St. Lawrence, in the Afternoon; came too late at Night, made Fires, but did not lie down to sleep; embarked long before Day, and after some Miles Progress down the River, we saw many Fires on our Right-Hand, which were made by the Men who left us, and went by land; with them we staid till Day, and then again embarked in our Battoes; the Weather was very bad (it snowed fast all Day) near Night arrived at Oswegotchy; I was almost starved to Death, but hoped to stay in this Indian Town till warm Weather; slept in an Indian Wigwam, rose early in the Morning (being Thursday) and soon to my Grief discovered my Disappointment! Several of the Prisoners had Leave to tarry here, but I must go 200 Miles farther down Stream, to another Indian Town; the Morning being extreamly cold, I applied to a French Merchant (or Trader) for some old Rags of Cloathing, for I was almost naked, but to no Purpose!

About Ten o'Clock, was ordered into a Battoe, on our Way down the River, with 8 or 9 Indians, one of which was the Man wounded in the Skirmish before mentioned; at Night we went on Shore, the Snow being much deeper than before, we cleared it away, and made a large Fire; here, when the wounded Indian cast his Eyes upon me, his old Grudge revived, he took my Blanket from me, and commanded me to dance round the Fire Bare-foot, and sing the *Prisoners Song*, which I utterly refused; this surprised one of my fellow Prisoners, who told me they would put me to Death (for he understood what they said) he therefore tried to persuade me to comply, but I desired him to let me alone, and was through great Mercy, enabled to reject his Importunity with Abhorrence! The Indian also continued urging, saying, you shall dance and sing; but apprehending my Compliance sinful, I determined to persist in declining it at all Adventures, and to leave the Issue to the divine Disposal! The Indian perceiving his Orders disobeyed, was fired with Indignation, and endeavoured to push me into the Fire, which I leapt over, and he being weak with his

Wounds, and not being assisted by any of his Brethern, was obliged to desist: For this gracious Interposure of Providence, in preserving me both from Sin and Danger, I desire to bless God while I live!

Friday Morning, was almost perished with Cold. Saturday, proceeded on our Way, and soon came in Sight of the Upper Part of the Inhabitants of Canada; here I was in great Hopes of some Relief, not knowing the Manner of the Indians, who do not make many Stops among the French, in their return from War, till they get Home: However when they came near some rapid Falls of Water, one of my fellow Prisoners, and several Indians, together with myself, were put on Shore, to travel by Land, which pleased me well, it being much warmer running on the Snow, than lying still in the Battoe; we past by several French Houses, but stopt at none; the Vessel going down a rapid Stream, it required haste to keep Pace with her, we crossed over a Point of Land, and found the Battoe waiting for us, as near the Shore as the Ice would permit: Here we left St. Lawrence and turned up Conasadauga River [10] but it being frozen up, we hauled our Battoe on Shore, and each of us took our Share of her Loading on our Backs, and marched towards Conasadauga, an Indian Town,[11] which was our designed Port, but could not reach it that Night; Came to a French House, cold, weary, and hungry; here my old Friend, the wounded Indian, again appeared, and related to the Frenchman, the Affair of my refusing to dance, who immediately assisted the Indian to

[10] "The River St. Lawrence, at Lake Ontario, takes its Beginning through several Islands, by which we are in no necessity of coming within Sight of Frontenac, when we go down the River; it is smooth Water from thence to Oswegotche (or as it is called by the French *Legalet*) but from hence to Montreal, the Water is more swift, with a Number of rapid Streams, though not dangerous to pass through with small Boats and Bark Canoes, provided the Stearsmen are careful, and acquainted with the Places. In transporting Provisions and warlike Stores up Stream from Canada to Lake Ontario, there is a necessity of unloading Battoes at several of the rapid Streams, and hauling them empty through shoal Water near the Shore; and carrying the Loading by Land to where the Water is more Slack; though there be several of these Places, yet the Land Carriage is not very far: The Land on both Sides the River, appears fertile a great Part of the Way from the Lake to Montreal; but the nearer the Latter the worse, more mirey and stony: The Timber is White Pine, Ash, Maple, Beach, Hickory, Hemlock, Spruce; and from the Lake about 150 Miles down, plenty of White Oak, but none about Montreal of that Kind." [Eastburn.]

[11] Another mission settlement of Iroquois and Algonquin Indians. It was also called the Lake of the Two Mountain mission.

Early colonial captivity scene. From John Frost, *Pictorial History of Indian Wars and Captivities* (New York, 1873).

Martyrdom of Father Jogues and other Jesuits. From François DeCreux, *Historiae Canadensis Libri Decem* (Paris, 1664).

Torturing a captive. From *Wonderful Adventures, A Series of Narratives of Personal Experiences among the Native Tribes of America* (Philadelphia, 1857).

strip me of my Flannel Vest, before mentioned, which was my All: Now they were resolved to compel me to dance and sing! The Frenchman was as violent as the Indian, in promoting this Imposition; but the Woman belonging to the House, seeing the rough Usage I had, took pity on me, and rescued me out of their Hands, till their Heat was over, and prevailed with the Indian to excuse me from dancing; but he insisted that I must be shaved, and then he would let me alone (I had at that Time a long Beard, which the Indians hate) with this Motion I readily complied, and then the Indian seemed content.

Sunday, April 11th, Set off towards Conasadauga, traveled about two Hours, and then saw the Town, over a great River, which was still frozen; the Indian stoped, and we were soon joined with a Number of our own Company, which we had not seen for several Days: The Prisoners, in Number Eight, were ordered to lay down our Packs, and be painted; the wounded Indian painted me, and put a Belt of Wampum round my Neck, instead of the Rope which I had worn 400 Miles. Then set off towards the Town on the Ice, which was four Miles over; our Heads were not allowed to be covered, lest our fine Paint should be hid, the Weather in the mean Time very cold, like to Freeze our Ears: after we had advanced nearer to the Town, the Indian Women came out to meet us, and relieved their Husbands of their Packs.

As soon as we landed at Conasadauga, a large Body of Indians came and incompassed us round, and ordered the Prisoners to dance and sing the Prisoners Song, (which I was still enabled to decline) at the conclusion of which, the Indians gave a Shout, and opened the Ring to let us run, and then fell on us with their Fists, and knocked several down; [12] in the mean Time, one ran before to direct us to an Indian House, which was open, and as soon as we got in, we were beat no more; my Head was sore with beating, and pained me several Days. The Squaws were kind to us, gave us boiled Corn and Beans to eat, and Fire to warm us, which was a great Mercy, for I was both cold and hungry: This Town lies about 30 Miles North-West from Montreal, I staid here till the Ice was gone, which was about Ten Days, and then was sent to Cohnewago, in Company with some Indians, who when they came within

[12] A variation of the gauntlet ritual. See Jogues, n. 13.

Hearing, gave Notice by their Way of shouting, that they had a Prisoner, on which the whole Town rose to welcome me, which was the more distressing, as there was no other Prisoner in their Hands; when we came near Shore, a stout Indian took hold of me, and hauled me into the Water, which was Knee-deep, and very cold: As soon as I got a-shore, the Indians gathered round me, and ordered me to dance and sing, now when I was stiff with Cold and Wet, and lying long in the Cannoe; here I only stamped to prepare for my Race, and was incompassed with about 500 Indians, who danced and sung, and at last gave a Shout, and opened the Circle; about 150 young Lads made ready to Pelt me with Dirt and gravel Stones, and on my setting off gave me a stout Volley, without my suffering great Hurt; but an Indian seeing me run, met me, and held me fast, till the Boys had stored themselves again with Dirt and small Stones, and let me run; but then I fared much worse than before, for a small Stone among the Mud hit my Right-Eye, and my Head and Face were so covered with Dirt, that I could scarce see my Way; but discovering a Door of an Indian House standing open, I run in: From this Retreat I was soon hauled, in order to be pelted more; but the Indian Women being more merciful interposed, took me into a House, brought me Water to wash, and gave me boiled Corn and Beans to eat. The next Day, I was brought to the Center of the Town, and cried according to the Indian Custom,[13] in order to be sent to a Family of Indians, 200 Miles up Stream, at Oswegotchy, and there to be adopted, and abused no more: To this End, I was delivered to three young Men, who said I was their Brother, and set forward on our Way to the aforesaid Town, with about 20 more Indians, but by reason of bad Weather, we were obliged to encamp on a cold, stony Shore, three Days, and then proceeded on; called at Conasadauga, staid there about a Week, in which Time, I went and viewed four Houses at a Distance from the Town, about a Quarter of a Mile from each other; in which, are represented in large Paint Work, the Sufferings of our Saviour, with Design to draw the Indians to the Papist's Religion; the Work is curiously done: A little farther stand three Houses near together, on the Top of a high Hill, which they call

[13] That is, the women cried over him. This ritualized weeping was preparatory to his being assigned back to Oswegatchy for adoption by an Indian family.

Mount Calvary,[14] with three large Crosses before them, which compleat the whole Representation: To all these Houses, the Priests and Indians repair, in performing their grand Processions, which takes up much Time.[15]

Set off on our Journey for Oswegotchy, against a rapid Stream, and being long in it, and our Provision growing short, the Indians put to Shore a little before Night; my Lot was to get Wood, others were ordered to get Fires, and some to Hunt; our Kettle was put over the Fire with some pounded Indian Corn, and after it had boiled about two Hours, my oldest Indian Brother, returned with a She Beaver, big with Young, which he soon cut to Pieces, and threw into the Kettle, together with the Guts, and took the four young Beavers, whole as they came out from the Dam,[16] and put them likewise into the Kettle, and when all was well boiled, gave each one of us a large Dishfull of the Broth, of which we eat freely, and then Part of the old Beaver, the Tail of which was divided equally among us, there being Eight at our Fire; the four young Beavers were cut in the Middle, and each of us got half of a Beaver; I watched an Opportunity to hide my Share (having satisfied myslf before that tender Dish came to Hand) which if they had seen, would have much displeased them. The other Indians catched young Musk-Rats, run a Stick through their Bodies, and roasted, without being skinned or gutted, and so eat them. Next Morning hastened on our Journey, which continued several Days, till we came near Oswegotchy, where we landed about three Miles from the Town, on the contrary Side of the River; here I was to

14 A Calvary and Way of the Cross erected by Abbé François Piquet, who also established the mission at Oswegatchy.

15 "The pains the Papists take to propagate such a bloody and absurd Religion as theirs, is truly amazing! This brings to my Remembrance, the following Discourse, I had with two French Priests in my Captivity; one of them asked me, if I was a Catholic; apprehending he meant the Romish Religion, I answered no; he replied, *no Bon*. On my relating the above to a fellow Prisoner, he said, I had answered wrong, because by the Word *Catholic* he meant a Christian: Some Time after, I was again asked by the other Priest, if I was a Catholic, I answered yes, but not a Roman Catholic; at which he smiled, and asked, if I was a Lutheran. I replied, no; he again inquired whether I was a Calvanist, I told him I was; to which he said, with warmth, *no Bon! no Bon!* which signifieth, it is not good. it is not good. O! may not the Zeal of the Papists, in propagating Superstition and Idolatry, make Protestants ashamed of their Lukewarmness, in promoting the Religion of the Bible!" [Eastburn.]

16 See Rowlandson, n. 36.

be adopted, my *Father* and *Mother* that I had never seen before were waiting, and ordered me into an Indian House, where we were directed to sit down silent for a considerable Time, the Indians appeared very sad, and my Mother began to cry, and continued crying aloud for some Time, and then dried up her Tears, and received me for her Son, and took me over the River to the Indian Town; the next Day I was ordered to go to Mass with them, but I refused once and again, yet they continued their Importunity several Days, saying it was good to go to Mass, but I still refused; and seeing they could not prevail with me, they seemed much displeased with their new Son.[17] I was then sent over the River, to be employed in hard Labour, as a Punishment for not going to Mass, and not allowed a Sight of, or any Conversation with my fellow Prisoners; the old Indian Man that I was ordered to work with, had a Wife, and some Children, he took me into the Woods with him, and made Signs that I must chop, giving me an Ax, the Indian soon saw that I could handle the Ax: Here I tried to reconcile myself to this Employ, that they might have no Occasion against me, except concerning the Law of my God; the old Man began to appear kind, and his Wife gave me Milk and Bread when we came Home, and when she got Fish, gave me the Gills to eat, out of real Kindness; but perceiving I did not like them, gave me my own choice, and behaved lovingly! Here I saw that God could make Friends of cruel Enemies, as he once turned the Heart of angry Esau into Love and Tenderness; when we had finished our Fence, which had employed us about a Week, I shewed the old Squaw my Shirt (having worn it from the Time I was first taken Prisoner, which was about seven Weeks) all in Rags, Dirt, and Lice; she said it was not good, and brought me a new One, with ruffled Sleeves (saying that is good) which I thankfully accepted. The

17 "When I was at Oswegotchy, the Indians took Notice, that I frequently retired alone, and supposing I had some bad Design, threatened if I did not desist, they would Tomahawk me; but my fellow Prisoner, who understood their Language, told them it would be a pity to hurt me on that Account, for I only went into a private Place to pray, which was true; the Indians replied, if so, it was good; but being yet suspicious, took Pains, by watching to find out how the Case was, and when they satisfied themselves, seemed pleased! and did not offer to interrupt me any more, which was a great Mercy, as the Contrary would have in some Degree, marred my Converse with God." [Eastburn.]

next Day they carried me back to the Indian Town, and admitted me to converse with my fellow Prisoners, who told me we were all to be sent to Montreal, which accordingly came to pass.

Montreal, at our Arrival here, we had our Lodging first in the Jesuit's Convent, where I saw a great Number of Priests, and People that came to Confession; after some stay, we were ordered to attend, with the Indians, at a Grand Council, held before the head General Vaudriel; [18] we Prisoners sat in our Rank (surrounded with our Fathers and Brethren) but were asked no Questions: the General had a Number of Officers to attend him in Council, where a noted Priest, called Picket, sat at his Right-Hand, who understands the Indian Tongue well, and does more Hurt to the English, than any other of his Order in Canada (his Dwelling is at Oswegotchy).[19] Here I was informed that some Measures were concerted to destroy Oswego, which they had been long preparing to execute; we in our Journey met many Battoes going up Stream, with Provision and Men for an Attack on our Frontiers, which confirmed the Report: The Council adjourned to another Day, and then broke up. My Indian Father and Mother took me with them to several of their old Acquaintance, who were French, to shew them their lately adopted Son; these Persons had been concerned with my Father and other Indians, in destroying many English Families in their younger Days; and (as one standing by who understood their Language, said,) were boasting of their former Murders! After some Days the Council was again called, before which, several of the Oneida Chiefs appeared, and offered some Complaint against the French's attacking our Carrying-Place, it being their Land; but the General laboured to make them easy, and gave them sundry Presents of Value, which they accepted: [20]

18 Pierre François de Rigaud, marquis de Vaudreuil-Cavagnal, governor of Canada from 1755 to 1759.

19 The same Abbé Piquet of Oswegatchy (see n. 14, above). Piquet was indeed, as Eastburn suggests, one of the most zealous priests in French America. He was present when Montcalm captured Oswego, and he subsequently accompanied raiding parties that invaded the British settlements.

20 "The French in Canada, well knowing the great Importance of having the Indians in their Interest, to promote their ambitious and unjust Designs, use a variety of Methods with them, among which, the following one is excellent in itself, and well worthy of Imitation, viz. They are exceeding careful to prevenr

After which, I knowing these Indians were acquainted with Captain Williams, at the Carrying-Place, sent a Letter by them, to let my Family and Friends know I was yet alive, and longed for Redemption; but it never came to Hand. The Treaty being ended, the General sent about ten Gallons of red Wine to the Indians, which they divided among us; after came the Presents, consisting of Coats, Blankets, Shirts, Skins (to make Indian Shoes) Cloth (to make Stockings) Powder, Lead, Shot, and to each a Bag of Paint, for their own Use, &c. After we Prisoners had our Share, my Mother came to me with an Interpreter, and told me I might stay in the Town, at a Place she had found for me, if I pleased (this was doubtless the Consequence of my declining to obey her Orders, in some Instances that affected my Conscience) this Proposal I almost agreed to; but one of my fellow Prisoners, with whom I had before some Discourse, about making our Escape from the Indian Town, opposed the Motion, and said, "pray do not stay, for if you do, we shall not be able to form a Plan for our Deliverance;" on which I told her I chose to go Home with her, and soon set off by Land in our Way thither, to Lascheen,[21] distant from Montreal about 9 Miles, where we left our Cannoes, and then proceeded, without Delay, on our Journey; in which I saw, to my Sorrow, great Numbers of Soldiers, and much Provisions, in Motion towards Lake Ontario.

After a painful and distressing Journey, we arrived at Oswegotchy, where we likewise saw many Battoes, with Provision and

spirituous Liquors being sold to the Indians, and if any of the Inhabitants are proved guilty of it, their temporal Interest is quite broke, and corporal Punishment inflicted on them; unless the General, on some particular Occasion, orders his Commissioners to deliver some to them. I may add, that knowing their Number is small, compared with the British Inhabitants on this Continent, and must quickly fall into their Hands, in case we united, and entered boldly into the Heart of their Country with a sufficient Force; for that very Reason, they choose to keep us continually on the Defencive, by sending when Occasion requires, large Bodies of Regulars, together with great Numbers of Indians, upon long and tedious Marches, that we may not come near their Borders; and especially by employing the Latter, constantly to waste and ravage our Frontiers, by which we are murdered by Inches, and beat without a Battle! By what I could learn when I was among them, they do not fear our Numbers, because of our unhappy Divisions, which they deride, and from them, strongly expect to conquer us entirely! which may a gracious God, in Mercy, prevent!" [Eastburn.]

[21] *La Chine* (China), the name given to LaSalle's frontier trading post by his competitors after he had mortgaged and lost it to finance an expedition to China, which LaSalle supposed could be reached by following the Ohio River south.

Soldiers, daily passing by in their Way to Frontenac,[22] which greatly distressed me for Oswego! Hence I resolved, if possible, to give our People Notice of their Danger: To this End, I told two of my fellow Prisoners, that it was not a Time to sleep, and asked if they would go with me, to this they heartily agreed; but we had no Provision, were closely eyed by the Enemy, and could not lay up a Stock out of our Allowance: However, at this Time, Mr. Picket (before mentioned) had concluded to dig a large Trench round the Town; I therefore went to a Negro, the principal Manager of this Work (who could speak English, French, and Indian, well) and asked him, if he could get Employ for two others, and myself, which he soon did; for which we were to have Meat and Wages. Here we had a Prospect of procuring Provision for our Flight; this, I in some Time effected for myself, and then asked my Brethren if they were ready, who replied they were not yet, but said, Ann Bowman, our fellow Prisoner, had brought 130 dollars from Bull's Fort, and would give them all they had Need of; I told them it was not safe to disclose such a Secret to her, but they blamed me for my Fears, and applied to her for Provision, letting her know our Intention, who immediately informed the Priest of it; on which we were apprehended, the Indians apprised of our Design, and a Court called; by Order of which, four of us were confined under a strong Guard, in a Room within the Fort, for several Days.

From hence, another and myself were sent to Cohnewago, under a strong Guard of 60 Indians, to prevent my ploting any more against the French, and banish all Hope of my Escape! However, when we arrived at this Place, it pleased that gracious God, who has the Hearts of all Creatures in his Hand, to incline the Captain of the Guard, to shew me great Kindness, in giving me Liberty to walk or work where I pleased, within any small Distance; on which I went to work with a French Smith, for six Livers and five Souse per Week;[23] which the Captain let me have to myself, and farther favoured me with the Priviledge of Lodging at his Mother's House, an English Woman (named Mary Harris,

[22] The fort, trading post, and settlement established in 1673 by LaSalle and Count de Frontenac. It was located where Kingston, Ontario, now stands.

[23] That is, six livres, five sous.

taken Captive when a Child, from Dearfield, in New-England) [24] who told me she was my Grand-mother, and was kind; but the Wages being small, and not sufficient to procure such Cloathing as I was in Want of, I proceeded no farther with the French Smith, but went to my Uncle Peter, and told him I wanted Cloaths, and that it would be better to let me go to Montreal, and work there, where I could Cloath myself better, than by staying with him, and that without any Charge to him, who after some Reasoning consented.

Set off on my Journey to Montreal, and on my entring the City met an English Smith, who took me to work with him; after some Time, we settled to work in a Shop, opposite to the General's Door, where we had the Opportunity of seeing a great Part of the Forces of Canada (both Soldiers and Indians) who were commonly brought there, before their going out to War; and likewise all Prisoners, by which Means we got Intelligence how our People were preparing for Defence; but no good News from Oswego, which made me fear, knowing that great Numbers of French were gone against it, and hearing of but few to defend it. Prayers were put up in all the Churches of Canada, and great Processions made, in order to procure Success to their Arms, against poor Oswego; but our People knew little of their Danger, till it was too late: Certainly if more frequent and earnest Application (both in private and public) was made to the God of Battle, we might with greater Probability, expect Success would crown our military Attempts! To my Surprize, the dismal News came, that the French had taken one of the Oswego Forts; in a few Hours, in Confirmation of this, I saw the English Standards (the melancholly Trophy of Victory) and the French rejoicing at our downfal, and mocking us poor Prisoners, in our Exile and Extremity, which was no great Argument either of Humanity, or true Greatness of Mind; great Joy appeared in all their Faces, which they expressed by loud Shouts,

24 Mary Harris was one of a number of New England children made captive at an early age who quickly forgot white culture and chose to remain with the Indians. Eunice Williams, daughter of the Reverend John Williams and niece of Cotton Mather, is perhaps the most notable example: captured and carried to Canada in 1704, she later took an Indian husband and turned Catholic. See Erwin H. Ackerknecht, "White Indians," *Bulletin of the History of Medicine*, XV (Jan., 1944), 15–36, and Clifton Johnson, *An Unredeemed Captive* (Holyoke, Mass., 1897).

firing of Cannon, and returning Thanks in their Churches; but our Faces were covered with Shame, and our Hearts filled with Grief —Soon after, I saw several of the Officers brought in Prisoners, in small Parties, and the Soldiers in the same Manner, and confined within the Walls, in a starving Condition, in order to make them Work, which some complied with, but others bravely refused; and last of all came the Tradesmen, among whom was my Son, who looking round saw his Father, who he thought had long been dead; this joyful Sight so affected him, that he wept!—nor could I, in seeing my Son, remain unconcerned!—no; the Tenderness of a Father's Bowels, upon so extraordinary an Occasion, I am not able to express, and therefore must cover it with a Vail of Silence!— But he, with all my Philadelphia Friends, being guarded by Soldiers, with fixed Bayonets, we could not come near each other, they were sent to the common Pound; but I hastened to the Interpreter, to try if I could get my Child at Liberty, which was soon effected! When we had the Happiness of an Interview, he gave me some Information of the State of our Family, and told me, as soon as the News were sent Home, that I was killed, or taken, his Mother was not allowed any more Support from my Wages, which grieved me much, and added to my other Afflictions! [25]

[25] "In the mean Time, it gave me some Pleasure, in this Situation, to see an Expression of equal Duty and Prudence in my Sons Conduct, who, though young in Years (about 17) and in such a confused State of Things, had taken care to bring, with much Labour and Fatigue, a large Bundle of considerable Value to me, it being Cloathing, &c. which I was in great Need of; he likewise saved a Quantity of Wampum, which we brought from New-York, and afterwards sold here, for 150 Livers. He traveled with me Part of the Journey toward Oswego, but not being so far on his Way, as I was when taken, he did not then fall into the Enemy's Hands, but continued free till Oswego was taken, and was then remarkably delivered from the Hands of the Indians, in the following Manner, 15 young Lads were drafted out to be delivered to them (which from their known Custom, it is reasonable to conclude, was to fill up the Number they had lost in the Battle) among which he was one: This barbarous Design, which is contrary to the Laws of War, among all civilized Nations, the French artfully concealed, under the Pretext of sending them to work in the Battoes; but my Child taking Notice, that all that were chosen were small Lads, doubted their real Intention was bad, and therefore slipt out of his Rank and concealed himself, by which Means, under God, he was preserved from a State of perpetual Captivity; his Place being filled up in his Absence, the other unhappy Youths were delivered up a Sacrifice to the Indian Enemy, to be instructed in Popish Principles, and employed in Murdering their Countrymen; yea, perhaps, their Fathers and Brethren, O horrible! O lamentable! How can the French be guilty in cold Blood, of such prodigious Iniquity? Besides their insatiable Thirst of Empire,

When the People taken at Oswego, were setting out on their Way to Quebec, I made Application for Liberty to go with them; but the Interpreter replied, that I was an Indian Prisoner, and the General would not suffer it, till the Indians were satisfied; and as they lived Two Hundred Miles from Montreal, it could not be done at that Time: Finding that all Arguments, farther on that Head, would not avail, because I was not included in the Capitulation; I told the Interpreter, my Son must go and leave me! in order to be ready at Quebec to go Home, when the Oswego People went, which probably would be soon; he replied, "It would be better to keep him with me, for he might be a Mean to get me clear much sooner."

The Officers belonging to Oswego, would gladly have had me with them, but found it impracticable; this is an Instance of Kindness and Condescension, for which I am obliged! Captain Bradley, gave me a good Coat, Vest, and Shirt; and a young Gentleman, who formerly lived in Philadelphia, gave four Pistoles (his Name is James Stone, he was Doctor at Oswego). These generous Expressions of Kindness and Humanity, I am under great Obligations to remember with affectionate Gratitude, and if ever it be in the Compass of my Power, to requite: This Money, together with what my Son brought, I was in Hopes would go far towards procuring my Release, from my Indian Masters; but seeing a Number of Prisoners in sore Distress, among which were, the Captains Grant and Shepherd, and about Seven more in Company, I thought it my Duty to relieve them, and commit my Release to the Disposal of Providence! Nor was this suffered to turn to my Disadvantage in the Issue, for my Deliverance was brought about in due Time, in another, and unexpected Way. This Company informed me of their Intention to Escape, accordingly I gave them all the Help in

Doubtless the Pardons they get from their Pope, and their Priests, embolden them, which brings to my Mind, what I saw when among them: On a Sabbath Day, perceiving a great Concourse of People at a Chapel, built on the Commons, at some Distance from the City, I went to see what was the Occasion, and found a kind of a fair, at which were sold Cakes, Wine, Brandy, &c. I likewise saw many Carts and Chases [chaises] attending, the Chapel Doors in the mean Time open, Numbers of People going in and out, and a Board hanging over the Door, on which was written, in large Letters, INDULGENCE PLENARY, or FULL PARDON." [Eastburn.]

my Power, saw them clear of the Town, on a Saturday Evening, before the Centries were set at the Gates, and advised them not to part from each other, and delivered to Captain Shepherd two Pocket Compasses; but they contrary to this Counsel parted, and saw each other no more: By their separating, Captain Grant, and Serjeant Newel, were deprived of the Benefit of a Compass; the other Part got safe to Fort William Henry, as I was informed by Serjeant Henry, who was brought in Prisoner, being taken in a Battle, when gallant, indefatigable Captain Rogers, made a brave Stand, against more than twice his Number! But I have not heard any Account of Captain Grant! Was enabled, through much Mercy, to continue communicating some Relief to other Prisoners, out of the Wages I received for my Labour, which was 40 Livers per Month!

In the latter Part of the Winter, Coal and Iron were so scarce, that I was hard set to get any more Work; I then offered to work for my Diet and Lodging, rather than be thrust into a stinking Dungeon, or sent among the Indians: The Interpreter took some Pains (which I thankfully acknowledge) but without Success; however, as I offered to work without Wages, a Frenchman took me and my Son in, upon these Terms, till a better Birth presented; here we staid one Week, but heard of no other Place, then he offered me and my Son, 30 Livers per Month, to strike and blow the Bellows, which I did for about two Months, and then was discharged, and traveled about from Place to Place, having no fixed Abode, and was obliged to lay out the small Remains of my Cash, in buying a little Victuals, and took a Hay-Loft for my Lodging: I then made my Case known to the kind Interpreter, and requested him to consider of some Means for my Relief, who replied he would; in the mean Time, as I was taking a walk in the City, I met an Indian Prisoner, that belonged to the Town where my Father lived, who reported, that a great Part of the Indians there, were just come, with a Resolution to carry me back with them; and knowing him to be a very honest Fellow, I believed the Truth of it, and fled from the Town to be concealed from the Indians; in the mean while, Schemes were formed for an Escape, and well prosecuted: The Issue of which was fortunate. General Vaudriel gave me and my Son, Liberty (under his Hand) to go to Quebec, and work there at our Pleasure, without Confinement, as Prisoners of War; by which Means, I was freed from paying a Ransom.

The Commissary, Monsieur Partwe, being about to set off for Quebec, my Son informed me that I must come to Town in the Evening, a Passage being provided for us; I waited till near Dark, and then entered the Town, with great Care, to escape the Indians, who kept watch for me (and had done so for some Time) which made it very difficult and dangerous to move; however, as they had no Knowledge of my Son, he could watch their Motions, without their Suspicion (the Providence of God is a great Deep, this Help was provided for my Extremity, not only beyond my Expectation, but contrary to my Design.) In the Morning, upon seeing an Indian set to watch for me, over against the House I was in, I quickly made my Escape, through the back Part of the House, over some high Pickets, and out of the City, to the River Side, and fled! A Friend knowing my Scheme for Deliverance, kindly assisted me to conceal myself: The Commissary had by this Time got ready for his Voyage, of which my Son giving me Notice, I immediately, with no lingering Motion, repaired to the Boat, was received on board, set off quite undiscovered, and saw the Indians no more! A very narrow and surprizing Escape, from a violent Death! (For they had determined to kill me, in case I ever attempted to leave them) which lays me under the strongest Obligations, to improve a Life rescued from the Jaws of so many Deaths, to the Honour of my gracious Benefactor!—But to return, the Commissary, upon seeing the Dismission I had from the General, treated us courteously! [26]

Arrived at Quebec, May 1st, The honorable Colonel *Peter Schuyler*,[27] hearing of my coming there, kindly sent for me, and

26 "Saw many Houses and Villages in our Pass along the River St. Lawrence towards the Metropolis; and here it may be with Justice observed, that the Inhabitants of Canada in general, are principally (if not wholly) settled upon Rivers, by reason that their back Lands being flat and swampy, are therefore unfit to bear Grain; Their Wheat is sown in the Spring of the Year, because the Winter is long, and would drown it; they seem to have no good Notion of making Meadow (so far as I had an Opportunity of observing); their horned Cattle are few and poor, their Living in general mean, they eat but little Flesh, nevertheless they are strong and hardy." [Eastburn.]

27 Schuyler had been in command of a New Jersey regiment at Oswego when it fell to the French.

after enquiries about my Welfare, &c. generously told me I should be supplied, and need not trouble myself for Support! This public spirited Gentleman, who is indeed an Honour to his Country, did in like Manner, nobly relieve many other poor Prisoners at Quebec!—Here I had full Liberty to walk where I pleased, and view the City, which is well situated for Strength, but far from being impregnable.

Here, I hope, it will not be judged improper to give a short Hint of the French Governor's Conduct; even in Time of Peace, he gives the Indians great Encouragement to Murder and Captivate the poor Inhabitants on our Frontiers; an honest, good Man, named William Ross, was taken Prisoner twice in the Time of Peace; when he was first taken, he learned a little of the French Tongue, was after some Time redeemed, and got to his Place of Abode: Yet some Years after, he, with two Sons, was again taken, and brought to Quebec; the Governor seeing the poor Man was Lame, and one of his Legs smaller than the other, reproved the Indians for not killing him, asking, "what they brought a lame Man there for, who could do nothing but eat; you should, said he, have brought his Scalp!" However, another of his Countrymen, more merciful than his Excellency, knowing the poor Prisoner to be a quiet, hard-working Man, redeemed him from the Indians; and two other Frenchmen bought his two Sons: Here they had been Slaves more than three Years, when I first arrived at Quebec; this Account I had from Mr. Ross himself, who farther added, that the Governor gave the Indians Presents, to encourage them to proceed, in that kind of Work, which is a Scandal to any civilized Nation, and what many Pagans would abhor! Here, also, I saw one Mr. Johnson, who was taken in a Time of Peace, with his Wife, and three small Children (his Wife was big with Child of a Fourth, and delivered on the Road to Canada, which she called Captive) all which, had been Prisoners between three and four Years, several young Men, and his Wife's Sister, were likewise taken Captive with them, and made Slaves!

Our Cartel being ready, I obtained Liberty to go to England in her; we set Sail the 23d of July, 1757, in the Morning, and discharged our Pilot about 4 o'Clock in the Afternoon; after which, we neither cast Anchor or Lead, till we got clear of the great River

St. Lawrence, from which, I conclude, the Navigation is much safer than the French have reported; in 28 Days we arrived at Plymouth, which occasioned great Joy, for we were ragged, lowsy, sick, and in a Manner, starved; and many of the Prisoners, who in all were about 300 in Number, were sick of the Small-Pox: My Son and Self, having each a Blanket Coat (which we bought in Canada to keep us warm) and now expecting Relief, gave them to two poor sick Men, almost naked! But as we were not allowed to go on Shore, but removed to a King's Ship, and sent to Portsmouth, where we were still confined on board, near two Weeks, and then removed to the Mermaid, to be sent to Boston; we now repented our well ment, though rash Charity, in giving our Coats away, as we were not to get any more, all Application to the Captain for any Kind of Covering being in vain; our Joy was turned into Sorrow, at the Prospect of coming on a cold Coast, in the Beginning of Winter, almost naked, which was not a little increased, by a near View of our *Mother Country*, the Soil and Comforts of which, we were not suffered to touch or taste.[28]

September the 6th, Set Sail for Boston, with a Fleet in Convoy, at which we arrived on the Seventh of November, in the Evening; it being Dark, and we Strangers, and poor, it was difficult to get a Lodging (I had no Shoes, and but Pieces of Stockings, and the Weather in the mean Time very Cold) we were indeed directed to a Tavern, but found cold Entertainment there, the Master of the House seeing a ragged and lowsy Company, turned us out to

[28] "On board the Mermaid Man of War, being in a distressed Condition, and hearing little from the Mouths of many of my Countrymen, but Oaths and Curses (which much increased my Affliction) and finding it difficult to get a retired Place, I crept down into the Hold among the Water Casks, to cry to God; here the Lord was graciously pleased to meet with me, and give me a Sense of his fatherly Love and Care; here he enabled me (blessed be his Name for ever) to look back and view how he had led me, and guarded me with a watchful Eye and strong Arm, and what Pains he had taken to wean me from an over-love of time Things, and make me content that he should choose for me: Here I was enabled to see his great Goodness in all my Disappointments, and that Afflictions were not Evidence of God's Wrath, but the Contrary, to all that honestly Endeavour to seek him with Faith and Love; here I could say, God is worthy to be served, loved, and obeyed, though it be attended with many Miseries in this World! What I have here mentioned, so far as I know my heart, is neither to exalt myself, or offend any one upon Earth, but to glorify God, for his Goodness and Faithfulness to the Meanest of his Servants, and to encourage others to trust in him!" [Eastburn.]

Wander in the Dark; he was suspicious of us, and feared we came from Halifax, where the Small-Pox then was, and told us, he was ordered not to receive such as came from thence: We soon met a young Man, who said he could find a Lodging for us, but still detained us by asking many Questions; on which I told him we were in no Condition to Answer, till we came to a proper Place, which he quickly found, where we were used well; but as we were lowsy, could not expect Beds. The next Morning, we made Application for Cloathing; Mr. Erwing, Son-in-Law to the late General Shirley,[29] gave us Relief, not only in respect of Apparel, but also Three Dollars per Man, to bear our Charges to Newport: When I put on fresh Cloaths, I was seized with a cold Fit, which was followed by a high Fever, and in that Condition obliged to Travel on Foot, as far as Providence, in our Way to Rhode-Island (our Money not being sufficient to hire any Carriage, and find us what was needful for Support:) In this Journey, I was exceedingly distressed! Our Comforts in this Life, are often allaved with Miseries, which are doubtless great Mercies, when suitably improved; at Newport, met with Captain Gibbs, and agreed with him for our Passage to New-York, where we arrived, November 21st, met with many Friends, who expressed much Satisfaction at our Return, and treated us kindly, particularly Messrs. Livingston, and Waldron.

November 26th, 1757. Arrived at Philadelphia, to the great Joy of all my friends, and particularly of my poor afflicted Wife and Family, who thought they should never see me again, till we met beyond the Grave; being returned, sick and weak in Body, and empty-handed, not having any Thing for my Family's and my own Support, several humane and generous Persons, of different Denominations, in this City (without any Application of mine, directly or indirectly) have freely given seasonable Relief; for which, may God grant them Blessings in this World, and in the World to come everlasting Life, for Christ's sake!

Now, God, in His great Mercy, hath granted me a temporal Salvation, and what is a Thousand Times better, he hath given me

29 William Shirley, governor of Massachusetts when the war began. After the Virginia conference with Braddock, Shirley was put in charge of the expedition to reduce Niagara. At the time of Eastburn's capture, Shirley was commander in chief of the British forces in America.

with it, a Soul-satisfying Evidence of an eternal in the World to come!

And now, what shall I render to the Lord for all his Benefits, alas I am nonplust! O that Saints and Angels might praise thee, for I am not worthy to take thy Name into my Mouth any more! Yet notwithstanding, thou art pleased to accept poor Endeavours, because *Jesus Christ* has opened the Door, whereby we may come boldly to the Throne of Thy Grace, praised be the Lord God Jehovah, by Men and Angels, throughout all Eternity!

But to hasten to the Conclusion, suffer me with Humility and Sorrow to observe that our Enemies seem to make a better Use of a bad Religion, than we of a good One; they rise up long before Day in Winter, and go through the Snow in the coldest Seasons, to perform their Devotions in the Churches; which when over, they return to be ready for their work as soon as Day-Light appears: The Indians are as zealous in Religion, as the French, they oblige their Children to Pray Morning and Evening, particularly at Conasadauga; are punctual in performing their stated Acts of Devotion themselves, are still and peaceable in their own Families, and among each other as Neighbours!

When I compared our Manner of Living with theirs, it made me fear that the righteous and jealous God (who is wont to make Judgment begin at his own House first) was about to deliver us into their Hands, to be severely punished for our Departure from him; how long has he waited for our Return, O that we may therefore turn to him, before his Anger break out into a Flame, and there be no Remedy!

Our Case appears to me indeed very gloomy! notwithstanding our Enemies are inconsiderable in Number, compared with us; yet they are *united as one Man*, while we may be justly compared to a House divided against itself, and therefore cannot stand long, in our present Situation.

May Almighty God, graciously incline us to look to him for DELIVERANCE, to *repent* of our Sins, *reform* our Lives, and *unite* in the *vigorous* and *manly* Use of all proper Means to this End. Amen.

FINIS.

VI

A Narrative of the Lord's wonderful Dealings with John Marrant, a Black, (Now gone to Preach the Gospel in Nova-Scotia) Born in New-York, in North-America, Taken down from his own Relation, arranged, corrected and published, By the Rev. Mr. Aldridge.

†††

The narrative of John Marrant's captivity among the Cherokees is one of the first American books by a Negro and one of the three most popular stories of Indian captivity, surpassed in number of editions only by those of Peter Williamson (1757) and Mary Jemison (1824). The first edition of the Marrant narrative was published in 1785 in London, followed by four successive editions in the same year, two with the same imprint and collation, and two (the fourth and fifth) "with additions" by Marrant. Subsequent editions include the sixth, of London (1788) and those of Dublin (1790); London (1802); Halifax (1808, 1812, 1813); Leeds (1815); a Welch version, Adroddiad am Ymdriniaethau Rhyfeddol yr Arglwydd a Ioan Marrant *(Caerdydd, 1818); and that of Middletown, Connecticut (1820). A complete listing of the Marrant editions is in Dorothy B. Porter,* Early American Negro Writings, a Bibliographical Study, *in the Bibliographical Society of America* Papers *for 1945. Although his narrative is often mistakenly classed with American "slave narratives," John Marrant was an educated freeman from a family of some means. Born in New York in 1755, moved to Florida and then to Georgia, Marrant was sent at the age of eleven to Charleston, South Carolina, to learn a trade. He became instead an acomplished musician. When about fourteen he was converted by George Whitefield, famous Methodist evangelist from England, and became a religious zealot. As a consequence his family thought him insane, and he left home to live in the wilderness. Sometime during the year 1770 he was found by an Indian deer hunter and taken to live among the Cherokees. Of the principal tribes in the Indian South (Cherokees, Creeks, Choctaws, and Chickasaws) only the Cherokees belonged to the Iroquoian family; the others comprised the Muskhogean family. The Cherokees were the mountaineers of the southern Indians, their villages located at the four corners of Tennessee, Georgia, and the Carolinas. Their forty or so towns numbered a population of about 15,000 at the time of Marrant's captivity. Like most Indian tribes, the Cherokees were named not by themselves but by their neighbors. The name Cherokee, "People of the Cave Country," was given by the Choctaws; the Cherokees called themselves* Aniyunwiya, *"the Principal People." Marrant remained with the Indians nearly two years, then returned home until the outbreak of the Revolution, when he was pressed into the British naval service for seven years. After the war he stayed in England, was ordained in 1785, and went to preach the gospel to the Indians of Nova Scotia. The text of the London, 1788 edition of the Marrant narrative, which follows the enlarged ("with additions") 1785 edition, is reprinted here.*

††

Preface

READER, *The following Narrative is as plain and artless, as it is surprising and extraordinary. Plausible reasonings may amuse and delight, but facts, and facts like these, strike, are felt, and go home to the heart. Were the power, grace and providence of God ever more eminently displayed, than in the conversion, success, and deliverances of* John Marrant? *He and his companion enter the meeting at* Charles-Town *together; but the one is taken, and the other is left. He is struck to the ground, shaken over the mouth of hell, snatched as a brand from the burning; he is pardoned and justified; he is washed in the atoning blood, and made happy in his God. You soon have another view of him, drinking into his master's cup; he is tried and perplext, opposed and depised; the neighbours boot at him as he goes along; his mother, sisters and brother, hate and persecute him; he is friendless, and forsaken of all. These uneasy circumstances call forth the corruptions of his nature, and create a momentary debate, whether the pursuit of ease and pleasure was not to be preferred to the practice of religion, which he now found so sharp-and severe? The stripling is supported and strengthened. He is persuaded to forsake his family and kindred altogether. He crosses the fence, which marked the boundary between the wilderness and the cultivated country; and prefers the habitations of brutal residence, to the less hospitable dwellings of enmity to God and godliness. He wanders, but Christ is his guide and protector.—Who can view him among the* Indian *tribes without wonder? He arrives among the* Cherokees, *where gross ignorance wore its rudest forms, and savage despotism exercised its most terrifying empire. Here the child, just turned fourteen, without sling or stone, engages, and with the arrow of prayer pointed with faith,* wounded Goliah, *and conquers the king.*

The untutor'd monarch feels the truth, and worships the God of the Christians; the seeds of the Gospel are disseminated among the Indians *by a youthful hand, and Jesus is received and obeyed.*

The subsequent incidents related in this Narrative are great and affecting; but I must not anticipate the readers pleasure and profit.

*The novelty or magnitude of the facts contained in the following pages, may dispose some readers to question the truth of them. My answer to such is,—*1. *I believe it is clear to great numbers, and to some competent judges, that God is with the subject of them; but if he knowingly permitted an untruth to go abroad in the name of God, whilst it is confessed the Lord is with him, would it not follow, that the Almighty gave his sanction to a falsehood?—*2. *I have observed him to pay a conscientious regard to his word.—He appeared to me to feel most sensibly, when he related those parts of his Narrative, which describe his happiest moments with God, or the most remarkable interpositions of Divine Providence for him; and I have no reason to believe it was counterfeited.*

I have always preserved Mr. Marrant's *ideas, tho' I could not his language; no more alterations, however, have been made, than were thought necessary.*

I now commit the whole to God.—That he may make it generally useful is the prayer of thy ready servant, For Christ's sake,

W. ALDRIDGE.[1]

London
July 19th, 1785.

A Narrative, &c.

I John Marrant, born June 15th, 1755, in New-York, in North-America wish these gracious dealings of the Lord with me to be published, in hopes they may be useful to others, to encourage the fearful, to confirm the wavering, and to refresh the hearts of true believers. My father died when I was little more than four years of age, and before I was five my mother removed from New-York to St. Augustine, about seven hundred miles from that city. Here I was sent to school, and taught to read and spell; after we had resided here about eighteen months, it was found necessary to remove to Georgia, where we remained; and I was kept to school until I had attained my eleventh year. The Lord spoke to me in my early days, by these removes, if I could have understood him, and said, "Here we have no continuing city." We left Georgia, and went to Charles-Town, where it was intended I should be put apprentice to some trade. Some time after I had been in Charles-Town, as I was walking one day, I passed by a school, and heard music and dancing, which took my fancy very much, and I felt a strong inclination to learn the music. I went home, and informed my sister, that I had rather learn to play upon music than go to a trade. She told me she could do nothing in it, until she had acquainted my mother with my desire. Accordingly she wrote a letter concerning it to my mother, which, when she read, the contents were disapproved of by her, and she came to Charles-Town to pre-

1 The Reverend William Aldridge (1737–97), nonconformist minister trained in theology at the Countess of Huntingdon's college at Trevecca in South Wales (see n. 19, below). Aldridge was minister of the Jewry-street Chapel (Calvinistic Methodist) for twenty years.

vent it. She persuaded me much against it, but her persuasions were fruitless. Disobedience either to God or man, being one of the fruits of sin, grew out from me in early buds. Finding I was set upon it, and resolved to learn nothing else, she agreed to it, and went with me to speak to the man, and to settle upon the best terms with him she could. He insisted upon twenty pounds down, which was paid, and I was engaged to stay with him eighteen months, and my mother to find me every thing during that term. The first day I went to him he put the violin into my hand, which pleased me much, and, applying close, I learned very fast, not only to play, but to dance also; so that in six months I was able to play for the whole school. In the evenings after the scholars were dismissed, I used to resort to the bottom of our garden, where it was customary for some musicians to assemble to blow the French-horn. Here my improvement was so rapid, that in a twelve-month's time I became master both of the violin and of the French horn, and was much respected by the Gentlemen and Ladies whose children attended the school, as also by my master: This opened to me a large door of vanity and vice, for I was invited to all the balls and assemblies that were held in the town, and met with the general applause of the inhabitants. I was a stranger to want, being supplied with as much money as I had any occasion for; which my sister observing, said, "You have now no need of a trade." I was now in my thirteenth year, devoted to pleasure, and drinking in iniquity like water; a slave to every vice suited to my nature and to my years. The time I had engaged to serve my master being expired, he persuaded me to stay with him, and offered me any thing, or any money, not to leave him. His intreaties proving ineffectual, I quitted his service, and visited my mother in the country; with her I staid two months, living without God or hope in the world, fishing and hunting on the Sabbath-day. Unstable as water I returned to town, and wished to go to some trade. My sister's husban being informed of my inclination provided me with a master, on condition that I should serve him one year and a half on trial, and afterwards be bound, if he approved of me. Accordingly I went, but every evening I was sent for to play on music, somewhere or another; and I often continued out very late, sometimes all night, so as to render me incapable of attending my master's business the next day; yet in this manner I served him a year and four months, and was much approved of by him. He wrote a letter to my mother to come and have me bound, and whilst my mother was weighing the matter in her own mind, the gracious purposes of God, respecting a perishing sinner, were now to be disclosed. One evening I was sent for in a very particular manner to go and play for some Gentlemen, which I agreed to do, and was on my way to fulfil my promise; and passing by a large meeting-house I saw many lights in it, and crowds of people going in. I enquired what it meant, and was answered by my companion, that a crazy man was hallooing there; this raised my curiosity to go in, that I might hear what he was hallooing about. He persuaded me not to go in, but in vain. He then said, "If you will do one thing I will go in with you." I asked him what that was? He replied, "Blow the French-horn among them." I liked the proposal well enough, but expressed my fears of being beaten for disturbing them; but upon his promising to stand by and defend me, I agreed. So we went, and with much difficulty got within the doors. I was pushing the people to make room, to get the horn off my shoulder to blow it, just as Mr. Whitefield [2] was naming his text, and looking round, and, as I thought, directly upon me, and pointing with his finger, he uttered these words, "PREPARE TO MEET THY GOD, O ISRAEL." The Lord accompanied the word with such power, that I was struck to the ground, and lay both speechless and senseless near half an hour. When I was come a little too, I found two men attending me, and a woman throwing water in my face, and holding a smelling-bottle to my nose; and when something more recovered, every word I heard from the minister was like a parcel of swords thrust into me, and what added to my distress, I thought I saw the devil on every side of me. I was constrained in the bitterness of my spirit to halloo out in the midst of the congregation, which disturbing them, they took me away; but finding I could neither walk or stand, they carried me as far as the vestry, and there I remained till the service was over. When the people were dismissed Mr. Whitefield came into the vestry, and being told of my condition he came immediately, and the first word he said to me was, "JESUS

[2] George Whitefield (1714–70), English evangelist and founder of Calvinistic Methodism.

CHRIST HAS GOT THEE AT LAST." He asked where I lived, intending to come and see me the next day; but recollecting he was to leave the town the next morning, he said he could not come himself, but would send another minister; he desired them to get me home, and then taking his leave of me, I saw him no more. When I reached my sister's house, being carried by two men, she was very uneasy to see me in so distressed a condition. She got me to bed, and sent for a doctor, who came immediately, and after looking at me, he went home, and sent me a bottle of mixture, and desired her to give me a spoonful every two hours; but I could not take any thing the doctor sent, nor indeed keep in bed; this distressed my sister very much, and she cried out, "The lad will surely die." She sent for two other doctors, but no medicine they prescribed could I take. No, no; it may be asked, a wounded spirit who can cure? as well as who can bear? In this distress of soul I continued for three days without any food, only a little water now and then. On the fourth day, the minister [3] Mr. Whitefield had desired to visit me came to see me, and being directed upstairs, when he entered the room, I thought he made my distress much worse. He wanted to take hold of my hand, but I durst not give it to him. He insisted upon taking hold of it, and I then got away from him on the side of the bed; but being very weak I fell down, and before I could recover he came to me and took me by the hand, and lifted me up, and after a few words desired to go to prayer. So he fell upon his knees, and pulled me down also; after he had spent some time in prayer he rose up, and asked me now how I did; I answered much worse; he then said, "Come, we will have the old thing over again," and so we kneeled down a second time, and after he had prayed earnestly we got up, and he said again, "How do you you do now?" I replied worse and worse, and asked him if he intended to kill me? "No, no," said he, "you are worth a thousand dead men, let us try the old thing over again," and so falling upon our knees, he continued in prayer a considerable time, and near the close of his prayer, the Lord was pleased to set my soul at perfect liberty, and being filled with joy I began to praise the Lord immediately; my sorrows were turned into peace, and joy, and love. The minister said, "How is it now?" I answered, all is well, all happy. He then

[3] "Mr. HALL, a Baptist Minister, at Charles-Town" [Marrant's note].

took his leave of me; but called every day for several days afterwards, and the last time he said, "Hold fast that thou hast already obtained, 'till Jesus Christ come." I now read the Scriptures very much. My master sent often to know how I did, and at last came himself, and finding me well, asked me if I would not come to work again? I answered no. He asked me the reason, but receiving no answer he went away. I continued with my sister about three weeks, during which time she often asked me to play upon the violin for her, which I refused; then she said I was crazy and mad, and so reported it among the neighbours, which opened the mouths of all around against me. I then resolved to go to my mother, which was eighty-four miles from Charles-Town. I was two days on my journey home, and enjoyed much communion with God on the road, and had occasion to mark the gracious interpositions of his kind providence as I passed along. The third day I arrived at my mother's house, and was well received. At supper they sat down to eat without asking the Lord's blessing, which caused me to burst out into tears. My mother asked me what was the matter? I answered, I wept because they sat down to supper without asking the Lord's blessing. She bid me, with much surprise, to ask a blessing. I remained with her fourteen days without interruption; the Lord pitied me, being a young soldier. Soon, however, Satan began to stir up my two sisters and brother, who were then at home with my mother; they called me every name but that which was good. The more they persecuted me, the stronger I grew in grace. At length my mother turned against me also, and the neighbours joined her, and there was not a friend to assist me, or that I could speak to; this made me earnest with God. In these circumstances, being the youngest but one of our family, and young in Christian experience, I was tempted so far as to threaten my life; but reading my Bible one day, and finding that if I did destroy myself I could not come where God was, I betook myself to the fields, and some days staid out from morning to night to avoid the persecutors. I staid one time two days without any food, but seemed to have clearer views into the spiritual things of God. Not long after this I was sharply tried, and reasoned the matter within myself, whether I should turn to my old courses of sin and vice, or serve and cleave to the Lord; after prayer to God, I was fully persuaded in my mind, that if I turned to my old ways I should perish eternally. Upon this I went home, and finding them all as hardened, or worse than before, and every body saying I was crazy; but a little sister I had, about nine years of age, used to cry when she saw them persecute me, and continuing so about five weeks and three days, I thought it was better for me to die than to live among such people. I rose one morning very early, to get a little quietness and retirement, I went into the woods, and staid still eight o'clock in the morning; upon my return I found them all at breakfast; I passed by them, and went up-stairs without any interruption; I went upon my knees to the Lord, and returned him thanks; then I took up a small pocket Bible and one of Dr. Watts's hymn books,[4] and passing by them went out without one word spoken by any of us. After spending some time in the fields I was persuaded to go from home altogether. Accordingly I went over the fence, about half a mile from our house, which divided the inhabited and cultivated parts of the country from the wilderness. I continued travelling in the desart all day without the least inclination of returning back. About evening I began to be surrounded with wolves; I took refuge from them on a tree, and remained there all night. About eight o'clock next morning I descended from the tree, and returned God thanks for the mercies of the night. I went on all this day without any thing to eat or drink. The third day, taking my Bible out of my pocket, I read and walked for some time, and then being wearied and almost spent I sat down, and after resting awhile I rose to go forward; but had not gone above a hundred yards when something tripped me up, and I fell down; I prayed to the Lord upon the ground that he would command the wild beast to devour me, that I might be with him in glory. I made this request to God the third and part of the fourth day. The fourth day in the morning, descending from my usual lodging, a tree, and having nothing all this time to eat, and but a little water to drink, I was so feeble that I tumbled half way down the tree, not being able to support myself, and lay upon my back on the ground an hour and a half, praying and crying; after which getting a little strength, and trying to

4 Isaac Watts (1674–1748), English clergyman and religious poet, known especially for his hymns (e.g., "There is a land of pure delight" and "O God, our help in ages past").

stand upright to walk, I found myself not able; then I went upon my hands and knees, and so crawled till I reach a tree that was tumbled down, in order to get across it, and there I prayed with my body leaning upon it above an hour, that the Lord would take me to himself. Such nearness to God I then enjoyed, that I willingly resigned myself into his hands. After some time I thought I was strengthened, so I got across the tree without my feet or hands touching the ground; but struggling I fell over on the other side, and then thought the Lord will now answer my prayer, and take me home: But the time was not come. After laying there a little, I rose, and looking about, saw at some distance bunches of grass, called deer-grass; I felt a strong desire to get at it; though I rose, yet it was only on my hands and knees, being so feeble, and in this manner I reached the grass. I was three quarters of an hour going in this form twenty yards. When I reached it I was unable to pull it up, so I bit it off like a horse, and prayed the Lord to bless it to me, and I thought it the best meal I ever had in my life, and I think so still, it was so sweet. I returned my God hearty thanks for it, and then lay down about an hour. Feeling myself very thirsty, I prayed the Lord to provide me with some water. Finding I was something strengthened I got up, and stood on my feet, and staggered from one tree to another, if they were near each other, otherwise the journey was too long for me. I continued moving so for some time, and at length passing between two trees, I happened to fall upon some bushes, among which were a few large hollow leaves, which had caught and contained the dews of the night, and lying low among the bushes, were not exhaled by the solar rays; this water in the leaves fell upon me as I tumbled down and was lost, I was now tempted to think the Lord had given me water from Heaven, and I had wasted it. I then prayed the Lord to forgive me. What poor unbelieving creatures we are! though we are assured the Lord will supply all our needs. I was presently directed to a puddle of water very muddy, which some wild pigs had just left; I kneeled down, and asked the Lord to bless it to me, so I drank both mud and water mixed together, and being satisfied I returned the Lord thanks, and went on my way rejoicing. This day was much chequered with wants and supplies, with dangers and deliverances. I continued travelling on for nine days, feeding upon grass, and not knowing whither I was going; but the Lord Jesus Christ was very present, and that comforted me through all. The next morning, having quitted my customary lodging, and returned thanks to the Lord for my preservation through the night, reading and travelling on, I passed between two bears, about twenty yards distance from each other. Both sat and looked at me, but I felt no fear; and after I had passed them, they both went the same way from me without growling, or the least apparent uneasiness. I went and returned God thanks for my escape, who had tamed the wild beasts of the forest, and made them friendly to me; I rose from my knees and walked on, singing hymns of praise to God, about five o'clock in the afternoon, and about 55 miles from home, right through the wilderness. As I was going on, and musing upon the goodness of the Lord, an Indian hunter, who stood at some distance, saw me; he hid himself behind a tree; but as I passed along he bolted out, and put his hands on my breast, which surprised me a few moments. He then asked me where I was going? I answered I did not know, but where the Lord was pleased to guide me. Having heard me praising God before I came up to him, he enquired who I was talking to? I told him I was talking to my Lord Jesus; he seemed surprised, and asked me where he was? for he did not see him there. I told him he could not be seen with bodily eyes. After a little more talk, he insisted upon taking me home; but I refused, and added, that I would die rather than return home. He then asked me if I knew how far I was from home? I answered, I did not know; you are 55 miles and a half, says he, from home. He farther asked me how I did to live? I said I was supported by the Lord. He asked me how I slept? I answered, the Lord provided me with a bed every night; he further enquired what preserved me from being devoured by the wild beasts? I replied, the Lord Jesus Christ kept me from them. He stood astonished, and said, you say the Lord Jesus Christ do this, and do that, and do every thing for you, he must be a very fine man, where is he? I replied, he is here present. To this he made me no answer, only said, I know you, and your mother and sister, and upon a little further conversation I found he did know them, having been used in winter to sell skins in our town. This alarmed me, and I wept for fear he would take me home by force; but when he saw me so affected, he said he would not take me home if I would go with him. I objected against that, for fear he would rob me of my comfort and communion with God: But at last, being much pressed, I consented to go. Our employment for ten weeks and three days, was killing deer, and taking off their skins by day, which we afterwards hung on the trees to dry till they were sent for; the means of defence and security against our nocturnal enemies, always took up the evenings: We collected a number of large bushes, and placed them nearly in a circular form, which uniting at the extremity, afforded us both a verdant covering, and a sufficient shelter from the night dews. What moss we could gather was strewed upon the ground, and this composed our bed. A fire was kindled in the front of our temporary lodging-room, and fed with fresh fuel all night, as we slept and watched by turns; and this was our defence from the dreadful animals, whose shining eyes and tremendous roar we often saw and heard during the night.

By constant conversation with the hunter, I acquired a fuller knowledge of the Indian tongue: [5] This, together with the sweet communion I enjoyed with God, I have considered as a preparation for the great trial I was soon after to pass through.

The hunting season being now at an end, we left the woods, and directed our course towards a large Indian town, belonging to the Cherokee nation; and having reached it, I said to the hunter, they will not suffer me to enter in. He replied, as I was with him, nobody would interrupt me.

There was an Indian fortification all round the town, and a guard placed at each entrance. The hunter passed one of these without molestation, but I was stopped by the guard and examined. They asked me where I came from, and what was my business there? My companion of the woods attempted to speak for me, but was not permitted; he was taken away, and I saw him no more. I was now surrounded by about 50 men, and carried to one of

5 Cherokee groups were the Lower (on the Savannah waters), Middle (on the Little Tennessee), and Upper (comprising the inhabitants of the valley towns on the Hiwassee and the Overhills on the lower reaches of the Little Tennessee). Between the Lower and the others was a difference of dialect sufficient to distinguish, but not separate, them. Their language revealed their Iroquoian ancestry, the dialect being an ancient separation from the parent stock.

their chiefs to be examined by him. When I came before him, he asked me what was my business there? I told him I came there with a hunter, whom I met with in the woods. He replied, "Did I not know that whoever came there without giving a better account of themselves than I did, was to be put to death?" I said I did not know it. Observing that I answered him so readily in his own language, he asked me where I learnt it? To this I returned no answer, but burst out into a flood of tears, and calling upon my Lord Jesus. At this he stood astonished, and expressed a concern for me, and said I was young. He asked me who my Lord Jesus was?—To this I gave him no answer, but continued praying and weeping. Addressing himself to the officer who stood by him, he said he was sorry; but it was the law, and it must not be broken. I was then ordered to be taken away, and put into a place of confinement. They led me from their court into a low dark place, and thrust me into it, very dreary and dismal; they made fast the door, and set a watch. The judge sent for the executioner, and gave him his warrant for my execution in the afternoon of the next day. The executioner came, and gave me notice of it, which made me very happy, as the near prospect of death made me hope for a speedy deliverance from the body: And truly this dungeon became my chapel, for the Lord Jesus did not leave me in this great trouble, but was very present, so that I continued blessing him, and singing his praises all night without ceasing: The watch hearing the noise, informed the executioner that somebody had been in the dungeon with me all night; upon which he came in to see and examine, with a great torch lighted in his hand, who it was I had with me; but finding nobody, he turned round, and asked me who it was? I told him it was the Lord Jesus Christ; but he made no answer, turned away, went out, and locked the door. At the hour appointed for my execution I was taken out, and led to the destined spot, amidst a vast number of people. I praised the Lord all the way we went, and when we arrived at the place I understood the kind of death I was to suffer, yet, blessed be God, none of those things moved me. The executioner shewed me a basket of turpentine-wood, stuck full of small pieces, like skewers; he told me I was to be stripped naked, and laid down in the basket, and these sharp pegs were to be stuck into me, and then set on fire, and when they had burnt to my body,[6] I was to be turned on the other side, and served in the same manner, and then to be taken by four men and thrown into the flame, which was to finish the execution. I burst into tears, and asked what I had done to deserve so cruel a death! To this he gave me no answer. I cried out, Lord, if it be thy will that it should be so, thy will be done: I then asked the executioner to let me go to prayer; he asked me to whom? I answered, to the Lord my God; he seemed surprized, and asked me where he was? I told him he was present; upon which he gave me leave. I desired them all to do as I did, so I fell down upon my knees, and mentioned to the Lord his delivering of the three children in the fiery furnace, and of Daniel in the lion's den, and had close communion with God. I prayed in English a considerable time, and about the middle of my prayer, the Lord impressed a strong desire upon my mind to turn into their language, and pray in their tongue. I did so, and with remarkable liberty, which wonderfully affected the people. One circumstance was very singular, and strikingly displays the power and grace of God. I believe the executioner was savingly converted to God. He rose from his knees, and embraced me round the middle, and was unable to speak for about five minutes; the first words he expressed, when he had utterance, were, "No man shall hurt three till thou hast been to the king." [7]

I was taken away immediately, and as we passed along, and I was reflecting upon the deliverance which the Lord had wrought out for me, and hearing the praises which the executioner was singing to the Lord, I must own I was utterly at a loss to find words to praise him. I broke out in these words, what can't the Lord Jesus do! and what power is like unto his! I will thank thee for what is passed, and trust thee for what is to come. I will sing thy praise with my feeble tongue whilst life and breath shall last, and when I

[6] "These pegs were to be kindled at the opposite end from the body" [Marrant]. This method of execution was a trait of the northern tribes in the late eighteenth century (see Manheim anthology, n. 5), evidently shared in the southeast.

[7] That is, the head chief. Prior to contact with Europeans, southern Indian tribes operated under systems of near-anarchy, without head, or even regional, chiefs. These positions seem to have been instituted by the French and English in order to create responsible agents with whom they could deal.

fail to sound thy praises here, I hope to sing them round thy throne above: And thus, with unspeakable joy, I sung two verses of Dr. Watts's hymns:

> "My God, the spring of all my joys,
>   The life of my delights;
> The glory of my brightest days,
>   And comfort of my nights.
> In darkest shades, if thou appear,
>   My dawning is begun;
> Thou art my soul's bright morning star,
>   And thou my rising sun."

Passing by the judge's door, he stopped us, and asked the executioner why he brought me back? The man fell upon his knees, and begged he would permit me to be carried before the king, which being granted, I went on, guarded by two hundred soldiers with bows and arrows. After many windings I entered the king's outward chamber, and after waiting some time he came to the door, and his first question was, how came I there? I answered, I came with a hunter whom I met in the woods, and who persuaded me to come there. He then asked me how old I was? I told him not fifteen. He asked me how I was supported before I met with this man? I answered, by the Lord Jesus Christ, which seemed to confound him. He turned round, and asked me if he lived where I came from? I answered, yes, and here also. He looked about the room, and said he did not see him; but I told him I felt him. The executioner fell upon his knees, and intreated the king, and told him what he had felt of the same Lord. At this instant the king's eldest daughter came into the chamber, a person about 19 years of age, and stood at my right-hand. I had a Bible in my hand, which she took out of it, and having opened it, she kissed it, and seemed much delighted with it. When she had put it into my hand again, the king asked me what it was? and I told him, the name of my God was recorded there; and, after several questions, he bid me read it, which I did, particularly the 53d chapter of Isaiah, in the most solemn manner I was able; and also the 26th chapter of Matthew's Gospel; and when I pronounced the name of Jesus, the particular effect it had upon me was observed by the king. When I had finished reading, he asked me why I read those names [8] with so much reverence? I told him, because the Being to whom those names belonged made heaven and earth, and I and he; this he denied.[9] I then pointed to the sun, and asked him who made the sun, and moon, and stars, and preserved them in their regular order? He said there was a man in their town that did it. I laboured as much as I could to convince him to the contrary. His daughter took the book out of my hand a second time; she opened it, and kissed it again; her father bid her give it to me, which she did; but said, with much sorrow, the book would not speak to her. The executioner then fell upon his knees, and begged the king to let me go to prayer, which being granted, we all went upon our knees, and now the Lord displayed his glorious power. In the midst of the prayer some of them cried out, particularly the king's daughter, and the man who ordered me to be executed, and several others seemed under deep conviction of sin: This made the king very angry; he called me a witch, and commanded me to be thrust into the prison, and to be executed the next morning. This was enough to make me think, as old Jacob once did, "All these things are against me;" for I was dragged away, and thrust into the dungeon with much indignation; but God, who never forsakes his people, was with me. Though I was weak in body, yet was I strong in the spirit: The Lord works, and who shall let it? The executioner went to the king, and assured him, that if he put me to death, his daughter would never be well. They used the skill of all their doctors that afternoon and night; but physical prescriptions were useless. In the morning the executioner came to me, and, without opening the prison door, called to me, and hearing me answer, said, "Fear not, thy God who delivered thee yesterday, will deliver thee to-day." This comforted me very much, especially to find he could trust the Lord. Soon after I was fetched out; I thought it was to be executed; but they led me away to the king's chamber with much bodily weakness, having been without food two days. When I came

[8] "Or what those parts were which seemed to affect me so much, not knowing what I read, as he did not understand the English language" [Marrant].

[9] What religion the Cherokees had was private, unorganized for public expression, without missionary duties, and wholly unrelated to their morality, which was drawn from tribal custom.

Capture of Mrs. Hanson and her daughter. From John Frost, *Pictorial History of Indian Wars and Captivities* (New York, 1873).

Death at the stake. From John Frost, *Pictorial History of Indian Wars and Captivities* (New York, 1873).

into the king's presence, he said to me, with much anger, if I did not make his daughter and that man well, I should be laid down and chopped into pieces before him. I was not afraid, but the Lord tried my faith sharply. The king's daughter and the other person were brought out into the outer chamber, and we went to prayer; but the heavens were locked up to my petitions. I besought the Lord again, but received no answer: I cried again, and he was intreated. He said, "Be it to thee as thou wilt;" the Lord appeared most lovely and glorious; the king himself was awakened, and the other set at liberty.[10] A great change took place among the people; the king's house became Gods' house; the soldiers were ordered away, and the poor condemned prisoner had perfect liberty, and was treated like a prince. Now the Lord made all my enemies to become my great friends. I remained nine weeks in the king's palace, praising God day and night: I was never out but three days all the time. I had assumed the habit of the country, and was dressed much like the king, and nothing was too good for me. The king would take off his golden ornaments, his chain and bracelets, like a child, if I objected to them, and lay them aside. Here I learnt to speak their tongue in the highest stile.

I began now to feel an inclination growing upon me to go farther on, but none to return home. The king being acquainted with this, expressed his fears of my being used ill by the next Indian nation, and, to prevent it, sent 50 men, and a recommendation to the king, with me. The next nation was called the Creek Indians, at 60 miles distance. Here I was received with kindness, owing to the king's influence, from whom I had parted; here I staid five weeks. I next visited the Catawar [11] Indians, at about 55 miles distance from the others: Lastly, I went among the Housaw [12] Indians, 80 miles distant from the last mentioned; here I staid seven weeks. These nations were then at peace with each other, and I passed among them without danger, being recommended from one to the other. When they recollect, that the white people drove them from the American shores, the three first nations have often

[10] That is, Marrant himself.

[11] Choctaw. The name is derived from the Creek word *cate*, or *chate*, meaning "red."

[12] Chickasaw.

united, and murdered all the white people in the back settlements which they could lay hold of, man, woman, and child. I had not much reason to believe any of these three nations were savingly wrought upon, and therefore I returned to the Cherokee nation, which took me up eight weeks. I continued with my old friends seven weeks and two days.

I now and then found, that my affections to my family and country were not dead; they were sometimes very sensibly felt, and at last strengthened into an invincible desire of returning home. The king was much against it; but feeling the same strong bias towards my country, after we had asked Divine direction, the king consented, and accompanied me 60 miles with 140 men. I went to prayer three times before we could part, and then he sent 40 men with me a hundred miles farther; I went to prayer, and then took my leave of them, and passed on my way. I had 70 miles now to go to the back settlements of the white people. I was surrounded very soon with wolves again, which made my old lodging both necessary and welcome. However it was not long, for in two days I reached the settlements, and on the third I found a house: It was about dinner-time, and as I came up to the door the family saw me, were frightened, and ran away. I sat down to dinner alone, and eat very heartily, and after returning God thanks, I went to see what was become of the family. I found means to lay hold of a girl that stood peeping at me from behind a barn. She fainted away, and it was upwards of an hour before she recovered: it was nine o'clock before I could get them all to venture in, they were so terrified.

My dress was purely in the Indian stile; the skins of wild beasts composed my garments; my head was set out in the savage manner, with a long pendant down my back, a sash round my middle, without breeches, and a tomahawk by my side. In about two days they became sociable. Having visited three or four other families, at the distance of 16 or 20 miles, I got them altogether to prayer on the Sabbath days, to the number of 17 persons. I staid with them six weeks, and they expressed much sorrow when I left them. I was now one hundred and twelve miles from home. On the road I sometimes met with a house, then I was hospitably entertained; and when I met with none, a tree lent me the use of its friendly shelter and protection from the prowling beasts of the woods during the night. The God of mercy and grace supported me thus for eight days, and on the ninth I reached my uncle's house.

The following particulars, relating to the manner in which I was made known to my family, are less interesting; and yet, perhaps, some readers would not forgive their omission: I shall, however, be as brief as I can. I asked my uncle for a lodging, which he refused. I enquired how far the town was off; three quarters of a mile, said he. Do you know Mrs. Marrant and family, and how the children do? was my next question. He said he did, they were all well, but one was lately lost; at this I turned my head and wept. He did not know me, and upon refusing again to lodge me, I departed. When I reached the town it was dark, and passing by a house where one of my old school-fellows lived, I knocked at the door; he came out, and asked me what I wanted? I desired a lodging, which was granted: I went in, but was not known. I asked him if he knew Mrs. Marrant, and how the family were? He said, he had just left them, they were all well; but a young lad, with whom he went to school, who, after he had quitted school, went to Charles-Town to learn some trades; but came home crazy, and rambled in the woods, and was torn in pieces by the wild beasts. How do you know, said I, that he was killed by wild beasts? I, and his brother, and uncle, and others, said he, went three days into the woods in search of him, and found his carcase torn, and brought it home, and buried it, and they are now in mourning for him. This affected me very much, and I wept; observing it, he said, what is the matter? I made no answer. At supper they sat down without craving a blessing, for which I reproved them; this so affected the man, that I believe it ended in a sound conversion. Here is a wild man, says he, come out of the woods to be a witness for God, and to reprove our ingratitude and stupefaction! After supper I went to prayer, and then to bed. Rising a little before day-light, and praising the Lord, as my custom was, the family were surprised, and got up: I staid with them till nine o'clock, and then went to my mother's house in the next street. The singularity of my dress drew every body's eyes upon me, yet none knew me. I knocked at my mother's door, my sister opened it, and was startled at my appearance. Having expressed a desire to see Mrs. Marrant, I was answered, she was not very well, and that my business with her could be done by the person at the door, who also attempted to shut me out, which I prevented. My mother being called, I went in, and sat down, a mob of people being round the door. My mother asked, "what is your business;" only to see you, said I. She was much obliged to me, but did not know me. I asked, how are your children? how are your two sons? She replied, her daughters were in good health, of her two sons, one was well, and with her, but the other,—unable to contain, she burst into a flood of tears, and retired. I was overcome, and wept much, but nobody knew me. This was an affecting scene! Presently my brother came in: He enquired who I was, and what I was? My sister did not know; but being uneasy at my presence, they contrived to get me out of the house, which being over-heard by me, I resolved not to stir. My youngest sister, eleven years of age, came in from school, and knew me the moment she saw me: She goes into the kitchen, and tells the woman her brother was come; but her news finding no credit there she returns, passes through the room where I sat, made a running curtsey, and says to my eldest sister in the next room, it is my brother! She was then called a foolish girl, and threatened; the child cried, and insisted upon it. She went crying up-stairs to my mother, and told her; but neither would my mother believe her. At last they said to her, if it be your brother, go and kiss him, and ask him how he does? She ran and clasped me round the neck, and, looking me in the face, said, "Are not you my brother John?" I answered yes, and wept. I was then made known to all the family, to my friends, and acquaintances, who received me, and were glad, and rejoiced: [13] Thus the dead was brought to life again; thus the lost was found. I shall now close the Narrative, with only remarking a few incidents in my life, until my connection with my Right Honourable Patroness, the Countess of HUNTINGDON.

I remained with my relations till the commencement of the American troubles.[14] I used to go and hear the Word of God, if

13 "I had been absent from them about 23 months" [Marrant].

14 The Revolution.

any Gospel ministers came into the country, though at a considerable distance, and thereby got acquainted with a few poor people, who feared God in Will's-Town, and Borough Town, Dorchester Town, and other places thereabouts; and in those places we used to meet and associate together for Christian conversation, and, at their request, I frequently went to prayer with them, and at times enjoyed much of the Lord's presence among them; and yet, reader, my soul was got into a declining state. Don't forget our Lord's exhortation, "What I say unto you, I say unto all, WATCH."

About this time I was an eye-witness of the remarkable conversion of a child seven and a half years old, named Mary Scott, which I shall here mention, in hopes the Lord may make it useful and profitable to my young readers. Her parents lived in the house adjoining to my sister's. One day, as I was returning from my work, and passing by the school where she was instructed, I saw the children coming out, and stop'd and looked among them for her, to take her home in my hand; but not seeing her among those that were coming out, I supposed she was gone before, and went on towards home; when passing by the church-yard, which was in my way, I saw her very busy walking from one tomb to another, and went to her, and asked her what she was doing there? She told me, that in the lesson she had set her at school that morning, in the Twentieth of the Revelations, she read, "I saw the dead, small and great, stand before God," &c. and she had been measuring the graves with a tape she then held in her hand, to see if there were any so small as herself among them, and that she had found six that were shorter. I then said, and what of that? She answered, "I shall die, Sir." I told her I knew she would, but hoped she would live till she was a grown woman; but she continued to express her desire to depart, and be with Christ, rather than to live till she was grown up. I then took her by the hand and brought her home with me. After this, she was observed to be always very solid and thoughtful, and that passage appeared always to be fresh upon her mind. I used frequently to be with her when in town, and at her request we often read and prayed together, and she appeared much affected. She never afterwards was seen out at play with other children; but spent her leisure time in reading God's word and prayer. In about four months after this she was taken ill, and kept her room about three weeks; when first taken, she told me she should never come down stairs alive. I frequently visited her during her illness, and made light of what she said about her dying so soon; but in the last week of her illness she said to me, in a very solemn manner, "Sir, I shall die before Saturday-night." The physicians attended her, but she took very few (if any) medicines, and appeared quite calm and resigned to God's will. On Friday morning, which was the day she died, I visited her, and told her that I hoped she would not die so soon as she said; but she told me that she should certainly die before six o'clock that evening. About five o'clock I visited her again. She was then sitting in a chair, and reading in her Bible, to all appearance pretty well recovered. After setting with her about a quarter of an hour, she got up, and desired me to go down, and send her mother up with a clean shift for her, which I did; and after a little time, when I went up again, I found her lying on the bed, with her eyes fixed up to Heaven; when turning herself and seeing me, she said, "Mr. Marrant, don't you see that pretty town, and those fine people, how they shine like gold? —O how I long to be with my Lord and his redeemed Children in Glory!" and then turning to her parents and two sisters (who were all present, having by her desire been called to her) she shook hands with them, and bade them farewell; desiring them not to lament for her when she was dead, for she was going to that fine place where God would wipe away all tears from her eyes, and she should sing Hallelujahs to God and the Lamb for ever and ever, and where she hoped afterwards to meet them; and then turning again to me, she said, "Farewell, and God bless you," and then fell asleep in the arms of Jesus. This afterwards proved the conversion of her mother.

In those troublesome times, I was pressed on board the Scorpion sloop of war, as their musician, as they were told I could play on music.—I continued in his majesty's service six years and eleven months; and with shame confess, that a lamentable stupor crept over all my spiritual vivacity, life and vigour; I got cold and dead. My gracious God, my dear Father in his dear Son, roused me every now and then by dangers and deliverances.—I was at the siege of Charles-Town,[15] and passed through many dangers. When the town was taken, my old royal benefactor and convert, the king of the Cherokee Indians, riding into the town with general Clinton, saw me, and knew me: He alighted off his horse,[16] and came to me; said he was glad to see me; that his daughter was very happy, and sometimes longed to get out of the body.

Some time after this I was cruising about in the American seas, and cannot help mentioning a singular deliverance I had from the most imminent danger, and the use the Lord made of it to me. We were overtaken by a violent storm; I was washed overboard, and thrown on again; dashed into the sea a second time, and tossed upon the deck again. I now fastened a rope round my middle, as a security against being thrown into the sea again; but, alas! forgot to fasten it to any part of the ship; being carried away the third time by the fury of the waves, when in the sea, I found the rope both useless and an incumbrance. I was in the sea the third time about eight minutes, and the sharks came round me in great numbers; one of an enormous size, that could easily have taken me into his mouth at once, passed and rubbed against my side. I then cried more earnestly to the Lord than I had done for some time; and he who heard Jonah's prayer, did not shut out mine, for I was thrown aboard again; these were the means the Lord used to revive me, and I began now to set out afresh.

I was in the engagement with the Dutch off the Dogger Bank, on board the Princess-Amelia, of 84 guns.[17] We had a great number killed and wounded; the deck was running with blood; six men were killed, and three wounded, stationed at the same gun with me; my head and face were covered with the blood and brains of the

[15] The British, under Gen. Henry Clinton, had called up troops from Savannah and New York and had massed some ten thousand soldiers for the attack on Charleston. The siege began on March 31, 1780, and ended with the capitulation of Maj. Gen. Benjamin Lincoln on May 12. It was the greatest American surrender of the war.

[16] "Though it is unusual for Indians to have a horse, yet the king accompanied the general on the present successful occasion riding on horse-back. If the king wished to serve me, there was no opportunity; the town being taken on Friday afternoon, Saturday an express arrived from the commander in chief at New-York, for a large detachment, or the town would fall into the hands of the Americans, which hurried us away on Sunday morning" [Marrant].

[17] "This action was on the 5th of August, 1781" [Marrant].

slain: I was wounded, but did not fall, till a quarter of an hour before the engagement ended, and was happy during the whole of it. After being in the hospital three months and 16 days, I was sent to the West-Indies, on board a ship of war, and, after cruising in those seas, we returned home as a convoy. Being taken ill of my old wounds, I was put into the hospital at Plymouth, and had not been there long, when the physician gave it as his opinion, that I should not be capable of serving the king again; I was therefore discharged, and came to London, where I lived with a respectable and pious merchant three years,[18] who was unwilling to part with me. During this time I saw my call to the ministry fuller and clearer; had a feeling concern for the salvation of my countrymen: I carried them constantly in the arms of prayer and faith to the throne of grace, and had continual sorrow in my heart for my brethren, for my kinsmen, according to the flesh.—I wrote a letter to my brother, who returned me an answer, in which he prayed some ministers would come and preach to them, and desired me to shew it to the minister whom I attended. I used to exercise my gifts on a Monday evening in prayer and exhortation, and was approved of, and ordained at Bath. Her Ladyship [19] having seen the letter from my brother in Nova-Scotia, thought Providence called me there: To which place I am now bound, and expect to sail in a few days.

I have now only to intreat the earnest prayers of all my kind Christian friends, that I may be carried safe there; kept humble, made faithful, and successful; that strangers may hear of and run to Christ; that Indian tribes may stretch out their hands to God; that the black nations may be made white in the blood of the Lamb; that vast multitudes of hard tongues, and of a strange speech, may learn the language of Canaan, and sing the song of Moses, and of the Lamb; and, anticipating the glorious prospect, may we all with fervent hearts, and willing tongues, sing hallelujah; the

[18] "About three years; it might be a few weeks over or under" [Marrant]. This merchant was John Marsden; see n. 20, below.

[19] The Countess of Huntingdon (Selina Hastings, 1707–91), Marrant's "Right Honourable Patroness" mentioned earlier in the narrative. The Countess was a Methodist convert and friend of Whitefield, who was her chaplain in 1747. She founded the Methodist religious community, "Lady Huntingdon's Connexion," in 1768 to supply ministers for the congregations under her patronage. Marrant was trained and received his ordination here.

kingdoms of the world are become the kingdoms of our God, and of his Christ. Amen and Amen.[20]

London,
Prescott-Street, No. 60,
July 18, 1785.

[20] The following notices are appended to the narrative:

[1] "SINCE MR. MARRANT's arrival at Nova-Scotia, several letters have been received from himself by different persons, and some by Mr. ALDRIDGE, the Editor of this Narrative; from which it appears, that Mr. MARRANT has travelled through that province, preaching the Gospel, and not without success; that he has undergone much fatigue, and passed through many dangers; that he has visited the Indians in their Wigwams, who, he relates, were disposed to hear and receive the Gospel.—This is the substance of the letters transmitted by him to the Editor above-mentioned."

[2] "London, August 16, 1785

MR. *John Marrant liv'd with us about 3 years, which he did with honesty and sobriety—he feared God, and had a desire to save his soul before he ever came to live with us;—he shewed himself to be such while he lived with us, by attending the means of Grace diligently, and by being tender hearted to the poor, by giving them money and victuals if he had left himself none. He left us with no misunderstanding whatever, about April last.*

This is nothing but the truth.

(Signed)
John Marsden,
H. Marsden."

Cotton-Merchant,
No. 38, Dowgate-Hill.

VII

Affecting History of the Dreadful Distresses of Frederic Manheim's Family. To Which Are Added, the Sufferings of John Corbly's Family. An Encounter Between a White Man and Two Savages. Extraordinary Bravery of a Woman. Adventures of Capt. Isaac Stewart. Deposition of Massey Herbeson. Adventures and Sufferings of Peter Williamson. Remarkable Adventures of Jackson Johonnot. Account of the Destruction of the Settlements at Wyoming.

†††

The Manheim anthology, a commercially inspired potpourri of captivity horrors, was first compiled and published in 1793. Subsequent editions include Mathew Carey's Philadelphia edition of 1794, the shortened Farnsworth version in 1798, a Boston reprint in 1799 retitled Horrid Indian Cruelties! Affecting History of . . . , *and three early nineteenth-century editions of the full anthology: one by Chapman Whitcomb in 1800; a reissue by Carey, also in 1800; and the Collins and Stockwell edition of 1802. Variations of the Manheim collection were subsequently printed in many captivity collections, including Loudon (1808), Drake (1839), and Pritts (1859). The Williamson, Herbeson, and Johonnot narratives are all previously published captivities and were simply reprinted in the Manheim anthology. The others (the Manheim account itself, the Reverend Mr. Corbly's letter, the "Extraordinary Bravery of a Woman," and Isaac Stewart's narrative) appeared for the first time in the Manheim anthology and are otherwise undocumented as to provenance, veracity, and, in some cases, authorship. The Williamson narrative contains some doubtful or specious passages; and the Johonnot account may not be a true story at all (see n. 25), but rather a later fabrication from contemporary evidence, in which case it stands as an interesting example of early American historical fiction. The Manheim anthology, with its choice bits of savage barbarity playing up the most sensational aspects of Indian attack and captivity, was published with an eye to the profitable pulp-thriller market. Shock value, through fulsomely described instances of Indian tortures and the piling of horror upon horror, was the stock-in-trade and principal object of collections of this kind. That four of the accounts in the Manheim anthology are not strictly captivities but bloody and violent sketches of Indian encounters further indicates the sensationalized and commercial nature of the collection. For this reason, and because these encounters also provide insight into Indian-white relations during the period, the complete anthology is reprinted here. The text is Carey's first edition (Philadelphia, 1794).*

††

IN the following pages are collected together several histories of the dreadful cruelties exercised by the Indians on persons so unfortunate as to fall into their hands. All the instances are authenticated in the most satisfactory manner; some by deposition, and others by the information of persons of unexceptionable credibility.[1]

THE AFFECTING HISTORY, &C.

FREDERIC Manheim,[2] an industrious German, with his family, consisting of his wife, Catherine, a daughter of eighteen years of age,

1 These prefatory remarks attesting the veracity of the materials are characteristically confident and vague (see headnote).

2 Manheim's first name, Frederick, is consistently misspelled throughout.

and Maria and Christina, his youngest children (twins,) about sixteen, resided near the river Mohawk, eight miles west of Johnston. On the 19th of October, 1779,[3] the father being at work at some distance from his habitation, and the mother and eldest daughter on a visit at a neighbour's, two hostile Canasadaga Indians [4] rushed in, and captured the twin sisters.

The party to which these savages belonged, consisted of fifty warriors, who, after securing twenty-three of the inhabitants of that neighbourhood, (among whom was the unfortunate Frederic Manheim,) and firing their houses, retired for four days with the utmost precipitancy, till they were quite safe from pursuit. The place where they halted on the evening of the day of rest, was a thick pine swamp, which rendered the darkness of an uncommonly gloomy night, still more dreadful. The Indians kindled a fire, which they had not done before, and ordered their prisoners, whom they kept together, to refresh themselves with such provisions as they had. The Indians ate by themselves. Instead of retiring to rest after supping, the appalled captives observed their enemies busied in operations which boded nothing good. Two saplings were pruned clear of branches up to the very top, and all the brush cleared away for several rods around them. While this was doing, others were splitting pitch pine billets into small splinters about five inches in length, and as small as one's little finger, sharpening one end, and dipping the other in melted turpentine.

At length, with countenances distorted by infernal fury, and with hideous yells, the two savages who had captured the hapless Maria and Christina, leaped into the midst of their circle, and dragged those ill-fated maidens, shrieking, from the embraces of their companions. These warriors had disagreed about whose property the girls should be, as they had jointly seized them; and, to terminate the dispute, agreeably to the abominable usage of the savages, it was determined by the chiefs of the party, that the prisoners, who gave rise to the contention, should be destroyed; and that their captors should be the principal agents in the execrable busi-

3 Less than two months after Maj. Gen. John Sullivan's expedition into the Iroquois heartland. Despite Sullivan's rout of Col. John Butler's Tory-Iroquois forces, the Indian war was far from having been won and in fact blazed up more furiously than ever.

4 Probably Senecas from Geneva, New York.

ness. These furies assisted by their comrades, stripped the forlorn girls, already convulsed with apprehensions, and tied each to a sapling, with their hands as high extended above their heads as possible; and then pitched them from their knees to their shoulders, with upwards of six hundred of the sharpened splinters above described, which, at every puncture, were attended with screams of distress, that echoed and re-echoed through the wilderness. And then to complete the infernal tragedy, the splinters, all standing erect on the bleeding victims, were every one set on fire, and exhibited a scene of monstrous misery, beyond the power of speech to describe, or even the imagination to conceive. It was not until near three hours had elapsed from the commencement of their torments, and that they had lost almost every resemblance of the human form, that these helpless virgins sunk down in the arms of their deliverer, Death.[5]

Sufferings of the rev. John Corbly and family from the Indians. Related in a letter to the rev. William Rogers, late pastor of the Baptist church in Philadelphia.

Muddy creek, Washington county, July 8, 1785.

Dear Sir, THE following is a just and true account of the tragical scene, of my family's falling by the savages, which I related when at your house in Philadelphia, and you requested me to forward in writing. On the second sabbath in May, in the year 1782, being my appointment at one of my meeting houses, about a mile from my dwelling house, I set out with my dear wife and five children, for public worship. Not suspecting any danger, I walked behind 200 yards, with my bible in my hand, meditating—as I was thus employed, all on a sudden, I was greatly alarmed with the frightful shrieks of my dear family before me—I immediately ran with

[5] The burning of the twins Maria and Christina is unusual in the light of Iroquois respect for twins, who were often considered magical. The method of turpentine-soaked pine splinters, however, is in accord with the fate of Lieutenant Boyd of Leicester, New York, during Sullivan's campaign in the same year, 1779 (cf. also "Account of the Destruction of the Settlements at Wyoming," below, n. 35, and the Marrant narrative, n. 6).

all the speed I could, vainly hunting a club as I ran, till I got within 40 yards of them: my poor wife seeing me, cried to me to make my escape—an Indian ran up to shoot me. I had to strip, and by so doing out-ran him. My wife had a sucking child in her arms: this little infant they killed, and scalped. They then struck my wife at sundry times, but not getting her down, the Indian, who aimed to shoot me, ran to her, shot her through the body, and scalped her: my little boy, an only son, about six years old, they sunk the hatchet into his brains, and thus dispatched him. A daughter, besides the infant, they also killed and scalped. My eldest daughter, who is yet alive, was hid in a tree, about 20 yards from the place where the rest were killed, and saw the whole proceedings. She seeing the Indians all go off, as she thought, got up, and deliberately crept out from the hollow trunk; but one of them espying her, ran hastily up, knocked her down, and scalped her—also her only surviving sister, on whose head they did not leave more than one inch round, either of flesh or skin, besides taking a piece out of her skull. She, and the before-mentioned one, are still miraculously preserved, though, as you must think, I have had, and still have, a great deal of trouble and expense with them, besides anxiety about them, insomuch that I am, as to worldly circumstances, almost ruined. I am yet in hopes of seeing them cured; they still, blessed be God, retain their senses, notwithstanding the painful operations they have already and must yet pass through. At the time I ran round to see what was become of my family, and found my dear and affectionate wife, with five children, all scalped in less than ten minutes, from the first outset—no one, my dear brother, can conceive how I felt—this, you may well suppose, was killing to me. I instantly fainted away, and was borne off by a friend, who by this time had found us out—When I recovered, oh the anguish of my soul!—I cried—would to God I had died for them, would to God I had died with them. O how dark and mysterious did this trying providence then appear to me! but—

"Why should I grieve—when grieving, I must bear?"

This, dear sir, is a faithful, though short narrative of that fatal catastrophe—and my life amidst it all, for what purpose, Jehovah only knows, redeemed from surrounding death—Oh, may I spend it to the praise and glory of his grace, who worketh all things after the council of his own will. The government of the world and of the church, is in his hands.—May it be taught the important lesson of acquiescing in all his dispensations. I conclude with wishing you every blessing, and subscribe myself,

Your affectionate, though afflicted friend, and unworthy brother in the gospel ministry.
JOHN CORBLY.

Remarkable encounter of a white man with two Indians. In a letter to a gentleman of Philadelphia.

Westmoreland, April 26, 1779.

Dear Sir, I WROTE you a note a few days ago, in which I promised you the particulars of an affair between a white man of this country, and two Indians: now I mean to relate the whole story, and it is as follows:

The white man is upwards of sixty years of age; his name is David Morgan, a kinsman to col. Morgan, of the rifle battalion.[6] This man had, through fear of the Indians, fled to a fort about twenty miles above the province line, and near the east side of Monogahela river. From thence he sent some of his younger children to his plantation, which was about a mile distant, there to do some business in the field. He afterwards thought fit to follow, and see how they fared. Getting to his field, and seating himself upon the fence, within view of his children, where they were at work, he espied two Indians making towards them; on which he called to his children to make their escape. The Indians immediately bent their course towards him. He made the best haste to escape away, that his age and consequent infirmity would permit; but soon found he would be overtaken, which made him think of defence. Being armed with a good rifle, he faced about, and found himself under the necessity of running four or five perches[7] towards the

[6] Col. Daniel Morgan, a Virginia frontiersman and veteran of the French and Indian War, had been put in command of the American rifle companies in 1775 and achieved renown for his leadership and exploits against the British.

[7] Five rods (see Gyles, n. 25).

Indians, in order to obtain shelter behind a tree of sufficient size.

This unexpected manoeuvre obliged the Indians, who were close by, to stop, where they had but small timber to shelter behind, which gave mr. Morgan an opportunity of shooting one of them dead upon the spot. The other, taking the advantage of Morgan's empty gun, advanced upon him, and put him to flight a second time, and being lighter of foot than the old man, soon came up within a few paces, when he fired at him, but fortunately missed him. On this mr. Morgan faced about again, to try his fortune, and clubbed his firelock. The Indian, by this time, had got his tomahawk in order for a throw, at which they are very dextrous. Morgan made the blow, and the Indian the throw, almost at the same instant, by which the little finger was cut off Morgan's left hand, and the one next to it almost off, and his gun broke off by the lock. Now they came to close grips. Morgan put the Indian down; but soon found himself overturned, and the Indian upon him, feeling for his knife, and yelling most hideously, as their manner is, when they look upon victory to be certain. However, a woman's apron, which the Indian had plundered out of a house in the neighbourhood, and tied on him, above his knife, was now in his way, and so hindered him getting at it quickly, that Morgan got one of his fingers fast in his mouth, and deprived him of the use of that hand, by holding it, and disconcerted him considerably by chewing it; all the while observing how he would come on with his knife. At length the Indian had got hold of his knife, but so far towards the blade, that Morgan got a small hold of the hinder end; and as the Indian pulled it out of the scabbard, Morgan giving his finger a severe screw with his teeth, twitched it out through his hand, cutting it most grievously. By this time they were both got partly on their feet, and the Indian was endeavouring to disengage himself; but Morgan held fast by the finger, and quickly applied the point of the knife to the side of its savage owner; a bone happening in the way prevented its penetrating any great depth, but a second blow directed more towards the belly, found free passage into his bowels. The old man turned the point upwards, made a large wound, burying the knife therein, and so took his departure instantly to the fort, with the news of his adventure.

On the report of mr. Morgan, a party went out from the fort, and found the first Indian where he had fallen; the second they found not yet dead, at one hundred yards distance from the scene of action, hid in the top of a fallen tree, where he had picked the knife out of his body, after which had come out parched corn, &c. and had bound up his wound with the apron aforementioned; and on first sight he saluted them with, How do do, broder, how do do, broder? but alas! poor savage, their brotherhood to him extended only to tomahawking, scalping, and, to gratify some peculiar feelings of their own, skinning them both; and they have made drum heads of their skins.[8]

Signal prowess of a woman, in a combat with some Indians. In a letter to a lady of this city.

Westmoreland, April 26, 1779.

Madam, I HAVE wrote to mr.——of your city, an account of a very particular affair between a white man and two Indians.[9] I am now to give you a relation in which you will see how a person of your sex acquitted herself in defence of her own life, and that of her husband and children.

The lady, who is the burthen of this story, is named Experience Bozarth. She lives on a creek called Dunkard-creek, in the south-west corner of this county. About the middle of March last, two or three families who were afraid to stay at home, gathered to her house, and there stayed; looking on themselves to be safer than when all scattered about at their own houses.

On a certain day some of the children thus collected, came running in from play in great haste, saying, there were ugly red men. One of the men in the house stepped to the door, where he received a ball in the side of his breast, which caused him to fall back into the house. The Indian was immediately in over him, and engaged with another man who was in the house. The man tossed the Indian on a bed, and called for a knife to kill him. (Observe

8 Cf. the incident after Sullivan's defeat of Butler at Newton, where American soldiers skinned two dead Indians from the hips down to make boot leggings for their officers.

9 A reference to the account (letter) immediately preceding.

these were all the men that were in the house.) Now mrs. Bozarth appears the only defence, who not finding a knife at hand, took up an axe that lay by, and with one blow cut out the brains of the Indian. At that instant, (for all was instantaneous) a second Indian entered the door, and shot the man dead, who was engaged with the Indian on the bed. Mrs. Bozarth turned to this second Indian, and with her axe gave him several large cuts, some of which let his entrails appear. He bawled out, murder, murder. On this, sundry other Indians (who had hitherto been fully employed, killing some children out of doors) came rushing to his relief; one of whose heads mrs. Bozarth clove in two with her axe, as he stuck it in at the door, which laid him flat upon the soil. Another snatched hold of the wounded bellowing fellow, and pulled him out of doors, and mrs. Bozarth, with the assistance of the man who was first shot in the door, and by this time a little recovered, shut the door after them, and made it fast, where they kept garrison for several days, the dead white man and dead Indian both in the house with them, and the Indians about the house besieging them. At length they were relieved by a party sent for that purpose.

This whole affair, to shutting the door, was not perhaps more than three minutes in acting.

I am, &c.

NARRATIVE OF THE ADVENTURES OF CAPT. ISAAC STEWART; TAKEN FROM HIS OWN MOUTH, IN MARCH, 1782.

I WAS taken prisoner about 50 miles to the westward of Fort Pitt, about 18 years ago,[10] by the Indians, and was carried by them to the Wabash, with many more white men, who were executed with circumstances of horrid barbarity; it was my good fortune to call forth the sympathy of Rose, called the good woman of the town,

10 Presumably, if Stewart's account can be credited, during Pontiac's Conspiracy in 1763–64. In June, 1763, Delawares and Mingoes, acting on Pontiac's orders, swept up Pennsylvania's Monongahela Valley massacring settlers and beginning a siege of Fort Pitt.

who was permitted to redeem from the flames, by giving, as my ransom, a horse.

After remaining two years in bondage amongst the Indians, a Spaniard came to the nation, having been sent from Mexico on discoveries. He made application to the chiefs, for redeeming me and another white man in the like situation, a native of Wales, named John Davey; which they complied with, and we took our departure in company with the Spaniard, and travelled to the westward, crossing the Mississippi near la riviere Rouge, or Red River, up which we travelled 700 miles, when we came to a nation of Indians remarkably white, and whose hair was of a reddish colour, at least mostly so; they lived on the banks of a small river that empties itself into the Red River, which is called the River Post. In the morning of the day after our arrival amongst these Indians, the Welchman informed me, that he was determined to remain with them, giving as a reason that he understood their language, it being very little different from the Welch. My curiosity was excited very much by this information, and I went with my companion to the chief men of the town, who informed him (in a language I had no knowledge of, and which had no affinity to that of any other Indian tongue I ever heard) that their forefathers of this nation came from a foreign country, and landed on the east side of the Mississippi, describing particularly the country now called West-Florida, and that on the Spaniards taking possession of Mexico, they fled to their then abode; and as a proof of the truth of what he advanced, he brought forth rolls of parchment, which were carefully tied up in otter skins, on which were large characters, written with blue ink; the characters I did not understand, and the Welchman being unacquainted with letters, even of his own language, I was not able to know the meaning of the writing. They are a bold, hardy, intrepid people, very warlike, and the women beautiful, when compared with other Indians.[11]

11 Tale of "white" Indians and anomalous "lost" tribes were not uncommon among explorers and travelers of the period. The description of the Welsh-speaking nation reported here perpetuates a bit of pseudoscientific mythology arising from the discovery in 1738 of the light-skinned Mandan Indians of the Plains. Believed by their discoverers to be the survivors of a lost expedition of white men who had come to the New World long before Columbus, the Mandans

We left this nation, after being kindly treated and requested to remain amongst them, being only two in number, the Spaniard and myself, and we continued our course up the waters of the Red River, till we came to a nation of Indians, called Windots,[12] that never had seen a white man before, and who were unacquainted with the use of fire arms. On our way, we came to a transparent stream, which, to our great surprize, we found to descend into the earth, and, at the foot of a ridge of mountains, disappeared; it was remarkably clear, and, near to it, we found the bones of two animals, of such a size that a man might walk under the ribs, and the teeth were very heavy.

The nation of Indians who had never seen a white man, lived near the source of the Red River, and there the Spaniard discovered, to his great joy, gold dust in the brooks and rivulets; and being informed by the Indians, that a nation lived farther west, who were very rich, and whose arrows were pointed with gold, we set out in the hope of reaching their country, and travelled about five hundred miles, till we came to a ridge of mountains, which we crossed, and from which the streams run due west, and at the foot of the mountains, the Spaniard gave proofs of joy and great satisfaction, having found gold in great abundance. I was not acquainted with the nature of the ore, but I lifted up what he called gold dust from the bottom of the little rivulets issuing from the cavities of the rocks, and it had a yellow cast, and was remarkably heavy: but so much was the Spaniard satisfied, he relinquished his plan of prosecuting his journey, being perfectly convinced that he had found a country full of gold.

On our return he took a different route, and, when we reached the Mississippi, we went in a canoe to the mouth of the Missouri, where we found a Spanish post; there I was discharged by the Spaniard, went to the country of the Chickesaws, from thence to the Cherokees, and soon reached Ninety-six, in South Carolina.

---

were subsequently thought to have been descended from Welshmen belonging to the legendary Prince Madoc's expedition across the Atlantic in the year 1170. No real proof of this Welsh ancestry has ever been put forward. A smallpox epidemic in 1837 nearly wiped out the Mandan nation, and today the tribe numbers only about three hundred. (See Robert Silverberg, *Indian North America Before Columbus* [New York, 1963].)

[12] Wyandots (Wyandottes), a tribe of the Huron confederacy.

ACCOUNT OF THE SUFFERINGS OF MASSY HERBESON, AND HER FAMILY, WHO WERE TAKEN PRISONERS BY A PARTY OF INDIANS. GIVEN ON OATH BEFORE JOHN WILKINS, ESQ. ONE OF THE JUSTICES OF THE PEACE FOR THE COMMONWEALTH OF PENNSYLVANIA.[13]

Pittsburgh, May 28, 1792

MASSY HERBESON, in her oath, according to law, being taken before John Wilkins, esq. one of the commonwealth's justices of the peace in and for the county of Alleghany, deposeth and saith, that on the 22d day of this instant, she was taken from her own house within two hundred yards of Reed's block house, which is called twenty-five miles from Pittsburgh; her husband being one of the spies, was from home; two of the scouts had lodged with her that night, but had left her house about sunrise, in order to go to the block house, and had left the door standing wide open. Shortly after the two scouts went away, a number of Indians came into the house, and drew her out of bed by the feet, the two eldest children, who also lay in another bed, were drawn out in the same manner, a younger child, about one year old, slept with the deponent. The Indians then scrambled about the articles in the house; when they were at this work, the deponent went out of the house, and hollowed to the people in the block house; one of the Indians then ran up and stopped her mouth, another ran up with his tomahawk drawn, and a third ran and seized the tomahawk and called her his squaw; this last Indian claimed her as his, and continued by her; about fifteen of the Indians then ran down towards the block house, and fired their guns at the block and store house, in consequence of which one soldier was killed, and another wounded, one having been at the spring, and the other in coming or looking out of the store house. This deponent then told the Indians there were about forty men in the block house, and each man had two guns, the Indians then went to them that were firing at the block house, and

[13] Mrs. Mercy Herbeson was captured in 1792 during increased Indian depredations following the failure of St. Clair's expedition in the Ohio country (see n. 26, below). Her deposition was later expanded, edited, and published under the title *A Narrative of the Sufferings of Massy Harbison* (1825).

brought them back. They then began to drive the deponent and her children away; but a boy, about three years old, being unwilling to leave the house, they took it by the heels, and dashed it against the house; then stabbed and scalped it. They then took the deponent and the two other children, to the top of the hill, where they stopped until they tied up the plunder they had got. While they were busy about this, the deponent counted them, and the number amounted to thirty-two, including two white men, that were with them, painted like the Indians.

That several of the Indians could speak English, and that she knew three or four of them very well, having often seen them go up and down the Alleghany river, two of them she knew to be Seneccas, and two Munsees, who had got their guns mended by her husband about two years ago. That they sent two Indians with her, and the others took their course towards Puckty. That she, the children, and the two Indians had not gone two hundred yards, when the Indians caught two of her uncle's horses, put her and the youngest child on one, and one of the Indians and the other child on the other. That the two Indians then took her and the children to the Alleghany river, and took them over in bark canoes, as they could not get the horses to swim the river. After they had crossed the river, the oldest child, a boy of about five years of age, began to mourn for his brother: one of the Indians then tomahawked and scalped him. That they travelled all day very hard, and that night arrived at a large camp covered with bark, which, by appearance, might hold fifty men; that the camp appeared to have been occupied some time, it was very much beaten, and large beaten paths went out in different directions from it; that night they took her about three hundred yards from the camp, into a large dark bottom, bound her arms, gave her some bed clothes, and lay down one on each side of her. That the next morning they took her into a thicket on the hill side, and one remained with her till the middle of the day, while the other went to watch the path, least some white people should follow them. They then exchanged places during the remainder of the day; she got a piece of dry venison, about the bulk of an egg, that day, and a piece about the same size the day they were marching; that evening, (Wednesday the 23d) they moved her to a new place, and secured her as the night before:

during the day of the 23d, she made several attempts to get the Indian's gun or tomahawk, that was guarding her, and, could she have got either, she would have put him to death. She was nearly detected in trying to get the tomahawk from his belt.

The next morning (Thursday) one of the Indians went out as on the day before to watch the path. The other lay down and fell asleep. When she found he was sleeping, she stole her short gown, handkerchief and a child's frock, and then made her escape—the sun was then about half an hour high—that she took her course from the Alleghany, in order to deceive the Indians, as they would naturally pursue her that way; that day she travelled along Conequenessing creek. The next day she altered her course, and, as she believes, fell upon the waters of Pine creek, which empties into the Alleghany. Thinking this not her best course, took over some dividing ridges, fell in on the heads of Squaw run, she lay on a dividing ridge on Friday night, and on Saturday came to Squaw run, continued down the run until an Indian, or some other person shot at a deer; she saw the person about one hundred and fifty yards from her, the deer running and the dog pursuing it, which, from the appearance, she supposed to be an Indian dog.

She then altered her course, but again came to the same run, and continued down it until she got so tired that she was obliged to lie down, it having rained on her all that day and the night before; she lay there that night, it rained constantly; on Sunday morning she proceeded down the run until she came to the Alleghany river, and continued down the river till she came opposite to Carter's house, on the inhabited side, where she made a noise, and James Closier brought her over the river to Carter's house.

This deponent further says, that in conversing with one of the Indians, that could talk English very well, which she suspects to be George Jelloway, he asked her if she knew the prisoner that was taken by Jeffers and his Seneccas, and in gaol in Pittsburg? She answered no—he said, you lie. She again said she knew nothing about him; he said she did, that he was a spy, and a great captain; that he took Butler's scalp,[14] and that they would have him or twenty scalps; he again said, that they would exchange for him; that

14 Maj. Gen. Richard Butler, second in command to St. Clair, was killed during the expedition.

he and two more was sent out to see what the Americans were doing; that they came round from Detroit to Venango; the Indian took paper, and shewed her that he, at Fort Pitt, could write and draw on it;—he also asked her if a campaign was going out against the Indians this summer—she said no—he called her a liar, and said they were going out, and that the Indians would serve them as they did last year; he also said the English had guns, ammunition, &c. to give them to go to war, and that they had given them plenty last year; this deponent also says, that she saw one of the Indians have captain Crib's sword, which she well knew. That one of the Indians asked her if she knew Thomas Girty, she said she did—he then said that Girty lived near Fort Pitt; that he was a good man, but not as good as his brother at Detriot; [15] but that his wife was a bad woman; she tells lies on the Indians, and is a friend to America. Sworn before me the day and year first above written.

JOHN WILKINS

Sufferings of Peter Williamson, one of the Settlers in the back parts of Pennsylvania. Written by himself.[16]

I WAS born within ten miles of the town of Aberdeen, in the north of Scotland; of reputable parents; at eight years of age, being a sturdy boy, I was taken notice of by two fellows belonging to a vessel, employed (as the trade then was) by some of the worthy merchants of Aberdeen, in that villainous and execrable practice, of stealing young children from their parents, and selling them as slaves in the plantations abroad, and on board the ship easily cajoled by them, where I was conducted between decks, to some others they had kidnapped in the same manner, and in about a month's time set sail for America. When arrived at Philadelphia, the captain

15 Simon, "at Detroit," and Thomas Girty were infamous American turncoats. After his break with the colonists in 1778, Simon led British and Indian raiding expeditions until 1796, when the British gave up Detroit and he fled to Canada.

16 The original Williamson narrative, first published in 1757, was entitled *French and Indian Cruelty; Exemplified in the Life and Various Vicissitudes of Fortune of Peter Williams, a Disbanded Soldier*. The version in the Manheim anthology is somewhat truncated. Note also the title-page error: "Wilkinson" appears in place of "Williamson."

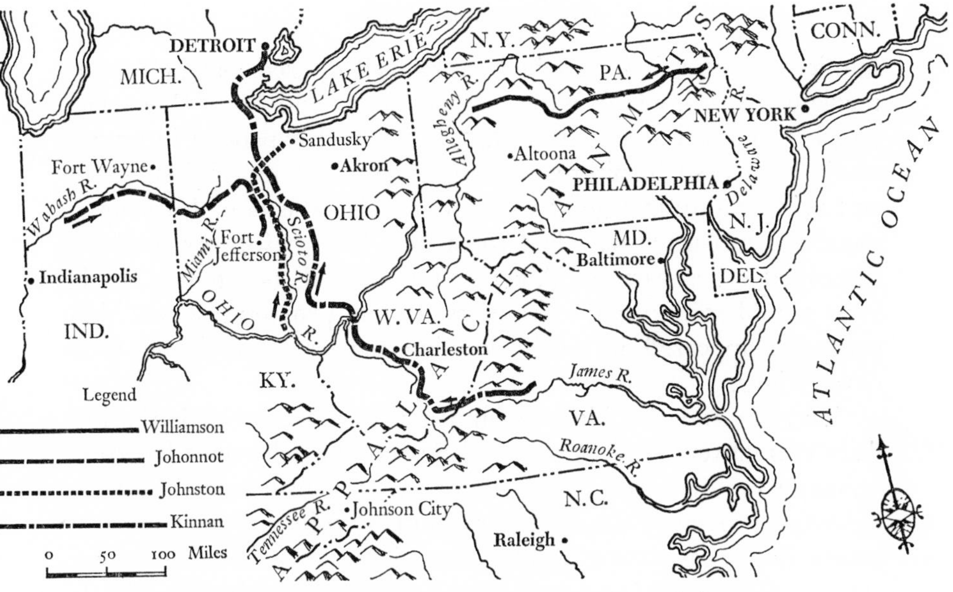

The journeys of Peter Williamson, Jackson Johonnot, Charles Johnston, and Mary Kinnan during captivity.

sold us at about sixteen pounds per head. What became of my unhappy companions I never knew; but it was my lot to be sold for seven years, to one of my countrymen,[17] who had in his youth been kidnapped like myself, but from another town.

Having no children of his own, and commiserating my condition, he took care of me, indulged me in going to school, where I went every winter for five years, and made a tolerable proficiency. With this good master, I continued till he died, and, as a reward for my faithful service, he left me two hundred pounds currency, which was then about an hundred and twenty pounds sterling, his best horse, saddle, and all his wearing apparel.

Being now seventeen years old, and my own master, having money in my pocket, and all other necessaries, I employed myself in jobbing for near seven years; when I resolved to settle, and married the daughter of a substantial planter. My father-in-law made me a deed of gift of a tract of land that lay (unhappily for me, as it has since proved) on the frontiers of the province of Pennsylvania, near the forks of Delaware, containing about two

[17] This man was Hugh Wilson.

hundred acres, thirty of which were well cleared and fit for immediate use, on which were a good house and barn. The place pleasing me well, I settled on it. My money I expended in buying stock, household furniture, and implements for out-of-door work; and being happy in a good wife, my felicity was compleat: but in 1754, the Indians,[18] who had for a long time before ravaged and destroyed other parts of America unmolested, began now to be very troublesome on the frontiers of our province, where they generally appeared in small skulking parties, committing great devastations.

Terrible and shocking to human nature were the barbarities daily committed by these savages! Scarce did a day pass but some unhappy family or other fell victims to savage cruelty. Terrible, indeed, it proved to me, as well as to many others; I that was now happy in an easy state of life, blessed with an affectionate and tender wife, became on a sudden one of the most unhappy of mankind: scarce can I sustain the shock which for ever recurs on recollecting the fatal second of October, 1754.[19] My wife that day went from home, to visit some of her relations; as I staid up later than usual, expecting her return, none being in the house besides myself, how great was my surprize and terror, when about eleven o'clock at night, I heard the dismal war-whoop of the savages, and found that my house was beset by them. I flew to my chamber window, and perceived them to be twelve in number. Having my gun loaded, I threatened them with death, if they did not retire. But how vain and fruitless are the efforts of one man against the united force of so many blood thirsty monsters! One of them that could speak English, threatened me in return, 'That if I did not come out, they would burn me alive,' adding, however, 'That if I would come out and surrender myself prisoner, they would not kill me.' In such deplorable circumstances, I chose to rely on their promises, rather than meet death by rejecting them; and accordingly went out of the house, with my gun in my hand, not knowing that I had it. Immediately on my approach they rushed on me like tigers, and instantly disarmed me. Having me thus in their power, they bound me to a tree, went into the house, plundered it of every thing they

18 Probably Shawnee or Delaware.
19 Shortly after Washington's surrender at Fort Necessity to the French.

could carry off, and then set fire to it, and consumed what was left before my eyes. Not satisfied with this, they set fire to my barn, stable, and out-houses, wherein were about 200 bushels of wheat, six cows, four horses, and five sheep, all which were consumed to ashes.

Having thus finished the execrable business, about which they came, one of the monsters came to me with a tomahawk [20] and threatened me with the worst of deaths, if I would not go with them. This I agreed to, and then they untied me, and gave me a load to carry, under which I travelled all that night, full of the most terrible apprehensions, lest my unhappy wife should likewise have fallen into their cruel power. At day break, my infernal masters ordered me to lay down my load, when tying my hands again round a tree, they forced the blood out at my fingers' ends. And then kindling a fire near the tree to which I was bound, the most dreadful agonies seized me, concluding I was going to be made a sacrifice to their barbarity. The fire being made, they for some time danced round me after their manner, whooping, hollowing and shrieking in a frightful manner. Being satisfied with this sort of mirth, they proceeded in another manner; taking the burning coals, and sticks flaming with fire at the ends, holding them to my face, head, hands, and feet, and at the same time threatening to burn me entirely if I cried out: thus tortured as I was, almost to death, I suffered their brutalities, without being allowed to vent my anguish otherwise, than by shedding silent tears; and these being observed, they took fresh coals, and applied them near my eyes, telling me my face was wet, and that they would dry it for me, which indeed they cruelly did. How I underwent these tortures has been matter of wonder to me, but God enabled me to wait with more than common patience for the deliverance I daily prayed for.

At length they sat down round the fire, and roasted the meat, of which they had robbed my dwelling. When they had supped, they offered some to me: though it may easily be imagined I had but little appetite to eat, after the tortures and miseries I had suffered,

20 "A tomahawk is a kind of hatchet, made something like our plaisterers' hammers, about two feet long, handle and all. They generally use it after firing their guns, by rushing on their enemies, and fracturing or cleaving their skulls with it, and very seldom fail of killing at the first blow" [Williamson's note].

yet was I forced to seem pleased with what they offered me, lest by refusing it, they should re-assume their hellish practices. What I could not eat, I contrived to hide, they having unbound me till they imagined I had eat all; but then they bound me as before; in which deplorable condition I was forced to continue the whole day. When the sun was set, they put out the fire, and covered the ashes with leaves, as is their usual custom, that the white people might not discover any traces of their having been there.

Going from thence along the Susquehanna, for the space of six miles, loaded at I was before, we arrived at a spot near the Apalachian mountains, or Blue-hills, where they hid their plunder under logs of wood. From thence they proceeded to a neighbouring house, occupied by one Jacob Snider and his unhappy family, consisting of his wife, five children, and a young man his servant. They soon got admittance into the unfortunate man's house, where they immediately, without the least remorse, scalped both parents and children: nor could the tears, the shrieks, or cries of poor innocent children, prevent their horrid massacre: having thus scalped them, and plundered the house of every thing that was movable, they set fire to it, and left the distressed victims amidst the flames.

Thinking the young man belonging to this unhappy family, would be service to them in carrying part of their plunder, they spared his life, and loaded him and myself with what they had here got, and again marched to the Blue-hills, where they stowed their goods as before. My fellow sufferer could not support the cruel treatment which we were obliged to suffer, and complaining bitterly to me of his being unable to proceed any farther, I endeavoured to animate him, but all in vain, for he still continued his moans and tears, which one of the savages perceiving, as we travelled along, came up to us, and with his tomahawk gave him a blow on the head, which felled the unhappy youth to the ground, whom they immediately scalped and left. The suddenness of this murder shocked me to that degree, that I was in a manner motionless, expecting my fate would soon be the same: however, recovering my distracted thoughts, I dissembled my anguish as well as I could from the barbarians; but still, such was my terror, that for some time I scarce knew the days of the week, or what I did.

They still kept on their course near the mountains, where they lay skulking four or five days, rejoicing at the plunder they had got. When provisions became scarce, they made their way towards Susquehanna, and passing near another house, inhabited by an old man, whose name was John Adams, with his wife and four small children, and meeting with no resistance, they immediately scalped the mother and her children before the old man's eyes. Inhuman and horrid as this was, it did not satisfy them; for when they had murdered the poor woman, they acted with her in such a brutal manner, as decency will not permit me to mention.[21] The unhappy husband, not being able to avoid the sight, intreated them to put an end to his miserable being; but they were as deaf to the tears and entreaties of this venerable sufferer, as they had been to those of the others, and proceeded to burn and destroy his house, barn, corn, hay, cattle, and every thing the poor man, a few hours before, was master of. Having saved what they thought proper from the flames, they gave the old man, feeble, weak, and in the miserable condition he then was, as well as myself, burdens to carry, and loading themselves likewise with bread and meat, pursued their journey towards the Great Swamp. Here they lay for eight or nine days diverting themselves, at times, in barbarous cruelties on the old man: sometimes they would strip him naked, and paint him all over with various sorts of colours: at other times they would pluck the white hairs from his head, and tauntingly tell him, 'He was a fool for living so long, and that they should shew him kindness in putting him out of the world.' In vain were all his tears, for daily did they tire themselves with the various means they tried to torment him; sometimes tying him to a tree, and whipping him; at other times, scorching his furrowed cheeks with red-hot coals, and burning his legs quite to the knees. One night after he had been thus tormented, whilst he and I were condoling each other at the miseries we daily suffered, 25 other Indians arrived, bringing with them 20 scalps and 3 prisoners, who had unhappily fallen into their hands in Conogocheague, a small town near the river Susquehanna, chiefly inhabited by the Irish. These prisoners gave us some shocking accounts of the murders and devastations committed in their parts; a few in-

21 Williamson apparently refers to mutilation. Sexual abuse of a dead woman is wholly inconsistent with what is known of Indian practices in this region (cf. Rowlandson, n. 54).

stances of which will enable the reader to guess at the treatment the provincials have suffered for years past. This party, who now joined us, had it not, I found, in their power to begin their violences so soon as those who visited my habitation; the first of their tragedies being on the 25th of October, 1754, when John Lewis, with his wife and three small children, were inhumanly scalped and murdered; and his house, barn, and every thing he possessed burnt and destroyed. On the 28th, Jacob Miller, with his wife and six of his family, with every thing on his plantations, shared the same fate. The 30th, the house, mill, barn, 20 head of cattle, two teams of horses, and every thing belonging to George Folke, met with the like treatment, himself, wife, and all his miserable family, consisting of nine in number, being scalped, then cut in pieces and given to the swine. One of the substantial traders, belonging to the province, having business that called him some miles up the country, fell into the hands of these ruffians, who not only scalped him, but immediately roasted him before he was dead; then, like cannibals, for want of other food, eat his whole body, and of his head made, what they called, an Indian pudding.

From these few instances of savage cruelty, the deplorable situation of the defenceless inhabitants, and what they hourly suffered in that part of the globe, must strike the utmost horror, and cause in every breast the utmost detestation, not only against the authors, but against those who, through inattention, or pusillanimous or erroneous principles, suffered these savages at first, unrepelled, or even unmolested, to commit such outrages, depredations, and murders.

The three prisoners that were brought with these additional forces, constantly repining at their lot, and almost dead with their excessive hard treatment, contrived at last to make their escape; but being far from their own settlements, and not knowing the country, were soon after met by some others of the tribes, or nations at war with us, and brought back. The poor creatures, almost famished for want of sustenance, having had none during the time of their escape, were no sooner in the power of the barbarians, than two of them were tied to a tree, and a great fire made round them, where they remained till they were terribly scorched and burnt; when one of the villains with his scalping knife, ripped open their bellies, took out their entrails, and burned them before their eyes, whilst the others were cutting, piercing, and tearing the flesh from their breasts, hands, arms, and legs, with red-hot irons, till they were dead. The third unhappy victim was reserved a few hours longer, to be, if possible, sacrificed in a more cruel manner; his arms were tied close to his body, and a hole being dug, deep enough for him to stand upright, he was put into it, and earth rammed and beat in all round his body up to his neck, so that his head only appeared above ground; they then scalped him, and there let him remain for three or four hours, in the greatest agonies; after which they made a small fire near his head, causing him to suffer the most excruciating torments; whilst the poor creature could only cry for mercy by killing him immediately, for his brains were boiling in his head; inexorable to all he said, they continued the fire, till his eyes gushed out of their sockets; such agonizing torments did this unhappy creature suffer for near two hours before he was quite dead. They then cut off his head, and buried it with the other bodies; my task being to dig the graves; which, feeble and terrified as I was, the dread of suffering the same fate enabled me to do.

A great snow now falling, the barbarians were fearful, lest the white people should, by their tracks, find out their skulking retreats, which obliged them to make the best of their way to their winter-quarters, about two hundred miles farther from any plantations or inhabitants. After a long and painful journey, being almost starved, I arrived with this infernal crew at Alamingo.[22] There I found a number of wigwams, full of their women and children. Dancing, singing, and shouting were their general amusements. And in all their festivals and dances, they relate what successes they have had, and what damages they have sustained in their expeditions; in which I now unhappily became part of their theme. The severity of the cold increasing, they stripped me of my cloaths for their own use, and gave me such as they usually wore themselves, being a piece of blanket, and a pair of mockasons, or shoes, with a yard of coarse cloth, to put round me instead of breeches.

At Alamingo I remained near two months, till the snow was off the ground. Whatever thoughts I might have of making my escape,

[22] A Delaware settlement, presumably several hundred miles from the other settlements.

to carry them into execution was impracticable, being so far from any plantations or white people, and the severe weather rendering my limbs in a manner quite stiff and motionless: however, I contrived to defend myself against the inclemency of the weather as well as I could, by making myself a little wigwam with the bark of the trees, covering it with earth, which made it resemble a cave; and, to prevent the ill effects of the cold, I kept a good fire always near the door. My liberty of going about, was, indeed, more than I could have expected, but they well knew the impracticability of my escaping from them. Seeing me outwardly easy and submissive, they would sometimes give me a little meat, but my chief food was Indian corn. At length the time came when they were preparing themselves for another expedition against the planters and white people; but before they set out, they were joined by many other Indians.

As soon as the snow was quite gone, they set forth on their journey towards the back parts of the province of Pennsylvania; all leaving their wives and children behind in their wigwams. They were now a formidable body, amounting to near 150. My business was to carry what they thought proper to load me with, but they never intrusted me with a gun. We marched on several days without any thing particular occurring, almost famished for want of provisions; for my part, I had nothing but a few stalks of Indian corn, which I was glad to eat dry: nor did the Indians themselves fare much better, for as we drew near the plantations they were afraid to kill any game, lest the noise of their guns should alarm the inhabitants.

When we again arrived at the Blue-hills, about thirty miles from the Irish settlements before-mentioned, we encamped for three days, though God knows, we had neither tents nor any thing else to defend us from the inclemency of the air, having nothing to lie on by night but the grass. Their usual method of lodging, pitching, or encamping, by night, being in parcels of ten or twelve men to a fire, where they lie upon the grass or brush, wrapped up in a blanket, with their feet to the fire.

During our stay here, a sort of council of war was held, when it was agreed to divide themselves into companies of about twenty men each; after which every captain marched with his party where he thought proper. I still belonged to my old masters, but was left behind on the mountains with ten Indians, to stay till the rest should return; not thinking it proper to carry me nearer to Conogocheague, or the other plantations.

Here I began to meditate an escape, and though I knew the country round extremely well, yet I was very cautious of giving the least suspicion of any such intention. However the third day after the grand body left us, my companions thought proper to traverse the mountains in search of game for their subsistance, leaving me bound in such a manner that I could not escape: at night when they returned, having unbound me, we all sat down together to supper on what they had killed, and soon after (being greatly fatigued with their day's excursion) they composed themselves to rest, as usual. I now tried various ways to try whether it was a scheme to prove my intentions or not; but after making a noise and walking about, sometimes touching them with my feet, I found there was no fallacy. Then I resolved, if possible, to get one of their guns, and, if discovered, to die in my defence, rather than be taken: for that purpose I made various efforts to get one from under their heads (where they always secured them) but in vain. Disappointed in this, I began to despair of carrying my design into execution: yet, after a little recollection, and trusting myself to the divine protection, I set forward, naked, and defenceless as I was. Such was my terror, however, that in going from them I halted, and paused every four or five yards, looking fearfully towards the spot where I had left them, lest they should awake and miss me; but when I was two hundred yards from them, I mended my pace, and made as much haste as I possibly could to the foot of the mountains; when, on a sudden, I was struck with the greatest terror at hearing the wood-cry,[23] as it is called, which the savages I had left were making, upon missing their charge. The more my terror encreased the faster I pushed on, and, scarce knowing where I trod, drove through the woods with the utmost precipitation, sometimes falling and bruising myself, cutting my feet and legs against the stones in a miserable manner. But faint and maimed as I was I continued my flight till day-break, when, without having any thing to sustain nature, but a little corn left, I crept into a hollow tree, where I lay very snug,

23 A cry of alarm, probably a variant of the war cry.

and returned my prayers and thanks to the divine being, that had thus far favoured my escape. But my repose was in a few hours destroyed at hearing the voices of the savages near the place where I was hid, threatening and talking how they would use me, if they got me again. However, they at last left the spot, where I heard them, and I remained in my apartment all that day without further molestation.

At night I ventured forwards again, frightened; thinking each twig that touched me a savage. The third day I concealed myself in like manner as before, and at night travelled, keeping off the main road as much as possible, which lengthened my journey many miles. But how shall I describe the terror I felt on the fourth night, when, by the rustling I made among the leaves, a party of Indians, that lay round a small fire, which I did not perceive, started from the ground, and, seizing their arms, ran from the fire amongst the woods. Whether to move forward or rest where I was, I knew not, when to my great surprize and joy, I was relieved by a parcel of swine that made towards the place where I guessed the savages to be; who, on seeing them, imagined that they had caused the alarm, very merrily returned to the fire, and lay again down to sleep. Bruised, crippled, and terrified as I was, I pursued my journey till break of day, when, thinking myself safe, I lay down under a great log, and slept till about noon. Before evening I reached the summit of a great hill, and looking out if I could spy any habitations of white people, to my inexpressible joy, I saw some which I guessed to be about ten miles distance.

In the morning I continued my journey towards the nearest cleared lands I had seen the day before, and, about four o'clock in the afternoon, arrived at the house of John Bell, an old acquaintance, where knocking at the door, his wife, who opened it, seeing me in such a frightful condition, flew from me, screaming, into the house. This alarmed the whole family, who immediately fled to their arms, and I was soon accosted by the master with his gun in his hand. But on making myself known, (for he before took me to be an Indian) he immediately caressed me, as did all his family with extraordinary friendship, the report of my being murdered by the savages having reached them some months before. For two days and nights they very affectionately supplied me with all necessaries, and carefully attended me till my spirits and limbs were pretty well recovered, and I thought myself able to ride, when I borrowed of these good people (whose kindness merits my most grateful returns) a horse and some cloaths, and set forward for my father-in-law's house in Chester county, about one hundred and forty miles from thence, where I arrived on the 4th day of January, 1775, (but scarce one of the family could credit their eyes, believing with the people I had lately left, that I had fallen a prey to the Indians) where I was received and embraced by the whole family with great affection; upon enquiring for my dear wife, I found she had been dead two months! This fatal news greatly lessened the joy I otherwise should have felt at my deliverance from the dreadful state and company I had been in.[24]

Remarkable adventures of Jackson Johonnot, a soldier under general Harmar and general St. Clair, containing an account of his captivity, sufferings, and escape from the Kickapoo Indians.[25]

THERE is seldom a more difficult task undertaken by man, than the act of writing a narrative of a person's own life; especially where the incident borders on the marvellous. Prodigies but seldom happen; and the veracity of the relaters of them is still less frequently vouched for; however, as the dispensations of Providence towards me have been too striking not to make a deep and grateful impression, and as the principal part of them can be attested to by living evidences, I shall proceed, being confident that the candid reader will pardon the inaccuracies of an illiterate soldier, and that

24 Williamson later joined the army and was captured by the French at the fall of Oswego, taken to Montreal, and sent with other prisoners to England. He died in Edinburg in 1799.

25 The "first edition" of this narrative (Lexington, 1791) is not extant and even may never have existed; it is referred to only in the imprint of the Providence edition of 1793. That Johonnot describes St. Clair's defeat at Fort Recovery, Ohio (which took place on Nov. 4, 1791), makes it seem unlikely that the narrative could have reached Lexington, Ky., in time to be printed in the same year. This apparent falsehood regarding publication, along with the fact that Johonnot reports having arrived at Fort Jefferson in September, 1791 (one month before that fort was in fact located and named), has cast doubt upon the authenticity of the narrative. See R. W. G. Vail, *The Voice of the Old Frontier*, 364–65.

the tender hearted will drop the tear of sympathy, when they realize the idea of the sufferings of such of our unfortunate country folks as fall into the hands of the western Indians, whose tender mercies are cruelties.

I was born and brought up at Falmouth, Casco-bay, where I resided until I attained to the seventeenth year of my age. My parents were poor, the farm we occupied, small, and hard to cultivate, their family large and expensive, and every way fitted to spare me to seek a separate fortune; at least these ideas had gained so great an ascendancy in my mind, that I determined, with the consent of my parents, to look out for a mean of supporting myself.

Having fixed on the matter firmly, I took leave of my friends, and sailed, the 1st of May, 1791, on board a coasting schooner for Boston. Being arrived in this capital, and entirely out of employ, I had many uneasy sensations, and more than once sincerely wished myself at home with my parents; however, as I had set out on an important design, and as yet met with no misfortune, pride kept me from this act, while necessity urged me to fix speedily on some mode of obtaining a livelihood.

My mind was severely agitated on this subject one morning, when a young officer came into my room, and soon entered into conversation on the pleasures of a military life, the great chance there was for an active young man to obtain promotion, and the grand prospect opening for making great fortunes in the western country. His discourse had the desired effect; for after treating me with a bowl or two of punch, I enlisted, with a firm promise on his side to assist me in obtaining a sergeant's warrant before the party left Boston.

An entire new scene now opened before me. Instead of becoming a sergeant, I was treated severely for my ignorance in a matter I had till then scarcely thought of, and insultingly ridiculed for remonstrating against the conduct of the officer. I suffered great uneasiness on these and other accounts, of a similar kind, for some time; at length, convinced of the futility of complaint, I applied my self to study the exercise, and in a few days became tolerable expert. The beginning of July we left Boston, and proceeded on our way to join the western army. When we arrived at fort Washington, I was ordered to join capt. Phelon's company, and in a few days set out on the expedition under general Harmar.[26] Those alone who have experienced, can tell what hardships men undergo in such excursions, hunger, fatigue and toil were our constant attendants; however as our expectations were raised with the idea of easy conquest, rich plunder, and fine arms in the end, we made a shift to be tolerably merry: for my own part, I had obtained a sergeancy, and flattered myself I was in the direct road to honour, fame and fortune. Alas! how fluctuating are the scenes of life! how singularly precarious the fortune of a soldier! Before a singular opportunity presented, in which I could have a chance to signalize myself, it was my lot to be taken in an ambuscade, by a party of Kickappoo Indians, and with ten others constrained to experience scenes, in comparison of which our former distresses sunk into nothing. We were taken on the bank of the Wabash, and immediately conveyed to the upper Miami, at least such of us as survived. The second day after we were taken, one of my companions, by the name of George Aikins, a native of Ireland, became so faint with hunger and fatigue, that he could proceed no further. A short council was immediately held among the Indians who guarded us, the result of which was that he should be put to death; this was no sooner determined on, than a scene of torture began. The captain of the guard approached the wretched victim who lay bound upon the ground, and with his knife made a circular incision on the scull; two others immediately pulled off the scalp; after this they each of them struck him on the head with their tomahawks, they then stripped him naked, stabbed him with their knives in every sensitive part of the body, and left him, weltering in blood, though not quite dead, a wretched victim to Indian rage and hellish barbarity.

We were eight days on our march to the upper Miami, during which painful travel, no pen can describe our sufferings from hunger, thirst, and toil. We were met, at the entrance of the town, by above five hundred Indians, besides squaws and children, who

26 Brevet Brig. Gen. Josiah Harmar, whom Gen. Arthur St. Clair had given command of 1,500 troops for an expedition against the Indians. Harmar began gathering his army at Fort Washington in September, 1790. The expeditionary force was defeated by Miamis in October, 1790, and Harmar resigned his commission in 1791. Johonnot's account here is inconsistent with these facts. St. Clair, governor of the Northwest Territory, was ambushed and defeated in 1791 by Miami and Wyandot war parties led by Little Turtle.

were apprized of our approach by a most hideous yelling made by our guard, and answered repeatedly from the village. Here we were all severely beaten by the Indians, and four of our number, viz. James Durgee, of Concord, Samuel Forsythe, of Beverly, Robert Deloy, of Marblehead, and Uzza Benton, of Salem, who all fainted under their heavy trials, were immediately scalped and tomahawked in our presence, and tortured to death with every affliction of misery that Indian ingenuity could invent.

It was the 4th of August when we were taken, and our unhappy companions were massacred the thirteenth. News was that day received of the destruction at L'Anguille, &c. of general Harmar's army,[27] numbers of scalps were exhibited by the warriors, and several prisoners, among whom were three women and six children, carried through the village destined to a Kickappoo settlement, further westward. The 15th of August, four more of my fellow prisoners, viz. Lemuel Saunders, of Boston, Thomas Tharp, of Dorchester, Vincent Upham, of Mistick, and Younglove Croxal, of Abington, were taken from us; but whether they were massacred or preserved alive, I am unable to say. After this nothing material occurred for a fortnight, except that we were several times severely whipped on the receipt of bad news, and our allowance of provisions lessened, so that we were apprehensive of starving to death, if we did not fall an immediate sacrifice to the fire or tomahawk: but heaven had otherwise decreed.

On the night following the 30th of August, our guard, which consisted of four Indians, tired out with watching, laid down to sleep, leaving only an old squaw to attend us. Providence so ordered that my companion had, by some means, got one of his hands at liberty, and having a knife in his pocket, soon cut the withes that bound his feet, and that which pinioned my arms, unperceived by the old squaw, who sat in a drowsy position, not suspecting harm, over a small fire in the wigwam.

I ruminated but a few moments on our situation; there was no weapon near us, except my companion's knife, which he still held; I looked on him to make him observe me, and the same instant

27 This actually occurred October 21–22, 1790.

sprung and grasped the squaw by the throat to prevent her making a noise, and my comrade in a moment cut her throat from ear to ear, down to the neck bone. He then seized a tomahawk and myself a rifle, and striking at the same instant, dispatched two of our enemies, the sound of these blows awakened the others, but before they had time to rise, we renewed our strokes on them, and luckily to so good effect, as to stun them, and then repeating the blow, we sunk a tomahawk in each of their heads, armed ourselves completely, and taking what provisions the wigwam afforded, we committed ourselves to the protection of Providence, and made the best of our way into the wilderness.

The compass of a volume would scarce contain the events of our progress through the wilderness; but as they were uninteresting to any but us, I shall only observe generally, that the difficulties of the journey, were too great to have been endured by any who had less interest than life at stake, or a less terrible enemy than Indians to fear. Hunger, thirst, and fatigue, were our constant companions. We travelled hard day and night, except the few hours absolutely requisite for repose, that nature might not sink under her oppression, at which period one constantly watched while the other slept. In this tiresome mode, we proceeded until the fifteenth of September, having often to shift our direction on account of impassable bogs, deep morasses and hideous precipices, without meeting any adventure worthy note. On the morning of the fifteenth, as we were steering nearly a north course in order to avoid a bog that intercepted our course, S. E. we found the bodies of one old man, a woman and two children newly murdered, stript and scalped. This horrid spectacle chilled our blood; we viewed the wretched victims; and from what we could collect from circumstances, we concluded that they had been dragged away from their homes, and their feet being worn out, had been inhumanly murdered, and left weltering in their blood. We were at a great loss now to determine what course to steer; at length we pitched upon a direction about northwest, and walked on as fast as possible to escape the savages, if practicable. About noon this day, we came to a good spring, which was a great relief to us; but which we had great reason a few minutes after to believe would be the last of our earthly comforts. My companion,

Richard Sackville, a corporal of captain Newman's company, stepped aside into the thicket, on some occasion, and returned with the account that a few rods distant he had discovered four Indians with two miserable wretches bound, sitting under a tree eating; and that if I would join him, he would either relieve the captives, or perish in the attempt. The resolution of my worthy comrade pleased me greatly; and as no time was to be lost, we set immediately about the execution of our design: Sackville took the lead, and conducted me undiscovered, within fifty yards of the Indians: two of them were laid down, with their musquets in their arms, and appeared to be asleep; the other two sat at the head of the prisoners, their musquets resting against their left shoulders, and in their right hands each of them a tomahawk, over the heads of their prisoners. We each chose our man to fire at, and taking aim deliberately, had the satisfaction to see them both fall; the others instantly started, and seeming at a loss to determine from whence the assault was made, fell on their bellies, and looked carefully around to discover the best course to take; mean time we had recharged, and shifting our position a little, impatiently waiting their rising; in a minute they raised on their hands and knees, and having as we supposed discovered the smoke of our guns rising above the bushes, attempted to crawl into a thicket on the opposite side. This gave us a good chance, and we again fired at different men, and with such effect, that we brought them both down; one lay motionless, the other crawled along a few yards, we loaded in an instant, and rushed towards him, yet keeping an eye on him, as he had reached his comrade's gun, and sat upright in a posture of defence. By our noise in the bushes he discovered the direction to fire; alas too fatally, for by his fatal shot I lost my comrade and friend Sackville. At this moment the two prisoners who were close pinioned, endeavoured to make their escape towards me, but the desperate savage again fired, and shot one of them dead, the other gained the thicket within a few yards of me: I had now once more got ready to fire, and discharged at the wounded Indian; at this discharge I wounded him in the neck, from whence I perceived the blood to flow swiftly, but he yet undauntedly kept his seat, and having new charged his guns, fired upon us with them both, and then fell, seemingly from faintness and loss of blood. I ran instantly to the pinioned white man, and having unbound his arms, and armed him with the unfortunate Sackville's musquet, we cautiously approached a few yards nearer the wounded Indian; when I ordered my new comrade to fire, and we could perceive the shot took effect. The savage still lay motionless. As soon as my companion had re-loaded, we approached the Indian, whom we found not quite dead, and a tomahawk in each hand, which he flourished at us, seemingly determined not to be taken alive. I, for my own part, determined to take him alive, if possible; but my comrade prevented me by shooting him through the body. I now enquired of my new companion what course we ought to steer, and whence the party came, from whose power I had relieved him. He informed me with respect to the course, which we immediately took, and on the way let me know, that we were within about three days march of fort Jefferson; that he and three others were taken by a party of ten Wabash Indians four days before, in the neighbourhood of that fort; that two of his companions being wounded, were immediately scalped and killed; that the party, at the time of taking him, had in their possession seven other prisoners, three of whom were committed to the charge of a party of four Indians. What became of them we knew not; the others being worn down with fatigue, were massacred the day before, and which I found to be those whose bodies poor Sackville had discovered in the thicket; that the other two Indians were gone towards the settlements, having sworn to kill certain persons whose names he had forgotten, and that destruction seemed to be their whole drift.

My comrade, whose name on enquiry, I found to be George Sexton, formerly a resident of Newport, Rhode-Island, I found to be an excellent woodsman, and a man of great spirit, and so grateful for the deliverance I had been instrumental in obtaining for him, that he would not suffer me to watch for him to sleep, but one hour in the four and twenty, although he was so fatigued as to have absolute need of a much greater proportion; neither would permit me to carry any of our baggage.

From the time of being joined by Sexton, we steered a south-east course, as direct as possible, until the 18th towards night, directing our course by the sun and the moss on the trees by day, and the moon by night: on the evening of the 18th, we providentially fell in with an American scouting party, who conducted us safely, in a few hours, to fort Jefferson, where we were treated with great humanity, and supplied with the best refreshments the fort afforded, which to me was very acceptable, as I had not tasted any thing except wild berries and ground nuts for above a week.

The week after our arrival at fort Jefferson, I was able to return to my duty in my own regiment, which the latter end of August joined the army on an expedition against the Indians of the Miami Village, the place in which I had suffered so much, and so recently, and where I had beheld so many cruelties perpetrated on unfortunate Americans. It is easier to conceive than describe the perturbation of my mind on this occasion. The risk I should run in common with my fellow soldiers, seemed heightened by the certainty of torture that awaited me in case of being captured by the savages. However, these reflections only occasioned a firm resolution of doing my duty, vigilantly, and selling my life in action as dear as possible, but by no means to be taken alive if I could evade it by any exertion short of suicide.

My captain shewed me every kindness in his power on the march, indulged me with a horse as often as possible, and promised to use his influence to obtain a commission for me, if I conducted well the present expedition;—poor gentleman! little did he think he was soon to expire gallantly fighting the battles of his country! I hasten now to the most interesting part of my short narrative, the description of general St. Clair's defeat, and the scenes which succeeded it.

On the 3d of November we arrived within a few miles of the Miami Village. Our army consisted of about 1200 regular troops, and nearly an equal number of militia. The night of the 3d, having reason to expect an attack, we were ordered under arms, about midnight, and kept in order until just before day-light, at which time our scouts having been sent out in various directions, and no enemy discovered, we were dismissed from the parade to take some refreshment. The men in general, almost worn out with fatigue, had thrown themselves down to repose a little: but the rest was of short duration, for before sunrise, the Indians began a desperate attack upon the militia, which soon threw them into disorder, and forced them to retire precipitately, into the very heart of our camp.[28]

Good God! what were my feelings, when, starting from my slumbers, I heard the most tremendous firing all around, with yellings, horrid whoopings and expiring groans in dreadful discord sounding in my ears. I seized my arms, ran out of my tent with several of my comrades, and saw the Indians with their bloody tomahawks and murderous knives butchering the flying militia. I fled towards them, filled with desperation, discharged my fire lock among them, and had the satisfaction to see one of the tawny savages fall, whose tomahawk was that instant elevated to strike a gallant officer, then engaged sword in hand with a savage in front. My example, I have reason to think, animated my companions. Our own company now reached the place we occupied, and aided by the regulars of other companies and regiments, who joined us indiscriminately, we drove the Indians back into the bush, and soon after formed in tolerable order, under as gallant commanders as ever died in defence of America. The firing ceased for a few minutes, but it was like the interval of a tornado, calculated by an instantaneous, dreadful reverse, to strike the deeper horror.—In one and the same minute seemingly, the most deadly and heavy firing took place on every part of our camp; the army, exposed to the shot of the enemy, delivered from the ground, fell on every side, and drenched the plains with blood, while the discharge from our troops directed almost at random, I am fearful did but little execution. Orders were now given to charge with bayonets. We obeyed with alacrity; a dreadful swarm of tawny savages rose from the ground, and fled before us; but alas! our officers, rendered conspicuous by their exertions to stimulate the men, became victims to savage ingenuity, and fell so fast in common with the rest, that scarce a shot appeared as spent in vain.—Advantages gained by the bayonet, were by this means, and want of due support, lost again, and our little corps obliged in turn, repeatedly to give way before the Indians.—We were now reduced to less than half our original number of regular troops, and less than a fourth part of our officers, our horses all killed or taken, our artillery men all cut off, and the

28 As was the case in Harmar's defeat the year before, the regulars stood ground but the untrained militia panicked in confusion.

pieces in the enemy's hands; in this dreadful dilemma we had nothing to do but to attempt a retreat, which soon became a flight, and for several miles, amidst the yells of Indians, more dreadful to my ears, than screams of damned fiends to my ideas, amidst the groans of dying men, and the dreadful sight of bloody massacres on every side, perpetrated by the Indians on the unfortunate creatures they overtook, I endured a degree of torture no tongue can describe, or heart conceive; yet I providentially escaped unhurt, and frequently discharged my musket, I am persuaded to effect.

Providence was pleased to sustain my spirits, and preserve my strength; and although I had been so far spent previous to setting out on the expedition, as to be unable to go upon fatigue for several days, or even to bear a moderate degree of exercise, I reached fort Jefferson the day after the action about ten in the morning, having travelled on foot all night to effect it.

Thus have I made the reader acquainted with the most interesting scenes of my life; many of them are extraordinary, some of them perhaps incredible; but all of them founded in fact, which can be attested by numbers. General St. Clair, in consequence of my sufferings and what he and others were pleased to call soldier-like exertions, presented me with an ensign's commission, on joining the remains of my old company, in which station I mean to serve my country again, as far as my slender abilities will permit; trusting that the same kind protecting providence, which hath covered my head in the day of battle, and shielded me repeatedly in the hour of danger, will dispose of me as to infinite wisdom seems best; and if I die in the cause of my country, may the rememberance of my sufferings, escapes, perseverance through divine support, and repeated mercies received, kindle a flame of heroism in the breast of many an American youth, and induce him, while he reads the sufferings of his unfortunate countrymen, to exert himself to defend the worthy inhabitants on the frontiers from the depredations of savages; whose horrid mode of war is a scene to be deprecated by civilized nature, whose tender mercies are cruelties and whose faith is by no means to be depended on, though pledged in the most solemn treaties.

Account of the dreadful devastation of the Wyoming settlements, in July 1778. From Gordon's history of the American war.[29]

SO early as the 8th of February, 1778, general Schuyler [30] wrote to congress—"There is too much reason to believe, that an expedition will be formed (by the Indians) against the western frontiers of this state (New-York) Virginia and Pennsylvania." The next month he informed them—"A number of Mohawks, and many of the Onondagoes, Cayugas, and Senecas, will commence hostilities against us as soon as they can; it would be prudent therefore early to take measures to carry the war into their country; it would require no greater body of troops to destroy their towns than to protect the frontier inhabitants." No effectual measures being taken to repress the hostile spirit of the Indians, numbers joined the tory refugees, and with these commenced their horrid depredations and hostilities upon the back settlers, being headed by colonel Butler, and Brandt, an half blooded Indian, of desperate courage, ferocious and cruel beyond example.[31] Their expeditions were carried on to great advantage, by the exact knowledge which the refugees possessed of every object of their enterprise, and the immediate intelligence they received from their friends on the spot. The weight of their hostilities fell upon the fine, new and flourishing settlement of Wyoming, situated on the eastern branch of the Susquehanna, in a most beautiful country and delightful climate.—It was settled and cultivated with great ardor by a number of people from Connecticut, which claimed the territory as included in its original grant from Charles II. The settlement consisted of eight townships, each five miles square, beautifully placed on each side of the river. It had increased so by a rapid population, that the settlers sent a thousand men to

29 The Wyoming settlements were located in the Wyoming Valley of Pennsylvania.

30 Gen. Philip Schuyler, commander of the American armies on the upper Hudson.

31 Col. John Butler and Joseph Brant, the famed Mohawk leader. Brant was the protégé, and probably the son, of Sir William Johnson, the English proconsul to the Iroquois. Brant was actually 70 miles away at the time of the attack.

serve in the continental army. To provide against the dangers of their remote situation, four forts were constructed to cover them from the irruptions of the Indians. But it was their unhappiness, to have a considerable mixture of royalists among them; and the two parties were actuated by sentiments of the most violent animosity, which was not confined to particular families or places; but creeping within the roofs and to the hearths and floors where it was least to be expected, served equally to poison the sources of domestic security and happiness, and to cancel the laws of nature and humanity.

They had frequent and timely warnings of the danger to which they were exposed by sending their best men to so great a distance. Their quiet had been interrupted by the Indians, joined by marauding parties of their own countrymen, in the preceding year; and it was only by a vigorous opposition, in a course of successful skirmishes, that they had been driven off. Several tories, and others not before suspected, had then and since abandoned the settlement; and beside a perfect knowledge of all their particular circumstances, carried along with them such a stock of private resentment, as could not fail of directing the fury, and even giving an edge to the cruelty of their Indian and other inveterate enemies. An unusual number of strangers had come among them under various pretences, whose behaviour became so suspicious, that upon being taken up and examined, such evidence appeared against several of them, of their acting in concert with the enemy, on a scheme for the destruction of the settlements, that about twenty were sent off to Connecticut to be there imprisoned and tried for their lives, while the remainder were expelled. These measures excited the rage of the tories in general to the most extreme degree; and the threats formerly denounced against the settlers, were now renewed with aggravated vengeance.

As the time approached for the final catastrophe, the Indians practised unusual treachery. For several weeks previous to the intended attack, they repeatedly sent small parties to the settlement, charged with the strongest professions of friendship. These parties, beside attempting to lull the people in security, answered the purposes of communicating with their friends, and of observing the present state of affairs. The settlers, however, were not insensible to the danger. They had taken the alarm, and col. Zebulon Butler [32] had several times written letters to congress and gen. Washington, acquainting them with the danger the settlement was in, and requesting assistance; but the letters were never received, having been intercepted by the Pennsylvania tories. A little before the main attack, some small parties made sudden irruptions, and committed several robberies and murders; and, from ignorance or a contempt of all ties whatever, massacred the wife and five children of one of the persons sent for trial to Connecticut, in their own cause.

At length, in the beginning of July, the enemy suddenly appeared in full force on the Susquehanna, headed by col. John Butler, a Connecticut tory, and cousin to col. Zeb. Butler, the second in command in the settlement. He was assisted by most of those leaders, who had rendered themselves terrible in the present frontier war. Their force was about 1600 men, near a fourth Indians, led by their own chiefs: the others were so disguised and painted, as not to be distinguished from the Indians, excepting their officers, who, being dressed in regimentals, carried the appearance of regulars. One of the smaller forts, garrisoned chiefly by tories, was given up or rather betrayed. Another was taken by storm, and all but the women and children massacred in the most inhuman manner.

Colonel Zeb. Butler, leaving a small number to guard fort Wilkesborough, crossed the river with about 400 men, and marched into Kingston fort, whither the women, children and defenceless of all sorts crowded for protection. He suffered himself to be enticed by his cousin to adandon the fortress.[33] He agreed to march out, and hold a conference with the enemy in the open field (at so great a distance from the fort, as to shut out all possibility of protection from it) upon their withdrawing, according to their own proposal, in order to the holding of a parley for the conclusion of a treaty. He at the same time marched out about 400 men well

[32] Zebulon Butler, a continental officer, shared command of the Wyoming garrison with Col. Nathan Dennison.

[33] This and much of what follows is inconsistent with what actually happened at Wyoming. The Americans, under Zeb Butler and Dennison, charged out of the fort headlong into a trap set by John Butler, whose rangers had simulated retreat. The American formation broke, and a general massacre ensued. Dennison reported his losses at over 300 men; the British and Indians suffered only eleven casualties.

armed, being nearly the whole strength of the garrison, to guard his person to the place of parley, such was his distrust of the enemy's designs. On his arrival he found nobody to treat with, and yet advanced toward the foot of the mountain, where at a distance he saw a flag, the holders of which, seemingly afraid of treachery on his side, retired as he advanced; whilst he, endeavouring to remove this pretended ill-impression, pursued the flag, till his party was thoroughly enclosed, when he was suddenly freed from his delusion, by finding it attacked at once on every side. He and his men, notwithstanding the surprise and danger, fought with resolution and bravery, and kept up so continual and heavy a fire for three quarters of an hour, that they seemed to gain a marked superiority. In this critical moment, a soldier through a sudden impulse of fear, or premeditated treachery, cried out aloud—"the colonel has ordered a retreat." The fate of the party was now at once determined. In the state of confusion that ensued, an unresisted slaughter commenced, while the enemy broke in on all sides without obstruction. Col. Zeb. Butler, and about seventy of his men escaped; the latter got across the river to fort Wilkesborough, the colonel made his way to fort Kingston; which was invested the next day on the land side. The enemy, to sadden the drooping spirits of the weak remaining garrison, sent in, for their contemplation, the bloody scalps of a hundred and ninety-six of their late friends and comrades. They kept up a continual fire upon the fort the whole day. In the evening the colonel quitted the fort and went down the river with his family. He is thought to be the only officer that escaped.

Colonel Nathan Dennison, who succeeded to the command, seeing the impossibility of an effectual defence, went with a flag to col. John Butler, to know what terms he would grant on a surrender: to which application Butler answered with more than savage phlegm in two short words—*the hatchet.*[34] Dennison having defended the fort, till most of the garrison were killed or disabled,

34 In point of fact, the essential terms of the capitulation were that after laying down their arms, every inmate of the fort was permitted to march away unharmed. There was no testimony by anyone present that any American man, woman, or child was killed after the surrender, and Dennison himself remarked in his report that Butler had made every effort to maintain control over his Indians and to abide by the terms of the capitulation. It was, indeed, one of the few instances in which Indians at war had even been kept under approximate control (see Gyles, n. 10).

was compelled to surrender at discretion. Some of the unhappy persons in the fort were carried away alive; but the barbarous conquerors, to save the trouble of murder in detail, shut up the rest promiscuously in the houses and barracks; which having set on fire, they enjoyed the savage pleasure of beholding the whole consumed in one general blaze.

They then crossed the river to the only remaining fort, Wilkesborough, which, in hopes of mercy, surrendered without demanding any conditions. They found about seventy continental soldiers, who had been engaged merely for the defence of the frontiers, whom they butchered with every circumstance of horrid cruelty. The remainder of the men, with the women and children, were shut up as before in the houses, which being set on fire, they perished altogether in the flames.

A general scene of devastation was now spread through all the townships. Fire, sword, and the other different instruments of destruction alternately triumphed. The settlements of the tories alone generally escaped, and appeared as islands in the midst of the surrounding ruin. The merciless ravagers having destroyed the main objects of their cruelty, directed their animosity to every part of living nature belonging to them; shot and destroyed some of their cattle, and cut out the tongues of others, leaving them still alive to prolong their agonies.

The following are a few of the more singular circumstances of the barbarity practised in the attack upon Wyoming. Capt. Bedlock, who had been taken prisoner, being stripped naked, had his body stuck full of splinters of pine knots,[35] and then a heap of pine knots piled around him; the whole was then set on fire, and his two companions, capts. Ranson and Durgee, thrown alive into the flames and held down with pitchforks. The returned tories, who had at different times abandoned the settlement in order to join in those savage expeditions, were the most distinguished for their cruelty; in this they resembled the tories that joined the British forces. One of these Wyoming tories, whose mother had married a second husband, butchered with his own hands, both her, his father-in-law,

35 "Pine knots are so replete with turpentine, that they are fired and used at night to illuminate the room; and lighted splinters are often carried about in the houses of Carolina planters instead of candles" [note in original]. See n. 5, above.

his own sisters and their infant children. Another, who during his absence had sent home several threats against the life of his father, now not only realized them in person, but was himself, with his own hands, the exterminator of his whole family, mother, brothers and sisters, and mingled their blood in one common carnage, with that of the ancient husband and father. The broken parts and scattered relics of families, consisting mostly of women and children, who had escaped to the woods during the different scenes of this devastation, suffered little less than their friends, who had perished in the ruin of their houses. Dispersed and wandering in the forests, as chance and fear directed, without provision or covering, they had a long tract of country to traverse, and many without doubt perished in the woods.[36]

[36] Distorted and sensationalized accounts such as this transformed the battle and surrender at Wyoming into a supreme example of monstrous Indian excesses and atrocities. It was never referred to as the Wyoming campaign, or battle, or attack, but always as the Wyoming massacre. Instead of gaining credit for a significant military victory, John Butler became the object of abuse even in his own country, from which personal aspersions his reputation never recovered.

VIII

A Narrative of the Incidents Attending the Capture, Detention, and Ransom of Charles Johnston, of Botetourt County, Virginia, Who Was Made Prisoner by the Indians, on the River Ohio, in the Year 1790; Together with an Interesting Account of the Fate of His Companions, Five in Number, One of Whom Suffered at the Stake.

†††

Charles Johnston, a Virginia attorney en route to the Kentucky country, was captured by a band of marauding Shawnee and Cherokee Indians on the Ohio River near the mouth of the Scioto on March 20, 1790. He and his traveling companions were divided among the Indians, Johnston being given to a Shawnee master. Although he was a prisoner only five weeks, the narrative of Johnston's captivity is a valuable repository of information about Shawnee hunting practices, warfare, ceremonies, and customs. Moreover, his encounters with Indianized whites as well as other captives and his relation of their stories extend the compass of his own adventure. Johnston's experiences also played a role in contemporary historical events. After his redemption Johnston, an educated man knowledgeable in current national affairs, was called to New York City to be interviewed by President Washington and Secretary of War Knox about conditions along the northern boun-

daries during the turbulent postwar period. With the close of the Revolution the stream of settlers to the westward of the Appalachians and the opening of lands in the Northwest Territory provoked the Indians north of the Ohio River, who saw these incursions as a violation of the Treaty of Fort Stanwix of 1768. It is estimated that from 1782 to 1790, the year of Johnston's capture, hostile Indians had killed, wounded, or taken prisoner nearly 1,500 persons along the Ohio River alone. Additionally, both Spain and England were still firmly, if illegally, established in the newly settled regions and were arming their Indian allies. Indian depredations became intolerable in 1789–90: attacks on the Kentucky, Virginia, and Pennsylvania frontiers and on Ohio River traffic increased; Miamis, Shawnees, and visiting Cherokees were especially active. Moved by the stories of these assaults, among which was Johnston's, Washington ordered an expedition against the Indians and began warfare that would last until 1795. The first edition of Charles Johnston's narrative was published in New York in 1827, almost thirty years after the events described, which, along with the fact that Johnston was a well-educated man, may account for its low-keyed presentation and unembellished style—uncharacteristic of most narratives of this period. The Cleveland, 1905 edition, a reprint of the first, is the basis for the text which follows.

††

INTRODUCTION

THE incidents of my capture on the River Ohio by the Indians, in the year 1790, and of my subsequent detention by them, have been considered, by many gentlemen, on whose candor and intelligence I can rely, of such interest as to merit the attention of the public. My earlier days have been so completely occupied by the business of a very active life, that I can with truth say, I could never spare the time necessary for such a work, until age is advancing upon me, and I find myself able to command a little leisure. But the strongest consideration which has operated on me to engage in this undertaking is, that an extremely incorrect and imperfect narrative was published by the Duke de Liancourt, in the account of his travels in America, which appeared some years ago.[1] Being called to Europe, on matters of business, in 1793, on my return in the following year I crossed the Atlantic in the ship Pigon, commanded by Captain Loxley, bound from London to Philadelphia. The Duke de Liancourt was one of my fellow-passengers. He assumed the name of Aberlib, which, as he informed me, was that of a Swiss servant formerly in his employment, because he was apprehensive, that in the event of our falling in with a French ship of war, his true name and title being known, might determine its commander to seize his person and carry him to France. On the voyage, as soon as we became acquainted, he selected me, from among a number of other passengers, as the object of his confidence, and imparted to me, and to no other person on board, except the Captain, the circumstances which had compelled him to fly from France, and to seek an asylum in a foreign country from the infuriated party, who had determined on the destruction of the French nobility. In the progress of our acquaintance, he ascertained that I had been a prisoner among the savages, and elicited from me a detail of the circumstances. We had frequent interviews in the cabin, while the other passengers were on deck. But the communication between us was of a nature, which subjected us both to the probability of mistaking the precise sense in which either of us meant to be understood: since he spoke the English language very imperfectly, and I was utterly ignorant of the French. I observed that he committed what I told him to paper, in his own tongue, and therefore inferred it was his intention to publish my story. Upon inquiry, whether this was his design, his answer left me in a state of uncertainty. But I obtained from him a positive assurance, that if he did publish, he would furnish me with an English translation, to be examined and corrected by me, before it should be issued from the press. The Duke did not execute his promise. I presume it escaped

1 François Alexandre Frederick Rochefoucauld-Liancourt D'Estissac (1747–1827), whose *Travels Through the United States* (1795) contains "The History of Mr. Johnston of Virginia, who in 1790 was taken prisoner by the Indians, written on board the Pigon in October, 1794." Rochefoucauld had fled the revolutionists in France; and during his residence in America from 1794 to 1799 he collected material for his book.

his memory, or, if he wrote me on the subject, his letter miscarried. The first intelligence I obtained on the subject was from the publication itself, which came to my hands not long after it was printed. It is replete with errors, particularly in relation to the names of persons and places.[2] Facts too are so coloured as to bear some resemblance to truth, while there is an essential variance from it; resulting, in all probablity, from the difficulty of our understanding each other accurately. I am perfectly confident, that the Duke has made no intentional misrepresentation. The excellence of his heart, and the correctness of his moral principles, place him above all suspicion. But another objection arises, from his omission of many striking details. It shall be my object to present as minute and faithful a narrative, of the occurrences when I was captured, and while in the hands of the savages, as my memory can supply after the lapse of so many years. I can confidently assert, that my recollection of incidents, during a period so calamitous to me, and while my faculties were vigorous, is sufficiently perfect to give them without danger of mistake. Every one, who has attained to my age, must have ascertained by experience, that the striking events of youthful life are fastened indelibly on the memory, and that their impression is more perfect, and is retained with greater precision, than those circumstances which occur to us in our declining years. I entertain no fears that my veracity will be questioned by those to whom I am known; and I appeal to others, who may read my details, whether they are distinguished by any features, which ought to bring upon them the frowns of incredulity.

2 "A few short specimens of the Duke's mistakes will be sufficient to show the general inaccuracy of his relation. He represents me as making a trip to Kentucky 'to examine some witnesses *before the supreme court of Virginia.*' He calls Kelly's Station '*Kekler's* Station.' Green Briar Court-House is '*Great Brayer* Court-House;' Jacob Skyles is '*James Skuyl;*' Mockasins are 'Macapins;' the boat in which our party descended the Ohio is a 'ship;' and I might cover pages with his errors. These, and his omission of facts, may be perceived by a comparison of his narrative with mine. I could, if necessary, give stronger proof of his imperfect knowledge of our language, by transcribing a letter from him now in my possession, which was written in reply to one that I had addressed to him on the subject of his errors" [Johnston's note]. Actually, Rochefoucauld's account does not differ so materially as one might expect from Johnston's statement here, and the additional light it sheds on the narrative makes it worth reading as a supplement.

NARRATIVE

CHAPTER I.

MR. John May, a gentleman of great worth and respectability, formerly resided at Belle-Vue, on the Appomattox river, five miles above the town of Petersburg, in Virginia. He was an early adventurer in the location and purchase of lands in Kentucky, after the settlement of that country commenced. His business was of such a nature and extent as to require the assistance of a clerk. In the year 1788, he offered me such inducements to enter his service, that I did not hesitate to accept his proposals. He was involved in some of those numerous litigations which have resulted, in Virginia and Kentucky, from the mode prescribed by law for acquiring title to unappropriated lands, and among others was engaged in a contest with the late Judge Mercer. In the progress of this contest, it became necessary for Mr. May to procure the depositions of witnesses who lived in the western country; and, in the month of August, 1789, I attended him in a journey made to Kentucky for the purpose of taking those depositions. No remarkable incident occurred in the course of this first trip, and we returned safely into the interior in the succeeding November. But having accomplished our object in part only, we set out again from his residence, with a view to its completion, in the latter part of February, 1790. We had travelled altogether by land on the first occasion.[3] But in this second journey, Mr. May determined to reach the point of his destination by descending the Kenhawa and Ohio rivers. We proceeded by the usual route to Green Briar Court-house, where the town of Lewisburg has been since built, which place we left about the 8th or 10th of March. The country between that place and the Kenhawa river, on which we were to embark, was then destitute of inhabitants, and the distance about eighty miles. On the evening

3 The route was probably up the James to the Shenandoah Valley, southward through the openings in the mountains along the headwaters of the Tennessee, westward through the Cumberland Gap, and then northwest to the settled portions of central Kentucky. This was the famous "Wilderness Road." In making their second journey, May and Johnston decided to avoid this circuitous course and to proceed over a shorter, but more difficult, route.

of the first day after our departure from Lewisburg, we came up with a party consisting of eight or ten persons, on their way to the Kenhawa. Among them were Col. George Clendiner,[4] and Mr. Jacob Skyles, the latter of whom was on a mercantile adventure, with a stock of dry goods, which he intended to carry down the river to Kentucky. The weather was uncommonly cold; and on that night there was so great a fall of snow, that in the morning we found it nine or ten inches thick on our blankets. We toiled on through a dreary country and unpleasant weather for two or three days longer, and then arrived at Kelly's Station, on the Great Kenhawa. There we contracted for one of those heavy, clumsy, slowly-moving structures, at that time employed on the Ohio for the conveyance of travellers and their property to the western settlements,[5] which had become considerable, and were rapidly increasing. But in the country now forming the State of Ohio, there was not, I believe, the habitation of a white man from Point Pleasant to Symmes's small settlement at the mouth of the Great Miami. At this day the same region comprehends a white population of perhaps seven or eight hundred thousand; [6] sends fourteen representatives to the congress of the United States; and may be fairly ranked among the most powerful states in the Union. On the margin of the river, then occupied by savages and wild beasts, flourishing towns have arisen, and productive farms appear. On the stream itself, numerous steam boats have supplied the place of the wrecked arks, formerly the only vehicles of trade and communication, which laboured along with difficulty, and without profit to their owners. Works of internal improvement have been commenced, which promise the highest benefits to a country enriched by nature with many of her choicest gifts. A great canal, already begun, will probably be completed in the course of a few years, which will yield all the benefits of a direct water communication with New Orleans, by the rivers

4 Clendennin.

5 These arks, or flatboats, were built without a keel, with high gunwales and sometimes a roof. Long poles bearing a sweep on the end kept the clumsy craft in the current. They were not usually returned to their place of origin, but were dismantled at the end of the journey and the lumber used for building purposes. Apparently the boat made for the May party had no roof.

6 "Mr. Wright, one of the representatives in Congress from that state, in his speech on the Judiciary bill, which I have lately seen, states the population at one million" [Johnston's note].

Ohio and Mississippi, and with New-York by Lake Erie and the New-York canal: [7] bearing on its bosom a commerce which will extend, by an interior navigation, from the northern to the southern extreme of the United States. This is a career of prosperity unequalled even by the rapid progress of other members of the American Union, and unparalleled in history. What a subject of reflection to the statesman and political economist! What a source of triumph, on the part of the free and thrifty institutions of the western hemisphere, over the strong systems of the eastern! Nor is this comparative view of the present, and former condition of the country to which it refers, unconnected with my subject. Many inhabitants of the states bordering on the Ohio river have come into existence since the occurrence of the incidents which I am about to relate; and might think the facts incredible, if not reminded of the state of things, so utterly different then from what it is now.

Our boat, or ark, for which we had bargained at Kelly's Station, was not ready to receive us until the lapse of several days. We were invited by Col. George Clendiner, who resided at the mouth of Elk river, some seven or eight miles from the Station, and where the town of Charleston has since been built, to spend this interval with him. At his house our time was passed in the utmost comfort, highly enhanced by the liberal, warm, and cordial hospitality, with which we were entertained by him and Mrs. Clendiner. From his dwelling we descended the Great Kenhawa to Point Pleasant, our party consisting of Mr. May, Mr. Skyles, and myself. Upon our arrival at that place, there was an accession to our number, composed of three persons: William Flinn, Dolly Fleming, and Peggy Fleming. Flinn was one of those hardy characters, bred in the young settlements of our country, accustomed to their usual pursuits; the sports of the chase, and hostilities with the Indians. The Miss Flemings were females of an humble condition in life. They were sisters. One of them was the particular friend of Flinn, and the other was her travelling companion. They were residents of Pittsburg, bound for the country down the Ohio river.

7 The "great canal, already begun" was the Ohio Canal, begun near Newark on July 4, 1825; it eventually linked Cleveland, on Lake Erie, with Portsmouth, on the Ohio. The "New-York canal" was the Erie, finished in 1825, which connected Buffalo, also on Lake Erie, with Albany, on the Hudson.

CHAPTER II.

We remained but a short time at Point Pleasant.[8] Having before heard a rumour, that the savages had decoyed a boat, which was descending the river, to the shore, and had killed all who were on board, we there came to the resolution, that no circumstances, no consideration, should induce us to venture on the land, until our arrival at Limestone. Those with whom we conversed at the Point, advised us, too, by no means to hazard ourselves on shore; since the intelligence received at that place was, that various parties of Indians were lurking about the banks of the Ohio. How far we adhered to our resolution, or attended to the information which we had obtained, will be seen in the sequel. The water was high in the river, which afforded us great facility in getting along. We had nothing more to do, than to gain the middle of the stream, and permit our heavy and unwieldly boat to float down. Our numbers were too few, and our experience as watermen too limited, to accelerate our progress beyond the rate at which the current flowed. But there was perfect safety, while we remained out of musket or rifle shot from the shore. In that there was no difficulty, as the part of the river, down which we were to pass, was about a mile in width. We apprehended no danger from any attempt which the savages might make to board us, while we were at a distance from land, because such attempts were not in conformity to their habits; the gunwales of our boat were so high that we were competent to the successful resistance of a party much larger than our own; and Mr. May, Skyles, Flinn, and I, were provided with fire arms. It is true, they were nothing better than ordinary fowling pieces, except Mr. Skyles's, which was a small neat rifle. But they seemed to us sufficient for our purposes, and would probably have proven so, if our indiscretion had not placed us completely in the power of our foes, and where the best weapons could not be employed with any chance of advantage.

Our boat was steered by an oar at the stern, and the male passengers performed that service in rotation. We had descended the river nearly to the junction of the Sciota, when about dawn of day, on the 20th of March, we were called up by Flinn, who stood at the

[8] Located at the junction of the Kanawha and Ohio rivers.

steering oar. He turned our attention to a smoke, which he had discovered and which was suspended in the atmosphere about the height of the tree-tops, on both sides of the river. We instantly determined to ascertain on which bank the fire that produced this smoke was burning, and then to bear from it towards the other. After a short time, we saw distinctly, that the smoke ascended from a fire on the north-western shore; and we began to turn towards the south-eastern, when we perceived two white men on the same side of the river where the fire was. They called to us, and implored us to receive them on board our boat, declaring, that they had been taken prisoners by the Indians some weeks before, at Kennedy's Bottom in Kentucky; had been led by their captors across the Ohio, and had been so fortunate as to escape from their hands: that they were suffering with the severest distress of cold and hunger, and must perish, or again fall into the power of their enemies, unless they were rescued by us from the miserable fate which awaited them. They continued down the bank of the river abreast of us, and repeated their story with cries and wailings, until the suspicions which had arisen in our minds on their first appearance, began to be weakened. At length they pressed their tale upon us with so much earnestness, and stated so many minute particulars connected with it, that our feelings were excited towards them, and we discussed the question of going on shore. We had first inquired from them as to the smoke which we had seen rising from their side of the river; but they denied that there was any fire. This falsehood, conclusively disproved by the evidence of our eyes, ought to have determined us to close our ears against all they told us. We proceeded, however, with the discussion. Flinn, and the two females, accustomed from their early lives, like most of the first settlers on our frontier, to think lightly of danger from Indians, urged us to land. Mr. May, Mr. Skyles, and I, opposed it. We laid great stress on the fact, that the two white men had not told the truth with respect to the fire, and therefore were not worthy of credit. But Flinn's reply was, that they were under the necessity of kindling fire in the cold weather which then prevailed, and were unwilling to acknowledge they had any, lest we might suspect there were Indians on the shore. By this time our progress on the water was so much faster than theirs on land, that we had gone far below them, and were almost out of reach of their voices. Flinn then proposed a scheme by which, according to his mode of reasoning, all the hazard of landing would be thrown upon himself alone, without exposure to the rest of our party. He said we had gained on them so much, that if there were any Indians, we must be greatly ahead of them; might touch the shore only long enough for him to leap on it, and immediately turn the boat into the stream again, where we would be safe: that if our apprehensions of Indians were well founded, he could perceive them as soon as they could see him; that he had no fears but he could escape by outrunning them; and that he would rejoin us the next day at Limestone, whither he would proceed on foot. On the contrary, should our fears prove groundless, we could put back, and take him and the two men on board. Believing this plan could be carried into effect in safety, and our hearts at the same moment yielding to the feelings of humanity, all on board immediately and fatally acceded to this proposition, without reflecting, that in crossing the current we should cease to move as rapidly as we had while going directly with it. The consequence was, we were so long in getting to the shore, that by the time we had reached it and had put Flinn out, to our utter asonishment and dismay, we beheld a party of Indians, completely armed after their manner, rushing upon us. Their number was not great, since none but the swiftest could gain the spot where we landed as soon as the boat reached it. We therefore determined on resistance. Mr. Skyles and I took up our guns for that purpose; but the main body of the Indians, who had concealed themselves from our view by keeping in the back ground as they ran at some distance from the river, began to come up. When Mr. May perceived their numbers thus increasing, he remonstrated against so unequal a contest, and urged that our attention and exertions should be directed to the single object of getting back into the current. But the height of the water was such, that our boat was involved among the numerous and strong branches of a large tree which bent from the bank; [9] and while we in vain endeavoured, by all the means in our power,

[9] This circumstance, as well as others in the Johnston narrative, may be seen recreated in Fenimore Cooper's *The Deerslayer* (1841); see my "Cooper and the 'Semblance of Reality': A Source for *The Deerslayer*," *American Literature,* XLII (Jan., 1971).

to extricate ourselves, the whole body of Indians, fifty-four in number, after firing a few scattering shot as they came up, took a position not farther than sixty feet from us, and, rending the air with the horrible war-whoop, poured their whole fire into our boat. Resistance was hopeless—to get from the shore impossible. In this state of despair, we protected ourselves from their fire by lying down in the bottom of the boat but not until the Indians had killed Dolly Fleming, who had taken shelter behind me, and received a ball in the corner of her mouth which passed close over my left shoulder. Skyles was wounded by a rifle bullet, which ranged across his back from one sohulder to the other. Our enemies continued to fire into the boat, until all our horses were killed. The danger to which we were already exposed was aggravated by these animals. They were so frightened by the smell of powder and the discharge of guns, that it was extremely difficult to avoid their trampling on us before they were shot; and after they fell, it was barely possible to keep clear of the kicks and struggles which they made in their dying agonies. After they were killed, the firing ceased, and all was quiet on board. Mr. May, who had not taken off his night-cap since he awoke in the morning, then rose on his feet, and, taking it from his head, held it up as a signal of surrender. Seeing him rise, I reminded him of the danger to which he would be exposed by standing up, and entreated him to lie down again. But it was too late. About the moment when I spoke, the fire recommenced, and this excellent man fell dead by a ball shot through his brain, while I supposed that he had taken my advice and had lain down of his own accord. Nor did I discover my mistake until, casting my eyes on him a short time afterwards, his face, covered with blood, and the mark of the ball in his forehead, too plainly indicated his fate. Once more the fire from the bank was discontinued. Flinn, by the time he had reached the top of the bank, was their prisoner: Mr. May and Dolly Fleming were killed: Mr. Skyles was wounded: Peggy Fleming and I remained unhurt. The savages then made their arrangements for taking possession of our boat, and immediately carried them into effect. About twenty of them plunged into the water and swam to us, with tomahawks in their hands, while the rest stood with their rifles pointed towards us, for the purpose of destroying us in the event of resistance to the boarding party.

When I found them climbing up the side of the boat, I rose, and reaching my hand to the Indian nearest me, assisted him in getting in; proceeding then to the others, I helped as many of them on board, in like manner, as I could. When they entered, they shook hands with me, crying out in broken English, "How de do! How de do!" I returned their salutation by a hearty squeeze of the hand, as if glad to see them. The truth was, I expected, at the moment when we were made prisoners, that all would be put to the tomahawk. Finding our reception so different from what I had anticipated, the kind greetings which I gave them were not altogether feigned. After the momentary confusion produced by the capture was over, they pushed the boat to the shore, when the remainder of the party entered it, with their rifles in their hands. They also shook hands with us, appearing to be highly delighted at the success of their enterprise. After the transports of the moment had in a degree subsided, some began to examine into the booty they had taken, consisting principally of the dry goods belonging to Mr. Skyles, whilst others were employed in scalping and stripping the dead. After this operation was performed, the bodies of Mr. May and Dolly Fleming were thrown into the river. The party then all went on shore, taking the prisoners and the booty along with them.

The first thing now to be attended to, was the kindling of a fire, which was soon done. We were immediately afterwards stripped of the greater part of our clothes. The weather was uncommonly cold for the month of March. I wore a surtout and broadcloth coat over a red waistcoat. When these were unbuttoned, and the red vest was discovered, an Indian of the name of Chick-a-tom-mo,[10] who had the chief command, and could speak some English, exclaimed, "Oh! you cappatain?" I answered in the negative. Then he said, pointing to his own breast, "Me cappatain—all dese," pointing to the other Indians, "my sogers." After taking my outer clothes, one of them repeated the word, "Swap—swap"—and demanded that I should give him my shirt for his, a greasy, filthy garment, that had not been washed during the whole winter. I was in the act of drawing it over my head, in compliance with

10 Shawnee chief Chickatommo was widely known for his successes in attacking traffic on the Ohio River. He was killed five years later by advance troops from Gen. Anthony Wayne's expedition, in action near Fort Defiance.

his demand, when another Indian behind me, whose name I afterwards learned was Tom Lewis, pulled it back, and after reproaching the first for his unkindliness, took the blanket from his own shoulders and threw it over mine. After this occurrence, I seated myself by the fire. Having now some leisure for reflection, I began to consider of the awful situation into which I had been thus suddenly plunged. No human being, who has not experienced a similar misfortune, is capable of conceiving the horror which thrilled through my frame upon finding myself a captive to these ruthless barbarians, and at the mercy of an enemy who knew no mercy. Bred up with an instinctive horror of Indians and of Indian cruelties, it was a situation which, of all others, I had most deprecated. I felt as if cut off for ever, from my friends and from the world: already my imagination placed me at the stake, and I saw the flames about to be kindled around me.

I had not remained long in this situation, when the scalps of Mr. May and Miss Fleming, which had been stretched upon sticks bent into a circular form, were placed before me at the fire to be dried. The sight of these scalps, thus unfeelingly placed immediately in my view; the reflection that one of them had been torn from the head of a female by our ferocious captors: the other from a man who had engaged my esteem and friendship; with whom I had embarked on a plan of business now utterly frustrated; and that a much more cruel destiny than his was probably reserved for me, operated with an effect which I should in vain attempt to describe.

CHAPTER III.

THE two white men, who had decoyed us on shore, now made their appearance. The name of one was Divine, the other Thomas. As soon as they came up, sensible of the strong imputation from us to which their conduct had subjected them, they began a course of apology and exculpation. They solemnly declared, that they had been compelled by the Indians to act the part which had brought us into their hands; that they had really been taken off from Kennedy's Bottom some weeks before; and expressed great concern, that they had been the unwilling instruments of our captivity. We hesitated to believe them: and our doubts were increased as far as related to Divine, when a negro man who had been captured by the Indians some time before, and had continued with them ever since, arrived. He informed us, that Thomas had been extremely averse to any share in the scheme of treachery which had been practised upon us: but that Divine alone had devised it [11] and carried it into effect, on a promise which he obtained from the Indians, that they would set him at liberty if he should procure for them other white prisoners in his stead. All the intelligence we obtained on this subject induced clearly the opinion with us, that Divine's guilt was unquestionable, and that Thomas had been an involuntary agent. About the time of the negro's arrival, six squaws, most of them old women, with two white children, a girl and a boy, the former about ten or eleven years of age, the latter perhaps a year or two older, joined us. They belonged to a family which had been taken prisoners in Kentucky, and from which they had been separated.

Skyles's wound was painful, and Flinn was permitted to examine it. He ascertained that the ball had entered at the point of one shoulder, had ranged towards the other, and was lodged against it. He then made an incision with a razor, and extracted it. One of the squaws washed the wound; caught the bloody water from it in a tin cup; and required Skyles to drink it, giving him to understand that by doing so the cure would be expedited.[12]

The fire, by this time, had been considerably extended: it was at least fifty feet in length. The Indians were all seated around it. Their rifles were arranged in a line in their rear, and so near, that each individual could lay his hand on his own in an instant. They were supported by long small poles, placed horizontally about three

[11] In fact, the stratagem of decoying travelers to shore along the banks of the Ohio River was extensively practiced. Numerous white renegades, including the infamous Simon Girty, were engaged in it.

[12] Blood-drinking was among many tribes considered specifically medicinal and generally salutary. Jonathan Carver, for example, reports that during the massacre of men, women, and children at Fort William Henry, "many of the savages drank the blood of their victims, as it flowed warm from the fatal wound" (*Captain Jonathan Carver's Narrative of His Capture, and Subsequent Escape from the Indians* [London, 1778]); Alexander Henry observed at the massacre at Fort Michilimackinac that "from the bodies of some, ripped open, their butchers were drinking the blood, scooped up in the hollow of joined hands and quaffed amid shouts of rage and victory" (*Travels and Adventures in Canada and the Indian Territories* [New York, 1809]). Cf. also the account in the Kinnan narrative about the Delawares who "quaff with extatic pleasure the blood of the innocent prisoner" undergoing torture.

feet high on forks, and were neatly and regularly disposed. Our captors consisted of Indians from various tribes. There were Shawanese, Delawares, Wyandots, and Cherokees. Much the largest number were Shawanese.[13] An old chief of that tribe took a position at one end of the line of fire, and harangued the party for ten or fifteen minutes. He frequently raised his eyes and pointed to the sun, sometimes to the earth, and then to me. We were incapable of comprehending the business which occupied them, and were in a state of the most disquieting alarm; but *my* apprehensions were peculiarly excited, because he pointed at me, and at neither of the other captives. This circumstance, however, was soon explained, when at the close of his speech, Chickatommo conducted me to an Indian seated on the ground, and placed me at his side, telling me, that was *my friend;* whose name I afterwards ascertained was Messhaw-a,[14] and that he belonged to the Shawanese tribe. Chickatommo then addressed the party from the same spot, on which the old Shawanese chief had stood, and very much after the same manner; but he pointed at Skyles, and when he had concluded his speech, delivered him to the custody of another Shawanese. The same ceremony was observed with respect to Peggy Fleming and Flinn. She was allotted to the Cherokees, and Flinn to the Shawanese. Why neither of us went to the Delawares or Wyandots, we were unable then to conjecture. But the probability is, that as those tribes were at peace with the whites, the individuals of them who belonged to the party of our captors, were unwilling to incur the hazard of involving their people in war, by accepting any of the prisoners. Their presence on this occasion is sufficiently accounted for by recollecting, that young men of all the savage tribes frequently go

13 The Shawnees, originally members of the Algonquian language family, had earlier removed southward along the Ohio River. Culturally more southern than any other Algonquins, they were associated with certain Creek and Cherokee bands. More than any other tribe, the Shawnees linked the Indians of the northeast with those of the southeast. The varied tribal composition of the band that attacked Johnston's party points up the effect of rapid white settlement and expansion westward after the war; these Indians no longer occupied separate hunting grounds but had become marauders in common. While the Shawnees had long resided in southern Ohio, the Delawares originally belonged in eastern Pennsylvania and the Cherokees in Tennessee and Kentucky. The Wyandots, of the Wendat (Huron) peoples, had come to northern Ohio from Canada.

14 The kindly Messhawa, still alive after the War of 1812, became one of the followers of Tecumseh.

out on predatory excursions, without consulting their chiefs or nation. The Cherokees, I believe, were not then engaged in open hostilities with us. Yet they were not influenced by any such scruples as those which governed the Delawares and Wyandots, because, perhaps, as it was their intention to bear off their captive to the Villages of Indians on the Sandusky, or Miami of the lake,[15] they did not apprehend a discovery of their conduct by the whites, or their own tribe, and were not disposed to forego the gratification of accepting a prisoner from the Shawanese as a reward for their assistance in making captures on the river. The Delawares and Wyandots were about to return to their own towns, and would have offended their people by bringing among them prisoners from a nation with whom they professed to be at peace.

After the distribution of the captives, Divine, Thomas, and Flinn, were required by the Indians to prepare four additional oars for the boat which they had taken from us, and with which it was their intention to attack any other boat, or boats, that might be passing down while they remained on the river. The first night of our captivity was spent in the most painful anticipations. Next morning, at an early hour, our foes were busily occupied in rendering their aspects as terrific as possible, by painting their faces in the manner which will be hereafter described, when I shall speak of the war-dance. Each individual was provided with a small looking-glass, which he held before him while laying on the paint, and which was placed in a frame with a short handle, and a string through a hole in the end of it, for the purpose of tying it to his pack. This process was preparatory to their intended attack on any white persons who might be passing on the river, and is never omitted by them when they expect to encounter an enemy.

About ten o'clock, a canoe, containing six men, was observed to ascend the river slowly under the opposite bank. All the prisoners were compelled to go to the side of the water, for the purpose of inducing those who were in the canoe to cross over, and to come under the command of the Indian rifles. I vainly hoped that it

15 On the banks of the Sandusky River, which flows through northern Ohio and empties into Lake Erie, were located the two great Indian villages of Upper and Lower Sandusky. Miami of the lake (the Maumee River) empties into Lake Erie near the northwestern corner of the state of Ohio. "Of the lake" was added to distinguish it from the Miami rivers that flow into the Ohio River.

would be in my power, by some signal or contrivance, to apprise these unfortunate persons of their danger, and to prevent their running headlong into such a snare as had succeeded against us. But in this hope I was disappointed. Divine, ingenious in wicked stratagems, seemed to be perfectly gratified to aid the savages in their views, and to feel no scruples in suggesting means for their accomplishment. He fabricated a tale, that we were passengers down the Ohio, whose boat had suffered so great an injury, that we were unable to proceed until it was repaired; but that, for want of an axe, it was impossible for us to do the necessary work. These unsuspecting canoe-men turned towards us: but the current bore them down so far below us, as to preclude all chance of my putting them on their guard. The Indians, as they had acted in our case, ran down the river at such a distance from it, and under cover of the woods, that they were not discovered until the canoe was close to the shore, when they fired into it, and shot every one on board. As they tumbled into the water, their little bark was overset. Two, who were not yet dead, kept themselves afloat, but were so severely wounded that they could not swim off. The Indians leaped into the river, and after dragging them to the shore, despatched them with the tomahawk. The bodies of the four who were killed were also brought to land, and the whole six were scalped.[16] All were then thrown into the river. Nothing I could then learn, or which has since come to my knowledge, has enabled me to understand who these unfortunate sufferers were.

On the same day, two or three hours afterwards, three boats, standing down the river, came into view. I do not know why, on this occasion, the Indians relinquished the plan of treacherous deception, which had in two preceding instances eventuated to their wish.

16 "They perform the process of scalping without regard to the size of the portion of skin taken from the crown of the head. If, in their haste to cut it off, they take more than is sufficient for their purpose, they afterwards, when at leisure, pare it down in a round shape to the diameter of about two inches. Doctor Robertson, in a note to his history of America, says: 'It was originally the practice of the Americans, as well as of other savage nations, to cut off the heads of the enemies they slew, and to carry them away as trophies. But as they found them cumbersome in their retreat, which they always made very rapidly, and often through a vast extent of country, they became satisfied with tearing off their scalps'" [Johnston]. Johnston refers to William Robertson's *History of America* (1777). For the primitive homeopathic/magical significance of the practice of scalping, see Jogues, n. 36.

They now waited until these boats reached the point in the river directly opposite to them; when they commenced an ineffectual fire with their rifles. The Ohio was there so wide, that their bullets fell far short of their objects; and after the boats had passed below us, the savages obliged all the male captives to get into the boat taken from Mr. May, now provided with the additional oars made on the day before. Every Indian too, jumped into that boat, and as they were unpracticed in the use of the oar, the labour of plying it was consigned to us. Our captors stood over us, and compelled us to exert our strength in rowing; an art, in which we had as little experience as themselves. But we took care, unskilful as we were, to avoid striking all at the same time with our oars. Yet as those whom we pursued had only one pair of oars in each boat, and we had two pair in ours, we shuddered for the event. Good management on the part of the passengers in the three boats, and intentional mismanagement on our part, saved them from the imminent dangers to which they were exposed. The middle boat waited for that in the rear, received the people from it, together with their oars, and pressed forward to overtake the headmost boat. By much effort they came alongside, and all entered it, having then many hands to relieve each other in rowing, and six oars to our four. To our great joy, they shot rapidly ahead of us; when the Indians, giving up the chase of the boat which they now perceived they could not overtake, turned their attention to the two which were adrift, and which contained the property that had been abandoned in them. A rich booty for our captors was found on board. It consisted principally of dry goods and groceries, intended for Lexington in Kentucky. There were some very fine horses too in them, among which I recognised two remarkable animals, a mare and a horse, belonging to Mr. Thomas Marshall, brother of the Chief Justice, with whom Mr. May and I had travelled through the wilderness on our return from the west in the preceding year.[17] That gentleman's

[17] Marshall's account of the incident (*History of Kentucky*, Vol. I) also includes the circumstances of Johnston's capture earlier: "A boat coming down [the Ohio] was decoyed to shore by a white man who feigned distress; when fifty savages rose from concealment, ran into the boat, killed John May and a young woman, being the first persons they came to, and took the rest of the people on board prisoners.... The 2nd of April, they attacked three boats on the Ohio near the confluence of the Scioto. Two, being abandoned, fell into the hands of the enemy, who plundered them; the other being manned with all the people,

hat was also among the relinquished articles. I recognized it at a glimpse. It was one of the cocked hats worn at that time, and a small piece had been cut or torn from the point which was worn in front. If we had overtaken strangers in these boats, and they had been captured or put to death by the savages, it would have been an affliction to me sufficiently bitter. But what would have been the aggravation of my sufferings, had the passengers, or any of them, in the event of our coming up with them, proved to be my intimates and friends.

The boats were taken to the shore, and their contents landed. The chiefs distributed the plunder among their followers, in a manner that seemed perfectly satisfactory to all. Flour, sugar, and chocolate, formed a part of their acquisitions. They probably believed that I understood the subject of making flour into bread better than they did, and that duty was required of me. I was furnished with the undressed skin of a deer, which was most disgustingly stained, by having been used as a saddle on the sore back of a horse, and was now to answer the purpose of a tray. I commenced my new employment by baking a number of loaves in the ashes. There was more dough than the fire would contain; and it struck me, that I would make the remainder into small dumplings and boil them in a kettle of chocolate than on the fire. All savages are particularly fond of sweet things. To gratify this taste, they had on the present occasion mixed a large portion of sugar with the chocolate, which in the operation of boiling infused itself into the dumplings and made them quite sweet. They were so delighted with this new, and, to them, delicious dish, that they appeared to consider me a very clever fellow as a cook, and continued me in that employment as long as I was their prisoner. They then indulged to the utmost excess in drinking whiskey found on board one of the boats. But they observed a precaution which, I believe, is never neglected by them in those situations which call on them for vigilance. A sufficient number for safe keeping and guarding their captives refrained from tasting the spiritous liquor, and had watchful eyes over us. The rest of the party drank to deep intoxication, in which Flinn went as far as any of them, and had a battle with

---

made its escape by hard rowing." Lost were twenty-eight horses and merchandise valued at £1,500.

one of the Indians, whom he easily vanquished. Some of the rest endeavoured to assist their combatant, when others interposed in Flinn's favour, and protected him from attack, declaring that such treatment as he had received would only be tolerated by women, and that having acted like *a man*, they would not suffer him to be abused. Their invariable habit is, not to quit the bottle or cask while a drop of strong drink remains; and they poured it down their throats until their stock was exhausted. This occurred in the course of the succeeding night.

In the mean time, we were separated by our guard from those who were intoxicated, and removed to some distance from them, when we laid down to sleep. Skyles and I were resolved on seizing the earliest occasion, which the course of incidents should present, for effecting our escape. We flattered ourselves, that the senseless intoxication into which the main party were plunged, the darkness of the night, or a momentary relaxation of vigilance on the part of our guard, might furnish the golden opportunity. Our scheme was, to get into one of the boats lying under the bank of the river, and to drop without noise down the stream. If we could get but a little distance from the shore unperceived, there would be a good prospect of success. We remained silent until we believed that all our sentinels were asleep. We then commenced a conversation in whispers, which we presumed would not be heard; or, if heard, would not be understood by our guard, who knew nothing of the English language. But the wakeful suspicions of our keepers were always on the alert; and when our whispers reached their ears, they deduced the most unfavourable inferences, and put an end, at least for the present, to all our hopes, by confining us closely with cords. Soon after this was done, one of the drunken Indians straggled from his companions, and came to us, brandishing his scalping knife. He quickly worked himself up into a great rage, and throwing himself across the body of Skyles, fastened on his hair and was determined to take off his scalp. It was with some difficulty that he was prevented, by those who were sober, from effecting his object. Resistance on the part of the prisoner was utterly beyond his power. They had secured both of us completely, by tying us down, in a manner which will be hereafter more minutely explained. During the night, Divine and Thomas secretly disappeared, without an effort, that we could discover, on the part of the Indians to detain them.

CHAPTER IV.

On the following day, the Indians seemed to think that their booty was of sufficient value to be worth carrying to their towns, and we took our departure from the Ohio in the afternoon. But all did not move off together. Those to whom Flinn belonged remained at the river, and we never saw them or him afterwards. When we began our march, a cow, taken in one of the boats which had been abandoned on the preceding day, as I have already related, was committed to my care. I was required to lead her by a rope secured to her horns. This creature perplexed me exceedingly. I suppose she had not been accustomed to travel in this way. She resisted my exertions to get her forward. She would leave the track on which we walked, and frequently when I passed on one side of a tree, she would insist on taking the other; to the great diversion of the Indians, who laughed immoderately at the difficulties into which they had brought me with this unmanageable animal.

Late in the evening we reached an encampment, where our captors had probably spent some time before we fell into their hands. It was about five miles from the river, and they had left a number of horses, stolen from the settlements of Kentucky, a quantity of dried bear's meat, venison, peltry, and some of their people, at this retired spot. It was a rich valley, where there was no undergrowth of timber, but a luxuriance of tender grass below a covering of thick weeds, which protected it from the effects of frost and cold. This encampment was provided with shelters from the weather, composed of skins stretched over poles in the form of a tent. The valley in which it was situated afforded subsistence for their horses. Here, to my great relief, they took the cow off my hands by slaughtering her. After breakfast, on the next day, Chickatommo, attended by a party belonging to his tribe, and by the Cherokees with Peggy Fleming, left the encampment. The horses, (all of which he took with him,) were packed with the meat and peltry. The rest of the party followed not long after these. We travelled through a trackless wilderness, abounding in game, on which the Indians depended entirely for subsistence during the journey. Their plan was, to carry home the dried meat for the summer use of their families. On the first or second day's progress, the Indians observed a tree, the bark of which was marked by the claws of a bear, easily distinguished by these sagacious and experienced hunters. They immedately went to work with axes which were found in the captured boats, and soon felled the tree. Two very small cubs were found in its hollow trunk. Their dam, attracted by the noise at her den, came up when the tree fell, and was shot. We regaled ourselves upon the flesh of the cubs, which to me was excellent eating, although the manner of dressing was not such as to improve its quality or to suit a delicate taste. Their entrails were taken out, and after the hair was thoroughly singed from their carcasses, heads, and feet, they were roasted whole. On the next day, a remarkably fat bear was killed, and we remained on the ground where he was taken, until all his meat was consumed.

The Indians now indicated a disposition to loiter and throw away time, very little in unison with the impatience which I felt to move on as rapidly as possible. I had conceived, and could not help cherishing the hope, that at our arrival at their towns it might be my good fortune to meet with some compassionate trader, who would, by ransom or otherwise, relieve me from the sufferings and dangers of my captivity. An accident, in other respects unimportant, subjected me to a night's torture. The savages, apprehensive of possible danger from pursuit, had left a few of their party in their rear, to watch on their track, and to give them timely intelligence of any attempt that might be made by the whites to overtake them, and wrest from them either their prisoners or their plunder. To the few, thus left in the rear, my sentinel and protector, Meshawa, belonged. In his absence, I was committed to the custody of another Shawanese, altogether unlike him in temper and character. When he was about to secure my arms at night, by lashing a rope around them, I injudiciously and without reflection complained that he drew the rope too tight. Upon which he exclaimed, "Damn you soul!" and tightened it with all the vigor he could exert, so closely, that by the morning it was buried in the flesh of one of my arms. I could obtain no rest; and when Meshawa came up with us the next day, it was exceedingly swelled and throbbed with agony. At the moment of his arrival he loosened the ligature from my limb, and harshly rebuked the other for the severity of his conduct towards me.

The Indians still continued the habit of daily lounging. If a bear was killed, and they swallowed a plentiful repast of it; or if any other food was procured, which afforded them an abundant meal; immediately after satisfying their appetites, they laid themselves down to sleep. When they awoke, if a sufficiency was yet in the camp, they would again eat plentifully, and sleep as before. Some packs of cards were found among other articles of their plunder from the boats. With these they amused themselves daily, by playing a game entirely new to me, which, when interpreted into English, was called "Nosey." Only two hands were dealt out, and the object of each player was, by a mode of play which I do not now recollect, to retain a part of the cards in his own possession at the close of the hand, and to get all from his adversary. When this was done, the winner had a right to a number of fillips, at the nose of the loser, equal to the number of cards remaining in the winner's hand. When the operation of the winner was about to begin, the loser would place himself firmly in his seat, assuming a solemn gravity of countenance, and not permitting the slightest change in any muscle of his face. At every fillip the bystanders would burst into a peal of laughter, while the subject of the process was required to abstain completely even from a smile; and the penalty was doubled on him if he violated this rule. It is astonishing to what an excess they were delighted with this childish diversion. After two had played for some time, others would take their places, and the game was often continued hour after hour.

While the Indians were employed in this amusement, I endeavoured to begin, and intended to keep, a journal of my travels. I was very imperfectly provided with the means of accomplishing my purpose. A copy of the Debates of the Convention of Virginia, assembled to decide on the adoption or rejection of the Federal Constitution,[18] was found in one of the boats taken on the Ohio. I had brought it from that river to serve as a source of amusement; and on the margins of its pages I determined to write my notes. The quill of a wild turkey was the best I could procure, of which I made a pen with a scalping knife. I furnished myself with ink by

18 This was the convention of Williamsburg in 1788.

mixing water and coal dust together, and began my daily minutes of our progress and its incidents. This attracted the attention, but did not excite the disquiet, of the Indians. Tom Lewis, the same who gave me the blanket, when another was about to strip me of my shirt, after I had written some lines of my journal, took it from my hands, carried it to the others who were sitting around the fire, and showed it to them all. They seemed gratified and surprised at what indicated, in their opinion, something extraordinary about me, which, however, they could not comprehend.

When the party had satisfied themselves with "Nosey," we resumed our march, and arrived at a large branch of the Sciota, which is, I believe, the same that is marked, on an excellent map of the State of Ohio in my possession, by the name of Salt Creek.[19] My shoes had been taken from me, and one of the squaws had made me a pair of mockasins from the leather of a greasy pair of old leggings. I was in front when we came to the edge of the water. The stream was rapid. I was unacquainted with its depth, could not swim, and hesitated to enter. An old woman, who was next behind me, took the lead, carrying a staff in her hand, with which she supported herself against the force of the current. If a man had gone in before me, I should still have hesitated; but being confident that I could wade safely wherever the old woman could get along, I followed her. The bed of the creek was formed entirely of round smooth stones, from which my greasy mockasins were so incessantly slipping, that I was every moment in extreme danger of losing my feet, and gained the opposite bank with the utmost difficulty.

CHAPTER V.

In the course of two or three days we came up with Chickatommo and his party, who had waited for us. The Cherokees, with their prisoner Peggy Fleming, had separated themselves from the Shawanese chief, and had taken a different route from that which we were to follow. The deportment of this girl was a subject of no little astonishment to me. I had expected, that the distressing occurrences which had befallen us, and the gloomy prospect before us; the destruction of nearly all the party, and the death of her sister

19 An eastern tributary to the Scioto; numerous salt springs were located along its banks.

before her eyes; her own captivity and probably dreadful fate; would have plunged her into grief and despondency. But no such effect was produced. On the contrary, from the day of our capture, up to the time when she was borne off by the Cherokees, she seemed to be perfectly indifferent to the horrors of her situation. She enjoyed a high flow of spirits; and, indeed, I had never seen any one who appeared to be more contented and happy.

About this period of our journey, we came to a line of trees which had been marked by surveyors: a class of persons against whom the savages entertain the deepest and most malignant hatred; because they consider them the agents by whom their lands are laid off and taken from them, and because they are invariably harbingers of occupancy and settlement by the whites.[20] The view of the trees, with the chops of the axe on their bark, irritated our party so highly, that we had reason to fear for our immediate safety. They poured forth curses on us, with a bitterness and fury that continued for some time: not did they become calm again, until we had gone some distance beyond the marked line.

Incidents of this kind, occurring every day, I might almost say every hour, necessarily subjected us to frequent and severe suffering. But the miseries of the night were more uniform. Before we went to rest, our captors adopted the most rigorous measures for securing us. Our arms were pinioned by a strong rope of buffalo hide, which was stretched in a straight line, and each end secured to a tree. Our keepers laid themselves by us on these ropes, three or four on each side: but they were at liberty to change their positions, while we could only lie on our backs. We were generally placed on different sides, sometimes on the same side of the fire. No covering was allowed me, except a child's blanket; for that which Tom Lewis had thrown over my shoulders on the first day of my captivity, had been restored to him as soon as the morning cold subsided. Skyles's blanket was much larger than mine, but we were not permitted to keep each other warm, by lying togther, or bringing our bed clothes into a joint stock. The fire usually burnt down about the time when we awoke, fatigued with our position, and be-

20 Survey of the public lands in the Northwest Territory had begun in 1787. The marks Johnston describes were probably made by surveyors engaged in running lines for the Ohio Company at Marietta.

numbed with cold. The residue of the night was nothing more than a series of severe pains; and when morning arrived, I was frequently incapable of standing on my feet, until the warmth of the fire restored my strength. A deer-skin under us formed our sole protection from the cold and dampness of the earth.

Skyles and I repeatedly conversed on a plan of escape which we meditated, but the execution of which we agreed, for the present, to delay. The weather had been for some time dry. The vast multitude of leaves, with which the ground was covered in the woods through which we travelled, rendered it impossible to pass over them in their present state, however cautiously, without producing a noise so loud as to reach with certainty the ears of the Indians, and to betray our flight. We hoped for rain before the expiration of many days, and were resolved on an attempt to regain our liberty as soon as the moist state of the leaves would permit us to walk among them unheard. Skyles had carefully concealed a knife in the pocket of his breeches, with which he intended to cut the cords that confined us at some favourable hour of the night; and it was our design then to run off into the woods, whatever might be the hazard of wandering about, destitute as we were, in the solitary wilds of the extensive forest by which we were surrounded. But unluckily, one morning, when he rose from the spot on which he had slept, I discovered the knife lying on his deer skin, and believing myself unobserved by the Indians, I pointed it out to him. They, however, perceived it as quickly as he did, and instantly stripped our breeches from both of us. To supply their place, we were furnished with such covering as the Indians themselves were accustomed to wear.

Skyles had, until this period, carried five English guineas in his watch pocket. When he was required to take off his breeches, several squaws were present. He therefore stepped a short distance aside; dropped the gold on the earth among the leaves; and pretending to employ himself in darning the legs of his stockings with a needle and thread, borrowed from one of the squaws, he took care to keep his back turned towards the party until he made a bag for his money out of a part of the linen of his shirt, which he cut off with a pair of scissors lent by the same squaw from whom he had obtained the needle and thread. This bag he carried under the covering which was around his waist, and we valued its contents as a fund from which we might derive substantial benefit, should we ever reach a place where comforts could be procured. But we had not travelled longer than three or four days, when the pieces of gold wore a hole through the linen bag, and were all lost.

The incident of the knife disposed the Indians to adopt a greater degree of rigour towards us than had been before practised. When we lay down to sleep at night, each of us had one end of a cord tied around his neck, and the other extended and fastened to a tree or stake five or six feet from his head. From this cord a small bell was suspended, which rattled with the slightest motion of our bodies, and announced to the whole party that we were stirring; and on every such occasion their vigilant attention was directed towards us. When this mode of confining us was first resorted to, the circumstances by which it was attended excited great alarm, and subjected us to the most painful terror for several hours. We had halted, early in the afternoon, in a small prairie. The Indians brought from an adjacent wood six strong stakes, which they drove securely into the ground. The bark was taken off; each stake was painted red; and a cord, fixed around the neck of each prisoner, seemed to indicate preparations for an awful event. Skyles was extremely terrified. My conjecture was, that nothing more was designed by the Indians than to take some new measures for retaining us securely in their power. The course of reasoning by which I endeavoured to allay the agitation of Skyles's mind, was ineffectual; and he at last begged that I would snatch up one of the rifles placed near us, and put him to death. The evening passed off; the hour of rest arrived; and we discovered that their arrangements looked no farther than to our safe keeping.

The cords put around our necks were, during the day, bound up at the ends into a sort of club, which hung down behind. This club on Skyles's neck reached precisely to his wound, which it severely annoyed and irritated. Yet the Indians loaded him with a very heavy pack, of which he could not venture to complain; because, in that event, he well knew, that his unfeeling master would aggravate the evil, by doubling his burden. As to myself, I had regularly borne a large weight of booty on my back from the encampment near the Ohio river, and was never permitted to travel without an uncommonly heavy rifle barrel, which, in addition to my pack, incommoded me most grievously.

It is the habit of these Indians, to treasure up all the bear's oil which they collect during the hunting season, and carry it to their villages for home use. It is put up in deer skins, which are stripped from the animal with as little splitting as possible, and the openings necessarily made are carefully and securely closed. These skins, when filled, are usually transported on horses, each horse bearing two. The oil is eaten with their jerked venison, and is as palateable an addition to that article of food, as butter is to bread. On one occasion, those of the party who had charge of the horses, had started from our encampment in the morning sooner than the rest, and had, perhaps inadvertently, left on the ground one of these skin-bags of bear's oil. When the foot party were about to commence their march they discovered it, and I was required to bear it. The bag was accordingly placed on my back, secured by a hoppas,[21] whilst my pack and rifle barrel were carried by one of the Indians. I found it a much heavier burden than I had before sustained. Ignorant as yet of their temper towards me, and apprehensive of mischief, should I manifest a refractory spirit, I determined to bear this oppressive load as long as my strength could endure it. I staggered along under its weight for perhaps a mile, or more; when, unable any longer to support it, I threw it down. My usual pack was then given to me, and the oppresive weight from which I had relieved myself was taken up by one of the party and carried forward till we overtook those who were mounted, without any appearance of displeasure on their part at my conduct.

Very soon after our capture, they invented names for Skyles and myself. I was called Ketesselo. Whether this word was in-

21 "The *hoppas* is a strap, fourteen or fifteen feet long, by which the pack is secured to the back. It is about two and a half inches wide in the middle, and gradually narrows towards each end to the width of one inch, or three fourths of an inch. A length of near two feet, in the middle, or broadest part, is very closely woven, and neatly ornamented with beads and porcupine's quills, stained of various colours, and tastefully wrought into fanciful forms. The *hoppas* is so tied to the pack, that this ornamented portion passes over the breast and upper part of the arms, and is all that can be seen in front. It is curiously plaited by the hand, and is made from the bark of a wild plant closely resembling hemp, and quite as strong" [Johnston]. Cf. the Mohawk burden-strap description in Eastburn n. 3.

tended to express any particular idea, or whether any precise meaning was conveyed by it, I could not learn. The appellation, in their language, by which they distinguished my fellow-prisoner, does not occur to my memory. But its English is, "Stinking white man;" applied to my unfortunate friend, because his wound had become offensive to the smell, although I was in the habit of washing it for him regularly every day.

At length, after a journey of ten or twelve days, we arrived on the eastern bank of the Sciota, at a point where our party determined to cross the river. But the water was too deep to be passed by fording; and all were soon employed in preparing a raft for the transportation of the men, women, prisoners, and baggage. The horses swam over. The dead timber, selected for constructing the raft, was felled and carried on the shoulders of the men to the waterside. A log had been cut, which was so large and heavy, that two persons were not able to carry it. Some of the party assisted a couple of their people to get the smaller end of this log on their shoulders, whilst I was required to bear the larger. They aided me in taking it up, but I quickly perceived that the burden was beyond my strength; and after staggering with it a short distance, there was no alternative but to throw it down. I called to the men who were in front of me with the smaller end, and told them in English, for I could not speak their language, what I was about to do. They probably did not understand me; and when I dashed the log to the ground, its whole weight by the sudden jolt was thrown so violently upon them, as to bring them to the earth with the log upon them. This roused them to a pitch of rage which might have seriously endangered my life, had not the injury which they received been so severe, that it was not in their power for some time to rise. But the incident was a subject of high sport to their brethren, who roared with laughter, while my fellow-labourers were repeatedly crying, "Damn Ketesselo!—Damn Ketesselo!" It is remarkable, that although only two Indians of this party understood or could speak our language, yet there was not one of them who did not utter curses in English; and all had caught the common salutation, "How-d'ye-do?" A consequence, which I did not regret, resulted from the adventure of the log. I was no longer required to aid in conveying the trunks of trees to the river. The raft was completed by securing together the logs which composed it with grapevines, and we all went over on it by making several trips.

CHAPTER VI.

Not long after passing the Sciota, we fell in with a hunting party, who encamped not far from us. Some of our Indians conducted me to their encampment; narrated boastfully the occurrences of our capture, and of their chasing the boats on the Ohio; and exulted in their success. Although I did not understand their language, their signs, gestures, and countenances, were so significant that I easily comprehended them. About this time, while I was crossing a creek upon a log, which lay over it at the height of five or six feet from its surface, the greasy mockasins which I wore were so slippery, that I tumbled off, over head and ears into the stream. But it was not deeper than my waist, and I had no difficulty in gaining the bank. Such is in general the stern gravity of face and deportment by which the savages are distinguished, that when we turn our attention to this trait in their manners, we are ready to infer, that they are entire strangers to mirth. But this, or any like trivial occurrence, never failed to produce from them loud and repeated bursts of merriment. It is perhaps worthy of notice, that although I had been little accustomed to exposure; had never been subjected to trials and hardships such as I was now compelled to undergo; yet no injurious effect on my health ensued from wading creeks, falling into the water, lying out in the open air, in all kinds of weather, nor from any other inconvenience which I encountered in the course of this long and painful march, the first I had ever made on foot.

Mr. Skyles and I soon found, that we had fallen into very different hands. Perhaps the characters of no two men ever formed a more striking contrast, than did those of his keeper and mine. Messhawa, to whom I had the good fortune to be allotted, had qualities which would have done honour to human nature in a state of the most refined civilization; whilst his keeper possessed such as disgraced even the savage. The one was humane, generous, and noble; the other was ferocious, cruel, and brutal. These distinguishing traits, which clearly showed themselves from the first, continued to mark the conduct of each throughout the whole of our subsequent journey. As regarded my safe keeping, Messhawa exerted a watchfulness and a fidelity to his trust, which never slumbered for a moment. But even in the execution of his duty, he evinced a regard to my feeling, and a desire to mitigate the severity of my sufferings: whilst the conduct of Skyles's keeper was calculated, in every respect, to wound his sensibility, and to aggravate his pain. At our meals, Messhawa would divide with me to the last morsel; but not so with the other. *His* object seemed to be, to afford his prisoner a sufficiency to sustain life, and nothing more. On one occasion, when we had penetrated far into the interior of the country after a fatiguing day's march, Skyles was eating some boiled racoon out of a kettle which was set before him. He had taken but a few morsels, when his keeper in an angry tone, snatched the kettle from him, and told him, he had ate enough, and should have no more!—It is true, we did not know these to be the words which he uttered, but from his gestures and manner we believed such to be the purport of them. Plentifully furnished with provisions for myself, from the bountiful hand of Messhawa, I felt the strongest inclination to supply the wants of my companion. But this could only be done by stealth; because I feared that discovery would draw upon me the vengeance of his brutal keeper, and place it out of my power to minister to the sufferings of my less fortunate fellowprisoner. The persons of these two Indians were as different as the qualities of their hearts. Messhawa was tall, straight, muscular, and remarkably well formed, of a very dark complexion, with a countenance free from the harshness and ferocity usually exhibited by the savage face, and expressive of mildness and humanity. He was distinguished as a swift runner. The other, whose name I have forgotten, was old, below the middle stature, lame, with a countenance on which the temper he continually displayed was very strongly marked.

My friend Skyles had procured a copy of the New Testament, which he frequently indulged himself in reading when we halted. One morning, when he was sitting at the fire with the book in his hand, endeavouring to extract that consolation from its pages which was inaccessible from any other source, the brutal old man, to whose custody he had been consigned, snatched it from him; harshly reproved him for reading it; and threw it into the flames.

The hour now arrived, when the man, who had been my companion in all the afflicting scenes of adversity through which I had passed since my capture; who was the sole individual with whom I could hold conversation; and the object of my warm and incessant sympathy, was separated from me. We had observed, that eyes of never-wearied vigilance were fastened upon us by our captors, and that their suspicions were always alive to every circumstance in our conduct. We therefore adopted the resolution, to deny ourselves the indulgence of a frequent interchange of thoughts and words, and to say little to each other, lest the Indians, apprehensive that a plan of escape might be the subject of our talk, should put an end to all communication between us. We strictly conformed to this resolution for some time, until a delightful state of the atmosphere on an April day so elevated our spirits, that we conversed much more freely than a discreet conformity to our own views of the subject would have prescribed. We were immediately punished for our imprudence. A party, consisting of eight or ten Indians, turned, with their prisoner Skyles, to the villages on the Miami of the lake. The others proceeded with me and the two white children towards the towns on the river Sandusky. My heart sunk within me when he was torn from my side. But the bitterness of the misfortune was greatest on his part; and I had yet some slender comforts left, while he had none. His wound, irritated by the pack which he carried, demanded care and attention. I had been in the daily habit of washing it; not a creature besides had touched it for a long time. He was now entirely in the hands of his unfeeling lame keeper, who cherished a savage delight in aggravating his sufferings; and there was not one among those around him who spoke his language. I was not wounded. Messhawa was of a kind, and even benevolent temper. Two of the Indians remaining with me were capable of expressing themselves in broken English; the little white boy and girl too were yet of my party.—Imagination may, perhaps, supply what the pen cannot describe, in relation to such a subject as the parting between Mr. Skyles and me. To say, that we cordially shook each other by the hand; that we embraced; that tears flowed in profusion from our eyes; would inadequately impart our emotions. Despair was the prevailing agent in the bosoms of both; and we quitted each other without a ray of hope to illumine our prospects.

Soon after our separation, the people to whom I belonged halted, about midday, for refreshment. An Indian, well advanced in years, retired fifteen or twenty steps from the fire, and, lying down with his face to the ground, fell asleep. A young man, who had kept his eyes on him, waited until he was perfectly in slumber. He then advanced, cautiously and without the slightest noise, to the spot where the other was quietly reposing; raised and dropped his tomahawk several times over his body; and at last struck its blade into his back with all the strength he could exert. The wounded man sprung on his feet, and ran off as fast as his legs could carry him. But he was not pursued; nor did he afterwards rejoin us. I was never able to obtain a clue to this assassinating attempt. Incidents of this nature, though followed by no interesting consequence, yet go far to show the character of the singular and savage people who had me in their possession.

A number of days subsequent to this were spent without any remarkable occurrence. The party sometimes travelled, often halted for the purpose of eating, sleeping, and playing their favorite game "Nosey," which they sometimes exchanged for a game like that called, among us, Five Corns.[22] They also occasionally amused themselves by dancing, invariably accompanied with a song composed of the words, "Kon-nu-kah,—He-ka-kah,—We-sa-too,—Hos-ses-kah"—repeated with a tone which did not strike the ear with a very musical effect. When they became fatigued with this exercise, they sometimes compelled Mr. Skyles, before he was separated from me, and myself, to imitate them in both the dance and the song, the words of which were repeated by me often enough to impress them so perfectly on my memory, that they are not yet forgotten. In one instance we were required, when the blaze of the fire was very high, to leap through it, and only escaped injury by performing the act as quickly as possible.

They carried two or three tobacco pipes, with which every man smoked when he chose, and they practised that amusement to great excess. A circle was frequently formed, and the pipe passed

[22] A game evidently similar to the Indian dice or bowl games. See Gyles, n. 28.

round from one to another, until all were satisfied. They are addicted, as I have before remarked, to taciturnity; and on these occasions, while enjoying the fumes of their tobacco, a word was rarely spoken by an individual among them. Sometimes a short, dry observation would escape one of those within the circle, to which the others would express their assent by a sort of grunt. They are much in the habit of conveying their ideas by a gesture or sign, always made with striking significancy.

We had now penetrated a great distance into the interior of a wild and uninhabited country; and I was compelled to abandon every thing like an effort or a hope to escape from my captors. Even though I had succeeded in eluding their incessant vigilance, so far as to get out of their power, I should have been unable to procure sustenance of any kind, or to explore my way through woods and deserts, for I knew not how many miles; and must have perished with hunger, or fallen into the hands of other Indians, parties of whom were wandering about in every direction. I was therefore reconciled to a continuance with them until we should arrive at their towns, where I flattered myself I might be purchased or ransomed by some benevolent trader.

During the whole march, we subsisted on bear's meat, venison, turkeys, and racoons, with which we were abundantly supplied, as the ground over which we passed afforded every species of game in profusion, diminishing, however, as we approached their villages. But we were destitute of bread and salt, necessaries of life to a white man, while they are considered mere superfluities by the Indian warrior or hunter, when he is occupied in war or the chase. A mode of living perfectly new to me; the fatigues of the journey; my exposure to all the inclemencies of the season and climate; and the uneasiness of mind under which I constantly laboured, wasted my strength and depressed my spirits. I had been nearly four weeks on this distressed journey. The vast wilderness through which I had passed, and that which still stretched before me, produced in my mind the frequent recollection of those beautiful lines from Goldsmith's Hermit, which were precisely adapted to my present condition:

For here forlorn and lost I tread,
With fainting steps, and slow,

Where wilds, immeasurably spread,
Seem length'ning as I go.[23]

But in addition to all these miseries, there was another source of painful apprehension, to which I could not advert with unconcern. I had heard enough of the Indian habits and manners to understand, that it is their usage, on reaching their towns with a prisoner, to subject him to the degrading and severe infliction of blows, while he runs the gauntlet.

All the women and boys are provided with staves, clubs, and such other weapons as they may choose. They are then arranged in two ranks, at a short distance from each other, and the captive is compelled to make his progress between these ranks at whatever pace he pleases, while every possible exertion is made to annoy and to beat him down.[24] Should he be fortunate enough, when thus exposed, to avoid extreme injury, yet he is not exempted from the most awful calamity which barbarism has invented for those who fall into its power. If the vindictive temper of the savages is unappeased; if they are not under the influence of those motives, or whims, or peculiar customs, which determine them on saving life; the miserable prisoner is fastened to a stake, a fire is kindled around him, his sufferings are aggravated and protracted by all the ingenuity of torture, until nature can bear it no longer, and he dies in agony inconceivable.

The gloom, which reflection on such subjects had spread over my mind, was in some degree dispelled by an incident, which, under ordinary circumstances would have been disregarded. We found a negro in the woods, under cover of a tent, which contained a quantity of whiskey and peltry belonging to his master, an Indian of the Wyandot tribe, then at peace with the United States. This negro was a runaway from the state of Kentucky, and had fled across the Ohio to the country of the savages; [25] among whom it was a law, as I was informed, that the first who should lay hands

[23] The lines that Johnston quotes are from "The Hermit, or Edwin and Angelina" (1764), a ballad by Oliver Goldsmith (1730?–74), English poet, novelist, essayist, and dramatist.

[24] See Jogues, n. 13.

[25] Although fugitive slaves among the Indians north of the Ohio were not so numerous as those among the southern tribes, Johnston came into contact with several; the number in the north must have been considerable.

on such runaway had a right to hold him as his property. The negro had been thus acquired by the Wyandot, who was, when we fell in with the negro, engaged in hunting, and had, on a trading expedition, recently visited the Muskingum, where he had obtained the whiskey now in the possession and care of his negro man.

I now felt myself quite at home; and the poor negro, whom under other circumstances, I should have kept at a distance, became my companion and friend. He treated me with great kindness and hospitality, offering me such refreshments as he had, the most acceptable of which were bread and salt. I had not tasted either since we left the Ohio river. My captors, as soon as they ascertained that the negro had whiskey for sale, began to barter for it a part of the booty which they had acquired on the Ohio. A pair of new boots, which they had taken from my saddlebags, and for which I had paid eight dollars at Petersburg, was given for a pint of whisky; and other articles were exchanged at a similar rate. The scenes which had passed on the Ohio were now to be acted over again. A disgusting revelry commenced, which lasted for three days, As usual, a sufficient number remained sober to guard the prisoners, consisting, at this time, only of the two children and myself.

On the first night, about the time when we were composing ourselves for rest, we were removed to some distance from the spot occupied by those who were in a state of intoxication, that we might not, while asleep, be disturbed by them. The two children had never been tied; but I was confined by cords, and Indians laid themselves on each side of me as before. In this situation I slept, until about midnight, when I was awaked by the falling of rain. Soon after, the negro, who had observed the direction in which we had gone when removed from the place where the drunken Indians were, arrived at our camp, and kindly proposed to me, that I should go with him to his tent, and sleep under it, protected from the rain. I pointed out the impossibility of accepting his invitation, without the consent of my guard, lying on each side of me, upon the rope with which I was confined. These men, hearing a conversation between the negro and myself which they did not understand, conceived a suspicion that he was concerting with me measures for my escape. They immediately sprung up, and seizing the negro, set up a tremendous yell, which was answered by the drunken party, and presently most of them came running towards us with their tomahawks in their hands. The negro, who could speak their language, was taken off a short distance and interrogated as to the object of his visit to me; after which I was separately questioned on the same point by one of those who spoke English. As there was an entire correspondence in our answers, the Indians did not doubt their truth; and I was permitted to accept the invitation of my new friend. I soon reached his tent, accompanied by nearly all the Indians, who appeared to have been much sobered by the incident which had just occurred. I then laid myself down within the tent, near its entrance, in front of which there was a fire. Sheltered from the rain, and no longer encumbered by ropes, I soon fell into a profound sleep, which I should probably have enjoyed till morning, had not my slumbers been interrupted by a sensation like that called the night-mare; but which was, in fact, produced by the weight of a large Indian sitting composedly on my breast, before the fire, and smoking his pipe. I turned over and dropped him on the ground, where he continued to sit, indulging, as if nothing had occurred, in his favourite amusement of smoking, until I again sunk into sleep.

CHAPTER VII.

In the morning, a frightful scene presented itself: they were preparing for the war-dance. A pole had been cut from the woods; after taking the bark from it, it was painted black, with streaks of red, winding like snakes around it: the lower end was sharpened, and at the top the scalps of my late companions, with others which they had obtained during their excursion, were suspended. Each Indian had dressed himself for the occasion. some had painted their faces black, with red round the eyes; others, reversing it, had painted their faces red, with black round the eyes: all with feathers stuck in their heads, and all with the aspect of so many demons. When they had finished adorning themselves in this manner, the pole was stuck fast into the ground. They formed themselves into a circle around it: and then the dance began. It commenced with the fell war-whoop, which had not ceased to ring in my ears since the fatal morning of our capture. They danced around the pole, writhing their bodies and distorting their faces in a most hideous manner. It is their practice, on such occasions, to repeat the injuries which have been inflicted on them by their enemies the whites; their lands taken from them—their villages burnt—their cornfields laid waste—their fathers and brothers killed—their women and children carried into captivity. In this instance, by these repetitions of their wrongs and sufferings, they had wrought themselves up to a pitch of the greatest fury.

The dance lasted for about half an hour. The scene being new to me, I had seated myself on a log to witness it. When it ended, Chickatommo, with eyes flashing fire, advanced towards me, and when in reach struck me a violent blow on the head. I immediately quitted my seat, seized him over the arms, and demanded why he struck me? He replied, by saying, "Sit down!—sit down!" I accordingly loosened my grasp, and resumed my seat on the log. At that moment, perceiving the two prisoner children near, who, like myself, had been attentive spectators of the dance, he snatched up a tomahawk that was at hand, and advanced towards them with a quick step and determined look. Alarmed at his menacing approach they fled:—he pursued. My humane friend Messhawa, seeing the imminent danger to which they were exposed, bounded like a deer to their relief. The boy being older and stronger than his sister, she was the first to be overtaken by Chickatommo, and would have been the first to fall a victim to his rage; but at the moment when the fatal instrument was raised to strike her dead, Messhawa had reached the spot. Coming up behind Chickatommo, he seized him around the arms, and with violence slung him back. He then darted towards the affrighted child, whom he reached in an instant, snatched her up in his arms, and pursued the boy. Misconstruing the good intentions of Messhawa, he redoubled his exertions to escape, and they had run a considerable distance before he was overtaken. When his deliverer came up with him, he thought all was over, and gave a bitter shriek, which was answered by one still more bitter from his sister, then in the arms of Messhawa and who had not yet understood his object. They were both, however, soon undeceived. Although he spoke to them in an unknown tongue, his language, from the manner of it, could not be misunderstood. They found that they had been mistaken, and that they had been pursued by a friend instead of an enemy. When this was ascertained, their little palpitating hearts were soon calmed into repose, and presently they arrived at our camp, walking by the side of Messhawa, who held each by the hand, and soothed them as they advanced with his caresses. The wood being an open one, I had viewed the scene with intense gaze; and nothing could exceed the delight I felt at finding my poor little companions thus relieved from the dangers of so perilous a situation.

On the next day two Mingo Indians [26] arrived and immediately participated in the drunken debauchery of our camp. One of these men had killed in the course of the preceding summer, an Indian of the Wyandot tribe, who was a husband, and the father of several children. Among all the savage nations of America, the usage prevails, of adopting prisoners taken in war for the purpose of supplying any loss incurred by those, who have had their friends slain in battle, or otherwise.[27] If one takes the life of another belonging to his own or a different tribe, he is bound to make reparation to the family of the dead man, either by the payment of a certain value in property, or by furnishing a substitute for the deceased, who occupies precisely the same station, and fills all the relations of such deceased in the community to which he belonged; becomes the husband of his widow, should he have left one, the father of his children, and is required to perform all the duties appertaining to these connexions. If reparation is not made for the death of a man by one of the modes which have been mentioned, within a period limited by their usages, the murderer becomes liable to be killed with impunity by the relatives of him who has fallen, or by any other of his tribe. In this instance, the Mingo stated to my captors his wretched situation. He declared himself so poor, that he was not able to render the requisite value for the Wyandot whom he had slain; and therefore that his own life must be forfeited, unless the alternative condition was fulfilled by him. While their hearts were warmed more by the operation of the spirituous liquor they had drank, than by any genuine emotions of

[26] A remnant of the Iroquois, the Mingos inhabited the country in the eastern part of Ohio.

[27] See Jogues, n. 20.

liberality, they did not hesitate to yield to his solicitations; and I was delivered over to this new master, to be substituted for the Wyandot whom he had murdered.

When I had ascertained, that those with whom I had travelled from the Ohio River, were preparing to resume their journey, and to leave me in the hands of my new possessor, I was utterly astonished and incapable of conceiving the cause of so unexpected a determination. For the purpose of relieving my mind from the anxiety and alarm necessarily produced by my transfer to the Mingo, I requested the negro to explain its object. He was equally ignorant with myself of the negotiations between my present and former proprietors, and applied to both parties for explanation. The intelligence, unreservedly communicated to him by each was perfectly concurrent, and the perturbation of my feelings was in a great degree diminished, when I learnt, that I was destined shortly to become a husband and a father. The prospect, indeed, was not very rapturous, of leading to the altar of Hymen an Indian squaw, already the mother of several children. But there was something extremely consoling in the hope, I might say in the persuasion, that such an event would bring within my reach those chances of escape from the savages, and for restoration to my country and friends, which I had thus far vainly exerted myself to obtain.

The Indians, whose captive I had heretofore been, took up their packs immediately after surrendering me to the Mingo, and continued their march. But before they set out, every individual made it a point to take leave of me, and to shake me by the hand. Several of them, by their countenances and manner, evinced feelings of kindness, and even of regret, at parting. My excellent friend Messhawa, who had certainly formed an attachment to me, seemed to partake more of this feeling than any of them.

After they left us, I had leisure to reflect on my new condition, and believed I had reason to congratulate myself on a change so auspicious. The matrimonial connexion, which had been designed for me, without my consent, occupied my mind, and I entertained an earnest curiosity with respect to the female, the place of whose husband I was to supply, and with whom I was to be allied by the ties of marriage. Whether she was old or young, ugly, or handsome, deformed or beautiful, were the questions not without their interest to me. I therefore inquired on those subjects from the Mingo, by the aid of my interpreter, the negro. But he had never seen her, and could give me no information, except that she was the mother of three or four children. But whatever might be her personal appearance, or the qualities of her heart; whether she was destitute of charms, or distinguished for them; the plan to be pursued by me was clear, and my resolution was not to deviate from it. I was not to be consulted in relation to the marriage intended for me by those who claimed the disposal of my person: whether it was to be productive of happiness or misery to me, was no concern of theirs. The only benefit which could result on my side would be, that I should be free, and no longer continue the object of suspicion and vigilance; and might seize on the first favourable opportunity which presented itself, of returning to the comforts, the security, and the enjoyments of civilized life. For the more certain attainment of my purpose, it was my intention, after assuming the charge of the family which I was about to enter by compulsion, thoroughly to devote myself to it, to reconcile myself as far as was in my power to the necesity by which I was overwhelmed; but by no means to delay my escape, when the moment should arrive at which there was a possibility of its being accomplished. It may well be conceived, that with such hopes and views, I became impatient for our arrival at the place of residence of my intended bride.

These reveries, which I continued hourly to indulge, were not of long duration. After the lapse of two or three days, the Mingo, who now considered me as his property, began to move on with me towards the town at which I was to be delivered, and where the bridal ceremony was to be performed at the proper period subsequent to my arrival. Before he fell in with the party from the Ohio, we had struck the war-path leading from the country on that river, to the Indian towns on the Sandusky and Miami. Upon this war-path my late proprietors had proceeded, when they took leave of the Mingo and myself; and as he conducted me along the same route in their rear, it would happen, that if delayed a few days, we should overtake them. The fact was, that my former possessors, after the generous feeling excited by the whiskey, which they were quaffing when the Mingo joined them, had subsided, began to repent of their liberality, and determined to reclaim me. They accordingly halted until we came up with them. We were received with smiles, and every indication of civility. They all shook us by the hand, and there was nothing which induced the slightest apprehension of ill humour. But this temper did not long display itself. A bitter altercation commenced, which soon proceeded to a high quarrel; in the course of which I was not exempt from uneasiness when I observed, by their frequent pointing to me, that I was the subject of controversy. The danger was, that one party might despatch me with the tomahawk or rifle, rather than yield me to the claim of the other. The dispute was terminated by the act of Messhawa, who caught two of the horses that were browzing in the immediate neighbourhood and in view of our position, mounted one of them, required me to get on the other, and conducted me, with his rifle on his shoulder, to the Indian town at upper Sandusky. This was done by instruction from Chickatommo.

We reached that place after riding about five miles.[28] Those of our party, who had been left in the rear by Messhawa and myself, did not long delay to follow us; and, when they arrived at the town, encamped about the centre of it. Mr. Francis Duchouquet, a Canadian trader, who had resided for some years among the Indians at this place,[29] had met us at the point where the party had waited for the Mingo and me, and had then, on my earnest solicitation, assured me, that overtures for my redemption should be made on our arrival at Upper Sandusky. He visited us in a short time after we had encamped in that village. At the first moment when I saw this gentleman, I was animated with the hope, that I

[28] "There were no streets in this town, but the Indian habitations were irregularly disposed, without regard to order or distance from each other. They were all constructed of bark, supported by corner posts and cross timbers, to which the bark was secured by strings made of its inner fibres. There was no chimney, but the fire was made about the centre of the hovel, and a hole was left in the roof over it for the escape of smoke. It requires no great labour to erect one of these frail dwellings; since the bark, which is the principal material, is obtained from large trees, when their sap begins to flow, in wide and long flakes. The corner posts and cross timbers are barely of sufficient size and strength to sustain the outer covering" [Johnston].

[29] French traders had been coming into the area south of the Great Lakes for over fifty years. That Duchouquet lived permanently at the Indian village is not unusual, for it was necessary that a trader establish some well-known place, or headquarters, to receive the pelts which he then carried to Detroit to be taken by boat to Quebec.

might prevail on him to treat with the Indians for my ransom, and that he might succeed in rescuing me from the pains and horrors of a captivity which I had then suffered for many weeks. I instantly renewed my application to him on this subject, and he did not hesitate to exert his good offices in my favour. But his propositions were decisively rejected; and the Indians expressed a determination not to let me go from their hands. The failure of this negotiation, when disclosed to me, produced an agonizing effect, which perhaps may be conceived, but cannot be expressed. All the terrors of a cruel death, inflicted by merciless savages, ingenious in the invention and practice of torture, recurred to my imagination, and filled me with despair.

CHAPTER VIII.

I HAD forgotten my copy of the Debates of the Virginia Convention, at the place from which I had been hurried by order of Chickatommo, on the day that we reached Upper Sandusky. Next morning the Mingo Indian, to whom I had been for a short time transferred, and from whom I had been reclaimed by my captors, appeared at our encampment. Recollection of the contest which he had lately maintained, for possession of my person, induced a suspicion, that his views were not propitious to my safety; and I was disposed to avoid him. My fears, however, were entirely dispelled, when, on his approach towards me, he drew from his bosom the book in which I had kept my journal, and presented it to me with a smiling face.

Soon afterwards, the party who held me a prisoner, was gladdened by the arrival of several Wyandots from Muskingum, with a quantity of whiskey in kegs, each of which contained about ten gallons, brought on horses, and lashed across their backs with hickory wythes. Immediately they began to barter with their guests for the article, with of all others, is most valuable in their eyes. The Wyandots turned their whiskey to good account. Five gallons were enough for the purchase of a horse worth two hundred dollars; a finely formed, handsome animal, now reduced in his plight by the journey from the Ohio River. Others of inferior value, were exchanged at a price proportioned to the first; and drunkenness soon spread itself over our encampment. But their customary precaution was not neglected; and a small number refusing to drink, remained sober, for the purpose of guarding me.

I had observed the liberality of their disposition while under the influence of drink, when they gratuitously yielded me to the Mingo; and therefore, pressed Mr. Duchouquet to renew his efforts for my ransom, at a moment which seemed favourable to my hopes. Again his propositions were rejected. I then begged him to ascertain, by inquiry from the Indians, to what point it was their intention to convey me; and what was the fate to which I was destined. To the first question they answered, by telling him that they intended to take me to their towns on the Miami river: to the second their reply was, that they did not know what final destination they should make of me. I had before this distinctly understood, that captives conveyed to the Miami towns, were certain of meeting the most dreadful fate; and that it is the invariable practice of the savages, to conceal their purposes from the prisoners whom they meant to sacrifice. When Mr. Duchouquet, therefore, reported to me the result of the inquiries which he had made at my request, my alarm and despondency were greater, if possible, than I had yet experienced; and every thing like hope was banished from my bosom.

The spirit of drunken debauchery prevailed, until the funds for purchasing whiskey, and the article itself, were about the same time exhausted. Four or five days of unbounded riot and intoxication had been passed, when the Indians to whom I belonged, finding themselves suddenly reduced from affluence to their usual poverty: ashamed of their wasteful expenditures, after having boasted of their exploits and their acquisitions on the Ohio; unwilling to return to their homes and their countrymen with nothing in their hands, of the wealth which they had recently possessed; adopted a resolution to go back to the river on which they had succeeded so well, and to make farther captures of white men and their property. They communicated their intention to Mr. Duchouquet, and informed him, that as the scalp of their captive might be transported with greater facility and safety than his person, they had determined to put me to death: but if he was in a temper to treat for my ransom, this was his time. A negotiation was then commenced, and concluded happily for me, without my knowledge or intervention.

It was agreed, that he should pay one hundred dollars worth of goods as the price of my liberation; and that I should be forthwith surrendered to him. The price was paid down in six hundred silver broaches; which answers all the purposes of a circulating medium with them.

This event, to me the most important of my life, by a singular coincidence occurred on the 28th of April, in the year 1790;[30] the day on which I attained the age of twenty-one years. It might be truly and literally denominated my second birth; since, within the preceding twenty-four hours, I might have been considered as dead to any prospect which my condition presented, except the most miserable, and sunk to the lowest depth of despair. The extravagance of my joy was such, that I know not any terms in our language adequate to its expression. Subsequent circumstances, presently to be noticed, threw me again into uneasiness and alarm.

After the Indians had disposed of me, they separated themselves into two parties. A small number of the Shawanese, the Mingo, the women, and the two captive children, set out for the Miami towns. Chickatommo, with the other Shawanese, commenced their route back to the Ohio River. Their departure seemed to ensure my safety, and therefore my mind was perfectly quieted. But there was a white man among the Wyandots at Upper Sandusky, who had been carried into captivity by those Indians when very young, and had been reared and naturalized with their tribe. He spoke the English language sufficiently to enable me to understand him; and we entered into conversation; in the course of which he intimated, that my emancipation was not yet reduced to certainty; and that he suspected it was the intention of Chickatommo and his party, to regain possession of my person. This suggestion, from a man who knew the savages well; their characteristic treachery; and the fact, that they had already once reclaimed me after having consigned me to the Mingo, induced an apprehension, that what I had heard was not to be disregarded. This apprehension was greatly strengthened, when on the succeeding day, the Shawanese chief with his followers, actually presented themselves again at Upper Sandusky.

Once more terror and despondency seized on me. I reflected on

[30] Johnston had been in captivity about five weeks and had traveled nearly two hundred miles.

the events which had passed; the miseries which I had endured; and the dreadful fate which was inevitable, should I now, for the third time, fall into the hands of my captors. I deliberately and solemnly resolved, to resist their whole force by exertion of all my powers, and to perish on the spot before they should ever again become my masters. I provided myself with a tomahawk, and calmly sat down on a log, fixed in my purpose should they approach, but chopping the log with the air of indifference. They made no attempt upon me, and retired to an encampment which they formed on the river near the town, yet out of our view. Mr. Duchouquet concurred with me in the opinion, that all the circumstances of their conduct were such, as to excite strong suspicion that they meditated my recapture. They had disappeared on the preceding day, after receiving the price for which I had been sold; had declared a design of returning to the Ohio; had suddenly returned, without any apparent reason or business; had encamped at a place different from that which they had before occupied, more remote from view, and better suited for a plan of surprise from it on us by night. We determined to prepare for the attack, and remain, with the utmost vigilance, on our guard. Mr. Duchouquet, and a labourer then in his service, continued to watch with me throughout the night. We locked and barred our door. We were in possession of an axe, several guns, and tomahawks. But there was no necessity for their use. The Indians permitted us to remain undisturbed; and on the next day quitted their camp. Their whole party, with their packs on their backs, came out of their course through the town; shook hands with Mr. Duchouquet and myself, declaring an intention to visit the British post at Detroit, and departed. I could not yet banish from my mind all disquiet, and continued under some apprehenhion that they might lurk in the neighbourhood, for a favourable opportunity to return and bear me off. But after several days of anxiety, we were informed by a party of strolling Indians from Lower Sandusky, that they had met Chickatommo and his followers, at a considerable distance from our village, pursuing their journey steadily towards Detroit. My fears and dangers were now at an end: my spirits became bouyant, and I indulged none but the most joyous feelings.

My mind became immediately occupied with the subject of my return to Virginia; which was embarrassed with some difficulties. I was alone, utterly ignorant of the country, and could reach home by one of two routes only. The first lay through the dreary wilderness which I had recently traversed; and the travellers who should attempt to pass, were subjected to all the perils from which I had been so lately delivered. The distance to the nearest settlement was great, and I was not possessed of the means of providing myself subsistence on the journey, which I should have been compelled to make to Pittsburg. The other was extremely circuitous, though less liable to danger. I could travel in perfect security under the protection of a trader: but there was no prospect of obtaining that advantage in a very short time, as the season of the year had not arrived, when the traders were in the habit of repairing to Detroit, with the peltry purchased in the course of the winter and spring, at the Indian villages. It was Mr. Duchouquet's intention, to convey his purchases to that place in person, in the course of about five weeks; and I had no choice but to remain at Upper Sandusky until that time; then to proceed with him to Detroit, and thence down the lakes into the state of New York, from which, the road to my native State would be perfectly easy and safe. The interval, between my liberation from captivity and the commencement of my homeward journey, was employed in assisting Mr. Duchouquet to sell his merchandise to the Indians, in attending to his books and accounts, and in occasional excursions; which I generally limited to the immediate vicinity of our village, because there was some hazard in venturing to a distance. On one occasion, however, I exceeded these limits, and walked two or three miles, for the purpose of visiting the spot where Col. Crawford had been tortured and burnt to death some years before, by the Delawares.[31] The sapling to which it was said he had been bound, when he suffered

[31] Col. William Crawford, leader of an expedition against the Indians of central Ohio in May, 1782, was captured and carried to Upper Sandusky. The details of his unspeakable death by torture, presided over by the Delaware war chief Captain Pipe, are fully recorded in the Knight and Slover captivity, *Narratives of a Late Expedition Against the Indians; with an Account of the Barbarous Execution of Col. Crawford; and the Wonderful Escape of Dr. Knight and John Slover from Captivity in 1782* (Philadelphia, 1783).

the most awful fate to which man can be subjected, was still alive, and was pointed out to me by my conductor—the white captive who was naturalized among the Wyandots.

A trivial incident exposed me yet again to the resentment and vengeance of one of those savage beings, whom it was hoped I had entirely escaped. The traders, and other white persons, at the Indian towns, were in the habit of wearing shirts made of calico. Mr. Duchouquet had furnished me with one of this description, which I had washed and hung out on a bush to dry. It had not remained there long, when I discovered a cow, belonging to an Indian of our village, in the act of eating it. She had devoured one sleeve, and was committing depredations on the other parts of it; when I contrived to get near her with a tomahawk in my hand, with which I gave her a blow on the forehead that felled her to the ground, apparently lifeless. Her owner, unobserved by me, was in view. He ran up to me with an infuriated, threatening face, and, at the moment when he appeared ready to execute his vengeance upon me for his fancied loss, the cow jumped up and ran away; thereby relieving me from the unpleasant necessity I should have been under of using the tomahawk in my own defence, had he made an attack on me.

About this time a Shawanese Indian arrived at Upper Sandusky, and brought the heart-chilling intelligence, that my late fellow-prisoner, William Flinn, had been burnt at the stake, and devoured by the savages, at one of the Miami towns. This monster declared, that he had been present when the miserable man was sacrificed; had partaken of the horrid banquet; and that his flesh was sweeter than any bear's meat!—a food of all others in highest repute with the Indians.

The small band of Cherokees, three in number, to whom Peggy Fleming had been allotted, in the distribution made of the prisoners on the Ohio, brought her to Upper Sandusky while I was there. She was no longer that cheerful, lively creature, such as when separated from us. Her spirits were sunk, her gayety had fled: and instead of that vivacity and sprightliness which formerly danced upon her countenance, she now wore the undissembled aspect of melancholy and wretchedness. I endeavoured to ascertain the cause of this extraordinary change, but she answered my inquiries only with her tears; leaving my mind to its own inferences. Her stay with us was only for a few hours, during which time, I could not extract a word from her, except occasionally the monosyllables *yes* and *no*. Gloom and despondency had taken entire possession of her breast; and nothing could be more touching than her appearance. Her emaciated frame, and dejected countenance, presented a picture of sorrow and of sadness, which would have melted the stoutest heart; and such was its effect upon me, that I could not abstain from mingling my tears with hers. With these feelings we parted. When we met again, it was under far different and more auspicious circumstances, as will hereafter be seen.

CHAPTER IX.

EARLY in June, Mr. Duchouquet, in conformity to his annual usage, set out for Detroit. All the traders, then occupied in the peltry business, were in the habit of repairing yearly, about the middle of autumn, with such articles of merchandise as were adapted to the Indian markets, to their towns, dispersed over the wide extended regions of the north-west. They carried with them ammunition, blankets, calico for shirts, coarse cloths for leggings, trinkets, vermillion, tomahawks, scalping-knives, and whatever else their experience informed them was suited to the taste, or to the necessities of their tawny customers. They received in exchange, the furs and skins collected by the Indians during their winter expeditions into the woods. But as these were not brought in until the spring, the traders sold the goods which the Indians wanted for winter use, on a credit until the spring; when they returned home, and paid for their fall purchases, as well as for the few light articles necessary to them through the summer. They were in general, punctual to their engagements; but there were some among them, who, like many of our white people, were apt to forget, or to disregard their promises. The collections of the traders at the Indian towns, were generally completed by the first of June, when all their furs and skins were conveyed to Detroit; whence they were sent down the lakes, and the St. Lawrence, to Montreal and Quebec. The quantities of peltry produced by this traffic, were immense and of very great value. They continue so at present; and the only change worthy of notice, which has since occurred, results from the great water communication, lately effected by New-York, between the lakes and the Hudson river,[32] which will probably transfer all the trade of which I have spoken, from the markets of Canada to those of New-York. The Canadians will, however, retain that share, which is afforded by the country to the north of the river St. Lawrence, and out of the range of that canal navigation.

Mr. Duchouquet was occupied in this trade. He sold his goods, and collected his peltry at Upper Sandusky. The season had arrived for transporting his purcheses to Detroit; and, with a light heart, I began the journey to that post, in his party. The Sandusky river is not navigable from the upper town; and Mr. Duchouquet's peltry was carried on packhorses to Lower Sandusky; whence there is a good navigation to Detroit. When we reached Lower Sandusky, a great degree of consternation prevailed there, produced by the incidents of the preceding day, and of the morning then recently passed. The three Cherokees, who had possession of Peggy Fleming, had conducted her to a place where they encamped, within a quarter of a mile's distance from the town. It was immediately rumoured that they were there, with a white female captive. The traders residing in the town, instantly determined to visit the camp of the Cherokees, and to see her. Among them was a man, whose name was Whitaker, and who, like the one that I had met with at Upper Sandusky, had been carried into captivity from the white settlements, by the Wyandots, in his early life. He was not so entirely the savage as the first; could speak our language better; and, though naturalized by his captors, retained some predilection for the whites. The influence which he had acquired with his tribe, was such that they had promoted him to the rank of a chief; and his standing with them was high. His business had led him frequently, before this period, to Pittsburg, where the father of Peggy Fleming then kept a tavern, in which Whitaker had been accustomed to lodge and board. As soon as he appeared with the other traders at the camp of the Cherokees, he was recognised by the daughter of his old landlord, and she addressed him by his name, earnestly supplicating his efforts to emancipate her from the grasp of her savage proprietors. Without hesitation, he

[32] Erie Canal.

acceded to her request. He did not make an application to the Cherokees, but returned to the town and informed the principal chief, distinguished by the appellation of King Crane,[33] that the white female captive was his sister: a misrepresentation greatly palliated by the benevolent motive which dictated it.

He had no difficulty in obtaining from the King a promise to procure her release. Crane went immediately to the camp of the Cherokees; informed them that their prisoner was a sister of a friend of his, and desired, as a favour, that they would make a present to him of Peggy Fleming, whom he wished to restore to her brother. They rejected his request. He then proposed to purchase her; this they also refused with bitterness, telling him "that he was no better than the white people, and that he was as mean as the *dirt*;" terms of the grossest reproach in their use of them. At this insult, Crane became exasperated. He went back to the town; told Whitaker what had been his reception, and declared his intention to take Peggy Fleming from the Cherokees by force. But fearing such an act might be productive of war between his nation and theirs, he urged Whitaker to raise the necessary sum in value for her redemption. Whitaker, with the assistance of the other traders at the town, immediately made up the requisite amount in silver broaches. This was not accomplished, until it was too late to effect their object on that evening. Early next morning, King Crane, attended by eight or ten young warriors, marched out to the camp of the Cherokees, where he found them asleep, while their forlorn captive was securely fastened, in a state of utter nakedness, to a stake, and her body painted black: an indication always decisive, that death is the doom of the prisoner. Crane, with his scalping knife, cut the cords by which she was bound; delivered her the clothes of which she had been divested by the rude hands of the unfeeling Cherokees; and, after she was dressed, awaked them. He told them, in peremptory language, that the captive was his, and that he had brought with him the value of her ransom. Then throwing down the silver broaches on the ground, he bore off the

33 One of the best-known of the Wyandot chiefs. His kindness to the whites is recorded in various accounts of the period. After the Treaty of Greenville in 1795, which ended Indian resistance in the Old Northwest, Crane removed to Upper Sandusky, where he died in 1818.

terrified girl to his town, and delivered her to Whitaker; who, after a few days, sent her, disguised by her dress and by paint as a squaw, to Pittsburg, under the care of two trusty Wyandots. I never learnt whether she reached her home or not; but as the Indians are remarkable for their fidelity to their undertakings, I presume she was faithfully conducted to her place of destination.

The Cherokees were so incensed by the loss of their captive, that they entered the Wyandot town of Lower Sandusky, declaring they would be revenged by taking the life of some white person. This was the cause of the alarm, which was spread among the traders at the time of our arrival, and in which our party necessarily participated; as it was indispensable that we should remain there several days, for the purpose of unpacking Mr. Duchouquet's peltry from the horses, and placing it on board the batteaux, in which it was to be conveyed to Detroit. The Cherokees painted themselves, as they and other savages are accustomed to do, when they are preparing for war or battle. All their ingenuity is directed to the object of rendering their aspect as horrible as possible, that they may strike their enemies with terror, and indicate by external signs the fury which ranges within. They walked about the town in great anger, and we deemed it necessary to keep a watchful eye upon them, and to guard against their approach. All the whites, except Whitaker, who was considered as one of the Wyandots, assembled at night in the same house, provided with weapons of defence, and continued together until the next morning; when, to our high gratification, they disappeared, and I never heard of them afterwards.

CHAPTER X.

At this place we found Mr. Angus McIntosh, who was extensively engaged in the fur trade. This gentleman was at the head of the connexion to which Mr. Duchouquet belonged, who was his factor or partner at Upper Sandusky, as a Mr. Isaac Williams was here. Williams was a stout, bony, muscular, and fearless man. On one of those days which I spent in waiting until we were ready to embark for Detroit, a Wyandot Indian, in his own language, which I did not understand, uttered some expression offensive to Williams. This produced great irritation on both sides, and a bitter quarrel ensued. Williams took down, from a shelf of the store in which the incident occurred, two scalping-knives; laid them on the counter; gave the Wyandot choice of them; and challenged him to combat with these weapons. But the character of Williams for strength and courage was so well known to his adversary, that he would not venture on the contest, and soon afterwards retired.

Lower Sandusky was to me distinguished by another circumstance. It was the residence of the Indian widow, whose former husband I had been destined to succeed, if the Mingo had been permitted to retain and dispose of me according to his intentions. I felt an irresistible curiosity to have a view of this female, and it was my determination to find her dwelling, and see her there, if no other opportunity should occur. She was at last pointed out to me as she walked about the village, and I could not help chuckling at my escape from the fate which had been intended for me. She was old, ugly, and disgusting.

After the expiration of four or five days from that on which we reached Lower Sandusky, our preparations were completed; the boats were laden with the peltry of the traders; and the whole trading-party embarked for Detroit. On the afternoon of the second day, having descended the river into Sandusky Bay, we landed on a small island, near the strait by which it enters into Lake Erie.[34] Here we pitched a tent which belonged to our party. The island was inhabited by a small body of Indians, and we were soon informed, that they were preparing for a festival and dance. If I then understood the motive or occasion which induced this dance, it is not now within my recollection. Several canoes were employed in bringing guests from the main, which is at a short distance, sep-

34 "Nothing can more strikingly illustrate the rapid march of population and improvement than the changed condition of things on this Lake and its borders. In little more than twenty years from the period of which I am speaking, the hostile fleets of civilized nations encountered each other on its bosom; and the name of Perry, and the glories of the 10th of September, 1813, will not soon be forgotten by Americans. Lower Sandusky, too, then a rude assemblage of huts, the dwellings of men equally rude, is rendered memorable by the defeat of a numerous British and Indian force, by a handful of Americans, commanded by the young and gallant Major, now Colonel Croghan" [Johnston]. Johnston here refers to events of the War of 1812: Commodore Oliver Hazard Perry's victory in the battle for control of Lake Erie ("We have met the enemy and they are ours"); and Major George Croghan's successful defense of the outnumbered garrison at Fort Stephenson earlier the same year.

arated from the island by a narrow arm of the bay. We were all invited to the dance by short sticks, painted red, which were delivered to us, and seemed to be intended as tickets of admission. A large circular piece of ground was made smooth, and surrounded by something like a pallisade, within which the entertainment was held. We had expected that it would commence early in the evening; but the delay was so long, that we laid down to sleep in the tent, which stood near the spot of ground prepared for the dance.

About eleven o'clock, we were awaked by the noise of the Indian mirth. One hundred, perhaps, of both sexes, and assembled. Their music was produced by an instrument much resembling the tambourine. Both men and women were dressed in calico shirts. Those of the women were adorned with a profusion of silver broaches, stuck in the sleeves and bosoms; they wore, besides, what is called a match-coat, formed by cloth, confined around the middle of their bodies by a string, with the edges lapping over toward the side, and the length of the garment extending a little below the knees. They wore leggings and mockasins. Their cheeks were painted red, but no other part of their face. Their long, black hair was parted in front, drawn together behind, and formed into a club. The liberal use of bear's oil gave it a high gloss. Such are the ornaments and dress of an Indian belle, by which she endeavours to attract the notice of admiring beaux. The men had a covering around their waists, to which their leggings were suspended by a string, extending from their top to the cord which held on the covering of the waist; and a blanket, or robe, thrown over the shoulders, and confined by a belt around the body, of various colours, and adorned with beads. The women were arranged together, and led the dance, the men following after them, and all describing a circle. The character of this dance differed essentially from that of the war-dance, which I had witnessed on a former occasion. The one was accompanied by horrid yells and shrieks, and extravagant gestures, expressive of fury and ferocity, with nothing like a mirthful cheerfulness. The other, which I saw in this last instance, was mere festivity and lively mirth. The women were excluded in the first, but had an active share in the last; and both sexes were highly animated by the music of the tambourine. An abundant supper had been provided, consisting altogether of the fresh meat of bears and deer, without bread or salt, and dressed in no other manner than by boiling. It was served up in a number of wooden trenchers, placed on the ground, and the guests seated themselves around it. We were invited to partake, but neither the food nor the cookery were much to our taste; yet we were unwilling to refuse their hospitality, and joined in their repast. We were not gainers by it; for when we were faring, not very sumptuously, on their boiled fresh meat, without bread or salt, they entered our tent, and stole from our basket, which contained provision enough for our voyage, a very fine ham, on which we had intended to regale ourselves the next day.

In the morning, we recommenced our progress to Detroit. In our open batteaux we could not venture along the direct course, across a bay of Lake Erie, which would have taken us to a hazardous distance from the land. We therefore hugged the shore, and landed whenever we required refreshment. To this we were in a great degree induced by the multitude of turtles' eggs with which the beach abounded, and which we easily procured in plenty. They were deposited in cavities a short distance below the surface, and their position was discovered by penetrating the sand with a stick. The sand is generally firm; but in those places where the turtles have formed their nests, there is only a thin crust above them, which yields to a slight touch of a stick, and, by the facility with which it is penetrated, shows where the eggs lie. We fried them in bear's oil, and found them very delicious food.

Two or three days after leaving the island where we feasted with the Indians, we gained the entrance of Detroit river, and ascended it to the post of Detroit, on its western bank, then occupied by a British garrison.[35] There I was informed that my friend and brother in misfortune, Mr. Jacob Skyles, had spent several days in concealment from a band of Indians, who had pursued him to that place, after he had escaped from his captivity by a most remarkable series of adventures. I had not obtained the slightest intelligence with respect to him since our separation, and was in

35 British forts on the American side of the boundary line after the close of the Revolution included Detroit, Schlosser, Michilimackinac, Erie, Niagara, and Oswego. Britain had refused to withdraw her forces from them until the Americans paid certain claims owed to British merchants before the war; the forts were vacated under the terms of Jay's Treaty in 1795.

the highest degree gratified to learn that he was safe, and on his way into the United States. It would, however, have been an additional pleasure to me, could we have returned into Virginia together, in a state of feeling so different from that which we had experienced when in the power of those captors, from whom we had every thing to fear and nothing to hope. Several years afterwards we met at the Sweet Springs, when he detailed to me the singular history of his flight from the Miami town, where the Indians had made every arrangement for subjecting him to torture and death. These details I shall relate, after stating the particulars of Flinn's sufferings and end, more minutely than heretofore, as they were communicated to me by a trader whom I saw at Detroit, and who was an eyewitness of the scene. The tale is horrible, and must shock every feeling of humanity. But my narrative would be imperfect without it; and although similar acts of barbarism and unrelenting cruelty have been related by others, this will, perhaps, interest the hearts of those who may read it, and will exhibit the savage character in a strong light.

It has been already stated, that the Indians cautiously conceal from a prisoner their intention, when they have determined that he shall be brought to the stake. The miserable Flinn had no intimation of his fate, and was perhaps indulging the fond hope, that he was yet to recover his liberty, and to be restored to civilized society. He had been conducted to one of those Miami towns which were, at that period, fatal to white captives; was not rigorously confined, though closely watched; and was suddenly seized by several Indians, at a place about a quarter of a mile from the village, where every preparation was immediately made for his sacrifice. Incisions were made through the muscular parts of his arm, between the elbows and shoulders, and, by thongs of buffalo hide passed through them, he was secured to a strong stake. A fire was kindled around him. A group had collected, among whom he discerned a white man. Flinn asked, if he was so destitute of humanity, as to look on and see a fellow-creature suffering in this manner, without an effort for his relief? This man instantly went into the adjacent village, informed the traders there of the plight Flinn was in, and of the necessity for interposition in his favour without loss of time. They made up the customary value of a prisoner in silver broaches, which they delivered to the white man; and he hastened back, not doubting that the ransom which he carried would be accepted: but it was peremptorily rejected. He then returned to the village, and applied again to the traders for their assistance, after reporting to them the failure of the proffered ransom. From their knowledge of the Indian habits and temper, they determined, as a last experiment, to send a keg of rum, in addition to the silver broaches; under a persuasion, that their extravagant love of that spirit would effect more than any other offer. But when the rum was presented by the white man, they split the head of the keg which contained it with their tomahawks, and the liquor flowed unheeded on the ground. Flinn's agent, who had in vain made every exertion in his power to save him, then told him that his case was desperate, and advised him to prepare for death. He exclaimed, "Then all I have to say is, may the Lord have mercy on my soul!"—and never again, while he retained his senses, uttered a word or a groan. All the ingenuity of the savages was exerted in aggravating his torments, by all those means which they know so well how to employ. His firmness remained unshaken; and he acted the same part which their own warriors perform on such awful trials.[36] Nothing could break his heroic resolution. At length the fire around him began to subside. An old squaw advanced to rekindle it. When she came within his reach, he kicked her so violently, that she fell apparently lifeless. His tormentors were then exasperated to the highest point, and made incisions between the sinews and bones at the back of his ankles, passed thongs through them, and closely fastened his legs to the stake, in order to prevent any repetition of their exertion. The old squaw, who by this time had recovered, was particularly active in wreaking her vengeance for the blow he had inflicted upon her. She lighted pine torches, and applied their blaze to him; while the men bored his flesh with burning splinters of the same inflammable wood. His agonies were protracted until he sunk into a state of insensibility, when they were terminated by the tomahawk.

[36] This is one of the few accounts, albeit secondhand, since Johnston himself was not an eyewitness, of a white victim able to maintain the same composure under torture that the Indians were themselves capable of. See Jogues, n. 15.

CHAPTER XI.

Mr. Skyles, after leaving the party to which I belonged, was led by the Indians, in whose possession he was, to one of the towns on the Miami of the Lake, in the neighbourhood where the wretched Flinn was tortured and put to death. Upon his arrival, he was compelled to run the gauntlet. A single fact will convey some idea of the spirit which directs the conduct of the savages on occasions of this sort. One of the lads belonging to the ranks through which Mr. Skyles passed, provided himself with the branch of a tree, from which the smaller limbs were all cut, except one. This he suffered to remain, near the large end of the weapon, about an inch and an half or two inches long, and sharpened it well at the point, giving it the form of a cock's spur. As the prisoner ran by the young savage, he drove the keen point of this instrument into his back with such force, that it remained firmly fixed in the flesh; was wrested from the hands of the boy; and was carried by Mr. Skyles, hanging down his back, to the end of his painful career. The same keeper, to whose custody he was first committed, had charge of his person, and never relaxed his vigilance, until the last night of Mr. Skyles's continuance with the Indians.

In the mean time, he had experienced much kindness from the wife of his surly sentinel, whose temper was altogether unlike that of her husband, and had been acted on in his favour by a variety of little attentions and services, which, from motives of policy, he rendered her every day; such as kindling her fire, and bringing her wood and water. At length she informed him, that his destiny was decided, and that he was, on the following day, to be tied to a stake and burnt to death. As the Indians are extremely addicted to falsehood, he at first doubted the truth of this appalling intelligence. But on that night it was completely confirmed. When the hour of rest arrived, it was the regular habit of his keeper to lie down in the same cabin with him, attended by four or five other men, whose business it was to assist in watching and guarding him. His mind was so alarmed and agitated by what the squaw had communicated, that he could not compose himself to sleep, but remained awake until a late hour. The old squaw, who had imparted to him the awful tidings of his intended fate, and a young girl, with the guard who were asleep, formed the party in his lodgings. He feigned sleep so well as to deceive the women, who sat up by the fire, and entered into a conversation, of which he was the subject. He had acquired so much of their language, as to enable him to understand many of their expressions. The elder squaw lamented the event which was next day to befall the white prisoner, and spoke in terms of compassion for the sufferings which he was to endure; while the girl exulted in the prospect of his torments, which in her own opinion every white man justly deserved. Mr. Skyles, after hearing what passed between the women, waited in impatient vigilance until they were overpowered by sleep, and every one else was quietly at rest. He then carefully rose from the fire, near which he had lain, took up a small bag of parched corn which he had before observed in the cabin, with one of the rifles and ammunition belonging to the men, and cautiously creeping to the door, gained the open ground. He made all possible haste to the Miami of the Lake, which flowed not far from the town, and swam across it; but perceiving he would be impeded by the gun, he determined to abandon the possession of it, and left it on the bank of the river.

Soon after passing the stream, he heard a bell, which he supposed was worn by a horse; and anxious to travel with speed, he directed his course to the spot from whence the sound came. He was not mistaken in his supposition. He took the bell from the horse's neck, converted its leathern collar into a substitute for a bridle, by cutting it up into strings with a knife which he had brought from his lodge, and mounted on his back. The night was extremely dark, and the growth in the woods very thick. His progress on the horse was therefore tardy and unpleasant. After riding a few miles, he determined to quit him, and march forward on foot. His intention was, to steer a course which would lead him to the settlements of Kentucky. He left the river, but was so unskillful a woodsman, that he pursued a direction quite opposite to that which he wished to follow, and which led him to the north, instead of the south. His plan was, to lie concealed all day, lest he should be seen, pursued, and be again captured by the Indians; and to go forward in the darkness of the of the night, when he would be little exposed to the danger of discovery. But he was incessantly environed with perplexing difficulties and perils. Frequently while he was endeavouring to explore his way through thick woods and wilds, utterly dark, he came suddenly on the encampments of parties of Indians, whose dogs would give him alarm by flying at him and barking, with a noise which excited great apprehension, that their masters would discover and seize on him. Groping his course, from necessity, in the night, a more experienced woodsman might have blundered far from the right tract. Sometimes he found himself, when day appeared, on, or near, the ground which he had left the evening before. While beset with all these perplexities, his only means of subsistence, the little bag of parched corn, was exhausted; and a new danger, that of perishing by hunger, stared him in the face.

In this extremity, there was no alternative, but to die for want of food in the wilderness; or to march boldly onward in open day, and find something to support life. He did not hesitate in the choice, and adopted the hazardous resolution of entering the first village he could reach, and of applying to any trader, who might reside in it, for relief from starving, and assistance in gaining a point of safety. But he wisely decided, that such an attempt was not to be made, unless under cover of night. Pursuing, therefore, in the day, the course before him, without knowing whither it would lead, he had approached so near to one of the Miami towns before he discovered it, that he feared, should he then retire, he would be exposed to the view of some of the inhabitants, who in such an event would certainly again make him a prisoner. Concealment until dark was his only resource. He laid himself down behind a log, which screened him from the view of the people in the town, and quietly kept his position as long as there was any daylight. When darkness began, he repaired to some charred fragments of a fire, which had lately burnt out near his log. By reducing a small quantity to dust, and mixing it with water, he made a black colouring, which he spread over his face and hands. His disguise was so complete, that he was quite satisfied he would not be recognised as a white man; and he entered the village. The wigwams of the Indians, as I have before said, are composed of bark; the houses of traders, who reside among them, are built of logs. He knew the distinction, and availed himself of it. Proceeding with great caution, he came to a house of logs, looked through the chinks between them, and ascertained that it was occupied by a family of Indians. It had probably been erected by a trader, who, from some cause or other, had left it. In his farther progress through the town, he identified the house of a trader, entered it, and asked for rum. He was told by its occupant, that he had no rum, but would procure him some. When Mr. Skyles had waited this man's return for a short time, having observed the course in which he walked off, he went out to meet him. He then disclosed to the trader, who had not yet discovered he was a white man, that rum was not his object; that he was an unfortunate citizen of the United States, who some weeks before had been captured by a band of Indians on the Ohio river; had been conducted by a party of them to one of the Miami villages, where it was their intention to take his life, if he had not fortunately escaped their clutches; that he was then famishing with hunger; and that without some charitable aid he must soon perish, or become again the captive of enemies who would show him no mercy. The trader told him, that his own life would be hazarded by affording him shelter; that there had been a party of Indians on that day in his village, from the tribe which had held him a prisoner, in search of him; but that he would do for him what was in his power. He conducted Mr. Skyles into a thicket of hazel bushes near the village, where he left him, until he prepared some refreshment. He then informed him, that if he would embark in a canoe on the Miami of the Lake, flowing along the edge of the town where they were, he might, by paddling industriously, overtake a boat belonging to certain traders, who had gone down the river that day to Detroit, but would probably lie to during the night. Mr. Skyles eagerly embraced this plan of making good his retreat. The trader led him to the water side, where a canoe was lying, into which he stepped without delay, and determined to exert himself in descending the river, that he might fall in with the traders and obtain passage in their boat to Detroit.

Between dawn and sunrise next morning he approached the entrance of Lake Erie, and discovered the boat not far ahead of him. He soon brought his canoe along side of it, but all on board were asleep. He awakened them. He had before revolved in his mind the question, whether he should make himself known or not; and his first decision was in the negative. He was induced to this by an apprehension of treachery, and by that timid caution to which a man in his condition is liable. His principal fear was, that these traders, for the purpose of keeping on good terms with the Indians, might make a merit with them of placing him again in their power. They inquired who he was?—He answered, that he was an adventurer, who had been looking out for land such as he wished to acquire, on the river AuGlaize, but had been driven from the country by the fear of danger from the Indians, who had lately practised horrid cruelties on certain white men captured on the river Ohio. They told him, it was true that one man had been burnt at a town on the Miami, and another had evaded the same fate by escaping from them a few nights before; and that they had, at a town which they had left on the preceding day, seen a party in pursuit of the fugitive. After a little hesitation, he ventured to disclose the fact, that he was that fugitive; threw himself on their humanity; and entreated, that they would receive him into their boat and permit him to pass in it with them to Detroit. He was overjoyed, when they promptly acceded to his request, and conveyed him to the British post in safety. His pursuers followed him to that place, where he was under the necessity of remaining in concealment for several days, until their departure; when he went on his journey into the United States. I am happy to add, that he recommenced business, some years afterwards moved to Kentucky, and succeeded in acquiring considerable property. But he has now gone to his long home, and has left an estimable family in comfort and independence.[37]

CHAPTER XII.

I RETURN to the incidents which relate to myself. I staid nine or ten days at Detroit, for a conveyance down Lake Erie. During that time, I enjoyed the warmest kindness and hospitality from Mr.

37 "A singular incident, and for that reason only do I think it worthy of relation, has been communicated to me since Mr. Skyles's removal to Kentucky. He travelled by water down the Ohio River. As he passed the mouth of the Sciota, near which he knew we were taken, he recollected that when taken, he had concealed about two hundred dollars in gold, of which he was then possessed, under a log. He did not think he could identify the spot, at that distance of time. But he landed, and searched under every trunk of a tree which he saw lying on the ground near the place where he believed his money was deposited, until he had the good fortune to strike on the right one, and recovered his money" [Johnston].

McIntosh and his family. My first reception by his lady and brother displayed on their part a liberality of feeling towards me, which did not abate while I remained, and which will be remembered by me with the deepest gratitude as long as my life shall last. I was badly provided with clothing. Mr. McIntosh supplied me with such as was decent, comfortable, and adapted to the season of the year. I was destitute of cash for my expenses on the long journey homeward, which I was most anxious to commence. A subscription was circulated, I have reason to believe by Mr. McIntosh and his brother James, among the inhabitants of the town of Detroit, which furnished me with a sufficient sum of money for my purposes. The population of the town then consisted of about one thousand persons, according to my present recollection.[38]

A state of things existed at this period, in the country where I then was, which subjected any citizen of the United States, passing through it, to considerable embarrassment. Although nearly seven years had elapsed since the conclusion of the war of independence, which had been ended by the definitive treaty of peace, entered into between the government of Great Britain and the American Congress, in September 1783, one of its important stipulations was yet unexecuted. The correspondence between Mr. Jefferson, when Secretary of State, and Mr. Hammond, the British minister then resident in the United States, contained in General Washington's message to both houses of Congress on the 5th day of December 1793, exhibits the ground taken by these agents of their respective governments, on the subject of those infractions of the treaty of 1783 with which each government charged the other. The correspondence itself has been published; and those who desire accurate and extensive information on the topics which it involves,

[38] "Mr. Schoolcraft, whose journal was written in 1820, says, at page 51, 'Detroit occupies an eligible situation on the West bank of the Strait that connects Lake Erie with Lake St. Clair, at the distance of six miles below the latter, and in North latitude of 42° 30″ according to the received observation. The town consists of about two hundred and fifty houses, including public buildings, and has a population of fourteen hundred and fifteen inhabitants, exclusive of the garrison. It enjoys the advantages of a regular plan, spacious streets, and a handsome elevation of about forty feet above the river, of which it commands the finest views' " [Johnston]. Johnston here draws from Henry Rowe Schoolcraft (1793–1864), American geologist, ethnologist, and author of numerous volumes on the history and conditions of the Indian tribes of the United States. Schoolcraft had accompanied the Lewis Cass expedition to Lake Superior in 1820.

will find ample compensation in the gratification afforded by the display in it of distinguished talents, especially on the part of Mr. Jefferson. The North Western posts, of which Detroit was one, were detained by Great Britain, and her garrisons occupied them, until after the victory obtained by Gen. Wayne over the Indians in that country, and the negotiation of Mr. Jay in 1794.

Many of the Indian tribes had continued hostilities with the United States through the revolutionary war, and for a long period after its conclusion. The detention of the posts, by the British troops, gave them an extensive influence in the surrounding territory; and no man was permitted to pass by those posts, without the consent of the commanding officer, at each of them, regularly declared by a written passport. In my case, the form usually observed was dispensed with; and Major Patrick Murray, who was the Commandant at Detroit, politely furnished me with a permission to go down the Lakes, which I here transcribe. It was directed to "Officers commanding British garrisons," and expressed in the following words:

"The bearer, Mr. Johnston, of Virginia, had the misfortune last winter to fall into the hands of the Indians on the Ohio; but having been redeemed by some British traders of this post, is now on his way to his home, and is hereby recommended to the protection of all officers commanding British garrisons, through which he may pass.

(Signed)
PAT. MURRAY, Major 60th Reg't.
Commanding at Detroit."
(Dated, Detroit, 22nd June, 1790.)

My obligation to this officer did not stop here. Several vessels, suited to the navigation of the Lakes, were employed in the transportation of stores, provisions, and other necessaries, to the garrisons of the different posts, and were subject to the orders of their commandants. Major Murray invited me to take a passage in one of these vessels. She was a sloop, called the "Felicity," commanded by Capt. Cowan, and bound for Fort Erie, which was situated at the lower extremity of the Lake, where the river Niagara leaves it. I cheerfully accepted this advantageous invitation, and embarked in the sloop as soon as she was ready to sail.

We steered our course down the lake, but were compelled, after going on for one or two days, by adverse winds, to lie to under the lee of an island. Here Capt. Cowan and I amused ourselves in catching the fine fish of the Lake, which were very abundant around us. They afforded us excellent sport, and we succeeded in getting as many of them as we desired. Our bait consisted of a red rag and the rind of bacon, tied to our hooks with a string. We had nothing to do, but sit in the stern of the jolly-boat; and as it was rowed about by two sailors, our lines were thrown behind us, the bait floated on the surface, the fish rose eagerly at it, and we were incessantly occupied for several hours in drawing them on board.

After a voyage of five or six days, we arrived at Fort Erie, where I continued a very short time, as I found a boat ready to proceed down the Niagara to Fort Schlosser; in which I obtained a passage, by the civility of the British officer commanding at Fort Erie, and reached Fort Schlosser in the evning. It is situated about a mile above the celebrated cataract of Niagara,[39] on the American side of the river. I was politely received, and entertained for the night, at the post, by its British commandant, who, on the next morning, visited the falls with me. It would be vain presumption on my part, to attempt a minute description of this "most sublime of nature's works;" a distinction which Mr. Jefferson would not have conferred on the Natural Bridge across Cedar creek, in Virginia, if he had seen this stupendous cataract. Some conception may be formed of those emotions of wonder which the view excites, by recollecting, that here all the waters of the great Lakes, Superior, Michigan, Huron, and Erie, one of them fifteen hundred miles in circumference, and none less than five hundred, are collected into a space of three fourths of a mile, and rush over a precipice of rock one hundred and fifty feet high. Such was the effect produced on me by surveying this magnificent object, that when I

[39] "Schoolcraft, in his Journal, page 33, says, 'This is an Iroquois word to signify *the thunder of Waters*, and the word as still pronounced by the Senecas is *O-ni-aa-garah*'" [Johnston].

attempted to express the astonishment of my feelings to the officer who accompanied me, I could find no language to give it utterance, and remained absolutely dumb: and no wonder it had this effect. The tremendous roar of waters producing such a sound as had never before fallen on my ear, the spray formed into white clouds and rising up to heaven, the rainbow [40] with its beautiful tints, all form an assemblage of objects so sublime, as at once to defy and mock description.

From the Falls I traveled on foot to fort Niagara, at the point where the river of that name enters Lake Ontario, and where the British commandant was Col. John Rodolphus Harris. I was stopped at the gate of the fortification by a sentinel, who called the officer of the day. He conducted me to the Colonel; and when I came into his presence, he inquired sternly, "Who are you, Sir?" I answered by telling him my name, and that I was from Virginia. "From Virginia! and what brought you here, sir?" I then handed him Major Murray's passport. He read it, and threw it back to me rudely. "Go about your business," said he; "when you wish to leave this place, I will give you a passport." I then retired to a tavern, under a bitter sense of that mortification which was inflicted by the unfeeling rudeness of Col. Harris. But I experienced a gratification next morning, which perfectly relieved me from its unpleasant effects. Having returned from the landing, to which I had walked for the purpose of ascertaining whether any boat would shortly go from it to Oswego, I entered my lodgings, and amused myself with a book, when an officer knocked at my door. He entered, and announced himself as Captain Lethbridge, of the garrison at Niagara. He informed me that he had heard of my captivity by the Indians, and presumed I had been stripped of every thing and was destitute of money. He then offered me a purse, containing a number of guineas, and desired that I would take from it such a sum as would be sufficient to disburse my expenses to Virginia, and refund it when my convenience would permit. I told him, that by the liberality of the inhabitants of Detroit, I was supplied with money for my journey, and therefore declined his gentlemanly and obliging offer. We entered into conversation, and by the ame-

40 "There is always a rainbow at the falls when the sun shines" [Johnston].

nity of his manners and language, he evinced a solicitude to counteract the operation of those feelings produced by the gross incivility of his commandant; and begged me to disregard and to forget the conduct of a man, whose temper was naturally churlish, and his manners habitually morose. After this, Capt. Lethbridge frequently visited me at my lodgings; introduced me to other officers; and exerted himself to render my stay at Niagara as pleasant as polite attentions and kindness could make it. I shall ever cherish a high sense and grateful recollection of his deportment. It is due to the gentlemen, who belonged to the different British garrisons which I passed, that I should declare, Col. Harris was the single individual among them of whose conduct towards me I had the slightest reason to complain.

CHAPTER XIII.

WHILE I waited for a conveyance by water to Oswego, Mrs. Forsyth and her son, of Detroit, came to Niagara, on their way to visit their friends in the state of New-York. This lady, her son, and I, engaged an open boat at our joint expense, to convey us along the Lake Ontario to Oswego. Our voyage was protracted, by the necessity to which we were subjected, in such a boat as ours, of clinging to the shore. At night we landed, and slept in a tent with which she was provided, and in the accommodation of which she invited me to partake. I was somewhat surprised to be persecuted, as we were, in that northern climate, by the swarms of moschettoes which infested our tent, and obliged us to keep up fires during the night for protection from their annoyance. The only habitation of man which we saw on the margin of the lake, was a miserable hut, occupied by a fugitive from Massachusetts, who had been engaged in the insurrection not long before headed by Shays,[41] and had retired to the border of Ontario for concealment. We lodged one night under his shelter.

Five or six days after we left Fort Niagara, we came to Fort

41 In 1786–87, Daniel Shays, who had been a captain in the revolutionary army, led an uprising of western Massachusetts farmers against the foreclosure of mortgages on their property. The insurrection, Shays' Rebellion, was put down, three of the insurgents were killed, and the remainder dispersed. Many fled to neighboring states and even to the frontier.

Oswego, and immediately proceeded up the river which bears the same name, and connects, by one of its branches, the lakes Ontario and Oneida. Between these lakes there is a short portage around a fall, which renders the navigation at that point impracticable. Our boat was there hauled to the shore, placed on rollers, and launched into the water above the fall. But this was done with so little caution and good management, that we narrowly, and with great difficulty, escaped the danger of dashing over the fall and wrecking our boat. Mrs. Forsyth was so alarmed, that she threw herself into the water, which was waist deep, and waded to the shore.

We continued on the river into Lake Oneida, which is of inconsiderable extent; steered to its eastern end; and, having gained the entrance of Wood Creek, ascended that little stream as far as it was navigable. We crossed another portage of about one mile,[42] and entered the Mohawk river, at or near Fort Stanwix, which, I believe, stood on the site of the town now called Rome. I had left the boat at the mouth of Wood Creek, and walked up its bank to Fort Stanwix. Between these points, I met a party of Oneida Indians, as I travelled alone. Their sudden and unexpected view startled me, and for a moment brought to my mind the horrors, which I hoped I had left behind me, never again to be encountered. They engaged me in talk, and I soon discovered that they were of a friendly tribe. This was then the course of communication between Upper Canada and the state of New-York; was much frequented; and boats were conveyed over the portage, from the head of the navigation of Wood Creek to Fort Stanwix, on a wagon always kept in readiness for that service.

On the first evening after we commenced our descent of the Mohawk, anxious to enjoy the comforts of a bed, which it had not been my good fortune to obtain since we left Niagara, when our little party went on shore to spend the night, I walked to a decent looking farm-house, and inquired if I could obtain lodging in it. I received an abrupt refusal from the mistress, who said that an out-house, to which she pointed, was open to my admission. But its appearance was comfortless, and I rejoined Mrs. Forsyth and her

[42] The spot where Robert Eastburn was captured in 1756; see Eastburn, n. 1.

son in the tent. My exterior and dress probably decided the good woman to withhold her hospitality, and were perhaps sufficiently unimposing to exempt her from reproach.

In our farther progress down the stream, we passed through the rich and beautiful country called the German Flats, consisting of widespread, fruitful bottoms, on both sides of the Mohawk. The mention of this fine river brings to my recollection those exquisite lines written by Mr. Thomas Moore on its banks, and I cannot resist the inclination to insert them.

From rise of morn, till set of sun,
I've seen the mighty Mohawk run;
And as I mark'd the woods of pine
Along his mirror darkly shine,
Like tall and gloomy forms, that pass
Before the wizard's midnight glass;
And as I viewed the hurried pace
With which he ran his turbid race,
Rushing, alike untired and wild,
Through shades that frown'd and flow'rs that smil'd
Flying by ev'ry green recess,
That wooed him to its calm caress,
Yet sometimes turning with the wind,
As if to leave one look behind!
Oh! I have thought, and thinking sigh'd,
How like to thee, thou restless tide!
May be the lot, the life of him,
Who roams along thy water's brim!
Through what alternate shades of wo,
And flow'rs of joy, my path may go;
How many an humble still retreat
May rise to court my weary feet;
While still pursuing, still unblest,
I wander on, nor dare to rest;
But urgent as the doom, that calls
Thy water to its destined falls,
I see the world's bewild'ring force
Hurry my heart's devoted course
From lapse to lapse, till life be done,
And the last current cease to run.

Oh! may my fall be bright as thine!
May Heav'n's forgiving rainbow [43] shine
Upon the mist that circles me,
As soft as now it hangs o'er thee! [44]

We arrived at Schenectady about noon of the third or fourth day after leaving Fort Stanwix; and I travelled on foot that evening to Albany, where I remained a single night only, and embarked on the next day in a sloop, which was commanded by Capt. Tenyke, and sailed for New-York. When I reached that city, the first Congress of the United States, assembled under the authority of the present Federal Constitution, was in session there.[45] It was a very high gratification, after having laboured my way from the river Ohio to Detroit, down the lakes, and across the state of New-York, a distance considerably exceeding one thousand miles, without the view of a human face which I had ever seen before, to meet the delegation from my native state; with two of whom, Col. Isaac Coles and Col. Josiah Parker, I was personally acquainted. Besides the members of Congress, several other Virginians were in the city, with whom, under the influence of that warm feeling of attachment cherished by the sons of the "Ancient Dominion" towards each other, I spent several days of social enjoyment. Among them was Col. William Davies, a gentleman whom I had well known at Petersburg, the place of his residence. He was occupied, at the seat of the general government, in adjusting, as a commissioner on the part of Virginia, the account of his state with the United States. My stock of cash, for which I was indebted to he good people of Detroit, was nearly exhausted. But Col. Davies promptly volunteered such supplies, as enabled me to complete my journey to my birth-place.

Such adventures and scenes, as those which had lately occurred to me, were rarely presented to the attention of the people of the

[43] "A rainbow always hangs over the falls of the Mohawk, when the sun shines. They are known by the name of the Cahoes; and at them Mr. Moore's verses were written" [Johnston].

[44] The poem quoted here, with numerous corruptions of the original text, is "Lines at the Cohoes or Falls of the Mohawk River." Thomas Moore (1779–1852), an Irish poet of the romantic period, composed the poem during his visit to America in 1804.

[45] This was the second session of the first Congress under the new Constitution.

northern cities; and mine excited some interest, and much conversation, in New-York. They came to the ears of Gen. Washington, then President of the United States; and his private secretary, Mr. Thomas Nelson, of Virginia, visited me at my lodgings, with a message from the President, that he wished to see me. I was conducted by Mr. Nelson to his house, and introduced to him. He congratulated me, with cordiality, on my fortunate release from the Indians, and made many inquiries with respect to the strength of the tribes in the country through which I had travelled while a captive. After answering his questions on that subject, as well as my limited opportunity of acquiring information would permit, he interrogated me as to the force of the British garrisons at the various military posts which I had passed, and the state of their fortifications. On these last points I could render him no reply from which the slightest benefit could be derived: because my character of an American citizen would have made me liable to suspicion, and even peril, while at the British fortifications, had I examined into such subjects; and therefore I had deemed it indispensable to abstain from them. Besides, military affairs were out of the range of my experience and observation. His inquiries were of such a nature as led me to infer, that the government of the United States contemplated the chastisement of the Indians, for the many depredations they had lately committed on the Ohio; and to wrest from the possession of the British troops the military posts which were then occupied by them within our territory, in violation of the treaty of 1783. That I did not err in my first inference, the disastrous expedition of General St. Clair, which soon followed, afforded sufficient proof;[46] and I have little doubt that the last would have been substantiated, but for the amicable arrangement afterwards adjusted by Mr. Jay's treaty.[47]

Nothing detained me longer from home, but the length of the road; and I began my way to Virginia, in the stage coaches plying on the mail route to Richmond. There I borrowed a gig and horse from a friend, and visited a small estate belonging to me in the upper part of Hanover, where I found some valued acquaintances, and my eldest brother, who had made a trip to my plantation for

46 The ill-fated expedition against the Indians north of the Ohio (see headnote).
47 Ratified by the Senate on June 24, 1795.

the purpose of looking into the state of my affairs during my absence. The unexpected meeting between us produced an effect on him, which, he has always declared, he never experienced before or since; he shed tears plentifully, but they were tears of joy. Thence I proceeded, on one of my own horses, to the neighbourhood of my mother's dwelling, in the county of Prince Edward, where no certain intelligence had been received with respect to me, and where the most distressful solicitude for my fate had prevailed. I feared that consequences to an aged and affectionate mother, which it was my duty carefully to avoid, might result from pressing into her presence without previous intimation. My arrangements were made in such a manner, that I rode to the house of a friend, Mr. Miller Woodson, in the evening, three miles distant. He kindly communicated to my mother, by letter, the prospect of my speedy arrival at home, and advised her to prepare for it the next day. My reception was distinguished by those evidences of strong emotion, which the occasion called forth. Tears of joy flowed from every eye. Even the sturdy slaves ran hastily from the field of labour, some of whom caught me in their arms and wept, whilst others fell upon their knees, and returned thanks to Heaven for my deliverance.

CHAPTER XIV.

THE anxiety of the neighbourhood, to hear the details of my capture, and of all my way-faring, brought them in great numbers, day after day, to my mother's house, and subjected me to narrations, which I was compelled so often to repeat, and which begat in me so many unpleasant recollections, that I almost dreaded the return of each succeeding day; my patience was severely tested, and I became quite fatigued with their inquiries, and my own answers.

I have always since regretted that when I left Mr. Duchouquet's abode, at Upper Sandusky, in my eagerness to set out for Detroit, where I should be perfectly secure from the mischiefs which had tormented me, and where I should be on my homeward route, I forgot the volume of the Debates of the Virginia Convention, in which my journal was written. If I had brought it with me, according to my intentions and wishes, my narrative would probably have been more minute, and my record would have supplied many things, for which I now draw, in vain, on my memory.

In the winter of the year 1802, I resided in the city of Richmond, where I then received a letter from Mr. Duchouquet, dated at Pittsburg, by which he informed me, that he was on his way to the city of Washington, in the character of interpreter to a band of Shawanese chiefs, who were going on business with the general Government; and that he feared his duties would not permit him to leave them, and pay me a visit, as he wished. He stated the time of his probable arrival at Washington, and requested me to meet him there. I most cheerfully acceded to this request. When we came together, I was utterly at a loss for adequate expression of that gratitude by which I felt myself bound to him. Our meeting was warmly cordial. Among the Indians composing this party, it gave me great pleasure to recognise Tom Lewis, who threw his blanket over me at the river Ohio, soon after my capture, and when I had been stripped of my upper clothing. He recollected me at the first glance, and shook my hand heartily. I made special inquiry for the excellent Messhawa, and learned that he was alive, and in good health. Tom Lewis was a young warrior when I was made a prisoner. At the time of which I am now speaking, he had acquired so much reputation and confidence with his tribe, that he had been promoted to the rank of a chief. Grateful for the former kindness of this man, I rendered him such attentions as were in my power, and on one occasion, invited him to come with Mr. Duchouquet, to a private dinner, which I had caused to be prepared for them, at the Hotel, in which I lodged. At the close of our repast, he was presented with a glass of syllabub.[48] He tasted it repeatedly; at length he inquired, what is this? Then answering his own question, he said "it is neither *meat* nor *drink*, it is *something*, yet it is *nothing!*"

Very soon after my return to Virginia, I had made a point of remitting to Mr. McIntosh at Detroit, through his friend Mr. Alexander McComb of New-York, the sum which Mr. Duchouquet had advanced when he relieved me from captivity, and this last

[48] A drink or, with gelatin added, a dessert, consisting of wine or liquor mixed with sweetened milk or cream.

named gentleman told me, that he had in many instances beside mine, rescued citizens of the United States from the hands of the Indians, by paying a ransom for them; but that he had not been fortunate enough to obtain repayment from all. I then advised him to apply to Congress for remuneration, in those cases where it had been withheld. I drew a petition to that body, which was presented by Mr. Giles, who advocated his application warmly and successfully, and Mr. Duchouquet drew from the public treasury the amount which he asked, on no other evidence than his own statements, and the fact of his having redeemed me from my captors. Mr. John Cotton Smith, of Connecticut, was then chairman of the committee of claims, and exerted himself in procuring justice to a man who had always practised benevolence towards those of our countrymen, whose misfortunes subjected them to the necessity of asking his aid. No objection was made to the passage of an act in his favour: a course dictated both by justice, and a humane policy, which without question, the community approves.

A correspondence was regularly continued between Mr. Duchouquet and myself, until within the last seven years, when no answers have been received to my letters, and my inference is, that he has either removed to some distant residence out of reach of communications, or is no longer in the land of the living.

CHAPTER XV.

AFTER the preceding narrative was written, I ascertained that my friend Mr. Duchouquet was yet alive, and that he resided at Piqua, on the head waters of the Miami of the Ohio. I lost no time in writing to him, and proposed that he should spend the present winter with me. I was highly gratified by his acceptance of my invitation, and by his arrival at my house early in November last. It is his intention to remain with me until the month of March next. He is now sixty-six years of age, and has spent upwards of forty of those years among the tribes of Indians, who until lately, occupied the country between the Ohio river, and Lake Erie. His earlier life was devoted to the pursuits of a trader with the Indians, and his success was, for a long time, equal to his expectations. But, it was his misfortune, immediately before the commencement of the last war with Great Britain, in the prosecution of his business, according to the plan which it was his custom to observe, that he gave credit to a considerable number of Indians for goods sold them, to a large amount, and for which they contracted to pay at the customary period. But before that period arrived, the British Government had engaged Tecumthe, and his brother the Prophet, in their interests. The influence of these characters among their red brethren was such, that they had no difficulty in rekindling a spirit of hostility against the Americans, which had never been entirely extinguished. The consequence was, that many of them followed Tecumthe: and participating in his disasters, never returned to their native towns.[49] Mr. Duchouquet sustained such serious losses by this event, that he relinquished the business of a trader, and has ever since been employed in the service of the United States, as an interpreter to the Indian agency established at Piqua, and now under the superintendence of Mr. John Johnston. My benefactor has ever sustained a fair character for integrity and veracity. He is not an enlightened scholar, but possesses a sounding understanding, and is capable of judicious observation. By him, I am enabled to add something to the history of the most remarkable individuals among my captors, and to report so much in relation to them, as may further gratify any curious inquirer.

Chickatommo was killed in a recounter with a detachment of General Wayne's army, near Fort Defiance, in the year 1795.

Messhawa was one of the followers of Tecumthe and the Prophet. He either fell in battle with the Americans, or went to the country west of the Mississippi; but it is believed he is dead.

Tom Lewis attached himself to the service of our Government, and fought on our side, at the battle of the Thames. He attained the rank of chief among the Shawanese on Stony Creek, where a part of their tribe established themselves at a town bearing his name, and remained for several years. He has not conducted himself correctly, and has lost the confidence of his people, as well as his chieftainship. He has removed with a band of his countrymen, beyond the Mississippi, and is yet alive.

49 The famous Shawnee chief and statesman Tecumseh (variously Tikamthi or Tecumthe) headed the Indian uprising in 1810 and was defeated by Gen. William Henry Harrison at the battle of Tippecanoe. His brother, Elkswatawa (Tenskwautawa), was a fanatic known as the Prophet. Tecumseh took the British side in the War of 1812 and was killed in the battle of the Thames.

Whitaker fought against the Americans, when General Wayne defeated the Indians at the Rapids of the Miami of the Lake, and has been dead many years.

King Crane acted the same part, at the same time. But in the war of 1813, he bore arms on our side, and fought for us at the battle of the Thames. He died eight or ten years ago.

IX

A True Narrative of the Sufferings of Mary Kinnan, who was Taken Prisoner by the Shawanee Nation of Indians on the Thirteenth Day of May, 1791, and Remained with them till the Sixteenth of August, 1794.

†††

Mary Kinnan was taken from her Virginia home by Shawnees on May 13, 1791, in the wake of increased Indian raids following the defeat of Gen. Josiah Harmar's expedition into the Ohio country in November, 1790 (see Manheim, n. 26). Encouraged by their victory over Harmar's forces and urged on by British representatives who promised every sort of military support short of direct intervention by the British regular army, the Indian nations of the Ohio-Great Lakes region launched a series of attacks early in 1791 against the settlements on the Ohio River. Other war parties then struck across the river into Pennsylvania, Kentucky, and Virginia. It was during one of these raids that Mary Kinnan was made captive. Sold by her Shawnee captors into a tribe of Delawares, Mrs. Kinnan remained a prisoner for over three years. She was rescued near Detroit in October, 1794, by her brother, Jacob Lewis, and was taken to New Jersey to live with relatives. Her brief but affecting narrative covers a long captivity in short space and is vague in many particulars of her experience. Historical detail or ethnological observation, however, is not the principal object of the memoir; rather, it is the development of the melo-

dramatic possibilities of the narrative, the workings of sensibility, and the opportunities for rhetorical refinement that occupy the narrator and to which most of her energies are directed. In this connection, and suggesting circumstances similar to those surrounding the 1760 edition of Elizabeth Hanson's account (see Hanson headnote), it is reported that, according to Mrs. Kinnan's grandniece, the Kinnan narrative was taken down and "improved" by Shepard Kollock, the printer of the first edition (Oscar M. Voorhees, "A New Jersey Woman's Captivity Among the Indians," New Jersey Historical Society Proceedings, *XIII [April, 1928], 152–65). In any case, the narrative proceeds with the expectation that the reader's heart will indeed be "melted with sorrow" on learning the heroine's misfortunes and sufferings, and the means of confirming that expectation are largely literary and stylistic. Mary Kinnan was in fact an Indian captive, and her narrative is in its outlines faithful to the record of her actual experience; yet, because of her treatment of that experience, it stands as a forerunner of later whole-cloth sentimental fiction and novels of sensibility that employ the context of Indian captivity solely as a fictive device for narrative management. In this more closely literary framework, then, lies the significance of the Kinnan narrative. The text reprinted here is that of the first edition (Elizabethtown, N.J., 1795).*

††

The Sufferings of Mary Kinnan, &c.

Whilst the tear of sensibility so often flows at the unreal tale of woe, which glows under the pen of the poet and the novelist, shall our hearts refuse to be melted with sorrow at the unaffected and unvarnished tale of a female, who has surmounted difficulties and dangers, which on a review appear romantic, even to herself.[1]

[1] The reader need only contrast these opening lines with the first paragraph of Mary Rowlandson's plain and direct narrative to glimpse the alteration of both conception and execution in a century of apprehending and reporting the captivity experience. Nothing about the circumstances of Indian captivity struck Mrs. Rowlandson in any way "romantic," nor did she think it necessary to press

Her history will not, perhaps, be without its use. It will display the supporting arm of a Divine Providence: it will point to the best and surest support under danger and adversity: and "it will teach the repiner at little evils to be juster to his God and to himself."

It would be unnecessary and tedious to describe the first part of my life, as it exhibited nothing which is not daily observed in the common walks of mankind. Suffice it to say, that, blest with the affections of the best of husbands, and the love and esteem of the most dutiful of children, my days passed sweetly on, and I had scarcely one single wish ungratified.[2] Happiness smiled on our cottage;—content spread her influence around;—the voice of grief was not heard;—and old age crept imperceptibly on. Alas! how soon was my horizon obscured by the dark clouds of misfortune! —how doubly poignant were rendered succeeding miseries by the recollection of such exalted happiness! [3]

The thirteenth day of May, 1791, will never be effaced from my mind. Although since that memorable period, four years have almost rolled their ample round, still at the recollection, my bosom heaves impetuous; the cold sweat of fear stands on my brow; and

---

the veracity of her account with a disclaimer emphasizing the "unaffected and unvarnished" nature of her story. The two narratives, indeed, serve by contrast to illustrate the accretion of melodrama and stylization in the narratives of Indian captivity and the consequent diminution of the sense of genuine human experience. For the matter of stylization in the narratives collectively, see Roy Harvey Pearce, "The Significances of the Captivity Narrative," *American Literature*, XIX (March, 1947), 1–20, and a development of that subject in my "A Surfeit of Style: The Indian Captivity Narrative as Penny Dreadful," *Research Studies,* XXXIX (December, 1971), 297–306.

[2] The Kinnan family had come in 1787 from Basking Ridge, New Jersey, and settled on the west side of the Tygart's Valley River in Randolph County, Virginia. Mary Lewis Kinnan was born on August 22, 1763. She was married at the age of fifteen to Joseph Kinnan and bore him three children: Lewis, Joseph Jr., and a daughter Mary. The Kinnans had taken into their home the widow of a neighbor, Mrs. George Ward, and her three children. Two other young men were members of the household as well: Jacob Lewis, Mrs. Kinnan's brother, and a young man named Canley. In all, eleven persons were in the Kinnan home when the Shawnees attacked.

[3] The device of first presenting scenes of tranquility and comfort in order to heighten the effect of the violence and suffering to follow is common to stylized and melodramatic narratives of this period and later ones. Cf., for example, *Life Among the Indians, or: The Captivity of the Oatman Girls Among the Apache and Mohave Indians* (1857) and Fanny Kelly's *Narrative of My Captivity Among the Sioux Indians* (1871).

the burning tear of anguish glistens in my eye. Our house was situated in a beautifully romantic and agreeable place, called Tiger's[4] Valley, in Randolph County, State of Virginia. Here I would mark nature progressing, and the revolutions of the seasons; and from these would turn to contemplate the buds of virtue and of genius, sprouting in the bosoms of my children. Employed in such a pleasing occupation, on that evening, I was startled by the bursting open of the door: I turned my affrighted eyes, and leapt with terror at the sight of three armed Indians. I saw the flash of the musket!—I heard the groan of my husband! Quick as thought, I seized my youngest child: fear added wings to my flight, and I ran with the swiftness of the wind. Alas! scarcely had I time to congratulate myself on my good fortune, before I was again caught; desperation gave me strength, and I again broke loose. I scarcely touched the ground as I coursed over the plain, when the cry of my child, supplicating me for help, arrested my ear. The yearnings of maternal affection extinguished my prudence; forgetting my imbecility,[5] I flew to assist her, and was taken. A third time I attempted to escape, but was knocked to the ground with a tomahawk; I then made signs of submission, and was carried to the house. Gracious God! what a scene presented itself to me! My child, scalped and slaughtered, smiled even then; my husband, scalped and weltering in his blood, fixed on me his dying eye, which, though languid, still expressed an apprehension for my safety, and sorrow at his inability to assist me; and accompanied the look with a groan that went through my heart. Spare me the pain of describing my feelings at this scene, this mournful scene, which racked my agonizing heart, and precipitated me to the verge of madness.

In happier times, I should have thought that my heart would cease to beat, and my pulse forget to throb under such an accumulated weight of misery. But the soul often acquires vigor from misfortune, and by adversity is led to the exertion of faculties, which till then were not possessed, or at least lay dormant. Thus it was with me; I have supported *in reality* what, *in idea*, had appeared impossible.

4 Tygart's.
5 That is, weakness.

After plundering the house of the most valuable articles, and pinioning my arms behind me, they departed; with them I too was forced to go.[6] Under the most favorable circumstances, this journey would have been painful: how much more so was it now, when the arrow of calamity was rankling in my bosom; when I was faint through loss of blood; and without refreshment, without rest. Nature too seemed to conspire against me: the rain descended in torrents; the lightnings flashed dreadfully, and almost without intermission; whilst the thunder rolled awfully on high. We rested not during the whole of that night,

> "Wherein the cub-drawn bear would couch
> "The lion and the belly-pinched wolf
> "Keep their fur dry." [7]

It was on Friday night that I was taken; on Saturday night they rested, and trimmed their scalps.[8] Ah! what did I not feel at the sight of these memorials of savage cruelty. I became indifferent to my existence; I was willing to bid adieu to that world, whence all the lovely relatives of life were borne before me; and, had I not been restrained by the spirit of Christianity, I had terminated my existence by my own hand. I appeared, as it were, insulated to the civilized world—nay, worse than insulated, for the poor lonely mariner, who is shipwrecked on some desart coast, has far greater cause to rejoice than I then had.

The next day we continued our march over the most rugged rocks and mountains, wet and slippery with the rain which had so

[6] At this point, three of the household were dead: Mr. Kinnan had been shot, and Mary's daughter and Mrs. Ward's daughter had been tomahawked. Mrs. Ward escaped with her two remaining children through an opening in the wall of a back room; the two Kinnan boys escaped through the kitchen. Mary's brother, Jacob, and the youth Canley fled without offering resistance or lending help to the family. See Boyd B. Stutler, "The Kinnan Massacre," *West Virginia History*, XVIII (October, 1939), 107–28.

[7] The use of literary allusions (in this case to *King Lear*, Act III, scene 1, lines 12–14) is commonplace in the stylized narrative of Indian captivity. Cf. *A True and Wonderful Narrative of the Surprising Captivity and Remarkable Deliverance of Mrs. Frances Scott* (1786) and *A Genuine and Correct Account of the Captivity, Sufferings, and Deliverance of Mrs. Jemima Howe* (1792), as well as the Oatman and Kelly captivities (n. 3, above).

[8] For a fuller description and commentary on Shawnee scalping practices, see Johnston, n. 16.

lately fallen. Nature was now so far exhausted, that I could not advance, except in a very slow manner, when, instead of compassionating my sufferings, my weariness, and misfortunes, I was beaten severely for not performing impossibilities. About this time they frequently threatened me with death; though I recked not[9] his approach in genuine form, yet, I must confess, my soul shrunk from him, when thus cloathed in vengeance, too much for man to bear.

In this manner we continued our journey, sorrow and fatigue still making increased ravages on my constitution, when one of the Indians was bitten by a snake. We were obliged to stay nineteen days, before he was cured and able to proceed: during this period I again recovered spirits and health sufficient to follow my savage conductors. In this accident I beheld and blest the good providence of God, thus eminently exerted in rescuing me from that world, "from whose bourn no traveller returns."[10]

In a few days after this we arrived at the Ohio.[11] Dark and rainy was the night in which we formed a raft, and crossed the river: dangerous as was the passage, we arrived in safety at the opposite bank;—the period of my misfortunes had not yet arrived; many bitter calamities were yet to be felt.[12]

After this we travelled for two days through the gloomy ridges of pine. Although their extreme wetness subjected us to many inconveniencies, not to say dangers, yet the Indians were fearful of being discovered, if they made a fire, and, of consequence, remained without one. From these we passed into a fine country, where we had plenty of venison, and other game; nevertheless so deeply was I afflicted that I cared not for the food, which was absolutely necessary to preserve life, and I was compelled by their threats of death, in its most horrid form, to eat those victuals for which I had no relish.

On the 29th of June we approached the Shawanee towns; when we arrived within about half a mile of them they fired their guns,

9 That is, took no heed of; was not concerned with.

10 *Hamlet*, Act III, scene 1, lines 79–80.

11 The route to the Ohio River was probably down the beaten warrior's path along the Little Kanawha River.

12 Breaking from the usual narrative sequence by the use of foreshadowing to pique the reader's attention is yet another dramatic device of these narratives.

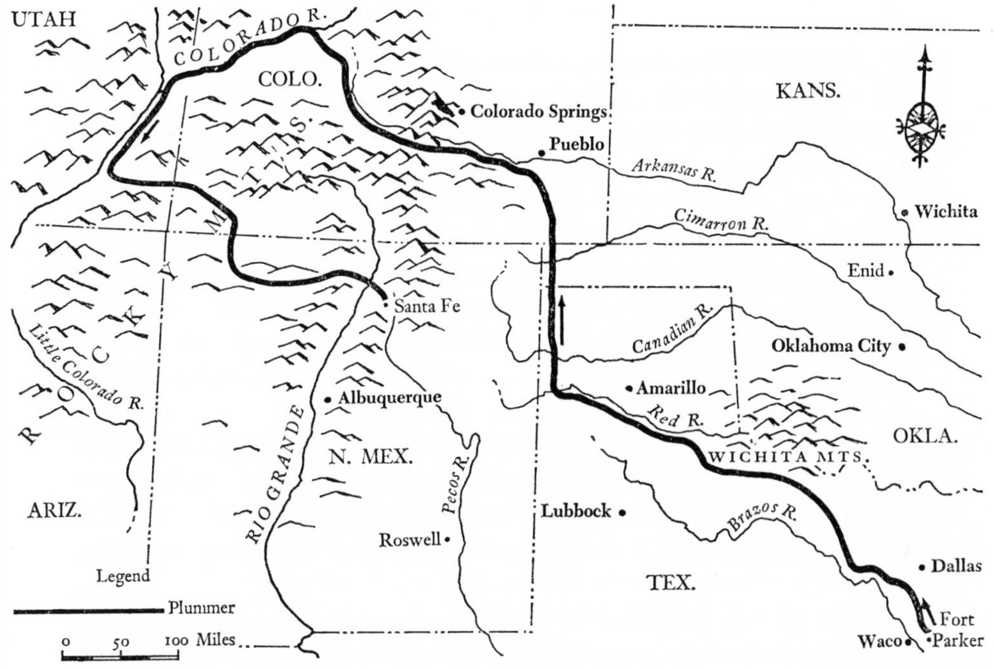

The long route suffered by Rachel Plummer.

stripped the bark from five trees, painted themselves and me in a most horrid manner, and commenced the scalp-whoop: [13] never did I hear a sound so calculated to inspire terror: my blood curdled within me at the sound, and fear took possession of all my faculties. This they repeated five times: they then seated themselves, until a vast number of people, attracted by the well-known and pleasing sound, came from the town and shook hands with them: each persen then struck me with great violence over the head and face, till I could not see, and till I finally dropt down senseless. They then recovered me and assisted me to walk into the town; having previously explained to me, that all the abuse which had been so liberally bestowed upon me, was to welcome me amongst them.[14]

13 The repetition of the scalp-whoop five times coincided with the stripping of bark from five trees also mentioned; the former announced to the village the number killed in the foray from which the band was returning, and the latter served as a war-record accounting at or near the camp. Of the five scalps, three were from the Kinnan settlement and two others from some Virginia home not identified.

14 A variation of the gauntlet ritual, or introduction to the village. See Jogues, n. 13.

During my journey, the sense of present danger blunted the remembrance of past misery, and prevented me from indulging in gloomy anticipations of future woe;—but now the whole weight of my affliction pressed heavily on my heart. The picture of my life was deeply, too deeply dashed with shade, and but a few faint strokes of light were intermingled with the numerous touches of the *sombre* pencil. But when my spirits were surcharged with sorrow's dew, I breathed out a fervent prayer to heaven, and relied on the beneficence of the Father of All. Uniformly my efforts were successful, and a calm resignation diffused itself through my frame, or the rays of hope danced sweetly round my heart.

I lived during four days with the sister of the savage who tore me from my peaceful home, and often contemplated with a sigh the depth of degradation, of which the human character is capable. On the third of July I was bought by a Delaware squaw,[15] and by her was put to the most menial and laborious offices.

One of the principal objects of my attention, whilst I lived amongst the Indians, was the humiliating condition of their women. Here the female sex, instead of polishing and improving the rough manners of the men, are equally ferocious, cruel, and obdurate. Instead of that benevolent disposition and warm sensibility to the sufferings of others, which marks their characters in more civilized climes, they quaff with extatic pleasure the blood of the innocent prisoner, writhing with agony under the inhuman torments inflicted upon him—whilst his convulsive groans speak music to their souls.

With my new mistress I continued until the defeat of St. Clair;[16] then another scene was presented to me, which opened afresh the sluices of sorrow. The numerous scalps of my unfortunate countrymen, which were then exhibited to my view—the rejoicings which took place on that lamentable occasion—and the brutal scenes which were then transacted, sorely wounded my bosom, already pierced so deeply by misfortune's shaft.—Still my sufferings were not alleviated; fed in a very scanty manner, I was

[15] Uprooted Shawnee and Delaware parties had banded together during this period of westward incursions by white settlers and army expeditions. See Johnston, n. 13.

[16] The disastrous rout of Gen. Arthur St. Clair's expeditionary force by Miamis and Wyandots on Nov. 4, 1791. See Manheim anthology, n. 26.

forced, nevertheless, to chop and carry wood to a considerable distance: in this occupation I had my feet frozen, and this added one more to my already long list of woes.

In the spring, for fear of my countrymen, the Indians removed from the Miami towns to Grand Glaize,[17] a most beautiful place. Here my sufferings became still more aggravated, although they had before appeared at their highest possible height. A new piece of ground was now to be cleared, and my heart grew more heavy in proportion as I was separated from my beloved country.

About this time there were prospects of peace. Hope, at all times easily enkindled, blazed forth at this prospect, and gilded my solitary footsteps: but the year passed away, and the devastations of war still continued. At this time an Indian trader engaged to convey a letter from me to my friends in New-Jersey, which he did by my direction, and this was the first news they had heard of me since my captivity, and, in the end, was the means of procuring my escape.[18]

The succeeding year commissioners came from the United States to conclude a treaty;[19] they departed, however, without attaining their object. The Indians, finding peace was not to be expected, turned out very generally for war, and left me, a prey to all the gloomy horrors of despair. In a short time they returned, bringing with them some horses and two prisoners; one of whom, Peter Tuttle, was afterwards redeemed—the other was killed by one of their chiefs.

17 Au Glaize, a group of towns clustered about the confluence of the Auglaize and Maumee rivers in what is now Defiance County, Ohio. At the time it was often called Grand Glaize, The Glaize, or simply, Glaize.

18 Mrs. Kinnan gave a hasty draft of the letter to the trader, one Robert Albert (Abbott), who took it to Detroit where it was copied by William Hindman on July 29, 1793. The messenger carrying it to Basking Ridge died of yellow fever in Philadelphia, and all of his personal effects were buried as a precautionary measure. It was only after the plague had abated that the letter was dug up and sent on its way again. It is now preserved in the records of the old Pension Bureau at Washington, D. C. See Oscar M. Voorhees, "The Pension Secured for 'Aunt Polly' Kinnan," *Somerset County Historical Quarterly*, V (April, 1916), 106–108.

19 The peace deputation sent by President Washington in May, 1793, consisting of Benjamin Lincoln, a former general in the Continental army; Timothy Pickering, who had been postmaster general and was to become secretary of war in 1794; and Beverly Randolph, a former governor of Virginia. The Indian nations resolved not to make peace on any other terms than the Ohio River boundary established by the Treaty of Fort Stanwix in 1768, and the negotiations collapsed.

In November the Indians began to be weary of war, and, in the beginning of January, sent in a talk to General Wayne by a Robert Wilson, an Indian trader, together with three Indians. General Wayne insisted, as a preliminary article, that all the prisoners should be delivered up: accordingly they came home, and collected a great number of us, unfortunate sufferers, and prepared to set out the next day to General Wayne at Fort Jefferson. But previously to our departure, one of the British agents came to them, and persuaded them, that perfidy was a leading trait in the character of the people of the United States; that they had placed ambuscades for them; and that they would never return alive. By these and other arts, they persuaded the Indians to persevere in their warfare,[20] and we were again dismissed to our laborious occupations.

O Britain! how heavy will be the weight of thy crimes at the last great day! Instigated by thee, the Indian murderer plunges his knife into the bosom of innocence, of piety, and of virtue; and drags thousands into a captivity, worse than death. The cries of widows, and the groans of orphans daily ascend, like a thick cloud, before the judgment-seat of heaven, and

"Plead like angels, trumpet-tongued,
"For your damnation:
"And pity, like a naked, new-born babe,
"Striding the blast, or heav'n's cherubin, hors'd
"Upon the sightless couriers of the air,
"Shall blow your horrid deeds in every eye,
"That tears shall drown the wind." [21]

I had by this time witnessed so many disappointments, that I yielded myself up entirely to despondency, and endeavored to

[20] Gen. Anthony Wayne had been appointed to command the United States Army and directed to compel the western Indian confederacy to acknowledge the sovereignty of the United States. The work of such British agents as mentioned here by Mrs. Kinnan was to counsel Indian resistance. The best-known and most troublesome of these agents was Alexander McKee, who had married a Shawnee woman and whose son was an important Shawnee chief.

[21] *Macbeth,* Act I, scene 7, lines 19–25. Mrs. Kinnan's application and alteration of the lines wrench the meaning to her own purpose. Macbeth here refers to Duncan, whose virtues "Will plead like angels, trumpet-tongued, against / The deep damnation of his taking off; / And pity, like a naked new-born babe, / Striding the blast, or heav'n's cherubim, hors'd / Upon the sightless couriers of the air, / Shall blow the horrid deed in every eye, / That tears shall drown the wind."

stifle the few scattered rays of hope, which faintly twinkled, like the glimmerings of a lamp just ready to expire.—In consequence of these impressions, I fell dangerously ill of a fever, which was accompanied by an excessive pain over my whole frame. The Indians now abated, in some degree, of the rough treatment which I had before experienced: but what contributed principally to my recovery was a letter, which I received from my brother, Jacob Lewis, mentioning that he was at Detroit, but that he dared not at present come to assist me because of the antipathy which the Indians evidenced against him, on account of his being a native of the United States.[22] To know that I was not immured beyond the knowledge of my friends and relatives; that they still entertained for me a warm, impassioned affection, was a delicious cordial to my drooping spirits. In return to this letter I wrote, that as it would be in the highest degree dangerous to come to the place where I then was, I advised him still to continue at Detroit, and if it were possible by any means to ameliorate my condition, I made no doubt he would exert himself to the utmost of his power. For six months, we enjoyed the pleasure of each other's correspondence, being but one hundred and forty miles distant, and enjoying a constant communication by means of the Indian traders. In the darkest and most gloomy seasons, his letters inspired me with comfort; and whilst I traced in them with joy the sentiment of friendship, and the warmth of fraternal affection, I would for a time forget my griefs in the extacy of delight.

On the first day of August, 1793,[23] we heard of the approach of General Wayne's army.[24] Fearful and perturbed, they immediately started for the Rapids of the Miami; taking only those things with which they could not dispense, and hiding or burying the rest. On the tenth I had resolved to make my escape; my plan was

[22] Jacob Lewis reached Detroit on Feb. 3, 1794, having been more than three months on the way. Detroit, and in fact all of the eastern portion of the present State of Michigan, were in the hands of the British.

[23] 1794.

[24] Wayne's approach was preparatory to the final and decisive encounter of the western wars. Later in the same month, Wayne's forces defeated the Indian nations at the Battle of Fallen Timbers near Fort Miami. With this defeat, the British withdrew their support of the Indians; attacks on the frontier ceased in the south as well as in the north. Indian hostility was never again to prove a significant factor in the continued advancement of the American frontier.

thoroughly matured, and I waited with impatience the approach of night to put it in execution. But how frail and uncertain are the schemes of mankind! how easily are even their best projects overturned! Going out on that day to get a tent-pole, I accidentally cut my foot in a most dangerous manner; this being at the distance of eighteen miles from the Rapids, and being unable to walk, I was obliged to be carried thither on a horse.

Soon after I arrived I heard from my brother, who had joined a party of British traders, and was coming down to the Rapids that he might see, and perhaps assist me to escape. He sent a Frenchman to me, who behaving in a manner which displeased the Indians, I requested him not to come again. He returned, and in a short time my brother came himself. As he was passing through the Indian camp I accidentally saw him: my joy was so great that I involuntarily gave a scream of pleasure:—the Indian who was with me, surprized at this singular behaviour, viewed me with an inquisitive eye; I fully comprehended the meaning of his look, and excused myself in a manner which, I believe, dissipated his apprehensions.

In order to concert some means of escape, my brother sent a friend to exchange bread for milk. After performing this errand he opened to me his real business, and appointed a tree where I might meet my brother that night. According to these directions I went, and how great was my surprize and disappointment to find nobody there. But the person who had previously appointed the tree as a place to meet, explained to me the next day the reason why we missed of each other, we having gone to different trees. The next night, however, the Indians having fallen asleep, I stole out about eleven o'clock. I found the brother of my heart anxiously expecting my arrival: after those congratulations which might be expected from two so dear to each other, who had been so long separated, we started and ran two miles to the British camp. I then, with a beating, fearful heart, crept into a brush-heap, where I lay during all that night, and on the next day my brother came and carried me from the place where I was lodged on board a vessel, which was about to descend the Miami river, the captain of which he had interested in my behalf—having previously drest me in one of his own suits of clothes and tied an handkerchief over my eyes, in order, as much as possible, to conceal my features. When we came to the mouth of the river, we anchored in full view of the Indians, who had come to the Lake, as well to avoid General Wayne, as to receive their provision, which was given them at this place. In this situation I remained some time, fearful of being recognized and re-claimed by some of the Indians: but finally, I prevailed with the master of a batteau, who was going to Turtle Island in Lake Erie, to carry me thither with him. When we arrived there we went on board a ship which was then lying at anchor there, bearing twelve guns, and were strictly examined by a Commodore Grant, who, when informed of my sufferings, used his interest to have me taken on board a brig going to Detroit. Having arrived at this last-mentioned place, I was so overcome by the joy which I felt at my delivery and the fatigue which attended it, that I continued unwell and unable to proceed for eight days. At the expiration of this period, I crossed Lake Erie and came to Niagara, where I was again examined, and having produced the pass given us by Commodore Grant, obtained another from Simcoe to the United States.[25] We descended in a batteau to the Genesee river, and thence travelled to New Jersey, where I arrived amongst my friends on the eleventh day of October, 1794.

If my history has been marked with woe-worn incidents—if I have been in a peculiar manner the child of misfortune;—if my cup of life has been deeply mixed with gall;—if despair has brooded over my soul, with all its horrors;—and finally, if I have been obliged to dismiss even dear delusive hope, having so often felt "what kind of sickness of the heart that was, which proceeds from hope deferred:" [26]—yet, by these very woes, I have been led to place my dependence on the beneficient dispenser of good and evil, and to withdraw my affections from that world, where the ties by which mankind are in general so firmly bound are indissolubly broken. Since the consequences of my affliction have been so beneficial, I repine not at it; ye, who are pierced by the darts of mis-

[25] John Graves Simcoe was the British commander at Niagara. The examinations and passes Mrs. Kinnan describes were necessary because the British still occupied their line of forts well after the Revolution. See Johnston, n. 35.

[26] A paraphrase of Prov. 13:12.

fortune, imitate my example, and like me recline on the bosom of your Father and your God.[27]

[27] Mary Kinnan never returned to her former home in Virginia, not even to visit the graves of her husband and daughter. She was thirty-one years of age when she was brought back to New Jersey, and she remained there for over fifty years. She died on Mar. 12, 1848.

X

Narrative of the Capture and Subsequent Sufferings of Mrs. Rachel Plummer, Written by Herself.

†††

Rachel Plummer was captured by Comanches on May 19, 1836, in the attack on Parker's Fort in Texas during Indian incursions following the Battle of San Jacinto. Even before the remnants of Santa Anna's defeated army had recrossed the Río Bravo, *the Mexican congress had decided to continue the war against Texas. With rumors of the return of the Mexican army to Texas, Indian movements of a hostile nature increased. A band of over seven hundred Comanches, Wichitas, and Kiowas attacked Parker's Fort, commanded by the Reverend James W. Parker, located at the headwaters of the Novasota (Navisott) River. At the fort when the Indians attacked were Parker's wife and four of their children, his father, Elder John Parker, his two brothers Benjamin and Silas, his daughter Rachel and her baby, and members of several other families. Parker himself had gone to work in a cornfield nearby with his oldest son and two sons-in-law, one of whom was L. T. M. Plummer, Rachel's husband. In the attack at the fort five were killed, one badly wounded, and five taken prisoner; twenty-three escaped. Those taken were Rachel and her eighteen-month-old baby James, her cousins Cynthia Ann and John Parker, aged eight and six, and her aunt, Mrs. Elizabeth Kellogg. When the Indians split their party and divided the prisoners, Mrs. Kellogg was taken by a band of Wichitas, Cynthia Ann and John were carried off by Quahada Comanches, while Rachel and her child remained with the original group of Comanches. Comanche Indians, members of the*

Shoshonean language family, had in the eighteenth century made a series of permanent migrations, separating from their fellow Shoshones in Wyoming and traveling south. Aggression from the northeast and the lure of trade and loot drew the Comanches to the Spanish frontier, where they became one of the earliest tribes to acquire horses. There they succeeded in adopting the war patterns of the Plains tribes. The Comanches in the nineteenth century roamed the entire Southern Plains as hunters following the buffalo and as warriors raiding through the Pueblo country deep into Mexico. But the real Comanche territory extended from the Wichita Mountains across the plains and streams to the Red River in Texas. The narrative of Rachel Plummer's captivity among them contains excellent detail on Southern Plains Indians' life and on the animals of the area, as well as on Comanche life and customs. The first edition of the Plummer narrative appeared in January, 1839, under the title Narrative of the Capture and Subsequent Sufferings of Mrs. Rachel Plummer, During a Captivity of Twenty-One Months Among the Cumanche Indians, *but the story of her captivity achieved its widest circulation from the reprinting of it in her father's* Narrative of the Perilous Adventures, Miraculous Escapes and Sufferings of Rev. James W. Parker . . . to which is appended a Narrative of the Capture and Subsequent Sufferings of Mrs. Rachel Plummer, His Daughter *(Louisville, 1844). This version follows the text of the "revised and corrected" second edition of December, 1839, and is reprinted here with additional corrections from an errata sheet in the 1844 edition. Correction of other errors made by the printer but not listed on the errata sheet have also been made in the interest of clarity.*

Narrative

On the 19th of May, 1836, I was living in Fort Parker, on the head waters of the river Favasott. My father, (James W. Parker,) and my husband and brother-in-law were cultivating my father's farm, which was about a mile from the fort.[1] In the morning, say 9

[1] The fort itself was located two-and-one-half miles northeast of what is now Grosbeak in Limestone County. James Parker and his brother Silas had built Parker's Fort in 1835.

o'clock, my father, husband, brother-in-law, and brother, went to the farm to work. I do not think they had left the fort more than an hour before some one of the fort cried out, "Indians!" The inmates of the fort had retired to their farms in the neighborhood, and there were only six men in it, viz: my grandfather, Elder John Parker, my two uncles, Benjamin and Silas Parker, Samuel Frost and his son Robert, and Frost's son-in-law, G. E. Dwight. All appeared in a state of confusion, for the Indians (numbering something not far from eight hundred) had raised a white flag.

On the first sight of the Indians, my sister (Mrs. Nixon,) started to alarm my father and his company at the farm, whilst the Indians were yet more than a quarter of a mile from the fort, and I saw her no more. I was in the act of starting to the farm, but I knew I was not able to take my little son, (James Pratt Plummer.) The women were all soon gone from the fort, whither I did not know; but I expected towards the farm. My old grandfather and grandmother, and several others, started through the farm, which was immediately adjoining the fort. Mr. G. E. Dwight started with his family and Mrs. Frost and her little children. As he started, uncle Silas said, "Good Lord, Dwight, you are not going to run?" He said, "No, I am only going to try to hide the women and children in the woods." Uncle said, "Stand and fight like a man, and if we have to die we will sell our lives as dearly as we can."

The Indians halted; and two Indians came up to the fort to inform the inmates that they were friendly, and had come for the purpose of making a treaty with the Americans. This instantly threw the people off their guard, and uncle Benjamin went to the Indians, who had now got within a few hundred yards of the fort. In a few minutes he returned, and told Frost and his son and uncle Silas that he believed the Indians intended to fight, and told them to put every thing in the best order for defence. He said he would go back to the Indians and see if the fight could be avoided. Uncle Silas told him not to go, but to try to defend the place as well as they could; but he started off again to the Indians, and appeared to pay but little attention to what Silas said. Uncle Silas said, "I know they will kill Benjamin;" and said to me, "Do you stand here and watch the Indians' motions until I run into my house"—I think he said for his shot-pouch. I suppose he had got a wrong shot-pouch, as he had four or five rifles. When uncle Benjamin reached the body of Indians they turned to the right and left and surrounded him. I was now satisfied they intended killing him. I took up my little James Pratt, and thought I would try to make my escape. As I ran across the fort, I met Silas returning to the place where he left me. He asked me if they had killed Benjamin. I told him, "No; but they have surrounded him." He said, "I know they will kill him, but I will be good for one of them at least." These were the last words I heard him utter.

I ran out of the fort, and passing the corner I saw the Indians drive their spears into Benjamin. The work of death had already commenced. I shall not attempt to describe their terrific yells, their united voices that seemed to reach the very skies, whilst they were dealing death to the inmates of the fort. It can scarcely be comprehended in the wide field of imagination. I know it is utterly impossible for me to give every particular in detail, for I was much alarmed.

I tried to make my escape, but alas, alas, it was too late, as a party of the Indians had got ahead of me. Oh! how vain were my feeble efforts to try to run to save myself and little James Pratt. A large sulky looking Indian picked up a hoe and knocked me down. I well recollect of their taking my child out of my arms, but whether they hit me any more I do not know, for I swooned away. The first I recollect, they were dragging me along by the hair. I made several unsuccessful attempts to raise my feet before I could do it. As they took me past the fort, I heard an awful screaming near the place where they had first seized me.[2] I heard some shots. I then heard uncle Silas shout a triumphant huzza! I did, for one moment, hope the men had gathered from the neighboring farms, and might release me.

I was soon dragged to the main body of the Indians, where they had killed uncle Benjamin. His face was much mutilated, and many arrows were sticking in his body. As the savages passed by, they thrust their spears through him. I was covered with blood, for my wound was bleeding freely. I looked for my child but could not

[2] "I think Silas was trying to release me, and in doing this he lost his life; but not until he had killed four Indians" [Plummer's note].

see him, and was convinced they had killed him, and every moment expected to share the same fate myself. At length I saw him. An Indian had him on his horse; he was calling, mother, oh, mother! He was just able to lisp the name of mother, being only about 18 months old. There were two Cumanche women with them, [their battles are always brought on by a woman,] one of whom came to me and struck me several times with a whip. I suppose it was to make me quit crying.

I now expected my father and husband, and all the rest of the men were killed. I soon saw a party of the Indians bringing my aunt Elizabeth Kellogg and uncle Silas' two oldest children, Cynthia Ann, and John; also some bloody scalps; among them I could distinguish that of my old grandfather by the grey hairs, but could not discriminate the balance.[3]

Most of the Indians were engaged in plundering the fort. They cut open our bed ticks and threw the feathers in the air, which was literally thick with them. They brought out a great number of my father's books and medicines. Some of the books were torn up, and most of the bottles of medicine were broken; though they took on some for several days.[4]

I had but few minutes to reflect, for they soon started back the same way they came up. As I was leaving, I looked back at the place where I was one hour before, happy and free, and now in the hands of a ruthless, savage enemy.

They killed a great many of our cattle as they went along. They soon convinced me that I had no time to reflect upon the past, for they commenced whipping and beating me with clubs, &c., so that my flesh was never well from bruises and wounds during my captivity. To undertake to narrate their barbarous treatment would only add to my present distress, for it is with feelings of the deepest mortification that I think of it, much less to speak or write

3 Scalps were used by Comanches in the Victory Dance and were also desirable as fringe decoration for shirts and shields.

4 "Among them was a bottle of pulverized arsenic, which the Indians mistook for a kind of white paint, with which they painted their faces and bodies all over, after dissolving it in their saliva. The bottle was brought to me to tell them what it was. I did not do it, though I knew it, for the bottle was labelled. Four of the Indians painted themselves with it as above described, and it did not fail to kill them" [Plummer].

of it; for while I record this painful part of my narrative, I can almost feel the same heart-rending pains of body and mind that I then endured, my very soul becomes sick at the dreadful thought.

About midnight they stopped. They now tied a plaited thong around my arms, and drew my hands behind me. They tied them so tight that the scars can be easily seen to this day. They then tied a similar thong around my ankles, and drew my feet and hands together. They now turned me on my face and I was unable to turn over, when they commenced beating me over the head with their bows, and it was with great difficulty I could keep from smothering in my blood; for the wound they gave me with the hoe, and many others, were bleeding freely.

I suppose it was to add to my misery that they brought my little James Pratt so near me that I could hear him cry. He would call for mother; and often was his voice weakened by the blows they would give him. I could hear the blows. I could hear his cries; but oh, alas, could offer him no relief. The rest of the prisoners were brought near me, but we were not allowed to speak one word together. My aunt called me once, and I answered her; but, indeed, I thought she would never call or I answer again, for they jumped with their feet upon us, which nearly took our lives. Often did the children cry, but were soon hushed by such blows that I had no idea they could survive. Then commenced screaming and dancing around the scalps; kicking and stamping the prisoners.

I now ask you, my christian reader, to pause. You who are living secure from danger—you who have read the sacred scriptures of truth—who have been raised in a land boasting of christian philanthropy—I say, I now ask you to form some idea of what my feelings were. Such dreadful, savage yelling! enough to terrify the bravest hearts. Bleeding and weltering in my blood; and far worse, to think of my little darling Pratt! Will this scene ever be effaced from my memory? Not until my spirit is called to leave this tenement of clay; and may God grant me a heart to pray for them, for "they know not what they do."

Next morning, they started in a northern direction. They tied me every night, as before stated, for five nights. During the first five days, I never ate one mouthful of food, and had but a very scanty allowance of water. Notwithstanding my sufferings, I could not but admire the country—being prairie and timber, and very rich. I saw many fine springs. It was some 70 or 80 miles from the fort to the Cross Timbers. This is a range of timber-land from the waters of Arkansas, bearing a southwest direction, crossing the False Ouachita, Red River, the heads of Sabine, Angelina, Natchitoches, Trinity, Brazos, Colorado, &c., going on south-west, quite to the Rio Grande. This range of timber is of an irregular width, say from 5 to 35 miles wide, and is a very diversified country; abounding with small prairies, skirted with timber of various kinds—oak, of every description, ash, elm, hickory, walnut and mulberry. There is more post oak on the uplands than any other kind; and a great deal of this range of timber land is very rough, bushy, abounds with briers, and some of it poor. West, or S. W. of the Brazos, it is very mountainous. As this range of timber reaches the waters of the Rio Grande, (Big River) it appears to widen out, and is directly adjoining the timber covering the table land between Austin and Santa Fe. This country, particularly south-west of the Brazos, is a well watered country, and part of it will be densely inhabited. The purest atmosphere I ever breathed was that of these regions.

After we reached the Grand Prairie, we turned more to the east; that is, the party I belonged to. Aunt Elizabeth fell to the Kitchawas,[5] and my nephew and niece to another portion of the Cumanches.[6]

I must again call my reader to bear with me in rehearsing the continued barbarous treatment of the Indians. My child kept crying, and almost continually calling for "Mother," though I was not allowed even to speak to it. At the time they took off my fetters, they brought my child to me, supposing that I gave suck. As soon as it saw me, it, trembling with weakness, hastened to my embraces.

5 Wichitas.

6 There was no political unit which could be termed the Comanche tribe. The tribe was no more than a congeries of bands held together by the bonds of a common tongue and culture. The population of the Comanche tribe was distributed among a number of autonomous bands, each loosely organized and each centering its activities in a vaguely defined territory within the Comanche country. The Comanche band, or local group, ranged in size from a single family camping alone, through the small camp of related individuals who formed a composite extended family, up to the large band of several hundred persons. See E. Adamson Hoebel, "The Political Organization and Law-Ways of the Comanche Indians," *Memoirs of the American Anthropological Association* LIV (1940), 5-149.

Oh, with what feelings of love and sorrow did I embrace the mutilated body of my darling little James Pratt. I now felt that my case was much bettered, as I thought they would let me have my child; but oh, mistaken, indeed, was I; for as soon as they found that I had weaned him, they, in spite of all my efforts, tore him from my embrace. He reached out his hands towards me, which were covered with blood, and cried, "Mother, Mother, oh, Mother!" I looked after him as he was borne from me, and I sobbed aloud. This was the last I ever heard of my little Pratt. Where he is, I know not.[7]

Progressing farther and farther from my home, we crossed Big Red River, the head of Arkansas, and then turned more to the north-west. We now lost sight of timber entirely.

For several hundred miles after we had left the Cross Timber country, and on the Red River, Arkansas, &c., there is a fine country. The timber is scarce and scrubby. Some streams as salt as brine; and others, fine water. The land, in part, is very rich, and game plenty.

We would travel for weeks and not see a riding switch. Buffalo dung is all the fuel. This is gathered into a round pile; and when set on fire, it does very well to cook by, and will keep fire for several days.

In July, and in part of August, we were on the Snow Mountains.[8] There it is perpetual snow; and I suffered more from cold than I ever suffered in my life before. It was very seldom I had any thing to put on my feet, but very little covering for my body. I had to mind the horses every night, and had a certain number of buffalo skins to dress every moon. This kept me employed all the time in day-light; and often would I have to take my buffalo skin with me, to finish it whilst I was minding the horses. My feet would

7 Mrs. Plummer did not live to learn the fate of her son. Broken in health and probably suffering from tuberculosis, she died February 19, 1839, a year after her release and only one month after the publication of her narrative. In December, 1842, her father learned that two boys had been ransomed from Indians and brought to Fort Gibson in eastern Oklahoma. Parker reached the fort in January, 1843, and discovered that the boys were his nephew John Parker, now aged fourteen, and Rachel's little James, now eight. Parker took them home with him, taught them English, and raised them.

8 The old name for the Rockies of that region. Mrs. Plummer's captors were traveling into what is now the state of Colorado.

be often frozen, even while I would be dressing skins, and I dared not complain; for my situation still grew more and more difficult.

In October, I gave birth to my second son.[9] As to the months, &c., it was guess work with me, for I had no means of keeping the time. It was an interesting and beautiful babe. I had, as you may suppose, but a very poor chance to comfort myself with any thing suitable to my situation, or that of my little infant. The Indians were not as hostile now as I had feared they would be. I was still fearful they would kill my child; and having now been with them some six months, I had learned their language. I would often expostulate with my mistress [10] to advise me what to do to save my child; but all in vain. My child was some six or seven weeks old when I suppose my master thought it too much trouble, as I was not able to go through as much labor as before. One cold morning, five or six large Indians came where I was suckling my infant. As soon as they came in I felt my heart sick; my fears agitated my whole frame to a complete state of convulsion; my body shook with fear indeed. Nor were my fears vain or ill-grounded. One of them caught hold of the child by the throat; and with his whole strength, and like an enraged lion actuated by its devouring nature, held on like the hungry vulture, until my child was to all appearance entirely dead. I exerted my whole feeble strength to relieve it; but the other Indians held me. They, by force, took it from me, and threw it up in the air, and let it fall on the frozen ground, until it was apparently dead.

They gave it back to me. The fountain of tears that had hitherto given vent to my grief, was now dried up. While I gazed upon the bruised cheeks of my darling infant, I discovered some symptoms of returning life. Oh, how vain was my hope that they would let me have it if I could revive it. I washed the blood from its face; and after some time, it began to breathe again; but a more heart-rending scene ensued. As soon as they found it had recovered a little, they again tore it from my embrace and knocked me down. They tied a platted rope round the child's neck, and threw its naked body

9 Mrs. Plummer was four months pregnant when she was captured.

10 "Having fallen into the hands of an old man that had only his wife and one daughter, who composed his family, I was compelled to reverence the both women as mistresses" [Plummer].

into the large ledges of prickly pears,[11] which were from eight to twelve feet high. They would then pull it down through the pears. This they repeated several times. One of them then got on a horse, and tying the rope to his saddle, rode round a circuit of a few hundred yards, until my little innocent was not only dead, but literally torn to pieces. I stood horror-struck. One of them then took it up by the leg, brought it to me, and threw it into my lap. But in praise to the Indians, I must say, that they gave me time to dig a hole in the earth and bury it. After having performed this last service to the lifeless remains of my dear babe, I sat me down and gazed with joy on the resting place of my now happy infant; and I could with old David, say, "You cannot come to me, but I must go to you;" and then, and even now, whilst I record the awful tragedy, I rejoice that it has passed from the sufferings and sorrows of this world. I shall hear its deathly cries no more; and fully and confidently believing and solely relying on the imputed righteousness of God in Christ Jesus, I feel that my happy babe is now with its kindred spirits in that eternal world of joys. Oh! will my dear Saviour, by his grace, keep me through life's short journey, and bring me to dwell with my happy children in the sweet realms of endless bliss, where I shall meet the whole family of Heaven—those whose names are recorded in the Lamb's Book of Life.

I would have been glad to have had the pleasure of laying my little James Pratt with this my happy infant. I do really believe I could have buried him without shedding a tear; for, indeed, they had ceased to flow in relief of my grief. My heaving bosom could do no more than breathe deep sighs. Parents, you little know what you can bear. Surely, surely, my poor heart must break.

We left this place, and as usual, were again on a prairie. We soon discovered a large lake of water. I was very thirsty; and although we travelled directly towards it, we could never get any nearer to it. It did not appear to be more than forty or fifty steps off, and always kept the same distance. This astonished me beyond measure. Is there any thing like magic in this, said I. I never saw a lake, pond, or river, plainer in my life. My thirst was excessive, and I was panting for a drop of water; but I could get no nearer to it.

[11] That is, branches of cacti.

I found it to be a kind of gas, as I supposed, and I leave the reader to put his own construction upon it. It is, by some, called water gas. It looks just like water, and appears even to show the waves. I have often seen large herds of Buffalo feeding in it. They appeared as if they were wading in the water; and their wakes looked as distinct as in real water.[12]

In those places, the prairies are as level as the surface of a lake, and can better be described by at once imagining yourself looking at a large lake. I have but a faint idea of the cause; but from the number of sea shells, (oysters', &c.,) I have no doubt that this great prairie was once a sea.

I was often on the salt plains. There the salt some little resembles dirty snow on a very cold day, being very light. The wind will blow it for miles. I have seen it in many places half leg deep; whilst other parts of the ground would be naked, owing to the strong winds drifting it.

I was at some of the salt lakes, which are very interesting to the view. Thousands of bushels of salt—yea, millions—resembling ice; a little on the muddy or milky order. It appears that there would not be consumption for this immense amount of salt in all the world; for it forms anew when it is removed, so that it is inexhaustible.

These prairies abound with such a number and variety of beasts, that pages could not describe them.

1st. The little prairie dog is as large as a grey squirrel. Some of them are as spotted as a leopard; but they are mostly of a dark color, and live in herds. They burrow in the ground. As a stranger approaches them, they set up a loud barking; but will soon sink down into their holes. They are very fat, and fine to eat.

2d. The prairie fox is a curious animal. It is as tall as a small dog—its body not larger than a grey squirrel, but three times as long. Their legs are remarkably small; being but little larger than a large straw. They can run very fast. Seldom fat.

3d. The rabbit rivals the snow in whiteness, and is as large as a small dog. They are very active, and are delicious to eat. They

12 "This was the mirage, common to large deserts and prairies. Those travellers in the East, who have passed over the deserts of Asia and Africa, make frequent mention of these phenomena" [Plummer].

can run very fast. I have thought they were the most beautiful animal I ever saw.

4th. The mountain sheep are smaller than the common sheep, and have long hair. They will feed on the brink of the steepest precipice, and are very active. They are very plenty about the mountains.

5th. Buffalo, the next largest animal known, except the elephant. Their number no one can tell. They are found in the prairies and seldom in the timber even when there is any. Their flesh is the most delicious of all the beef kind I have seen. I have often seen the ground covered with them as far as the eye could reach.

The Indians shoot them with their arrows from their horses. They kill them very fast, and will even shoot an arrow entirely through one of these large animals.[13]

6th, The Elk, the largest of the deer species, with very large horns, and often more than six feet long. There are but few of them found in the same country with the buffalo; but they range along the Missouri river and in parts of the Rocky Mountains. Their flesh is like venison.

7th. The Antelope. This is, I believe, the fleetest animal in the world. They go in large flocks or herds. They will see the stranger a great way off, will run towards him till they get within twenty or thirty steps, and then the whole herd (perhaps some thousands) will wheel at the same moment, and are soon two or three miles off. They will again approach you, but not quite so near as at first, and then wheel again. They generally make about three or four of these visits, still wheeling from you at a greater distance. They will then leave you. They are much like the goat, and are by some called the wild goat.

8th. There are a great variety of wolves on the prairies: the large grey wolf, the large black wolf, the prairie wolf, and, I believe, the proper jackall. There is a large white wolf which will

[13] In food-getting, Comanche culture was basically a buffalo culture. The great communal hunts of the buffalo occurred during the summer months when hides were in their prime after the seasonal moulting. Sporadic and uncontrolled hunting of buffalo occurred whenever they were available during other seasons. Buffalo had to be killed as fast as possible so they would not get overheated in long running, as their meat would then spoil before it could be cured. Each buffalo was butchered by the women of the man who had killed it, his identification being made by characteristic markings on the arrows.

weigh 300 pounds, has very long hair of silvery white, and is very ferocious. They will kill a buffalo, and will not go out of the way of man or beast.

9th. There are four kinds of bears in the mountains; the white, grisley, red, and black bears. The grisley bear is the largest and most powerful. They will weigh 1200 or 1400 pounds. They cannot climb, but live in the valleys about the mountains. They are very delicious food. The white bear is very ferocious, and will attack either man or beast. They are hard to conquer. The Indians are very fearful of them, and will not attack them; and even if attacked by them, will try to make their escape. They are of a silvery white, and are found along the brows of the Rocky Mountains. They are very fat and delicious food. The common black bear is scarce, as is also the red bear. This last species of bear is alone heard of in the western part of the Rocky Mountains. They are the most beautiful beast I ever saw, being as red as vermillion.

10th. The common deer is in many places very plenty. In the mountains they grow much larger than they do in Texas.

11th. Turkies, on the heads of Columbia river, are very numerous. They do not range on the prairies nor about the Snow mountains.

12th. Wild horses (Mustangs) are very plenty on the prairies. Thousands of the very finest horses, mules, jacks, &c., may be seen in one day. They are very wild. The Indians often take them by running them on their horses and throwing the lasso over their heads. They are easily domesticated.[14]

13th. Man-Tiger. The Indians say that they have found several of them in the mountains. They describe them as being of the feature and make of a man. They are said to walk erect, and are eight or nine feet high. Instead of hands, they have huge paws and long claws, with which they can easily tear a buffalo to pieces. The Indians are very shy of them, and whilst in the mountains, will never separate. They also assert that there is a species of human beings that live in the caves in the mountains. They describe them

[14] As a beast of burden and as a means of personal transportation, the horse had a fundamental value to the Comanches. In this respect the horse was a capital good; the most notable form of wealth was in this form of chattel. Great herds of horses were accumulated, and the increase of herds through selective breeding was practiced by the Comanches.

to be not more than three feet high. They say that those little people are alone found in the country where the man-tiger frequents, and that the former takes cognizance of them, and will destroy any thing that attempts to harm them.[15]

14th. The beaver is found in great numbers in the ponds, which are very numerous on the heads of the Columbia, Missouri, Arkansas, Rio Grande, Platte, and all the country between; though it is very mountainous, and sometimes the ponds are on the highest ground.

These strange animals, in many instances, appear to possess the wisdom of human beings. They appear to have their family connections, and each family lives separate, sometimes numbering more than a hundred in a family. A stranger is not allowed to dwell with them. They burrow in the ground when they cannot get timber to build huts. In case they can get timber, they will cut down quite large trees with their teeth, then cut them off in lengths to suit their purposes; sometimes five or six feet long, and will then unite in hauling them to a chosen spot, and build up their houses in the edge of the water. The first story is some three feet high—one door under the water. The next story is not so high, has three doors, one next the water, one next the land, and one down through the floor into the first story. There is continually a sentinel at the door next the land, and on the approach of any thing that alarms them, they are soon in the water.

They will move from one pond to another, and it is strange to see what a large road they make in removing. Their fur and size need no description. They are generally very fat, but the tail only is fit to eat. The bait with which the traps are baited, is collected from this animal, and is difficult to prepare, as there has to be a precise amount of certain parts of the animal. If there is too much of any one ingredient they will become alarmed, and even leave the pond. In preparing the bait, no part of your flesh must touch it, or they will not come near it. The bait has to be changed every few days by adding something; a small piece of spignard or annis

15 The "man-tiger" description seems to fit the grizzly bear best; however, the relationship between the "man-tiger" and the "little people" suggests that Mrs. Plummer is passing along Comanche religious myth. Among such imaginary, as opposed to animistic, spirits as Water Babies from the swampy places, Comanche legend includes Dwarf People living in the mountains (see n. 26, below).

root [16] may be dropped into it. It is kept close in bladders, or skin bags, and nothing that goes into it must be touched with the hands.

15th. Muskrats in those ponds are beyond number. They also build houses in the ponds. They are built of any kind of trash they can find.

The most abrupt range of the Rocky Mountains embraces a large tract of country, and so incredibly high, and perpendicular are they in many places, that it is impossible to ascend them. At some places the tall sharp peaks of mountains resemble much the steeple on a church. Probably you can see twenty of these high peaks at one sight; and in other places the steep rock bluff, perhaps 200 feet high, will extend ten miles perfectly strait and uniform. In some places you will find a small tract of level country on the tops of the mountains. These levels are generally very rich. This range of mountains crosses the heads of the Missouri, and bears in a south-westerly direction to, and beyond the Rio Grande, even as far as I have ever been; also, bearing north, down the Columbia river as far as I went, and the head waters of the Platte, (perhaps I may be mistaken in the names of some of the rivers.) They can better be described by saying they are a dreadful rough range of mountains, I suppose as high as any others in the world. The bottoms are very rich. It will be winter on the top of the mountains, and spring or summer in the valleys. There is a kind of wild flax that grows in these bottoms which yields a lint, out of which the Indians make ropes. It is very strong. As far as I was down on the tributaries of the Columbia, the bottoms were seldom more than one half mile wide; in some places a mile. The timber is indifferent in the bottoms, and more indifferent on the high land.

The buffalo sometimes finds it very difficult to ascend or descend these mountains. I have sometimes amused myself by getting on the top of one of these high pinnacles and looking over the country. You can see one mountain beyond another until they are lost in the misty air. Where you can see the valleys, you will often see them literally covered with the buffalo, sometimes the elk, wild horse, &c.

North-west of the head of the Rio Grande, which is some 150 miles N. W. of Santa Fe, the country becomes more level. Part of

16 That is, spikenard (*Aralia racemosa*) and anise. Both are highly aromatic.

this country is inhabited by a nation of Indians, called Apatches, and another tribe called Ferbelows.[17] In this section of country there are some farms where fine wheat is raised.

This region of country is but very little known by the American people, being infested with such numerous tribes of Indians that Americans are very unsafe to be there. If the timber was not so indifferent, this country would be densely inhabited. The soil would fully justify the idea. In point of health it certainly is not surpassed in the world; and although very far to the north, is not excessively cold. I do not think it is colder than the state of Tennessee. The present inhabitants say there is nothing like fevers known in that country.

There are a great many caves in this high mountainous country. I must give my readers an account of one of my adventures in one of these caves. I am compelled to ask my reader to indulge me in the following adventure, as I am certain that this, as well as others of my adventures, will appear very remarkable; and reader, you will be compelled to fancy yourself in a condition where life has lost its sweetness, before you will be able to credit it. And here let me remark, that I have withheld stating many things, that are facts, because I well know that you will doubt whether any person could survive what I have undergone. I further assure you, my reader, that I have not written one word but what is fact. But to my story.

At one time, whilst on the Rocky Mountains, I had discovered a cave near the foot of the mountain. Having noticed some singular rocks, &c., at its mouth, that excited in me a curiosity to explore this singular looking place, and the time drawing nigh, that we were to leave this encampment, I was much afraid I would not have an opportunity of satisfying this curiosity. I had repeatedly asked my mistress to permit me to go into the cave, but she refused. A few days before we were to leave, however, she yielded a reluctant consent to my singular desire, and also permitted my young mistress to accompany me.

I immediately set about making my arrangements for this adventure. I procured some buffalo tallow, and made of a part of it some large candles, (if I may so call them) and took with me some tallow to make more, should I need them. I took with me the neces-

17 Pueblos.

sary instruments for striking fire, procured some light fuel, and thus prepared, we started into the cave. We had not proceeded more than 30 or 40 rods, when my companion became alarmed. I told her there was nothing alarming yet, and tried to persuade her to go on with me, but she refused to go any farther herself, or to let me go. I was, however, determined to proceed, and she appeared determined that I should return.—A combat now ensued, and she struck at me with a piece of the wood we had with us. I dodged the blow, and knocked her down with another piece. This made her yell most hideously; but being both out of sight and out of hearing of any person, I cared not for her cries, but firmly told her that if she attempted again to force me to return until I was ready, I would kill her. In the scuffle, being both down, the candle had fallen from my hand, and fortunately was not put out. I picked it up, and here a sight was presented to my view that surpasses all description. Innumerable stars, from the most diminutive size up to that of the full moon, studded the impenetrable gloom above and around us. I had not, until now, noticed the sublime and awful appearance of the cave. It was this sight that had alarmed my companion, and finding it impossible to induce her to proceed on the adventure with me, I agreed, on the condition that she would help me to mind the horses, to return with her to the mouth of the cave, which I did, and then returned to prosecute my adventure in the cave.

On reaching the battle-ground, I felt a great anxiety to find out the cause of this strange scene, which upon a close examination, was more splendid than the mind can conceive. Reader, you may fancy yourself viewing, at once, an entirely new planetary system, a thousand times more sublime and more beautiful than our own, and you fall far short of the reality I here witnessed. I soon discovered that these lights proceeded from the reflections of the light of the candle by the almost innumerable chrystalized formations in the rocks above, and on either side.—The room I was in was large, say 100 feet wide, and its length was beyond my sight. The ceiling was about twelve feet high, and the floor was nearly smooth, and in many places was as transparent as the clearest glass. The sides and ceiling were thickly set with the same material, from which projected thousands of knobs or lumps, varying from 1 to 30 inches in length. The reflections of the light of the candle, from these transparent lumps, exactly resembling the clearest ice, proved to be the stars that had caused so much alarm in my young mistress, and wonder in me. Having satisfied my curiosity by a full examination of this singular apartment, I pursued my journey in the bowels of the earth.

For a distance of three or four miles, the cave differed in appearance and width, but nothing worthy of notice was observed. I now came to another place that excited my admiration. The cave forked, the ceiling or roof of the right hand fork being about 10 feet high and 6 feet wide. This avenue was obstructed by the intervention of bars of these transparent formations, reaching from the ceiling to the floor. They were too close together to permit my body to pass between them, and the room, into which I could look, surpassing, in splendor, any thing I had yet seen, I was anxious to explore it. After much labor, I succeeded in breaking one of these bars, and I now entered one of the most spacious and splendid rooms my eyes ever beheld. It was about 100 feet in diameter, and 10 high. It was nearly circular, and the walls, ceiling and floor being entirely transparent, presented a scene of which the mind can form no just conception, much less the pen describe. I know my readers would not credit it if I were to attempt to describe it. I therefore leave my readers to their own conjectures of how such a room would look, prepared as a house of public worship, with a pulpit and three rows of seats around it, all of the same material, as has been described, on one side, and on the other a beautiful clear stream of water.

The water of this river, or creek, was so clear that I could have seen a pin on the bottom. It was about 50 yards wide, and varied from one to two feet deep. I crossed it, and after going down it a mile or more, I heard a most terrific roaring. I continued my course in the direction from whence it came until I reached a place where this stream fell down a precipice, the depth of which I could form no conjecture, but from the deafening roar that it made, it must have been immense.

Being much fatigued, and having come to the end of my journey, I sat down to rest. I had not been seated here long before I fell asleep, as I suppose, and in the confused roar of the waters I fancied I could hear the dying screams of my infant. I thought of home and my friends far away, that I must never see again.—My wounded body appeared to bleed afresh, as my mind reverted back to the cruelties inflicted upon me by my barbarian captivators, when there appeared to me the form of a human being. He held in his hand a bottle containing a liquid, with which he bathed my wounds, which ceased paining, and strange to say never hurt me afterwards. (This I know is not fancy, and sometimes, in reflecting upon this adventure, I am lost in doubt as to whether this whole scene was reality or only a dream.) [18] He consoled me with kind words, that I will remember, but shall not here relate. Oh, could it have been possible that He who comforts the afflicted and gives strength to the weak, that God, in His bountiful mercy could have extended His hand to a poor wretch like me. whilst thus buried in the earth. How inscrutible are thy ways, Oh, God; and thy mercy and wisdom, how unsearchable. Were I to give vent to my feelings, and possessed the mental capacity equal to the task, it would swell this humble narrative far beyond the limits I have prescribed to it.

Having renewed my light, I retraced my steps. I found the distance much greater, on returning, (or it appeared so,) than I thought. On reaching the place where my young mistress turned back, I found that the Indians had been in the cave looking for me. I reached the camp just as the sun was setting, and was astonished to learn that I had spent two days and one night in the cave. I never, in my life, had a more interesting adventure, and although I am now in the city of Houston, surrounded by friends and all the comforts of life, to sit alone, and in memory, retrace my steps in this cave, gives me more pleasurable feelings than all the gaudy show and pleasing gaity with which I am surrounded. The impressions made upon my mind in this cave, have since served as a healing balm to my wounded soul.

There are some interesting incidents connected with this adventure, which I do not think proper to give to the public at this time; they may, perhaps, be published hereafter. I have given but a very partial description of one of the most interesting scenes that occurred.

About the middle of March, all the Indian bands—that is, the

18 The reader of Mrs. Plummer's narrative must of course interpret this scene for himself; annotation cannot here supply him.

Cumanches, and all the hostile tribes, assembled and held a general war council. They met on the head waters of the Arkansas, and it was the largest assemblage I ever saw. The council was held upon a high eminence, descending every way.[19] The encampments were as close as they could stand, and how far they extended I know not; for I could not see the outer edge of them with my naked eye.

I had now been with them so long that I had learned their language, and as the council was held in the Cumanche language, I determined, (for I yet entertained a faint hope that I would be released,) to know the result of their proceedings. It being contrary to their laws to permit their squaws to be present in their councils, I was several times repulsed with blows, but I cheerfully submitted to abuse and persevered in listening to their proceedings.

A number of traditionary ceremonies were performed, such as would be of but little interest to the reader. This ceremony occupied about three days, after which they come to a determination to invade and take possession of Texas. It was agreed that those tribes of Indians who were in the habit of raising corn, should cultivate the farms of the people of Texas; [20] the prairie Indians were to have entire control of the prairies, each party to defend each other. After having taken Texas, killed and driven out the inhabitants, and the corn growing Indians had raised a good supply, they were to attack Mexico. There they expected to be joined by a large number of Mexicans who are disaffected with the government, as also a number that would or could be coerced into measures of subordination, they would soon possess themselves of Mexico. They would then attack the United States.

They said that the white men had now driven the Indian bands from the East to the West, and now they would work this plan to drive the whites out of the country; they said that the white people had got almost around them, and in a short time they would drive them again. I do believe that almost every band or nation of Indians was represented in that Council, and there was but one thing that was left unsettled, that was the time of attack—some said, the

[19] Apparently the council was held on a mesa in what is now central Colorado.

[20] The Comanches themselves cultivated no plants but obtained a certain amount of corn from the Kiowas and Wichitas. They got most of their tobacco in trade with the Mexicans of the southwest.

spring of 1838, and others said the spring of 1839; though this matter was to be left measurably to the Northern Indians, and to be communicated to the chiefs of the Cumanches. The Council continued in session seven days, and at the end of that period, they broke up. One Indian came to me on the prairie, and stated that he was a Beadie, that he lived on the San Jacinto river, and that they were determined to make servants of the white people, and cursed me in the English language, which were the only English words I had heard during my captivity.

On one occasion, my young mistress and myself were out a short distance from town. She ordered me to go back to the town and get a kind of instrument with which they dig roots. Having lived as long, and indeed longer than life was desirable, I determined to aggravate them to kill me.

I told her I would not go back. She, in an enraged tone, bade me go. I told her I would not. She then with savage screams ran at me. I knocked, or, rather, pushed her down. She, fighting and screaming like a desperado, tried to get up; but I kept her down; and in the fight I got hold of a large buffalo bone. I beat her over the head with it, although expecting at every moment to feel a spear reach my heart from one of the Indians; but I lost no time. I was determined if they killed me, to make a cripple of her. Such yells as the Indians made around us—being nearly all collected—a christian mind cannot conceive. No one touched me. I had her past hurting me, and indeed, nearly past breathing, when she cried out for mercy. I let go my hold of her, and could but be amazed that not one of them attempted to arrest or kill me, or do the least thing for her. She was bleeding freely; for I had cut her head in several places to the skull. I raised her up and carried her to the camp.

A new adventure this. I was yet undetermined what would grow out of it. All the Indians seemed as unconcerned as if nothing had taken place. I washed her face and gave her water. She appeared remarkably friendly. One of the big chiefs came to me, and appeared to watch my movements with a great deal of attention. At length he observed.—

"You are brave to fight—good to a fallen enemy—you are directed by the Great Spirit. Indians do not have pity on a fallen enemy. By our law you are clear. It is contrary to our law to show foul play. She began with you, and you had a right to kill her. Your noble spirit forbid you. When Indians fight, the conqueror gives or takes the life of his antagonist—and they seldom spare them."

This was like balm to my soul. But my old mistress was very mad. She ordered me to go and get a large bundle of straw. I soon learned it was to burn me to death. I did not fear that death; for I had prepared me a knife, with which I intended to defeat her object in putting me to death by burning, having determined to take my own life. She ordered me to cross my hands. I told her I would not do it. She asked me if I was willing for her to burn me to death without being tied. I told her that she should not tie me. She caught up a small bundle of the straw, and setting it on fire, threw it on me. I soon found I could not stand fire. I told her that I should fight if she burnt me any more, (she had already burnt me to blisters in many places.) An enraged tiger could not have screamed with more terrific violence than she did. She set another bundle on fire, and threw it on me. I was as good as my word. I pushed her into the fire, and as she raised, I knocked her down into the fire again, and kept her there until she was as badly burned as I was. She got hold of a club and hit me a time or two. I took it from her, and knocked her down with it. So we had a regular fight. I handled her with more ease than I did the young woman. During the fight, we had broken down one side of the house, and had got fully out into the street. After I had fully overcome her, I discovered the same diffidence on the part of the Indians as in the other fight. The whole of them were around us, screaming as before, and no one touched, I, as in the former case, immediately administered to her. All was silent again; except now and then, a grunt from the old woman. The young woman refused to help me into the house with her. I got her in, and then fixed up the side of the house that we had broken.

Next morning, twelve of the chiefs assembled at the Council House. We were called for, and we attended; and with all the solemnity of a church service, went into the trial. The old lady told the whole story without the least embellishment. I was asked if these things were so. I answered, "Yes." The young woman was asked, "Are these things true?" She said they were. We were asked if we had any thing to say. Both of the others said "No." I said I had. I told the Court that they had mistreated me—they had not taken me honorably; that they had used the white flag to deceive us, by which they had killed my friends—that I had been faithful, and had served them from fear of death, and that I would now rather die than be treated as I had been. I said that the Great Spirit would reward them for their treachery and their abuse to me. The sentence was, that I should get a new pole for the one that we had broken in the fight. I agreed to it, provided the young woman helped me. This was made a part of the decree, and all was peace again.[21]

This answered me a valuable purpose afterwards, in some other instances. I took my own part, and fared much the better by it.

I shall next speak of the manners and customs of the Indians, and in this I shall be brief—as their habits are so ridiculous that this would be of but little interest to any.

They never stay more than three or four days in one place, unless it is in very cold weather; in that case, they stay until the weather changes. Their houses are made of skins, stretched on poles, which they always carry with them.[22] Their poles are tied together, and put on each side of a mule, whilst one end drags on the ground. The women do all the work, except killing the meat. They herd the horses, saddle and pack them, build the houses, dress the skins, meat, &c. The men dance every night, during which, the women wait on them with water.

No woman is admitted into any of their Councils; nor is she allowed to enquire what their councils have been. When they move, the women do not know where they are going. They are no more than servants, and are looked upon and treated as such.[23]

[21] Nineteenth-century Comanche politico-legal practices were derived in part from the earlier Shoshone cultural affiliation, but modified by the Plains influence and its exuberant militarism. In many ways, Comanche law was geared to the preservation of status between individual males.

[22] The material culture of the Comanches was relatively meager and was of the general Plains type. Families lived in buffalo-hide tipis of the twenty-two pole variety laid upon a four-pole foundation. No pottery or weaving was known to them, and clothes were made of finely tanned and smoked hides. Theirs was a simple culture adapted to high mobility.

[23] The Comanche woman was placed largely in the category of property. Her legal disabilities and low status made her very much a chattel, first to her father and brother, later to her husband.

I knew one young man have his mother hung for refusing to get him feathers for his arrows, and appeared rejoiced at her death.

They are traditionary in their manner of cooking. It is considered a great sin, and sure defeat, to suffer meat to be broiled and boiled on the same fire at the same time. Every kind of provision has to be cooked and eaten by itself. When meat is broiling, or boiling, no person is allowed to pass so near as to suffer their shadow to pass over the meat, or it is not fit to eat. They often eat their meat entirely raw. When they kill meat, they suffer nothing to be lost. They have rigid laws,[24] and rigorously enforce them when violated. They know no such thing as mercy. They have no language to express gratitude, only to say I am glad.

Dancing is a part of their worship. Torturing their prisoners is another. They pay their homage to a large lump of platina, which lays in the Cross Timbers, on the waters of the Brazos.[25] Every year, the chiefs collect sacrifices, and offer them to this their God. These offerings consist of beads, muscle shells, periwinkles, &c. There are several bushels of beads that have been left there as sacrifices. They worship different things while on the prairie. Some worship a pet crow—some a deer skin, with the sun and moon pictured on it. The band that I was with, worshipped an eagle's wing. Those things are kept as sacredly by them, as the Holy Scriptures are by us.[26] They drink water every morning until they vomit—particularly when they are going to war.[27] They believe in a Supreme Being—the resurrection of the body, and in future rewards and punishments. I am informed, however, that some tribes

24 That is, taboos; in this case, those relating to food.

25 "Platina is a scarce and valuable metal, heavier and more durable than gold. The Indians make arrow spikes of it sometimes. It is very malleable. This lump will weigh some thousands of pounds" [Plummer]. Platinum, especially found naturally, was called platina.

26 Comanche religion showed affiliation with characteristic forms of the Plains Indians and was based on the concept of the guardian spirit. Success and excellence in any action or trait depended upon power given to man by supernatural beings—animistic objects of nature, such as birds, animals, reptiles, and fishes. All were living spirits who possessed special attributes or powers which they could give to men as medicine. (Cf. Iroquois beliefs; Jogues, n. 12). The essence of the religion was in the relation between the earthling and his guardian spirits. Power came in vision visitations—a dream phenomenon or hallucinatory experience—involving fasting and certain rituals. See Ruth Benedict, "The Concept of the Guardian Spirit in North America," *Memoirs of the American Anthropological Association*, XI (1924), 3–71.

27 Part of the Comanche purification ritual preparatory to battle.

do not believe in these things. These Indians are not countenanced by the others.

Their manner of doctoring by faith is amusing. When any of the men are sick, the principal civil chiefs order two of the wigwams to be joined together, though open between. A hole is dug in each of these camps, about two feet deep. In one of them, a fire is built; on the side of the other, is a lump of mud as large as a man's head. All around the hole, as well as this lump of mud, the ground is stuck full of willow sprouts. At sun-rise, the sick man and musicians enter the camps, and the music is kept up all day. No one must pass near enough to allow his shadow to fall on the camp, or the patient is sure to die; but if every thing is done right, he is sure to get well. If he die, it is attributed to a failure in some of the ceremonies.

Having said as much on this subject as is necessary, I shall now return to my narrative.

On the head of Columbia river, I could sometimes get some dry brush to make me a light to work by. We were now in a very deep valley. One evening, I was going in search of some dry brush, and discovered some shining particles on the ground.

I picked up one of them. It was about three-fourths of an inch in circumference, of an oblong shape. I found it gave light, which superseded, even afterward, the necessity of using dry brush. It was perfectly transparent. I leave my reader to judge what it was. I thought it was a diamond. There were unnumbered thousands of pieces. In some places, I could see the little ravine on which they were, at the distance of a mile, by the light which emanated from them. I lost this stone a few days before I was purchased. I have good reason to believe that one of the richest gold mines ever discovered may be found in that valley; and it would be a pity for so much wealth to remain undiscovered. The Indians often found pieces large enough to make arrow spikes, which is the only use they have for it. They would at any time exchange one of these arrow spikes for an iron one—the latter being harder and lighter. I may hereafter say more on this subject.

In the province or country called Senoro, I found many curiosities. (I, perhaps, may be mistaken as to the country; as all I know of it, I learned from the Indians and Mexican prisoners.) This country, I think, was a north-west course from Santa Fe, about 700 miles.[28] Here I found a great curiosity in a kind of thorn, which is as complete a fish-hook as ever I saw, having several strong beards on each hook; and what is still more strange, there are various sizes on the same shrub. These hooks are quite as strong as any that are made of steel, and more elastic. I have two of them now that I have caught many a fish with. I took them off the bush myself, and have kept them ever since I have been released. I have often been offered five dollars for one of them, but I have never been induced to part with them. They often bring to my recollection the distant country where I obtained them.

In this region of country, nearly every shrub and tree bears a thorn or briar. The timber, what little there is, is very low and scrubby. I wish I had language to give a fair description of this part of the country, with its present inhabitants. There are some Mexicans residing here. I tried to get one of them to buy me. I told him that even if my father and husband were dead, I knew I had land enough in Texas to fully indemnify him; but he did not try to buy me, although he agreed to do it. Some of the inhabitants are Indians. I am not certain of what tribe they are; but they cultivate the land, and raise some corn and potatoes. I was allowed to be among them but very little; neither do I believe them to be friendly with the Cumanches—though I saw no quarrel between them; but the Cumanches stole their horses and killed some of them as we were about leaving. I learned from the women that it was very seldom the Cumanches went into that country. I saw here, some springs that were truly a curiosity. The water, or kind of liquid, was about the consistency of tar, which would burn like oil, and was as yellow as gold. The earth, in many places, is also yellow. There are very few places in all this country, but what looks to be very poor. From the time that we left the country of the Rocky Mountains, and during the whole time we were in this region, I do not think I saw one tree more than fifteen feet high; and those, as before stated, covered with thorns. The healthiest looking Indians I ever saw,

[28] If, as Mrs. Plummer suggests, this "Senoro" was northwest of Santa Fe some 700 miles, it cannot have been the province of Sonora, Mexico. Mrs. Plummer's point of reference might have been the small Santa Fe, near Mexico City, but this is doubtful in the context of her travels.

lived here. Notwithstanding it is a healthy country, I do not think it ever will be settled by white men, as I saw nothing to induce white men to settle there. I have neglected to mention that the Indians have very rigid laws in the collection of debts. If one man owes another, it stands perpetually as a debt until paid. When a creditor brings a suit for a debt, it is done by informing the civil chiefs. They immediately find out the amount due, which is recovered in buffalo skins, furs, mules, horses, bows, arrows, &c., according to the amount. The debtor is immediately informed of the amount that stands against him, and if he does not at once discharge the debt, it is in the power of the creditor, at any time, to enforce his judgment—which amounts to disfranchisement—that is, the debtor can hold no office, not even that of musician. He is not allowed to dance with his tribe, nor to hunt with them. If the debt is still unpaid when the debtor dies, his children are held under the same restrictions as those incurred by the father; nor are their wives allowed to associate with other women.

There are among them delinquent debtors, who are doubtless now bound for debts contracted by their forefathers five hundred years ago. Some use great exertions to pay the debt; but the last cent must be paid.

They have their different grades of officers, both civil and military. In many cases, these offices are hereditary. They enforce their laws most rigorously, even among themselves. They are strangers to any thing like mercy or sympathy, unless it is in war. They appear to be much enraged at the death of one of their men—particularly if their dead are scalped. If their dead are not scalped, they do not mind it so much.[29] When they have a battle, every exertion to prevent their dead from falling into the hands of the enemy is made, even to the extent of risking their own lives, which they often lose in trying to save, or carry off their dead from the field of battle. If they cannot get the body, they take off the scalp or head of their slain—such is their aversion to the enemy becoming possessed of the scalp. The scalps of their enemies are kept as securities of good luck. This good luck is transferrable from the father to the son.

On one occasion, they had a very severe battle with the Osage

[29] See Jogues, n. 36.

Indians,[30] in which the Cumanches lost several men. Part of them fell into the hands of the Osages. They secured the heads of some, and from others they took their scalps; yet the Osages got some of them. They grieved much more for those who had been scalped, than for those that were not.

In this battle, the Cumanches got hold of several of the Osages that were killed, and brought their bodies to the town. They cut them up, broiled and boiled and ate them.[31] My young mistress got a foot, roasted it, and offered me part of it. They appear to be very fond of human flesh. The hand or foot, they say, is the most delicious.

These inhuman cannibals will eat the flesh of a human being, and talk of their bravery or abuse their cowardice with as much unconcern as if they were mere beasts.

One evening as I was at my work, (being north of the Rocky mountains,) I discovered some Mexican traders.[32] Hope instantly mounted the throne from whence it had long been banished. My tottering frame received fresh life and courage, as I saw them approaching the habitation of sorrow and grief where I dwelt. They asked for my master, and we were directly with him. They asked if he would sell me. No music, no sounds that ever reached my anxious ear, was half so sweet as "*ce senure*," (yes, sir.) The trader made an offer for me. My owner refused. He offered more, but my owner still refused. Utter confusion hovers around my mind while I record this part of my history; and I can only ask my reader, if he can, to fancy himself in my situation; for language will fail to describe the anxious thoughts that revolved in my throbbing breast when I heard the trader say he could give no more. Oh! had I the treasures of the universe, how freely I would have given it; yea, and then consented to have been a servant to my countrymen. Would that my father could speak to him; but my father is no more. Or one of my dear uncles; yes, they would say

30 A tribe of Siouan-speaking Indians.

31 See Jogues, n. 35. See also Williamson narrative, p. 222, and Johnston narrative, p. 290.

32 "I had dreamed, the night before, that I saw an angel, the same I saw in the cave. He had four wings. He gave them to me, and immediately I was on the wing, and was soon with my father. But, when I awoke, behold! it was all a dream" [Plummer].

"stop not for price." Oh! my good Lord, intercede for me. My eyes, despite my efforts, are swimming in tears at the very thought. I only have to appeal to the treasure of your hearts, my readers, to conceive the state of my desponding mind at this crisis. At length, however, the trader made another offer for me, which my owner agreed to take. My whole feeble frame was now convulsed in an extacy of joy, as he delivered the first article as an earnest of the trade.

MEMORABLE DAY! Col. Nathaniel Parker, of Charleston, Illinois, burst into my mind; and although I knew he was about that time in the Illinois Senate, I knew he would soon reach his suffering niece, if he could only hear of her. Yes, I knew he would hasten to my relief, even at the sacrifice of a seat in that honorable body, if necessary.

Thousands of thoughts revolved through my mind as the trader was paying for me. My joy was full. Oh! shall I ever forget the time when my new master told me to go with him to his tent? As I turned from my prison, in my very soul I tried to return thanks to my God who always hears the cries of his saints:

My God was with me in distress,
  My God was always there;
Oh! may I to my God addresss
  Thankful and devoted prayer.

I was soon informed by my new master that he was going to take me to Santa Fe. That night, sleep departed from my eyes. In my fancy I surveyed the steps of my childhood, in company with my dear relations. It would, I suppose, be needless for me to say that I watched with eagerness the day spring, and that the night was long filled with gratitude to the Divine Conservator of the divine law of heaven and earth.

In the morning quite early, all things being ready, we started. We travelled very hard for seventeen days, when we reached Santa Fe. Then, my reader, I beheld some of my countrymen, and I leave you to conjecture the contrast in my feelings when I found myself surrounded by sympathising Americans, clad in decent attire. I was soon conducted to Col. William Donoho's residence.

I found that it was him who had heard of the situation of myself and others, and being an American indeed, his manly and magnanimous bosom, heaved with sympathy characteristic of a christian, had devised the plan for our release.[33] Here I was at home. I hope that every American that reads this narrative may duly appreciate this amiable man, to whom, under the providence of God, I owe my release. I have no language to express my gratitude to Mrs. Donoho. I found in her a mother, to direct me in that strange land, a sister to condole with me in my misfortune, and offer new scenes of amusement to me to revive my mind. A friend? yes, the best of friends; one who had been blessed with plenty, and was anxious to make me comfortable; and one who was continually pouring the sweet oil of consolation into my wounded and trembling soul, and was always comforting and admonishing me not to despond, and assured me that every thing should be done to facilitate my return to my relatives; and though I am now separated far from her, I still owe to her a debt of gratitude I shall never be able to repay but with my earnest prayers for the blessing of God to attend her through life.

The people of Santa Fe, by subscription, made me up $150 to assist me to my friends. This was put into the hands of Rev. C*******,[34] who kept it and never let me have it; and but for the kindness of Mr. and Mrs. Donoho, I could not have got along. Soon after I arrived in Santa Fe, a disturbance took place among the Mexicans. They killed several of their leading men. Mr. Donoho considered it unsafe for his family, and started with them to Missouri, and made me welcome as one of his family. The road led through a vast region of prairie, which is nearly one thousand miles across. This, to many, would have been a considerable undertaking, as it was all the way through an Indian country. But we arrived safely at Independence, in Missouri, where I received many signal favors from many of the inhabitants, for which I shall ever feel grateful. I staid at Mr. Donoho's but I was impatient to learn something of my relatives.

My anxiety grew so great that I was often tempted to start on

33 "Mrs. Harris had also been purchased by his arrangements" [Plummer].

34 "At the request of my father I forbear publishing his name" [Plummer].

foot. I tried to pray, mingling my tears and prayers to Almighty God to intercede for me, and in his providence to devise some means by which I might get home to my friends. Despite of all the kind entreaties of that benevolent woman, Mrs. Donoho, I refused to be comforted; and who, I ask, under these circumstances, could have been reconciled?

One evening I had been in my room trying to pray, and on stepping to the door, I saw my brother-in-law, Mr. Nixon. I tried to run to him, but was not able. I was so much overjoyed I scarcely knew what to say or how to act. I asked, "Are my father and husband alive?" He answered affirmatively. "Are mother and the children alive?" He said they were. Every moment seemed an hour. It was very cold weather, being now the dead of winter.

Mr. Donoho furnished me a horse, and in a few days we started, Mr. Donoho accompanying us. We had a long and cold Journey of more than one thousand miles, the way we were compelled to travel, and that principally through a frontier country. But having been accustomed to hardships, together with my great anxiety, I thought I could stand any thing, and the nearer I approached my people, the greater my anxiety grew. Finally on the evening of the 19th day of February, 1838, I arrived at my father's house in Montgomery county, Texas. Here united tears of joy flowed from the eyes of father, mother, brothers, and sisters; while many strangers, unknown to me, (neighbors to my father) cordially united in this joyful interview.

I am now freed from my Indian captivity, enjoying the exquisite pleasure that my soul has long panted for.

Oh! God of Love, with pitying eye
  Look on a wretch like me;
That I may on thy name rely,
  Oh, Lord! be pleased to see.

How oft have sighs unuttered flowed
  From my poor wounded heart,
Yet thou my wishes did reward,
  And sooth'd the painful smart.

Closing Address

I am compelled, by my fast declining physical strength, to stop short of what I had intended to write. I feel assured that soon, very soon, I shall enter upon a more serious and hazardous an adventure than that detailed in the foregoing pages—an adventure upon the things of eternity—and may I not indulge the hope that my kind readers will properly appreciate my feelings in these, my last moments, when the "king of terrors" is staring me in the face and bidding me to prepare to yield up my scarred and emaciated form to its mother earth, and my afflicted and immortal soul to Him who gave it.

When I indulge in a retrospect of the past, and all my trials and sufferings are brought in view to memories eye; whilst my heart bleeds anew over those scenes of sorrow and tribulation, through which it was the will of God I should pass, I feel a joyous hope, that they were the means my Heavenly Master, in his wisdom, thought proper to make use of in preparing me to meet the angels of glory in realms of eternal bliss. When I reflect back and live over again, as it were, my past life—when I see my dear children torn from me by the barbarous hands of the savage—one of whom was inhumanly killed before my eyes, and its lifeless and mangled corpse thrown, with derision, into my arms—I feel rejoiced to think that all is well with it. Yes, with the eyes of faith, directed by a firm reliance on the promises of God, I can see its pure spirit mingling with those of the blessed around the eternal throne of the Most High God.

Where my dear child (James Pratt) is, I know not; but I sincerely hope, and have much consolation in believing that he too has been taken to his eternal home on high, where "the wicked cease from troubling and the weary are at rest." The firm hope I enjoy of meeting my dear babes in heaven, and of mingling with them and their kindred spirits, in eternal praises to "the Lamb of God, who taketh away the sins of the world," robs death of its sting and the grave of its victory. Yes—blessed be God—I feel a joy at the approach of death, which cannot be described—a joy which nothing earthly can impart, and none but pure spirits feel.

I feel that my days of probation on this earth are fast drawing to a close; and I know, dear reader, that long before you shall read this, my closing address to my fellow travellers to eternity, the mind that dictated it will have passed the just ordeal of a righteous and merciful God, and the hand that penned it, have become food for the worms of the grave.

To my dear parents and relatives—to all my fellow-travellers to the bar of God, I would say, murmur not at the ways of Providence. When the body is afflicted and the spirit is wounded in your pilgrimage through this vale of tears, murmur not; but look up, with an eye of unwavering faith, to Him who has said "come unto me, all ye that are weary and are heavy laden, and I will give you rest." Yes, He will pour a healing balm into your wounded soul, and through the merits of the redeeming blood of His blessed Son, Jesus Christ, bring you through all your trials and tribulations on this earth, and finally bear you to a place of eternal rest on high, where sorrows and afflictions will be felt no more. My dear father—my dear mother—my affectionate brothers and sisters—my kind readers, will you all prepare to meet there?

There is, in these, my last hours, but one doubt in my mind that gives me pain; and that is, the uncertainty that hovers around the fate of my helpless child. I have said that I hoped and believed that God has cut short his sufferings, by the intervention of the hand of death. This is merely a hope, founded upon the supposition that his tender frame could not withstand the cruelties of his inhuman captors. He may yet live, and if so, he is now, whilst I am penning these lines, suffering all the horrors of Indian barbarity. Oh, God, have mercy on him, if it be so. Thou, who art a father to the fatherless, wilt, I know, deal with him, according to thy mercy and wisdom. When I suffer myself to indulge in doubt, and permit myself to believe that he still lives in bondage, my bosom heaves like the waves of the ocean, when lashed into madness by the furious tempest, and phrenzy seizes my brain. How gladly would I give the whole world if it were mine—yea, my own life, were it in my power, to release him. But I have no hope of having this doubt removed. Soon, very soon, I must bid adieu to all the doubts, perplexities, and sorrows of this world; but I cannot nor shall cease to pray to God in his behalf. The fountain of my tears are dried up; I cannot weep for him—but may I not hope, that when I have passed into eternity, my dear parents and friends will breathe one prayer and shed one tear of sympathy for my poor lost child, James Pratt.[35]

January, 1839. RACHEL PLUMMER.

35 James was ransomed four years later (see n. 7, above). All of the five captives taken at Parker's Fort were eventually returned to white civilization. Rachel's aunt, Mrs. Elizabeth Kellogg, had been redeemed in Nacogdoches six months after the attack; the boy John Parker came in with Rachel's son James in 1843; the girl Cynthia Ann was the object of a long and nearly futile search. In 1846 an army officer spoke to Cynthia Ann and made an offer of ransom to her captors, but they refused. In 1852 she was again located, but by this time she had adopted the life of the Comanches, had taken an Indian husband, and was the mother of two children. She refused redemption, even when her brother John was sent to prevail upon her to return. Eight years later, in 1860, a band of Comanche raiders was captured by a cavalry force in northwest Texas, and Cynthia Ann was discovered among them. Her brother was made her guardian, and she lived with him in Anderson County, learning white ways and adjusting to her new environment with difficulty. She died in 1870. See James T. De Shields, *Cynthia Ann Parker* (St. Louis, 1886).

Bibliography

†††

Ackerknecht, Erwin H. "White Indians," *Bulletin of the History of Medicine*, XV (Jan., 1944), 15–36.

Barbeau, C. Marius. "Indian Captivities," *Proceedings of the American Philosophical Society*, XCIV (1950), 522–48.

Benedict, Ruth. "The Concept of the Guardian Spirit in North America," *Memoirs of the American Anthropological Association*, XI (1924), 3–71.

Birch, John J. *The Saint of the Wilderness*. New York, 1936.

Boas, Franz. *Race, Language and Culture*. New York, 1949.

Cotterill, R. S. *The Southern Indians*. Norman, Okla., 1954.

Culin, Stewart. *Games of the North American Indians*. 24th Annual Report, Bureau of American Ethnology. Washington, D. C., 1907.

DeShields, James T. *Cynthia Ann Parker*. St. Louis, 1886.

Dorson, Richard M. *America Begins: Early American Writings*. New York, 1950.

Drake, Samuel Gardner. *The Aboriginal Races of America*. New York, 1880.

———. *Indian Captivities; or Life in the Wigwam*. Boston, 1839.

———. *The Old Indian Chronicle*. Boston, 1867.

Fenton, William N. *American Indian and White Relations to 1830*. Chapel Hill, 1957.

———, ed. *Parker on the Iroquois*. Syracuse, 1968.

Foreman, Grant. *The Five Civilized Tribes*. Norman, Okla., 1934.

Hallowell, A. Irving. *Backwash of the Frontier: The Impact of the Indian on American Culture*. Annual Report, Smithsonian Institution. Washington, D.C., 1958.

Heckewelder, John. "An Account of the History, Manners, and Customs, of the Indian Nations," *Transactions of the Historical and Literary Committee of the American Philosophical Society* (Philadelphia, 1819), I, 180–242.

Heimann, Robert K. *Tobacco and Americans*. New York, 1960.

Hoebel, E. Adamson. "The Political Organization and Law-Ways of the Comanche Indians," *Memoirs of the American Anthropological Association*, LIV (1940), 5–149.

Jennings, Jesse D., and E. Norbeck, eds. *Prehistoric Man in the New World*. Chicago, 1964.

Johnson, Clifton. *An Unredeemed Captive*. Holyoke, Mass., 1897.

Josephy, Alvin F. *The Indian Heritage of America*. New York, 1969.

Knowles, Nathaniel. "The Torture of Captives by the Indians of Eastern North America," *Proceedings of the American Philosophical Society*, LXXXII (1940), 151–225.

Leach, Douglas E. *Flintlock and Tomahawk: New England in King Philip's War*. New York, 1958.

Lincoln, C. H., ed. *Narratives of the Indian Wars*. New York, 1913.

Lowie, Robert H. *Indians of the Plains*. New York, 1954.

Madison, Charles A. *Book Publishing in America*. New York, 1966.

Morgan, Lewis H. *League of the Ho-De-No-Sau-Nee or Iroquois*. Ed. by William N. Fenton. New York, 1962.

Pearce, Roy Harvey. *The Savages of America: A Study of the Indian and the Idea of Civilization*. Baltimore, 1953.

———. "The Significances of the Captivity Narrative," *American Literature*, XIX (Mar., 1947), 1–20.

Porter, Dorothy B. *Early American Negro Writings*. Bibliographical Society of America *Papers*. Washington, D. C., 1945.

Silverberg, Robert. *Indian North America Before Columbus*. New York, 1963.

Smith, Henry Nash. *Virgin Land*. Cambridge, Mass., 1950.

Speck, Frank G. *Penobscot Man*. Philadelphia, 1940.

Stone, Eric. *Medicine Among the American Indians*. New York, 1932.

Stutler, Boyd B. "The Kinnan Massacre," *West Virginia History*, XVIII (Oct., 1939), 107–28.

Swanton, John R. *Indian Tribes of North America.* Bureau of American Ethnology *Bulletin 145*. Washington, D. C., 1952.

Talbot, Francis, S. J. *Saint Among Savages.* New York, 1935.

Tebbel, John, and Keith Jennison. *The American Indian Wars.* New York, 1960.

Thomas, Isaiah. *The History of Printing in America.* Albany, 1874.

Thwaites, Reuben Gold, ed. *The Jesuit Relations and Allied Documents.* Cleveland, 1906.

Trueman, Stuart. *The Ordeal of John Gyles.* Toronto, 1966.

Underhill, Ruth. *Red Man's America.* Chicago, 1953.

Vail, R. W. G. *The Voice of the Old Frontier.* Philadelphia, 1949.

VanDerBeets, Richard. "The Indian Captivity Narrative as Ritual," *American Literature*, XLIII (Jan., 1972), 548–62.

———. "A Surfeit of Style: The Indian Captivity Narrative as Penny Dreadful," *Research Studies*, XXXIX (Dec., 1971), 297–306.

Van Every, Dale. *Ark of Empire.* New York, 1963.

———. *A Company of Heroes.* New York, 1962.

Vogel, Virgil J. *American Indian Medicine.* Norman, Okla., 1970.

Voorhees, Oscar M. "A New Jersey Woman's Captivity Among the Indians," *New Jersey Historical Society Proceedings*, XIII (Apr., 1928), 152–65.

———. "The Pension Secured for 'Aunt Polly' Kinnan," *Somerset County Historical Quarterly*, V (Apr., 1916), 106–108.

Wallace, Ernest, and E. Adamson Hoebel. *The Comanches.* Norman, Okla., 1952.

Washburn, Wilcomb E., ed. *The Indian and the White Man.* Garden City, N. Y., 1964.

Waugh, F. W. *Iroquois Foods and Food Preparation.* Ottawa, 1916.

Index

†††